A TO Z OF
AMERICAN WOMEN BUSINESS LEADERS AND ENTREPRENEURS

A TO Z OF

AMERICAN WOMEN BUSINESS LEADERS AND ENTREPRENEURS

VICTORIA SHERROW

✔®

Facts On File, Inc.

Facts On File, Inc.
132 West 31st Street
New York NY 10001

Library of Congress Cataloging-in-Publication Data

Sherrow, Victoria.
A to Z of American women business leaders and entrepreneurs/Victoria Sherrow.
p. cm.
Includes bibliographical references and indexes.
ISBN 0-8160-4556-9 (hard : alk. paper)
1. Businesswomen—United States—Biography—Dictionaries. 2. Women executives—United States—Biography—Dictionaries. 3. Entrepreneurship—United States. I. Title.

HD6054.4.U6 S5 2002
338′.0082′092273—dc21
[B]   2001051122

Facts On File books are available at special discounts when purchased in bulk quantities for businesses, associations, institutions, or sales promotions. Please call our Special Sales Department in New York at (212) 967-8800 or (800) 322-8755.

You can find Facts On File on the World Wide Web at http://www.factsonfile.com

Text design and cover design by Cathy Rincon

Printed in the United States of America

VB Hermitage 10 9 8 7 6 5 4 3 2 1

This book is printed on acid-free paper.

CONTENTS

ACKNOWLEDGMENTS

I would like to thank the people who helped me to complete this project. They include the living women in the book and their representatives, who took time to review and correct their profiles. Some also provided biographical information, spoke to me by phone, answered my questions, and supplied photographs. The staffs of libraries, universities, foundations, museums, newspapers, and archives helped me to locate and acquire photographs for the book and provided written materials for the text. I also thank my editor at Facts On File, Nicole Bowen, who assisted me in numerous ways during the preparation of the book.

AUTHOR'S NOTE

A *to Z of American Women Business Leaders and Entrepreneurs* describes the careers of some remarkable American women who have succeeded in business as founders, managers, directors, owners, and operating officers. Inevitably, many outstanding women could not be included in this volume, especially since the number of women in business has increased dramatically in recent decades. In making my selections, I looked for women from various periods in history and diverse nationalities, ethnic groups, and fields of endeavor, as well as women who overcame obstacles in order to succeed. I have also included women who achieved important "firsts"—for example, the nation's first woman bank president,

radio station owner, and founder of a million-dollar company. Many other women have certainly excelled as business leaders and entrepreneurs, but lack of space and, in some cases, the lack of enough research material, forced me to limit my selections.

Information on other women can be found in the list of recommended sources at the end of the book. For more information on a woman profiled, consult the further reading list that follows her entry. References to other women profiled in this book are set in small capital letters as an aid to readers. To further help readers locate information, I have provided lists of subjects arranged by area of activity and by year of birth.

INTRODUCTION

From colonial innkeepers, merchants, and printers, to 19th-century factory owners and dressmakers, to the financiers, founders, and corporate executives of today, American women have succeeded in business. Although many did not receive credit for their contributions, American women have made their mark in virtually every field, both in areas that were traditionally associated with women and areas that were considered for men only.

Along the way, women have faced numerous legal, political, and social barriers, including attitudes that said a woman's place was in the home and that women were too delicate—and not smart enough—for the business world. Often, women were denied access to the education and training, encouragement, professional associations, or funding and other resources that would enable them to start businesses or take on leadership positions. Those who did work outside the home also continued to bear the major responsibility for domestic duties. Hard work, talent, interpersonal skills, and persistence have enabled women to succeed in spite of these obstacles.

Records from colonial days show that American women were involved in business activities since the colonies were founded in the early 1600s. Life in colonial America presented women with new challenges and opportunities that were not always available in Europe. For example, to attract women

colonists, colonies in what would become Massachusetts and Pennsylvania offered unmarried women the chance to own land, something that was banned by English law at that time. Thousands of women also came as indentured servants, committed to work a specific number of years for an employer in exchange for their passage to America. Former indentured servants, both male and female, sometimes went into business after serving out their contracts, or they became farmers, after obtaining several acres of land as promised in their contract. Women who had been apprenticed to milliners, dressmakers, or hairdressers often continued to ply those trades.

As American settlers struggled to survive, women found themselves performing jobs that were regarded as men's work in their homelands. Their efforts were increasingly important as families worked together to run farms and plantations or stores or other businesses. In many cases, women and men worked side by side. One well-known example is Deborah Read Franklin, wife of Benjamin Franklin, who helped to run a store and later a post office beside her husband's printing office.

Some commercial enterprises were the outgrowths of work that women already did inside the home or on farms, such as spinning, weaving, and sewing, or cultivating and preparing food. Women who raised a surplus of crops or produced extra cloth or thread could sell or trade it. Often, these women traded for tools, sugar, or other things their families needed. Talented needlewomen sometimes went into business as dressmakers, tailors, and milliners. Other women earned money by curing fish, baking bread, or producing specialty foods, such as chocolate or mustard.

Colonial women ran various enterprises, including taverns, rooming houses, and inns, as well as shops offering dry goods, furniture, foodstuffs, tobacco, playing cards, glass, chinaware, garden seeds, tools, soap, candles, and other items. Some of the women who ran apothecaries sold their own herbal remedies. Women also ran gristmills, distilleries, and slaughterhouses, or operated taverns or inns, although laws in some colonies forbade them from handling liquor. In Boston during the early 1700s, women operated 12 of the city's 34 licensed inns.

In many cases, women took over the work of a sick, deceased, or absent husband, or they inherited businesses from their fathers. They managed to run these existing businesses and sometimes improved or expanded them. At the young age of 17, Eliza Lucas Pinckney began running her family's three rice plantations in South Carolina during the 1730s. In addition to her other duties, Pinckney studied botany and played a key role in making indigo a major commercial crop in her region.

Colonial women made important contributions to printing and publishing, which were usually run as family businesses. Before the American Revolution, 11 women supported their families by running a printing press. They included Ann Franklin of Newport, Rhode Island; Mary Katherine Goddard of Philadelphia; Cornelia Smith Bradford of Philadelphia; Margaret Draper of Boston; Hannah Bunce Watson of Hartford, Connecticut; Mary Crouch of Salem, Massachusetts; and Elizabeth Timothy of South Carolina. Like most of these women, Timothy took over her husband's business after he died. She managed to produce the very next issue of the *South Carolina Gazette* on schedule and earned high praise from the community for her efficiency as publisher. When her son Peter Timothy was old enough, he took over the busi-

ness; his widow, Ann, then became publisher after his death. In 1785, Ann Timothy was named state printer for South Carolina.

Some women thrived in ventures that were considered unusual for women of their era. For instance, Margaret Hardenbroek De Vries Philipse operated her late husband's sea-trading business and used the income to buy profitable new real estate. Susanna Wright, who owned land in the Pennsylvania colony, helped to launch and run a ferry business across the Susquehanna River and operated a commercial farm and silk business. Martha Turnstall Smith managed a whaling company and was known to go out on the ships herself.

American women found still more opportunities to prove their business skills during and after the Revolution. As the colonies broke away from Britain, markets for American-made goods expanded, so women could sell more of the cloth, clothing, hats, food products, and other things they made. Husbands and fathers went to war, leaving women in charge of businesses. After the war, widows and women whose husbands had been disabled became the sole breadwinners for their families.

Nonetheless, the social ideal called for women to remain in the home and stay out of the workplace unless they lacked another means of support. Most people urged women to devote themselves to supporting their husband's endeavors while caring for their homes and children. According to this line of thought, men operated in the public sphere while women remained in the private sphere. In some circles, a working wife was an embarrassment—a sign that her husband could not adequately support the family.

Women who did venture into the public sphere and assume new roles needed both energy and courage. They were still expected to tend to their homes and children and perform other domestic chores, often without any help. Wealthier women who could afford servants were expected to oversee their household staffs and to carry out various social obligations. The prevailing attitudes also held that women were not as intelligent or capable as men and could not deal with men in the business world.

During the late 18th century, women in the new United States continued to disprove such attitudes and prosper, despite the odds. These success stories included some remarkable women of color. Madeline La Framboise, born to French and Ottawan parents, became a fur trader who owned and operated trading posts in present-day Michigan during the late 1700s. After her husband Joseph was killed in 1806, La Framboise managed these trading posts alone, building a reputation for fairness and quality goods that enabled her to compete successfully with John Jacob Astor, the best-known fur trader in America. During these same years, in the Louisiana colony, French-African Marie-Therese Metoyer, a former slave whose African name was Coincoin, developed a large and profitable plantation—the first in the country to be owned and run by a black woman. Metoyer raised cattle and indigo, corn, and tobacco crops.

Across the country, women broke new ground in the 1800s as owners, managers, and entrepreneurs. As they had in colonial days, women ran printing businesses, producing newspapers, pamphlets, documents, and books. One of the most prominent early-19th-century printers was Jane Aitken of Philadelphia, who took charge of her deceased father's bindery and press. She achieved an important first in 1808 when she printed an edition of the Bible.

Women proved they could manage businesses in fields previously dominated by men. After her husband died in 1825, Rebecca Pennock Lukens became the first woman ironmaster in America when she took charge of the Brandywine Iron Works, founded by her father, in Coatesville, Pennsylvania. Lukens not only saved the company from bankruptcy but proceeded to build a large and successful business that became Lukens Steel (and later Bethlehem Steel).

The Industrial Revolution changed people's lives, as factories produced more of the goods that had once been made in the home. Although many women no longer had to make cloth, soap, candles, and other household goods, they were still discouraged from joining the labor force except when they were needed to fill jobs vacated by men. This happened during the Civil War, as women ran businesses and took over jobs men left when they joined the military. Hundreds of women went to work for the federal government, which offered women the clerical jobs men had held before the war. Businesses hired women as clerks, copyists, and bookkeepers, but women were usually paid much less than men holding the same jobs. However, as more women began working in offices, they learned firsthand how businesses operate and they acquired new skills.

After the war, widows and women whose husbands had been disabled continued to work for a living, as did unmarried women who needed to support themselves. Most of them were employed as clerks, bookkeepers, teachers, domestic servants, salespeople, or in other fields predominantly composed of women. Some war widows petitioned their state governments to lease them land and give them enough tools, seeds, and rations so they could raise their own food and cash crops running family farms.

Women who moved west during the late 1800s found new opportunities to earn money by providing services to other settlers. Some of these women were minorities who overcame substantial obstacles to build their businesses. Former slave Clara Brown, who provided laundry and meal services in a Colorado mining town, used some of the money she earned from her real estate and mining investments to help other African Americans relocate in the West. Bridget ("Biddy") Mason, who went to California as a slave, obtained freedom for herself and her daughters and amassed a real estate fortune in her adopted city, Los Angeles. Mason supported religious and educational institutions and other philanthropic works.

While some women started their own businesses during those years, many other American women found new jobs in offices. The typewriter was invented in 1868 and, by the 1870s, improvements had made it more efficient. Women were considered more nimble-fingered than men, so they were hired as secretaries and typists. To prepare women for business jobs, Mary Foote Seymour opened a stenography school, and, in 1889, she began publishing the *Business Woman's Journal.* Seymour said the goal of her magazine was to give women encouragement and information by "pointing out new occupations" in office work to those who might otherwise think their only choice was unskilled labor. Katharine Ryan Gibbs founded a chain of schools to prepare women for jobs as secretaries, stenographers, and clerks. The Gibbs schools promoted high standards in academics and personal conduct and aimed to prepare women to advance to higher positions.

Although most women were employees rather than owners or managers, some women rose to top positions. New Englander Margaret Swain Getchell La Forge began as a bookkeeper at Macy's, a New York City retail store. With her gift for merchandising and marketing, La Forge helped to build Macy's into a large, diverse business and rose up the hierarchy to become store manager in 1866, when she was only 25 years old. In Michigan, Anna Sutherland Bissell helped her husband build a company to make and sell carpet sweepers and took over as president of the BISSELL Company when he died in 1889, expanding to add new products and reach world markets. Ohio native Rose Markward Knox helped her husband build a food-products business, Knox Gelatine, and became president after his death. At first, Knox pretended that her son Charles was heading the company, even though he was still a student, but people who visited company headquarters realized the truth. One salesman who arrived on a snowy day began cleaning his boots when he noticed a broom at the entrance and concluded, "Only a woman would have the common sense to put that broom by the door." As president, Rose Knox instituted progressive labor policies, rebuilt the main factory and built another, and increased the company's profits.

While some women took charge of existing businesses, others became entrepreneurs, either alone or with partners. Finding a specific need in the marketplace, these women used their talents to fill it. Former slave Elizabeth Hobbs Keckley became one of the top dressmakers in the nation's capital and a confidante to her most famous client, First Lady Mary Todd Lincoln. When Lydia Estes Pinkham's husband could not support their family, which included five children, Pinkham began mass-producing and selling an herbal concoction she had previously been giving away. Advertisements featuring her healthy, grandmotherly face helped to sell millions of bottles of Lydia E. Pinkham's Vegetable Compound, which ads claimed was "A medicine for woman. Invented by a woman. Prepared by a woman." Ellen Curtis Demorest, who owned several hat shops, saw the need for standardized dress patterns, based on the latest fashions, that would help American women make stylish clothing at home—and millions of customers agreed. Harriet Hubbard Ayer, a divorcée with young daughters, built a beauty products business around a face cream formula she found in France. In the process, Ayer established herself as a beauty expert, writing books and newspaper columns on the subject.

Other women saw the need for better food processing methods. A native of New York State, Amanda Theodosia Jones developed a vacuum-canning process and established a factory, run by women, that used her patented technique. In California, Eloisa Jones Dawson, who had started a cannery business with her husband in their backyard, took over the operation after he died in 1885 and built it into the California Fruit Cannery Association, which later merged with other companies to become the California Packing Corporation.

Women also assumed new leadership roles in the entertainment arts. Actress Laura Keene, an English immigrant, became the first woman to manage her own theatrical company. In 1878, Emma Abbott became the first woman to form an opera company, the Emma Abbott English Opera Company, which she operated until one month before her death in 1890. A native of Illinois, Abbott performed in New York City as well as London before she formed her company.

The late 1800s found women owning and running a wide variety of businesses. A census conducted in 1870 in the states of Iowa, Illinois, Indiana, Wisconsin, Michigan, Minnesota, and Ohio showed about 30,000 women proprietors. They operated millinery shops, dressmaking businesses, bakeries, photography studios, groceries, and dry-goods stores, often marketing the skills they had gained as homemakers and mothers.

Through their involvement in business and related activities, more women became interested in political issues, and they joined forces with other women who shared their concerns. Before the Civil War, most women's groups had been organized for social reasons, but after the war, new groups were formed to promote women's rights, such as the right to vote. Through these groups, women expanded their social contacts and became more involved in the outside world.

During the late 1800s, women also gained more educational opportunities, as new women's colleges were founded and more existing colleges and universities became coeducational. An increasing number of women began attending college and earning degrees. By 1870, women made up about 20 percent of all college students, and that percentage rose to nearly 33 percent in 1880. Women with college degrees challenged old ideas about women's roles and capabilities, and they developed more self-confidence. They steadily entered male-dominated professions, such as medicine and law. One trailblazer, Victoria Claflin Woodhull, not only became, along with her sister, one of Wall Street's first women stockbrokers, but also went on to publish a controversial political newspaper, form a political party, and then run for president of the United States in 1872. The outspoken Woodhull told women they must "own themselves."

Although few women were as famous or as daring as Woodhull, more women openly asserted their rights to be recognized as man's equal and to be judged according to their abilities instead of stereotypes. More women made their way in professions such as law and medicine that had been restricted to men.

Women continued to prove they could run large companies. One of them was Nettie McCormick, whose husband, Cyrus McCormick, invented the mechanical reaper but lost interest in running his business and did not want to rebuild his plant after the great Chicago fire destroyed it in 1871. Nettie McCormick urged him to not only rebuild but to expand the business, which became International Harvester. After his death in 1886, as company president, she enlarged the business and helped it to adapt to changing times.

A number of entrepreneurial women became wealthy and even earned millions through their businesses, often in hair care and beauty products. Martha Matilda Harper launched what was probably the world's first true franchise, a chain of hair and beauty salons that sold her products. Annie Turnbo Malone and Sarah Breedlove McWilliams Walker, known as Madam C. J. Walker, developed independent hair-products businesses that made both women wealthy and enabled them to support African-American causes and other charitable organizations. Walker, the daughter of former slaves, often said, "I got my start by giving myself a start." Elizabeth Arden, the daughter of a truck farmer, advanced from "treatment girl" to salon owner to founder of a world-famous cosmetics company. Arden was a driven executive who played a major role in developing new products. An article in *Fortune* magazine commented, "She has probably earned more money than any other business woman in history by commanding the sun to stand still until she got the proper shade of pink in a bottle."

While some women managed urban-based businesses, more women were also in charge of agricultural enterprises and ranches. As of 1900, about 300,000 women were farmers, planters, and overseers. Many of them owned land and other property, much of it inherited from fathers and husbands.

Career choices continued to grow during the early 1900s as women excelled in new fields and became their own bosses. Elsie de Wolfe became an interior decorator at a time when men dominated that profession. Her friend Elisabeth (Bessie) Marbury ran a successful literary and theatrical agency. Other women entered the fields of aviation, advertising, and finance. Some women excelled in more than one field. Versatile Kate Gleason of Rochester, New York, ran a machine-tool company, became the first woman to head a national bank, and developed low-cost urban housing. "It pays to be the first in any field if you can," Gleason advised other women. In Richmond, Virginia, Maggie Lena Mitchell Walker became the first woman president of a local bank and skillfully guided her company through the crisis of the Great Depression.

Women still struggled to enter certain arenas. During the 1920s, in the newly emerging radio industry, most station managers maintained a policy of hiring only men as broadcasters and news announcers. If they did hire a woman, she was usually limited to traditional roles, such as talking about cooking, fashion, or child-rearing. Women who managed to obtain jobs as announcers were often harshly criticized. Some women managed to break through these barriers, however. When Marie Zimmerman and her husband, Robert, bought a station in Vinton, Iowa, she played a key role in planning and broadcasting.

During the early 1900s, women seldom held top jobs in retail and advertising, even though they were likely to understand what American consumers, primarily women, wanted and needed in the marketplace. A few women managed to reach the top. Ruth Fanshaw Waldo became one of the first women to become an executive at an advertising firm before 1950. A few women also became executives at major retail stores. When Dorothy Shaver earned $110,000 as president of Lord & Taylor in 1931, her salary was the highest then paid to a woman—but still only about one-fourth of what men earned in a comparable position.

As more women became executives and business owners, they provided role models and inspiration to others. Women in business formed local and regional organizations and clubs to promote their common goals. In 1918, during World War I, the War Department of the federal government organized a meeting in New York City where two representatives from every state gathered to begin forming a national businesswomen's committee. Although the war ended that same year, the plans continued and the National Federation of Business and Professional Women's Clubs, Inc., was formed the next year. Its goals were to promote legislation and public policy issues that concern women in the workplace and to provide services and training for members. The organization continued to grow, and in 1956, its affiliate organization, the BPW Foundation, was launched as a nonprofit research and educational organization.

In the meantime, another world war presented new challenges and thrust women into jobs that had been held only by men. During World War II, 6 million American women went to work, many of them in factories making planes, ships, tanks, and munitions. Women also assumed managerial positions in various corporations after men left for military service.

Some women worked their way up the ranks to become executives. In 1943, Ruth Leach (Amonette), who had worked her way from typewriter demonstrator to systems service representative at IBM (International Business Machines), became the first executive vice president of a major U.S. corporation. In her autobiography, *Among Equals,* Amonette later wrote, "[World War II] provided great opportunities for women in the business world, especially at IBM, where the systems service women helped break down the barriers the country had against accepting women as peers in the workplace. And the same goes for the women in the IBM factories all over the country, who operated the complicated machinery as well as any man."

Although many women were laid off when the war ended, a number of them chose to remain in the workplace, even if it meant taking lower-paid jobs. In 1950, 32 percent of the workforce was made up of women, compared to 16 percent in 1940. A large percentage of these were women who had stayed at home until their youngest child entered school.

During the postwar years, more women built successful fashion design and beauty products businesses, bringing their perspective as women who knew what other women wanted to wear or use. One of the most innovative was Russian-American Ida Rosenthal, whose company manufactured the brassiere her husband had designed to improve the fit of clothing made for clients in her custom-dress business. Women also excelled in the toy business. Ruth Handler and her husband, Elliot, founded the Mattel Toy Company, and Handler's Barbie doll, inspired by watching her daughter play with friends, became one of the top-selling toys of all time. She later said that when she first proposed the idea for the doll, "[My people] looked at me like I was asking the impossible."

Although a few women were finding fame and fortune in the business world, others felt relegated to lower-level jobs and and most received lower wages than men were paid for the same work. In addition, women who went to work were often criticized for neglecting their families and were called "unfeminine." Even the most successful women executives encountered discrimination. Ruth Handler recalled the day she arrived at a private club to give the keynote address to a group of investors and was escorted to the meeting through the alley and the kitchen. She later discovered that the club rules excluded women.

By the 1960s, more women challenged longstanding beliefs and asked for equal pay for equal work. They asked why women were expected to choose between work and family, while men were entitled to both. In 1963, Betty Friedan discussed these kinds of concerns in her book *The Feminine Mystique.* Friedan also noted that women working in the home made significant contributions to society, but their work was often taken for granted.

As women discussed Friedan's book, they described various problems they faced in the workplace, including lack of opportunities for promotion, a lack of affordable child care, and sexual harassment. Individual women and groups of women pushed for political changes. In response, the U.S. Congress passed several key pieces of legislation, including the Equal Pay Act of 1963 and the Civil Rights Act of 1964. The Equal Employment Opportunity Commission (EEOC) was created in 1972 to prohibit employers from discriminating on the basis of race, color, religion, national origin, or gender. Six years later, the Pregnancy Discrimination Act (PDA) banned discrimination against women employees because of pregnancy, childbirth, or related medical conditions. These laws enabled many women to pursue careers that led them to higher positions.

During the 1960s and 1970s, new organizations also emerged to address issues that concerned working women. Some organizations were formed for women in specific fields, such as advertising or banking, while others embraced broader agendas. In 1962, Felice N. Schwartz founded Catalyst, an organization that monitors the status of women in business and offers professional women tools for fulfilling leadership roles. Schwartz, who headed Catalyst for 30 years, said that her goal was to provide women with better access to the workplace and more top-level opportunities in corporations. In her books and articles, Schwartz described ways employers could help women employees by providing flexible work hours, quality day care, and parental leave. Critics said that employers would hire fewer women if their costs increased. In response, Schwartz said that companies would lose valuable talent if they ignored the fact that "Women face many, many obstacles in the workplace that men do not face." She also contended that policies in the workplace should enable both men and women to carry out parental responsibilities as partners, saying, "When a woman is faced with doing all the housework, all the childcare and then full-time work in the corporate area, she is stunted. The same applies to men."

Although by the late 1960s women had definitely made progress in the executive suite, many felt the sting of gender discrimination. Barriers were obvious in the financial sector, where women sought higher positions at banks and investment firms. The notion persisted that women were not as good with mathematics or money matters as men were. Qualified women found investment firms simply would not hire them except for secretarial positions. In *Wall Street Women,* author Anne B. Fisher interviewed Muriel "Mickey" Siebert, who, in 1967, became the first woman to buy a seat on the New York Stock Exchange. Siebert opened her own brokerage firm. Calling Wall Street "the last bastion of male supremacy," she recalls, "In the first year I was on the Exchange, hundreds of women came to see me. It seemed as though every woman in the world who wanted a job on Wall Street walked into my office. And so did every woman whose husband had died and left her a lot of money she didn't know how to invest. That got me thinking about how totally in the dark women were, in those days, about finance."

Many women found themselves bumping into a "glass ceiling"—a term that became familiar after it appeared in a 1986 *Wall Street Journal* article. The phrase was used to describe invisible but real barriers that kept women from rising to the top in business and industry or from earning as high a salary as male business leaders.

Sometimes, the glass ceiling prompted women to become entrepreneurs. A 1997 survey showed that among women in business for fewer than 10 years, 22 percent started their own businesses because they felt they had reached a glass ceiling in their previous careers. Of those who had owned businesses for at least 20 years, about 9 percent said they had encountered that situation. Other compelling reasons for starting a business are stated by author A. David Silver in his 1994 book *Enterprising Women:* "The woman entrepreneur is someone dissatisfied with her career path (though not with her chosen field) who decides to solve a problem that is causing her, and many other people, she believes, intense dissatisfaction." Silver points out that it takes not only insight to find a solution to a problem but also "the energy to build and launch a company to convey, on a continuing basis, the solution to the problem." An example of this type of entrepreneur is Bette McMurry Nesmith Graham, who invented a solution—Mistake Out, later called Liquid Paper—to the problem of typing errors in the workplace. Graham proceeded to build a company from the ground up, while working at her secretarial job and juggling her other roles as homemaker and single parent.

At the turn of the 21st century, women in the workplace continue to juggle multiple roles, as they have for centuries, and most carry a heavier burden than their male counterparts. Surveys showed that, as of the year 2000, women with outside jobs were still contributing more hours to household chores, child care, and community work than men. This heavy workload has impeded many women from rising to higher positions with more responsibilities. Often, they have not been able to spend as many hours at work as men, and some women have left the workforce, either temporarily or permanently, in order to raise a family. Women have also described feeling guilty and frustrated when they believed they were not able to give their all either at home or at work.

Is "having it all" a realistic goal? Women have said that in order to "have it all," they also have to "do it all." Top executives cope in different ways. Some women pursuing high-powered careers have remained single or chosen not to have children. Others have given up time with their families. Those with children depend on domestic help and child care, and some have spouses who work from home, which enables them to spend more time with their children. Some executives insist on being home in time for dinner each night, while others make time to take their children to school each morning before going to work. Some top executives say their husbands are equal partners at home, as well as in the workplace. In a 1999 interview with television journalist Neil Cavuto, Marion Sandler, cochairman and co-CEO of Golden West Financial Corporation, said, "My husband has always shared with me and he's shared the domestic kinds of things. So he has his things that he does and I have my things that I do. . . . I don't have the sole burden."

In her article "Life at the Top," which appeared in the March 2000 issue of *Working Mother,* author Diane Cyr found that "working Mom CEOs" were skilled at prioritizing. For example, Avon's Andrea Jung told Cyr, "I'm 120 percent with whatever I'm doing. It's never occurred to me to take work home." They also compromise, said Cyr: "CEO mothers will sacrifice plenty—exercise, meditation, gossiping with friends, to name a few—in order to meet those priorities." Commenting on this subject, Carol Bartz, the president and chief executive officer of Autodesk, told author Liane Enkelis, "I am not capable of being a good CEO, a good friend, a good mom, a good wife, a good public citizen all at the same time. I can't do this. I can only do a couple of these adequately at one time. And I can control which I am going to attend to and when."

Another problem women have faced in the business world is a lack of investment capital. Women who want to start businesses have found it more difficult to obtain financing from venture capital firms. For example, statistics showed that, between 1991 and 1996, companies founded or run by women received only 1.6 percent of the $33.5 billion invested in technology.

In spite of these kinds of difficulties, statistics also show steady growth in the number of women executives, administrators, business owners, and corporate board members. Since 1995, the number of women corporate officers and top earners in Fortune 500 companies (America's 500 largest corporations) has grown every year. The percentage of women corporate officers in these companies was 8.7 percent in 1995 and 11.9 percent in 2000. Women held 3.3 percent (77 of 2,353) of the top earner spots in 2000, as opposed to 1.2 percent in 1995. Women made up 5.1 percent (114 of 2,248) of the people who held such titles as CEO, vice chairman, president, chief operating officer, senior executive vice president or executive vice president.

A report issued in May 1999 by the National Foundation for Women Business Owners showed that the number of women-owned businesses in America more than doubled between 1987 and 1999, reaching 9.1 million. During that same period, the number of people employed in firms owned by women quadrupled (to 27.5 million) and sales grew fivefold (to more than $3.6 trillion).

Women-owned businesses composed about 38 percent of all U.S. businesses. As in previous surveys, most women-owned businesses were in the service industry but, between 1992 and 1999, the greatest growth was seen in the areas of construction, wholesale trade, transportation/communications, agriculture, and manufacturing. According to authors Gene Bylinsky and Alicia Hills Moore, "Between 1990 and 1999, the proportion of executive and administrative jobs held by women in the manufacturing sector jumped from 26 percent to 33 percent." Despite this increase, only a few women held top jobs at manufacturing companies.

The number of minority women business owners has also increased. Between 1987 and 1996, the number of firms owned by minority women rose by 153 percent. Employment in those companies rose by 276 percent, and sales rose by 318 percent. During those years, the number of businesses owned by African-American women rose by 135 percent, and the number of firms owned by Hispanic women rose by 206 percent. For companies owned by Asian women, the increase was 138 percent.

More women can also be found on the boards of directors of Fortune 500 companies. As of 1997, women held 10.6 percent (643 of 6,081) of the total seats on these companies, an increase of 18 percent since 1994. Women executives are encouraged by this development, saying that women board members provide role models for other women.

In recent decades, women with a strong interest in science and math have found new arenas for their talents. They have entered the rapidly growing fields of high technology and e-commerce. In 1997, Pamela Lopker, the founder of QAD, Inc., a leading software company, said, "In some other industries that have more traditional ways of operating it's sometimes hard for a woman to make headway. High technology is fast moving and fast growing—nothing is set in concrete. That gives everyone—including, of course, women—a lot of opportunity."

However, some women note there are still only a few women leading high-tech companies. After Sandra Kurtzig retired as head of ASK Computer

Systems, which she had founded, Carol Bartz was the only remaining female CEO of a large tech company in Silicon Valley. Some women working in high-tech companies claimed they had encountered "subtle sexism" and that their ideas were often ignored. Other analysts noted that fewer women were pursuing degrees in computer science. According to the National Center for Education Statistics, 28.4 percent of those degrees went to women in 1995, compared to 37.1 percent in 1984. Surveys showed that many girls of elementary and secondary school age still perceive mathematics and technology as men's areas. Women in technology have set out to help young people realize the many opportunities in their field.

As the 21st century began, several women had achieved top management positions at large U.S. corporations and had significant responsibilities, along with significant financial compensation. Three women—Marion Sandler of Golden West Financial Corporation, Andrea Jung of Avon Products, Inc., and Carly Fiorina of Hewlett-Packard Company—headed Fortune 500 companies. (A fourth, Jill Barad of Mattel, Inc., had resigned in February.) Katherine Giscombe, a senior director at Catalyst, said, "The proportion of women in senior positions is growing, slowly but steadily." A few women, including Sherry Lansing and Stacey Snider, were also at the helm of major motion picture studios, and Oprah Winfrey, Geraldine Laybourne, Kay Koplovitz, Judy McGrath, and Marcy Carsey had achieved major success in television. Self-made women entrepreneurs had built companies that made them millionaires and even billionaires. Three women who achieved the billionaire distinction are Muriel Siebert, founder of Siebert and Company; Martha Stewart, founder of Martha Stewart Omnimedia; and Donna Dubinsky, founder of Handspring, Inc. Oprah Winfrey was nearing the billion-dollar mark.

Shelly Lazarus, CEO of advertising giant Ogilvy & Mather, says, "I see a big jump, I feel a big jump. I feel the influence of women with the companies I deal with much more. They're at the tables now for the big decisions, and they occupy jobs now of enormous influence."

A

AHMANSON, CAROLINE LEONETTI
(1919–)   *Charm/Modeling School Founder, Executive, Philanthropist*

The founder of her own self-improvement center and talent agency, Caroline Leonetti Ahmanson has been involved in various business activities, including banking, and has worked to promote trade for the United States and the greater Los Angeles area.

Born in 1919 to Italian immigrant parents in San Francisco, Leonetti graduated from the University of California at Berkeley, where she also worked part time as the campus representative for a department store. She was married briefly and gave birth to a daughter, Margo, then taught at Marymount College and High School and Immaculate Heart High School.

In 1945, while still in her twenties, she founded Caroline Leonetti Ltd., (later the Caroline Leonetti School of Modeling and Commercials) a charm school in Hollywood, California, that offered young women courses in personal grooming, fashion, etiquette, and social graces. The business was a success and enabled Leonetti to support herself and her daughter. For 23 consecutive years, Leonetti

was featured on a popular television show as an expert who offered viewers tips on beauty and fashion. Leonetti later described her life at that time: "I had raised my daughter and educated her well, and I had a flourishing business. I had a life of my own choosing. I could take time off when I wished, and I traveled a great deal."

Leonetti had spent 17 years as a working single parent when she met and married Howard F. Ahmanson, a billionaire financier and philanthropist who resided in Beverly Hills, California. She called Ahmanson, who died in 1968, "a remarkable man."

After she was widowed, Caroline Leonetti Ahmanson entered other business fields, including banking. She chaired the Los Angeles branch of the Federal Reserve Bank of San Francisco from 1978 to 1979, and in 1981 she was appointed to serve a one-year term as chair of the Federal Reserve Bank of San Francisco, Twelfth District.

Ahmanson also devoted herself to philanthropy. Her lifelong interest in education and the arts prompted Ahmanson to promote the development of a comprehensive arts high school in Los Angeles during the late 1970s. At that time, funding for arts programs in public schools was declining. The

The founder of a successful self-improvement center and talent agency, Caroline Leonetti Ahmanson also served as chairperson on the Board of Directors of the Federal Reserve Bank of San Francisco.
(Photo courtesy of Caroline Leonetti Ahmanson and The Skirball Institute on Human Values)

Ahmanson Foundation helped to fund the Arts High Foundation, incorporated in 1984, for the purpose of offering students free professional arts training along with a strong academic program. Arts High opened in 1985, and Ahmanson remained on the board of the school as of 2000.

Much of Ahmanson's work has centered on improving trade and cultural relations with other nations. She has been vice chairman of the Board of Directors of the National Committee on United States–China Relations and the chairman of the Los Angeles–Guangzhou Sister City Association, as well as board member of the Los Angeles–St. Petersburg Sister City Association. She also served as director emeritus of American Women for International Understanding. In addition, she has served on the

Institute of International Education, the Peace Corps Advisory Council, and the President's Committee on the Arts and Humanities. She also serves as vice chairman of the California American Woman's Economic Development Corporation and on the Board of Directors of the Los Angeles Area Chamber of Commerce as "Special Director Emeritus."

Her numerous honors include the Certificate of Merit from the Council of the City of Los Angeles, the Northwood Institute Distinguished Women's Award for prominent business leaders (1978), and a Special Service Award from the Federation of Youth Clubs, where she has worked to provide programs for teenagers. In 1991 she received an honorary doctor of laws degree from the University of Notre Dame in South Bend, Indiana. In addition, she is a director emeritus for the Board of Directors of the Walt Disney Company, where she served on the board from 1985 to 1992.

Further Reading

Ahmanson, Caroline Leonetti. "Philanthropy in the 21st Century," *Skirball Institute Newsletter,* Fall 1998.

"Caroline Leonetti Ahmanson." Northwood University Distinguished Women—Caroline Leonetti Ahmanson. Available online. URL: http://www.northwood.edu/dw/1978/ahmanson.html. Downloaded on March 1, 2001.

Konolige, Kit. *The Richest Women in the World.* New York: Macmillan, 1985.

"Los Angeles County High School for the Arts Foundation." Available online. URL: http://www.lafn.org/education/arts/foun/foundation.html. Downloaded on May 13, 2001.

AITKEN, JANE
(1764–1832) *Business Operator, Business Owner, Printer*

Aitken operated a successful bindery and press business in Philadelphia and printed an 1808 edition of the Bible, a first for an American woman.

Born on July 11, 1764, Aitken grew up learning about the printing trade from her father, Robert Aitken, a native of Scotland, where Aitken was born. After the family moved to Philadelphia in

1771, he founded a bookbinding and printing business there and published the *Pennsylvania Magazine,* which was edited by the famous Revolutionary politician and author Thomas Paine. *Pennsylvania Magazine* kept readers informed about political events and the course of the American Revolution and contained the text of the Declaration of Independence in July 1776. Robert Aitken is believed to be the first printer to offer the New Testament in the United States; it was issued in 1782 in an edition of 10,000 copies. Despite his hard work, however, the business was usually not profitable.

After her father died in 1802, Jane Aitken took over the operation of the business and was regarded as one of the most important printers, male or female, of the early 19th century. She understood the mechanical aspects of the printing business, such as typesetting, and appreciated well-written articles and literature. She was also a good business manager. In 1808, Jane Aitken became the first woman printer in America to produce an edition of the Bible, the four-volume "Thomson Bible."

In addition to printing government documents, Aitken's business served various businesses and organizations, among them the Philadelphia Society for Promoting Agriculture. She printed the society's *Memoirs* in 1811.

Aitken, who never married, struggled for years to pay off her father's debts and support her younger sisters, one of whom had been widowed with three children just before Robert Aitken died. Sometime around 1813, she served time in prison for her debts and her equipment was seized, but a friend bought it back for her. Aitken seems to have retired from the business in 1815, and she died on September 5, 1832, after a long illness.

Further Reading

"Account of monies due to Jane Aitken," Available online. URL: http://www.library.upenn.edu/special/pspa/collections/Phila1.html. Downloaded on March 29, 2001.

"Jane Aitken Papers, 1784–1814." American Philosophical Society. Available online. URL: http://www.amphilsoc.org/library/browser/a/aitken.htm. Downloaded on November 2, 2001.

✳ ALVARADO, LINDA
(1952–)   *Executive, Business Owner, Contractor*

Linda Alvarado heads Alvarado Construction Inc., a general contracting firm that builds large commercial, industrial, telecommunications, and heavy engineering projects. Alvarado also became the first Hispanic majority owner of a major baseball franchise, the Colorado Rockies. She has said, "Perseverance and persistence have kept me going with the challenges faced in pursuring a nontraditional career."

Alvarado was born June 15, 1952, in Albuquerque, New Mexico, where she was the only girl in a family that included five brothers. While growing up, she played various sports, including softball, basketball, soccer, and field hockey and learned to be a tough competitor. At school, she worked hard and earned top grades, while also excelling as a varsity athlete. Religion was another important aspect of the family's life; both of Alvarado's grandfathers were Protestant ministers. She later said that she and her brothers received a great deal of encouragement from her parents, whom she described as "very, very positive people."

With the aid of a merit scholarship, Alvarado attended Pomona College in Claremont, California, where she earned a degree in economics. After she graduated, Alvarado worked as a landscaper and later as a laborer for a company that built retail centers and multifamily housing projects. She enjoyed the work and liked being on construction sites, despite encountering some men who expressed prejudice against women in this field, sometimes leaving insulting graffiti where she would see it. During the early 1970s, women made up only about 1 percent of the people in the construction industry.

However, Alvarado did not give up. She accepted a job as a contract administrator at a commercial development company and worked her way up to the position of office engineer. Eager to learn more, she returned to school and took classes in surveying and construction supervision—what she later called "unusual classes for women. . . . very non-traditional as you could imagine." During those years, the construction industry was undergoing changes, as people began to use computers for estimating and scheduling, and Alvarado wanted to learn more about that too.

Eager to start her own construction company, Alvarado put together a business plan, but six banks rejected her applications for a loan. Her parents mortgaged their home to provide her with $2,500 in start-up money until she finally obtained the business loan she needed. Alvarado Construction was founded in 1978, and she became its president and chief executive officer (CEO).

Through hard work, creative problem-solving, and determination, Alvarado expanded her com-

A native of New Mexico, Linda Alvarado is the CEO and president of her own construction company, based in Denver, Colorado.
(Photo courtesy of Linda Alvarado)

pany, which began to obtain contracts for larger projects, including auto dealerships, shopping centers, schools, telecommunications companies, and high-rise buildings. By 2000, it was one of the fastest-growing firms of its kind in the United States, with 450 employees and multimillion-dollar revenues. Alvarado Construction, which specializes in projects throughout the western part of the United States, has performed work for the city and county of Denver, including the Colorado Convention Center. Other projects include the Navy/Marine Training Center in Aurora and Colorado's Ocean Journey Aquarium. In 2001, Alvarado Construction was a partner in the construction management team building the Denver Mile High Stadium's Invesco Field and completing the landmark building renovation of the Bernard Valdez Heritage Center, also in Denver, a project Alvarado called "a labor of love."

Alvarado expanded her business holdings and scored another first when she became the first female entrepreneur to bid for ownership of a new Major League Baseball team. In 1991, she put together a proposal with a small group that acquired the franchise for the Colorado Rockies. She says that she hopes other women will view her experience in two traditionally male areas—construction and sports—and pursue their goals and dreams.

In addition, Alvarado is a director on the corporate boards of Pepsi Bottling Group, Pitney Bowes, and Minnesota Mining and Manufacturing (3M)—all Fortune 150 companies (150 largest American corporations). She serves as chairman of the board of the Denver Hispanic Chamber of Commerce and as commissioner of the White House Initiative for Hispanic Excellence in Education. President Bill Clinton appointed her to the President's Advisory Commission on Educational Excellence for Hispanic Americans on March 17, 1995. The commission advises the president about the progress Hispanic Americans are making to achieve national education goals. It also coordinates federal programs to promote educational excellence for Hispanic Americans and looks for ways to increase the involvement of state, private sector, and community resources.

Linda Alvarado has received many honors for her professional achievements, civic leadership, and philanthropy. In 1996, she was named Revlon "Business Woman of the Year," as well as the U.S. Hispanic Chambers of Commerce (USHCC) "Businesswoman of the Year" for the second year in a row. When she first received the latter award in 1995 at the organization's Miami convention, USHCC President José Niño said, "Ms. Alvarado's exceptional commitment to the Hispanic business community, along with her professional growth, make her the ideal recipient of this prestigious award." *Hispanic Business Magazine* named her as one of its 100 most influential Hispanics in America, and the Sara Lee Corporation honored her with its "Frontrunner Award" for achievement and leadership in business and the community. In 2001, the Horatio Alger Association named her as one of its 10 outstanding Americans, citing her achievements in overcoming significant economic circumstances and bias. Alvarado has often been a featured speaker at national business conferences, conventions, and schools.

Further Reading

"National Minority Supplier Development Council," *Minority Business Entrepreneur (MBE)*, December 31, 1998, p. 43.

Padilla, Wanda M. "Miami Hosts U. S. Hispanic Chamber National Convention," *La Voz de Colorado,* November 18, 1995, p. 11.

"President Names Linda Alvarado to the President's Advisory Commission on Educational Excellence for Hispanic Americans." The White House, Office of the Press Secretary. Available online. URL: http://www.ed.gov/PressReleases/03-1995/whpalvar.html. Posted on March 17, 1995. Downloaded on August 3, 2001.

Rebchook, John. "Historic Heritage Center Eyes the Future Denver Building Home to Number of Nonprofits," *Denver Rocky Mountain News,* July 7, 2001, p. 1B.

Reilly, Rick. "Maybe That's It . . ." *Sports Illustrated,* June 14, 1993, p. 46ff.

Tabak, Joyce. "Exploring the Americas." *Minority Business Entrepreneur (MBE),* December 31, 1995, p. 33.

Williamson, Richard. "Hispanic Group Honors Founders Today Recalling Past, Looking To Future," *Denver Rocky Mountain News,* April 24, 1998, p. 3B.

✵ AMONETTE, RUTH M. LEACH
(Ruth Pollock)
(1916–)   *Executive, Author*

In 1943, Ruth Leach became the first woman vice president at International Business Machines (IBM) and one of the first prominent women executives in the United States.

A native of Oakland, California, Ruth Leach was born in 1916. She grew up in nearby Piedmont and entered the University of California at Berkeley in 1933. Leach was an enthusiastic athlete who especially loved tennis and worked during the summers as a camp counselor, teaching young campers swimming, canoeing, and other skills. She later said that these responsibilities and experiences helped her to become more self-assured and confident. In 1937, Leach earned a degree in political science, having taken a variety of courses, ranging from anthropology to architecture and art because, as she said later, "Everything interested me. . . ."

Leach worked briefly as a dental assistant and then decided to explore job opportunities at the upcoming World's Fair, or Golden Gate International Exposition, in San Francisco in 1939. After an interview with IBM, she was offered a job demonstrating the company's electric typewriters at the company's Gallery of Science and Art at the exposition. After working there for eight and a half months, Leach and the other women at the IBM gallery were invited to remain with the company, and she moved to Endicott, New York, where she attended IBM's Systems Service Class 448.

When her training ended, Leach was assigned to work as a systems service representative at the IBM office in Atlanta. She was promoted in July 1940 to instructor in the IBM Department of Education, based in Endicott, New York. That October, she was promoted again, this time to the

When Ruth Leach (Amonette) became the first woman vice president at IBM in 1943, she was one of only five corporate vice presidents at that company.
(Photo courtesy of IBM Corporation)

position of secretary of education for women. Supervisors praised Leach's public relations skills and dedication. Leach described her new position as "a fabulous opportunity."

After being appointed manager of the systems service division, Leach selected, trained, and supervised hundreds of female employees. She also traveled extensively in the United States and Canada, meeting with people in the sales, service, and engineering departments of IBM.

Leach was promoted to the position of IBM vice president on November 16, 1943. The board of IBM said that her promotion was "in recognition of her ability and of the increasingly important part which women are playing in the operation of the company." At that time, few American women held executive positions at large companies, and IBM president Thomas J. Watson

Sr. was considered a pioneer in promoting women. In addition, during World War II, women had more employment opportunities when men left their jobs to join the military. In her autobiography, Leach later wrote, "Without the changes World War II created in the workforce and without the vision and foresight of Mr. Watson Sr., I never would have penetrated the man's world at the top of the corporate life, rising in four years from a typewriter demonstrator at the World's Fair to become one of five corporate vice presidents at IBM in 1943."

From 1941 to 1945, the United States was directly involved in World War II, and IBM contributed to the war effort by producing guns as well as artificial hands for injured veterans. After World War II ended, many women across the United States found themselves out of a job when returning male veterans took their places in industry and other areas where women had been working. IBM instituted a policy stating that married women would no longer be employed unless they had a special need, such as being the family breadwinner. After recovering from an episode of tuberculosis in 1947, Leach did return to her position at IBM and worked in the human relations department, but some of her colleagues who married left the company. Between 1947 and 1953, she served on the board of the Camp Fire Girls of America, the Women's Council of the New York Public Library, and the New York Tuberculosis and Health Association. She also belonged to the Business and Professional Women's Club of New York, the Academy of Political Science, the New York Women's Council of the Association of National Advertisers, and the American Association of University Women.

Various organizations recognized Ruth Leach as one of America's most prominent businesswomen, and she received numerous honorary degrees and awards. In 1945, *Mademoiselle* magazine selected her as one of its Merit Award winners, and she was chosen as one of the 11 outstanding American women of the year. The award ceremony was held in Washington, D.C., at the annual dinner of the Women's National Press Club. In 1946, Governor

Thomas E. Dewey of New York asked her to serve on his New York State Women's Council, along with other outstanding women in the fields of education, personnel, labor, the media and business. One of the other council members was her friend, cosmetics company founder ELIZABETH ARDEN. That same year, at age 29, Leach was honored by the Women's National Press Club and received an achievement award in Washington, D.C.

After 14 years with IBM, Ruth Leach retired in 1953. In January 1954, she married Walter (Bill) Pollock, and they settled outside Philadelphia. Ruth Leach Pollock pursued new interests, including horticulture, and was an active member of the board of the Pennsylvania Horticulture Society. The couple adopted a daughter, Elizabeth, in 1956. Later, the family moved to Switzerland and then to California, where Ruth Pollock devoted much of her time to volunteer organizations. She was widowed in 1977 and remarried in 1988 to Wilbur K. Amonette, a widower whom she had first met in college. In 1996, she was inducted into the Women in Technology International (WITI) Hall of Fame.

Ruth Leach Amonette wrote an autobiography, which was published in 1999. As of 2002, she was living with her husband in California.

Further Reading

Amonette, Ruth Leach. *Among Equals: The Rise of IBM's First Female Corporate Vice President.* Berkeley, Calif.: Creative Arts, 1999.

"WITI—Ruth Leach Amonette," Hall of Fame for Women in Technology. Available online. URL: http://www. witi.com. Downloaded on August 7, 2000.

McKenna, Patrick. "Hall of Fame for Women in Technology." Newsbytes News Network, June 10, 1996.

✸ ARDEN, ELIZABETH
(Florence Nightingale Graham)
(1878–1966) *Entrepreneur, Executive, Business Owner*

Elizabeth Arden founded one of the most famous and profitable cosmetics companies in the world. Arden, who was regarded as one of America's top beauty experts for several decades, received a special award in 1952 from a national press organization, which said she had "made beauty attainable to all American women."

On December 1, 1878, Florence Nightingale Graham was born in Woodbridge, Canada, near Toronto. Her Scots-born father, William Graham, was a truck farmer; her English-born mother, Susan Tadd Graham, was a homemaker who died when Florence was six years old. The family, which included four children, was quite poor, and Graham helped by selling produce from the back of a wagon when they went to market.

After high school, she entered nurses' training—in keeping with her name, after the British woman who had pioneered that profession. However, she was unsuited for nursing and later said, "I found I didn't really like looking at sick people. I want to keep people well, and young, and beautiful." During that time, she met a biochemist working in the hospital laboratory to develop creams for various skin diseases and wondered if healing creams might also beautify the complexion. At home, she tried to create her own skin cream formula by mixing various formulas in the kitchen. Her father said she was wasting her time and must either marry or seek employment.

Eager to see more of the world, Graham moved to Toronto, where she worked as a dental assistant and in clerical and sales jobs. At age 30, she relocated to New York City and became a bookkeeper at E. R. Squibb, a pharmaceutical company. Once again, she was drawn to visit the laboratories where scientists were developing new products.

The beauty culture business was growing rapidly during those years and Graham changed jobs again to work as a cashier in Eleanor Adair's beauty parlor. She soon became a "treatment girl" who gave facials and manicures to wealthy customers. As her wages increased, she rented a more comfortable apartment and sent her family money. In 1909, she left Adair to work with another beauty entrepreneur, Elizabeth Hubbard, who had created creams that Graham liked better than Adair's.

Elizabeth Arden rose from "treatment girl" to beauty salon owner, then founded her own highly successful cosmetics company.
(Photo by Alan Fisher, courtesy of Library of Congress)

Together, they operated a business on fashionable Fifth Avenue and advertised their salon and products in *Vogue* magazine. Their creams and oils were named Grecian Daphne. Because beauty treatments were only starting to gain wide respectability, they gave their salon snob appeal by saying that it was reserved for "women socially prominent in the Metropolis and suburbs."

The partnership dissolved when the two women disagreed about how to run the business. Florence Graham remained in the old salon and renamed herself and the business "Mrs. Elizabeth Arden." She redecorated the salon, using a $6,000 loan from her brother William, and painted the entrance door red, which would become an Arden signature in all her salons. Arden asked two hair-dressers to work in a room in her salon so customers could receive hair and skin care in the same place. Each morning, she arrived early to clean the salon, then gave treatments for nine hours. Afterward, she gave manicures and spent some of her time experimenting in her home laboratory.

As color cosmetics became more socially acceptable, Arden decided to sell rouge and tinted face powder and taught her staff how to apply them. Blessed with a clear, glowing complexion, Arden was a fine advertisement for her products and services, which attracted more and more customers. However, there was a high turnover among the staff, who described Arden as demanding and difficult. Some resigned, while others were fired.

In 1914, Arden visited France to examine beauty salons there, then opened another Arden salon, in Washington, D.C., and expanded the manufacturing end of her business. She introduced two successful new products: a face cream with a whipped-cream consistency, called Venetian Cream Amoretta, and a companion skin tonic. The next year, Arden married former banker Thomas Lewis, and he joined her in the business.

Within a few years, she added eye makeup and fragrances to her line and was selling products in Europe where she built salons in Cannes, France; Berlin, Germany; and Rome, Italy. Her sister Gladys de Maublanc, who had married a Frenchman, managed the salon in Paris. Arden is said to have boasted, "There are only three American names that are known in every corner of the globe: Singer Sewing Machines, Coca-Cola, and Elizabeth Arden." Because Arden targeted the "prestige" market, primarily women in the upper 3 percent income bracket, she insisted on beautiful packaging, with Arden models posed in opulent surroundings, and continued to price her products higher than average.

During the early 1920s, Arden developed hair-care products and bath preparations. She used yoga exercises to help relieve chronic hip pain and decided to add exercise rooms to her salons. Arden also made the first instructional exercise recordings.

By 1925, the company had a gross income of more than $2 million a year just from its U.S. wholesale division, and Elizabeth Arden was wealthy and famous as a beauty expert. Active and energetic, she looked younger than her age. The company continued to expand, opening a new and more luxurious office building in New York City in 1929. That year, Arden turned down an offer of $15 million to buy her business, to which she devoted most of her time and energy. She opened Maine Chance, the first American beauty spa/retreat facility, at her Maine country home. In addition to North America and Europe, she sold products in South America, Asia, Australia, and Africa.

She continued to introduce new products, such as kits containing several shades of lipstick to accompany different clothes, and new shades of powder, rouge, and eye makeup. In 1936, Arden launched her first fragrance, Blue Grass, named for the landscape around her Virginia estate, where she raised racehorses.

Her business continued to thrive during the Great Depression of the 1930s and World War II (1939–45). She created Montezuma Red lipstick during the war years to match the red trim on the uniforms of military women.

In 1935, Arden was divorced from Thomas Lewis. She married a Russian, Prince Michael Evlanoff, in 1942, when she was 64 years old, but the marriage ended after 13 months.

In addition to her business, Arden supported various charities, including the Lighthouse for the Blind, March of Dimes, and the Heart Fund. She served on the board of the American Women's Voluntary Services and helped to found the American Symphony.

Arden continued to work into her eighties, often from her 10-room apartment on Fifth Avenue, which was decorated mostly in shades of pink, her favorite color. Sometimes she surprised the staffs of her salons with impromptu visits. When she died in 1966, Elizabeth Arden had earned more money than any other business-woman in history, and her company was grossing about $600 million a year.

Elizabeth Arden, Inc., is still a prominent beauty products company with corporate offices in Miami Lakes, Florida.

Further Reading

ea magazine. "Elizabeth Arden: Profile of a Pioneer," Available online. URL: http://www.elizabetharden.com/heritage.today.asp. Downloaded February 8, 2002.

Lewis, Alfred Allan, and Constance Woodworth. *Miss Elizabeth Arden.* New York: Coward, McCann, & Geoghegan, 1972.

Peiss, Kathy. *Hope in a Jar: The Making of America's Beauty Culture.* New York: Metropolitan Books, 1998.

✳ ASH, MARY KAY (Mary Kathlyn Wagner)
(1918–2001)   *Entrepreneur, Business Owner, Executive*

Ash founded a multimillion-dollar business, Mary Kay Inc., that sells beauty products through an international network of direct sales representatives. The company provides opportunities for women to earn high incomes for top performance.

Mary Kathlyn Wagner was born on May 12, 1918, in Hot Wells, Texas. Her father suffered from tuberculosis and was an invalid, and her mother worked long hours in a restaurant to support the family. By age 7, Mary Kay was caring for her father, cleaning house, and preparing meals. She later said that these experiences strengthened her character and taught her to work hard. Despite her many responsibilities, she earned high marks in school and won special awards for public speaking and for her performance on the debate team.

After high school, Wagner could not afford to attend college and decided to marry a popular local musician, Ben Rogers. To boost the family income, she began working in direct sales, first for a book company, then for Stanley Home Products. Just one year after joining Stanley, she was crowned Queen of Sales at the annual convention in Dallas. During World War II, her husband served in the military; they divorced shortly after the war ended. She continued to work for Stanley Home Products and was able to support her daughter and two sons.

Although she won awards for her sales performance and was promoted to the position of manager, she concluded that the male branch manager would never promote her further because she was a woman. She left the company in 1952 and became national training director for another direct-sales firm, the World Gift Company, based in Dallas.

By 1963, she had remarried and decided to retire (when a man she hired and trained was promoted above her at twice her salary) and write a book about her work experiences. She later said that her goal was to "help other women overcome some of the obstacles I had encountered." She recalled, "First, I wrote down all of the good things the companies I had been with had done and then the changes I would make." During this time, Ash visualized a company that would offer new opportunities, especially for women, and reflect her personal values. She said, "My frustrations as a woman in the business world were based on the fact that I had often been paid far less than a man doing the same work." Employers had told her that men had families to support, but she knew many working women had the same responsibilities; besides, she believed that they should receive the same pay if they did the same work.

Instead of finishing her book, she was inspired to open the kind of company she had always wanted to work for, selling a skin-care product she had been using for more than 20 years. The formula she purchased had been developed by a hide tanner whose daughter was selling it.

While she was preparing to launch her business, her second husband and partner died unexpectedly of a heart attack. Although friends urged her to abandon her plans, she went forward, using her life savings of $5,000 to open the first Mary Kay offices in a 500-square-foot storefront in Dallas. Her 20-year-old son, Richard Rogers, left his job in insurance to join her in the business, which initially employed nine beauty consultants and was called Beauty by Mary Kay. Besides skin care products, the line expanded to include color cosmetics.

The company trained independent salespeople, called beauty consultants, who were paid commissions based on their sales. Consultants bought the products from Mary Kay, then demonstrated them to customers, using the party plan method, gathering a group of women at someone's home for a sales presentation. They were trained to show customers how to use the products, and customers could try them out before purchasing them. Mary Kay believed the groups should be small—about six to eight women—instead of large and impersonal.

As an experienced salesperson herself, Mary Kay inspired her employees with dynamic speeches and encouragement and offered them prizes and personal recognition. She believed in, as she put it, "praising people to success." Consultants attended regular sales meetings, where they were encouraged to share their positive experiences. For her company motto, she chose "God

Starting with $5,000 in 1963, Mary Kay Ash built a billion-dollar beauty empire.
(Photo courtesy of Mary Kay Company)

First, Family Second, Career Third." The color pink, used to package her products, became a Mary Kay signature, and Ash began rewarding top sales directors with pink Cadillacs like her own and with diamond jewelry and vacation trips. These sales methods attracted a growing base of repeat customers and fostered employee loyalty, as salespeople worked to advance their careers.

Ash went forward with the construction of a plant, which became one of the largest manufacturing facilities in its region. She married Mel Ash and became Mary Kay Ash. The company also continued to expand its product line. In 1964, Mary Kay became one of the first companies to offer a full line of men's products: its Mr. K. line. Packaged in brown and silver, the line included moisture balm and cleanser formulated for men's complexions.

When the company went public with its stock offering in 1968, Ash became a millionaire. Beginning in the 1970s, Mary Kay, Inc., expanded into Australia and Canada, as well as more than 20 other countries in Europe, Asia, and Latin America. Ash and her son decided to buy back the company in 1985. They paid $250 million for the stock, and Mary Kay once again became a privately held company.

By 1992, retail sales had reached $1 billion; worldwide retail sales for 1997 increased further, to $2 billion. During the 1990s, new factories opened in Switzerland and the People's Republic of China. Mary Kay consultants also operated in the former Soviet Union.

Mary Kay Cosmetics is considered a model of a well-run business because of its profitability, effective management, employee satisfaction, and personalized customer service. The company has an unusually high number of women in management. As of 1994, more women in the company were earning incomes greater than $100,000 per year than at any other American company.

In 1987, Ash, who was named chairman emeritus of her company, was actively involved in the company and held seminars for the consultants, inspiring them with her enthusiastic speeches. "I created this company for you," she often told them.

As of 2002, there are more than 850,000 independent beauty consultants in 37 countries worldwide, and company retail sales are $2.5 billion. As of 2001, more than 150 women have earned more than $1 million in their Mary Kay careers.

In addition to making public appearances and delivering motivational speeches, Ash wrote several books, all best-sellers, including her autobiography, *Mary Kay* (1981), *Mary Kay on People Management* (1993), and *You Can Have It All* (1995), which reached the best-seller list in one week. She received the Northwood University award as an outstanding business leader in 1990. In 1996, she established the Mary Kay Ash Charitable Foundation, which raises money for cancer research, screening, and treatment and for the prevention of violence against women. Her company, which develops and manufactures products in a modern plant in Texas, has also been praised for its sound environmental policies.

After suffering a stroke in 1996, Ash experienced declining health. She died of natural causes on November 22, 2001, at her home in Dallas.

Further Reading

Ash, Mary Kay. *Mary Kay*. New York: Perennial Library, 1986.

———. *Mary Kay on People Management*. New York: Warner Books, 1984.

———. *You Can Have It All*. Rocklin, Calif.: Prima, 1995.

Harrison, Patricia, editor. *America's New Women Entrepreneurs: Tips, Tactics, & Techniques of Women Achievers in Business*. Washington, D.C.: Acropolis Books, 1986.

Silver, A. David. *Enterprising Women*. New York: AMACOM, 1994.

ASTOR, SARAH TODD
(1768–1834) *Business Operator*

With her keen business sense and hard work, Sarah Todd Astor helped her husband develop successful fur, shipping, and real estate ventures that made him the richest man in mid-19th-century America.

Sarah Todd was born in New York City in 1768, the youngest daughter of a Scottish-American father and Dutch-American mother whose family, the Brevoorts, was socially prominent in the New York colony. Some of Mrs. Todd's relations were wealthy and prominent people, but she and her husband had a modest income. In 1770, Sarah's father died, leaving his widow and children nearly penniless. Aided by Sarah and her other daughters, Mrs. Todd opened a boardinghouse.

At that time, Sarah Todd met John Jacob Astor, who was selling cakes for a New York baker and beginning to open a small fur business. Astor's Dutch family had been living in Germany before he left for America. According to some historians, Todd and Astor met when Astor walked by the boardinghouse and saw Sarah outside, cleaning the entrance steps. Astor began visiting the Todd family, and he impressed Sarah and her mother as a hardworking and sensible man who would succeed. The couple married on September 19, 1785, and lived in two rooms at the boardinghouse.

Sarah Astor brought a dowry of $300 to the marriage and used both her money and business skills to help her husband develop and operate his fur trade and other endeavors. People who knew Sarah praised her as thrifty, religious, intelligent, and hard-working, and they said she played a major role when her husband opened his new fur shop in 1786. She had a keen eye for quality and her husband trusted her judgment in planning and marketing. It was rumored that Sarah Astor was a better judge of furs than her husband, and he did not contradict those reports.

While John Jacob Astor traveled to wilderness areas to buy and ship furs, Sarah Astor ran the store. She also sold the musical instruments that her husband ordered from his brother, who was living in London. When the instruments arrived, Sarah Astor displayed them in a room at the boardinghouse, which she turned into a shop. They were advertised in the New York *Packet* in May 1786, as "an elegant assortment of Musical Instruments, such as piano fortes, spinnets, pianoforte guitars, the best of violins, Herman flutes, clarinets, hautboys, fifes, the best Roman violin strings, and all other kinds of strings, music books

and paper, and every other article in the musical line . . . on very low terms for cash." In addition to the instruments, Sarah Astor displayed furs and offered them for sale.

In 1790, with two children and another on the way, the Astors moved to a larger apartment on the second floor above their store. As John Jacob Astor expanded his trading and shipping businesses, Sarah continued to advise him and helped him run various businesses while providing him with social contacts that would further their interests. She entertained bankers, merchants, and political figures and introduced Astor to people with business experience and social connections. Sarah Astor, who had relatives engaged in the shipping trade, also encouraged her husband to engage in trade with China and to explore fur-trading opportunities in the American Northwest. John Jacob referred to his wife as a business partner.

While raising five children (three others did not survive infancy), Sarah also helped to manage the couple's economic affairs. Only she and her husband knew their actual net worth. By 1800, this figure had reached about $250,000, and within 10 years it had climbed to about $2 million. By then, the Astors were buying real estate in New York City, which would add more millions to their fortune. Once again, Sarah Astor encouraged her husband in this new venture. Astor biographer Derek Wilson writes, "She became a useful junior partner who, in addition to bringing up her family, was fully conversant with the day-to-day running of the business."

In 1803, the family moved to a fine townhouse at 223 Broadway, and Astor operated from large, comfortable business offices. Sarah rarely saw her busy husband and had the major role in rearing the children and running the household. She was a stricter parent than John Jacob. Although she did not spend much time socializing or entertaining, she enjoyed attending the theater and inviting guests to musical performances at the Astor home.

Astor sold the fur business in 1834, the same year Sarah died while he was on a business trip in Europe. When Astor himself died in 1848, he was the richest man in America, with a fortune estimated at more than $20 million.

Further Reading

Cowles, Virginia. *The Astors.* New York: Knopf, 1979.

Kavaler, Lucy. *The Astors: A Family Chronicle of Pomp and Power.* New York: Dodd, Mead, 1966.

Stokesbury, James L. "John Jacob Astor, A Self-Invented Money-Making Machine," *American History,* December 1972. Available online. URL: http://www.thehistorynet.com/AmericanHistory/articles/1997/12972text.htm. Downloaded on January 3, 2001.

Wilson, Derek. *The Astors: 1763–1992.* New York: St. Martin's, 1993.

✳ AUERBACH, BEATRICE FOX

(1887–1968) *Entrepreneur, Executive, Philanthropist*

Beatrice Fox Auerbach built a family store into one of the largest privately owned retail businesses in America and one of the nation's finest department stores and implemented progressive labor reforms.

Beatrice Fox was born on July 7, 1887, in Hartford, Connecticut, where her ancestors had built a successful department-store business. Her parents, Theresa and Moses, both came from German-Jewish families that had moved to the United States during the mid-1800s. Beatrice's paternal grandfather, Gerson Fox, had opened the first G. Fox & Company department store in 1847, starting with a one-room dry-goods shop where he sold buttons, ribbons, and other specialty items. Moses Fox spent years working in the store and took charge after his father died in 1880. Under his leadership, Fox developed into a business that occupied a five-story building and sold an array of clothing, shoes, dry goods, household goods, and other items.

As a child, Beatrice enjoyed the privileges of wealth and was educated in private schools. During one of the family's frequent trips to Europe, Beatrice met George S. Auerbach and they were married. The couple settled in Salt Lake City, Utah, where George Auerbach operated a family-owned store, and they had two daughters: Georgette, born in 1916, and Dorothy, born in 1919.

Back in Hartford, a fire destroyed the Fox department store in 1917. Since a large inventory was stored in a warehouse, Moses Fox was able to continue the business by renting space in various buildings while a new store was constructed. The new 11-story G. Fox & Company store reopened in 1918. By then, Moses Fox was 66 years old, and he asked his son-in-law to move his family to Hartford and help him to run the store. George Auerbach took on the job of secretary-treasurer along with other duties at G. Fox.

Beatrice Auerbach also worked in the business part time but began working there full time after George Auerbach died in 1927. Two years later, she took over her husband's former job as secretary-treasurer and assumed other responsibilities to help her aging father. When Moses Fox died in 1938, Beatrice Auerbach became the manager of the store and president of G. Fox, a position she held from 1938 to 1965.

Under Beatrice Fox Auerbach, the store grew 10-fold to become one of the largest privately owned retail businesses in America and one of the nation's finest department stores. Auerbach offered customers more services, including a toll-free telephone order system and free delivery. Automated billing made that department more efficient. Auerbach also came up with creative ways to promote merchandise, and she hired efficient, innovative managers. Customers enjoyed the store's elegant surroundings and changing window displays. In 1947, her peers in the retail business awarded Auerbach the TOBE award as Connecticut's most outstanding merchant.

Auerbach also implemented labor reforms that benefited her 3,000 employees. Fox employees had a five-day, 40-hour workweek, and the store operated a nonprofit lunchroom on the premises. Employees received sick pay, medical care on the job, and retirement benefits, and they could borrow money from the company at no interest if they had a financial emergency. In addition, Auerbach was one of the first major department store owners to hire African Americans in higher-level jobs and to promote them.

Auerbach was also active in the community. She supported numerous charitable causes, and the community often sought her help when a problem arose. For example, in 1945, she sent a team of decorators to refurnish the Connecticut governor's mansion. The wife of Raymond E. Baldwin, the new governor, had reportedly refused to move into the mansion because the furnishings were mismatched. Auerbach's team located beautiful antiques and commissioned reproduction pieces from a respected Hartford cabinetmaker, Nathan Margolis, for the mansion.

In 1962, Auerbach received a special citation from the Connecticut Bar Association for her public service and charitable contributions. She devoted even more time to civic and philanthropic activities after she sold her stock in G. Fox to the May Department Store chain for $40 million in 1965. Auerbach established the Beatrice Fox Auerbach Foundation to fund worthwhile causes, including the Service Bureau for Women's Organizations, which helped to train women's groups in techniques of community organization. The University of Hartford, Connecticut College, and Hartford College for Women all benefited from Auerbach's generosity. She received honorary degrees from Wesleyan University, St. Joseph's College, the University of Hartford, and Trinity College.

Auerbach died on November 29, 1968. Her foundation continues to provide funds for a variety of educational, artistic, and social service programs and institutions.

Further Reading

Connecticut Forum. "Beatrice Fox Auerbach, 1887–1968." Available online. URL: http://www.ctforum.org/cwhf/auerbach.htm. Downloaded on March 1, 2001.

Reilly, Philip J. *Old Masters of Retailing: A History of Merchant Pioneers and The Industry They Built.* New York: Fairchild Publications, 1966.

State of Connecticut. "About the Governor's Residence." Available online. URL: http://www.state.ct.us/governor/tour/about.htm. Downloaded on May 3, 2001.

✳ AYER, HARRIET HUBBARD

(1849–1903) *Entrepreneur, Business Owner, Executive*

Harriet Hubbard Ayer was one of the first Americans to start a large cosmetics business and the first woman to make a fortune in this field. Her astute business methods and clever marketing techniques were especially remarkable during an era when few women owned or ran businesses.

Born in Chicago, Illinois, on June 27, 1849, to an affluent family, Harriet Hubbard graduated from the Convent of the Sacred Heart at age 15. Two years later, she married Herbert Ayer, a prominent Chicago businessman. They had three daughters, and Harriet Ayer became a patron of the arts and a society hostess. In 1886, she divorced her husband, who was rumored to be an alcoholic and a philanderer. Herbert Ayer also lost his fortune, leaving Harriet and her two surviving children without support.

Ayer moved to New York City and began working in the fine furniture industry, then started a decorating and antiques business, importing furniture, paintings, and other items from Europe. During a business trip to Paris in 1866, Ayer met a French chemist who sold a face cream she liked so much that she purchased the recipe. With financial help from her second husband, Ayer began to produce and market the cream under the label Recamier Preparations. (The French chemist had claimed that Madame Juliette Recamier, a famous beauty of the early 1800s, used the cream.) Ayer repeated this story in her newspaper ads. At that time, it was illegal to claim a product was a "beauty" cream, but Ayer managed to convey that message without using those precise words. She also paid American women known for their good looks to appear in ads and endorse the cream.

Through her social connections, Ayer was able to display and sell her product in top department stores, and sales grew steadily. Ayer, who also began writing about health and beauty, became wealthy. However, she spent substantial sums defending herself against lawsuits filed by people who claimed she had stolen her face cream formula from them.

In 1893, Ayer faced another serious problem: Her daughter Harriet's father-in-law had her committed to a mental institution, claiming that she was depressed over the death of a child that had occurred 22 years earlier. For 14 months, Ayer was confined in a private psychiatric hospital, then lost control of her cosmetics company after a bitter battle with the primary stockholders, one of whom was Harriet's father-in-law.

After her attorney and friends secured her release, Ayer embarked on a new career as a writer and lecturer. She spoke about the plight of the mentally ill. In those days, people could be committed without expert medical examinations or due process of law. Ayer criticized relatives who used involuntary commitment in order to seize control of a person's property, and she informed the public that some institutional supervisors were accepting bribes in exchange for confining people.

In 1896, Ayer began writing a new column in the New York *World* newspaper, offering advice about beauty. She emphasized good health habits, including nutrition, sleep, cleanliness, exercise, and fresh air. In 1899, Ayer published her best-selling book, *Harriet Hubbard Ayer's Book: A Complete and Authentic Treatise on the Laws of Health and Beauty.* She also produced new cosmetics, including La Belle Cocotte, which was promoted as an antiwrinkle face cream, and she served as a spokesperson for the Chesebrough Ponds Company, which made various creams. After Ayer died in 1903, her daughter Margaret took over writing the beauty advice column in the *World.*

Further Reading

Ayer, Margaret Hubbard, and Isabella Taves. *The Three Lives of Harriet Hubbard Ayer.* Philadelphia: Lippincott, 1957.

Decker, Jeffrey Louis. *Made in America: Self-Styled Success from Horatio Alger to Oprah Winfrey.* Minneapolis: University of Minnesota Press, 1997.

Mulvey, Kate, and Melissa Richards. *Decades of Beauty: The Changing Image of Women, 1890s–1990s.* New York: Checkmark Books, 1998.

B

✳ **BAJAJ, KAVELLE**
(1950–) *Entrepreneur, Business Owner, Executive*

Kavelle R. Bajaj founded I-Net, a leading computer service company, and has served as its president.

As a child growing up in India, Bajaj was taught that women should follow traditional roles as family caretakers, but she was interested in the family construction business from an early age. She later told interviewer Lavina Melwani, "I came from a business environment. My father, the whole family, was basically in business, but as a girl you're always discouraged, you're never encouraged." She decided to pursue higher education and earned a degree in home economics at the University of New Delhi.

In 1973, she was married; the next year, she and her husband, Ken, moved to the United States and settled in Maryland. Bajaj wanted to work but did not like the clerical jobs she was offered. She said, "I discovered that I really had no marketable skills per se." She began studying to become a professional dietitian but found she did not enjoy the work environment. Her husband encouraged her

desire to go into business, and she tried importing materials from India to create leather handbags and jewelry for sale. In addition, she decided to learn about computers and took courses at Montgomery College. During these years, she was also raising two sons.

Two years later, Bajaj, who had become a U.S. citizen in 1983, decided to go into the computer service industry. With $5,000 from the family budget, Bajaj founded I-Net, a business that sells computer hardware and software and constructs computer networks tailored specifically to the customer's needs. At first, the company operated out of the Bajaj home with eight employees.

Ken Bajaj was working for EDS Corporation at the time and was transferred to Detroit, Michigan, after General Motors bought the company. Kavelle stayed in Bethesda to run her own company, and for the next two years the couple spent weekends together while living in different cities. In 1988, Ken Bajaj left EDS to become executive vice president at I-Net, in charge of marketing and operations. Kavelle Bajaj remained in charge of finance and strategic planning. Their two sons later joined their parents in the business.

The company experienced extraordinary growth—a rate of 80–90 percent per year by 1988. I-Net provided systems for government clients, including the U.S. Army and the National Aeronautics and Space Administration (NASA), as well as Mobil, Shell, British Petroleum, and other large corporations. In 1994, its revenues reached more than $200 million. As president, Bajaj supervised 2,000 people in 38 offices in 22 states. In 1995, she won a local entrepreneur-of-the-year award in the Washington, D.C., area.

When asked by Lavina Melwani what special quality she brought to her job, Bajaj said, "The ability to listen and to understand what somebody is looking for and to put together a solution for them."

In 1996, I-Net was sold to Wang Laboratories for an undisclosed sum, and it became an independent subsidiary of Wang.

Further Reading

Melwani, Lavina. "Indian American Entrepreneurs Ride the Bull," *Little India,* November 30, 1994. Available online. URL: http://206.20.14.67/achal/archive/Oct96/nawab1.htm. Downloaded on May 3, 2001.

———. "Nawabs of Cyberspace," *Little India,* October 31, 1996. Available online. URL: http://www.elibrary.com/id/242/101/getdoc.cgi?id=196817370x...:US;EL&dtype=0~0&dinst. Downloaded on May 5, 2001.

Nelton, Sharon. "Inspiring Future Business Owners: An Income of Her Own," *Nation's Business* February 1, 1995, pp. 50–51.

"Notable Asian Americans: Kavelle Bajaj Founded Large Computer Firm," *Denver Rocky Mountain News,* May 30, 1998, p. 58A.

✳ BANDY, DICKSIE BRADLEY

(1890–1971)   *Entrepreneur, Business Owner*

Dicksie Bradley Bandy helped to build a small bedspread-making business into a large and successful textile company. Born in Bartow County, Georgia, in 1890, Dicksie Bradley, named after her country-doctor father, Dick, attended the Reinhart Normal College in Waleska, Georgia,

then graduated from Georgia State College for Women and became a schoolteacher. In 1915, she married Burl J. "B. J." Bandy, a Southern Railroad telegraph operator. During World War I, Dicksie Bandy began working as a telegraph operator at Southern Railroad, too, as men left their jobs to serve in the military. She continued to teach school during that time.

The Bandys had saved their money and opened country stores in Sugar Valley and Hill City, Georgia, but they experienced financial problems after the war, when the country went through a recession. Unable to sell their produce, local farmers could not afford to pay for goods they had purchased on credit before the harvest season. Bandy later said, "As times got worse and worse, many of our accounts took bankruptcy and never paid us anything. We owed our suppliers $22,000."

Determined to pay off their debts completely, Bandy and her husband looked for ways to earn money. They decided to sell hand-tufted, or chenille, bedspreads, a cottage industry that had evolved in the region at the turn of the century when Dalton, Georgia, native Catherine Evans Whitener revived this handicraft and sold some of her spreads. Other women in the region also made tufted bedspreads for various small companies or independent salespeople. Whitener let the Bandys use some of her patterns to make sample spreads.

Although Dicksie Bandy had never traveled beyond Atlanta before, she agreed to take a suitcase filled with samples to stores in northern cities, starting in Washington, D.C. Because they had worked for the railroad, the family could travel free with a railroad pass. Bandy first visited Woodward and Lothrop, a department store in Washington where the store buyer offered to purchase 400 bedspreads from Bandy at $4, which meant a profit of about $2 per spread. In Baltimore, Bandy sold another 200 spreads. After returning home to fill these orders, Bandy set off again, this time to Macy's, a famous New York City department store, where she secured an order for 1,000 bedspreads.

As demand increased, the Bandys operated from headquarters in Dalton and hired people to make the bedspreads from their homes, creating a business that would eventually employ numerous people. Women tufted the spreads at home, then sent them to be laundered and finished. The bedspreads were shipped around the country. The Bandys invested in machinery that helped to produce and finish the spreads, and they founded factories in Dalton, Rome, Cartersville, and Ellijay, all in Georgia.

The business boomed and was reportedly worth $1 million by the 1930s. With money to invest, the Bandys bought the Boycell Manufacturing Company in North Carolina, which made scatter rugs, bathrobes, and other tufted products, as well as bedspreads. The factory in Cartersville, eventually named Bartow Textiles, became the largest tufted textile mill in America.

Bandy's husband B. J. died in 1948. Their daughter Christine and her husband, Joe McCutchen, took over running the factory in Ellijay; son Jack Bandy also worked in the family businesses, which grew to include hotels; daughter Dicksie and her husband, David Tillman, took charge of Bartow Textiles in 1949. Chenille bedspreads remained popular throughout the 1950s, but then orders declined, so the family focused more on rugs and contributed to the growth of the carpeting industry. The family business grew to include Bartow Textiles, Universal Carpets, Coronet Industries, and Southern Craft Company.

Besides bringing many jobs to their region, the Bandys contributed money and time to various philanthropic causes. They donated the intensive-care unit to Dalton Hospital, and Dicksie Bandy became a major fund-raiser for the Salvation Army. She also supported the Dalton Regional Library System.

Bandy had a strong interest in the Cherokee Indians, who had been forced out of their ancestral lands in Georgia in 1828, a tragedy known as the Trail of Tears. She made speeches describing how thousands had died during their forced removal to a western reservation, saying, "I apologize to you, the Cherokee Nation, for what our gold-hungry, land-famished ancestors did." In the 1950s, Bandy spearheaded a campaign to dedicate the home of Cherokee chief Joseph Vann, located near Dalton, as a monument to the Cherokee Nation. The house was restored and officially dedicated in 1958. The Cherokee People of Oklahoma named Bandy an official ambassador to their nation and supported her award as a Georgia Woman of Achievement, an honor she received posthumously in 1993. Bandy died in 1971.

Further Reading

"Dicksie Bradley Bandy, 1890–1971." Georgia Women of Achievement: 1993 Inductee Dicksie Bradley Bandy. Available online. URL: http://www.gawomen.org/honorees/long/bandyd_long.htm. Downloaded on May 23, 2001.

Patton, Randall L. "B. J. Bandy and Bartow Textiles: Creating an Industry." Kennesaw State University Center for Regional History and Culture. Available online. URL: http://www.kennesaw.edu/research/crhc/articles/bandy.html. Downloaded on May 20, 2001.

✤ BARAD, JILL
(1951–) *Executive*

As president and chief executive officer (CEO) of Mattel, Inc., Barad headed one of the world's largest toy companies during the 1990s and was the second woman, after KATHARINE MEYER GRAHAM, to run one of America's top 500 companies.

Jill Ellikan was born on May 23, 1951 in Queens, New York, the daughter of Lawrence and Corky Ellikan. Her father was a television technician who went on to become a director of successful series programs. Jill, whose first job was operating the cash register at her grandparents' pharmacy, enjoyed performing and singing for her family when she was a child. At age 16, she modeled during the summer for a clothing company called Happylegs; later, she spent a year selling cosmetics. She received her bachelor of arts (B.A.) degree in 1973 from Queens College, majoring in English, psychology, and drama. Ellikan had planned to become a doctor but changed her mind after fainting in an operating room.

In 1974, she took a role in a film called *Crazy Joe* but decided she would prefer to go into business instead of acting. She accepted a job at Coty Cosmetics as a traveling cosmetician-trainer. During her business trips, she observed store displays and came up with ideas to improve the way Coty products were shown in the stores. One of her ideas for displaying face powder was adopted and used for 20 years.

She relocated to Los Angeles in 1977 after meeting Thomas K. Barad, now an independent film producer, whom she married in 1979. In Los Angeles, she took a job with an advertising agency that handled the Max Factor & Co. account until she became pregnant with the first of their two sons: Alex, born in 1980. Another son, Justin, was born in 1983.

In 1981, shortly after her first son was born, Barad returned to the business world, taking a job at Mattel (cofounded by RUTH HANDLER), where she earned $38,000 a year as a product manager. During the next two years, she helped to launch several successful new toys. In 1983, she was placed on the team that was in charge of Barbie, the popular teenage fashion doll Mattel had launched in 1959. Barad helped to dramatically improve Barbie sales, which also improved Mattel's earnings, as she suggested new ways to update Barbie and give her more diverse roles. In 1985, Barad suggested Day-to-Night Barbie, a doll that wore a business suit for day and elegant party clothes at night. Other new dolls for the 1980s were Dentist Barbie, Doctor Barbie, Executive Barbie, and Astronaut Barbie. Barad also came up with a popular advertising slogan to convey a positive message for young girls who played with the dolls: "We can do anything."

By the late 1990s, Mattel introduced Barbies with more diverse skin and eye colors, and a doll that used a wheelchair. Barbie came in white, Hispanic, and African-American versions. International, fairy-tale, and historical Barbies were manufactured, and the doll had appeared as a teacher, majorette, prom queen, nurse, ballerina, equestrian, flight attendant, physician, figure skater, archeologist, astronaut, and basketball player, among other things. A new, fuller-figured Barbie had a smaller bust and larger waist and hips.

Barbie sales increased from $200 million in 1982 to $1.9 billion in 1997. A Barbie fan herself, Barad had a six-foot-tall Barbie statue on the staircase of her home and hung Andy Warhol's painting of Barbie in her living room.

As a result of her success, Barad received several promotions and salary increases. She became an executive vice president, and, in 1989, she was promoted to copresident of Mattel's U.S. operations. In 1992, Barad was named president and chief operating officer (COO) of the company. Her colleagues said that she had a good sense for the kinds of toys that would appeal to children. Sheila Wellington, president of Catalyst, a group that does research on women in business, said of Barad: "She has proven you can work your way up from the bottom, that you can have a family and be a CEO, and that you can be very tough and very feminine."

Barad received awards and other recognition for her business achievements. In 1994, the Sara Lee Foundation gave her its Frontrunner Award, and she was on *Fortune* magazine's list of the Top 50 Women in Business in 1997, 1998, and 1999.

In 1997, Barad was named Mattel CEO. During the next three years, her compensation package totaled about $23 million, and she held options to buy 4.9 million shares of Mattel stock. Barad said that one of her goals was to build the company's high-tech toy division, including toys with built-in microprocessors and a Barbie digital camera. In addition to her responsibilities at Mattel, she sat on the boards of Microsoft Corporation and Pixar, Inc.

As of 1999, Barad was the top shareholder in the Mattel company. That year, she reportedly earned $780,000 and $4 million in bonuses. However, the company's stock had fallen and toy sales were declining. In 2000, Jill Barad resigned from Mattel and received a severance package that was reportedly worth $50 million.

Further Reading

Grant, Linda. "Mattel Gets All Dolled Up," *U.S. News and World Report,* December 13, 1993, pp. 74–76.

Morris, Kathleen. "The Rise of Jill Barad," *Business Week,* May 25, 1998, p. 63.
Wells, Jennifer. "Stuck on the Ladder," *Maclean's,* November 20, 1997, pp. 60ff.

BARTZ, CAROL
(1948–) *Executive*

Since 1992, Carol Bartz has been the president and chief executive officer (CEO) of Autodesk, which ranked as the world's fourth largest PC software company in 1997. Bartz believes that people can take charge of their own lives to create successful careers, and says, "I have worked for lousy management and great management, big companies and small companies, and I've had good relationships and bad relationships, and none of that matters. What matters is that it is my job to manage myself—mentor myself—through these things."

As president of Autodesk, Inc., Carol Bartz is one of the most prominent women in technology. (Courtesy of Autodesk, Inc.)

Carol Bartz was born in Wisconsin on August 28, 1948. Her father worked at a feed mill in their small town. Her mother was ill for several years and died when Carol was eight. After her mother's death, Carol helped to care for her younger brother, Jimmy, and did cooking, laundry, housecleaning, and other chores. A few years after her mother died, her maternal grandmother brought Carol and Jimmy to live on her farm.

In school, Bartz excelled in all her classes, especially science and math. She later told authors Liane Enkelis and Karen Olsen, "I actually loved those subjects—solving problems, getting answers, doing experiments. I got straight A's in everything: math and science weren't any different from any other subject." With a scholarship, she attended a women's college, William Woods, in Missouri, for two years, then went on to the University of Wisconsin, where she also won a scholarship. She graduated with honors in 1970 with a degree in computer science, then worked as a systems analyst at 3M, where she excelled at selling and servicing computer systems from 1972 to 1976.

After a few years, she hoped to rise to a management position but found few opportunities for women in her industry during the early 1970s. In 1976, she moved to Digital Equipment Corporation, a Boston-based company that had established itself as a leader in the computer industry. There, she worked as a sales manager and product-line manager.

By 1983, she was ready for a change and left for the Silicon Valley area of northern California to work at Sun Microsystems. This new company would eventually become a leader in its industry, providing network computing products, such as workstations, servers, storage subsystems, network switches, software, and microprocessors, along with customer support. At Sun Microsystems, Bartz began as a customer marketing manager, but before a year had passed, she was promoted to vice president of worldwide marketing. Under her direction, her division increased its revenues nearly 60 percent in two years. She rose to the second position in the company, vice president of worldwide field operations, which included customer service, with 6,500 people in her division. During the late 1980s, sales were booming and the service department had trouble keeping up with the demand, so Bartz worked with her team to resolve this problem and meet other challenges.

By 1990, Bartz had spent 20 years in the computer industry learning different skills and aspects of the business. Autodesk, Inc., a software company based in northern California, recruited her to head its company, which was growing and experiencing strong sales with its AutoCAD, a computer-aided design software product.

When Bartz arrived, she worked to give Autodesk more structure, clear leadership, and improved methods of communication among the different divisions. She assembled an experienced management team and implemented changes slowly enough to minimize the conflict that often accompanies changes in management. The company was geared to being creative and innovative, and she worked to channel those ideas into products customers want and need. Revenues increased nearly 15 percent by 1994, with an increase in net income of 42 percent over the previous year.

The same week she arrived at Autodesk, Bartz faced a serious health problem: She was diagnosed with breast cancer and required surgery, followed by other treatments. Bartz informed her coworkers about her situation and urged everyone to carry on as usual, something she tried to do herself. Since that time, Bartz has served on the boards of cancer organizations and says she wants to promote women's health and education after she retires, possibly in her fifties.

Bartz became CEO and chairman of the board of Autodesk in 1992. As of 1997, only 2 percent of technology company chief executives were women, yet Bartz found herself running the fourth-largest PC software company in the world. That year, she received the Women in Technology International (WITI) Hall of Fame award.

Married to Bill Marr, an executive at Sun Microsystems, Bartz is the mother of a daughter, Layne. She enjoys gardening and tennis and actively works to help young people excel in math and science. Bartz says that girls in particular should be encouraged to excel in science, math, and technology and prepared to assume leadership roles in those fields.

Bartz also tries to open new doors for women in the technology field. To that end, she sponsors Autodesk's Women's Manager Group and the Autodesk Foundation. She encourages all Autodesk employees to volunteer some time at their local schools, an activity they can fulfill as part of their work schedule.

Further Reading

Enkelis, Liane, and Karen Olsen. *On Our Own Terms.* San Francisco: Berrett-Kohler Publishers, 1995.

Gemperlein, Joyce, and Monique Talitenu. "An Interview With Carol Bartz," *San Jose Mercury News.* Available online. URL: http://www.thetech.org/revolutionaries/bartz/i_a.html. Downloaded on February 3, 2001.

Richards, Sally. "Changing the World, One Girl at a Time." An interview with Carol Bartz. Women in Technology International (WITI). Available online. URL: http://www.witi.com/wire/feature/cbartz.shtml. Downloaded on January 6, 2001.

BAY, JOSEPHINE PERFECT
(Josephine Holt Perfect)
(1900–1962)   *Financier, Executive*

Josephine Perfect Bay was the first woman to head a member firm of the New York Stock Exchange. Upon the death of her husband, she also ran a major shipping business.

Josephine Holt Perfect was born on August 10, 1900, in Anamosa, Iowa, but grew up in Brooklyn, New York. After graduating from Brooklyn Heights Seminary, she studied at Colorado College from 1918 to 1919, then returned to Brooklyn, where she became actively involved in community work, particularly the Junior League, a charitable group that offered volunteer opportunities for socially prominent young women. She was credited with helping to save the Brooklyn Junior League from serious financial problems during the 1930s. While continuing to work in community organizations, Josephine Perfect and her sister Tirzah also started a profitable Christmas card company.

In 1942, she married Charles U. Bay, a senior partner at the New York brokerage firm A.M. Kidder & Company and director of American Export Lines, a successful shipping business. When World War II ended, Charles Bay was appointed ambassador to Norway, and the couple lived there from 1946 to 1953. Josephine Bay organized and helped to implement relief programs for people in war-torn Europe.

After Charles Bay became ill in 1955, Josephine Bay was elected a limited partner at A.M. Kidder. Charles died that same year, and she became director of American Export Lines, which was then grossing about $60 million a year. Bay was elected chairman of the company's executive committee in 1956; that same year, she became president and chairman of the board of A. M. Kidder, a member of the New York Stock Exchange, making her the first woman to head a member firm.

Bay continued to actively work at both firms and was named chairman of the board of American Export in 1959. She remained in that position for one year and retained the presidency and chairmanship of A. M. Kidder until she died on August 6, 1962.

Further Reading

Bracken, Jeanne Munn. "Women in the Workplace: Business," *Women's History,* spring/summer 1996. Available online. URL: http://www.thehistorynet. com/WomensHistory/articles/19962_text.htm. Downloaded on May 27, 2000.

✳ BEECH, OLIVE ANN MELLOR
(1903–1993)   *Business Cofounder, Executive*

Called the First Lady of Aviation, Olive Ann Beech cofounded Beech Aircraft Corporation with her husband. After his death, she took charge of the company and expanded the business so that it became a leading manufacturer of private airplanes, with sales of more than $200 million by 1978.

Olive Ann Mellor was born on September 25, 1903, in Waverly, Kansas. Her father, Frank, was a carpenter and her mother, Suzannah, was a homemaker. Olive Ann attended grade school in Paola, Kansas, and later recalled that she was interested in mathematics at an early age. At age 7, she had her own bank account and was given the job of writing checks and paying the household bills. When she was 14, the family was living in Wichita, and she decided to enter the American Secretarial and Business College instead of the usual four-year high school. During those years, the secretarial field was one of the few careers women were encouraged to pursue. At the college, women learned bookkeeping, typing, and stenography.

After her graduation in 1920, Mellor took a job as office manager and bookkeeper at an electric company in Augusta, Kansas, where she lived in a boardinghouse. She returned to Wichita four years later and worked as a secretary at the Travel Air Manufacturing Company. The president was Walter H. Beech, a former World War I U.S. Army Air Corps pilot, engineer, and stunt flyer who had creative ideas for aircraft designs. Impressed by Mellor's financial skills, he hired her, and she became the only female employee, as well as the only nonpilot, at this new company.

Soon, Mellor was promoted from secretary to receptionist, then to bill collector and paymaster. She later recalled how the staff teased her because she knew very little about airplanes: "When I first started working at Travel Air, I didn't know the empennage [tail assembly of an aircraft] of an airplane from the wing." She asked the chief engineer to make her a detailed drawing of a plane with all the components labeled. After studying the parts of the plane, she learned how everything worked.

Mellor also learned the various aspects of the business and was promoted again, to office manager and executive secretary. As part of her job, she traveled with Walter Beech to meetings and air races, where he piloted Travel Air planes. The company received a major boost in 1925 when its planes won first, second, and third place in the 1925 Ford reliability tour. In 1926, the company introduced the first Travel Air cabin monoplane and then won the famous Woolaroc race from California to Hawaii.

Beech sold his company to Curtiss-Wright in 1929 and became an executive with the new, merged company. He and Olive Ann Mellor were married the next year. They settled in New York City, where Walter worked at his new job and she became a homemaker.

Within a few years, however, the couple decided to return to Wichita and start their own company, designing and producing airplanes. They invested their savings in the venture and rented space for a factory and offices. In 1932, they formed Beech Aircraft Corporation, with Walter as president and Olive as secretary-treasurer and director. Their goal was to build the finest planes in the world. Founded in the midst of the Great Depression, the company, which produced private and commercial planes, had no sales its first year and only one sale the second. The business improved steadily after they introduced their Model 17 Staggerwing, a single-engine cabin biplane with a comfortable five-seat interior, in 1934. The plane was speedier than the fastest military plane. In 1937, they brought out another successful plane, the Model 18 Twin Beech, which was popular with both civilians and the air corps. Their company motto became "It takes a Beechcraft to beat a Beechcraft!" Both planes remained in production for years.

Olive Beech handled the company's finances but also worked in numerous ways to build the business. In 1936, she suggested they let a female pilot race the Staggerwing for that year's Bendix trophy, America's premier cross-country flying race, so that people would be impressed to see a woman, not a muscular man, at the controls. Pilots Louise Thaden and Blanche Noyes won the race, setting a new transcontinental speed record. By 1938, sales would top $1 million.

In 1937, the Beeches welcomed their first daughter, SuzAnne. A second daughter, Mary Lynn, was

In 1951, the year after Olive Beech took over as head of the company she and her husband had cofounded, the Women's National Aeronautics Association named her its Woman of the Year.
(Photo courtesy of Wichita State University, Special Collections)

born in 1940. While Olive was in the hospital giving birth, Walter Beech was stricken with encephalitis and was hospitalized with swelling in his brain. He lapsed into a coma, and from her hospital bed Olive Beech had to take over managing the company. Although Walter Beech survived, he was hospitalized for nearly a year. When he did return to work, he was no longer physically strong, so Olive Beech assumed many of his functions at Beech Aircraft during this critical time.

For the next few years, World War II brought a tremendous demand for airplanes, which were needed for combat, transport, and training purposes. Olive Beech took out more than $75 million in loans to expand the plants. The company supplied 7,400 military aircraft during the war, and most American navigators and bombardiers trained in a Beech Aircraft Navigator, Kansan, or Wichita. Olive Beech gained national recognition as an outstanding businesswoman, and, in 1943, the *New York Times* named her as one of America's 12 most distinguished women.

When the war ended, the company produced some outstanding new civilian planes, including the Twin Beech and the Mentor, a military training plane. Sales of planes sagged in the late forties, so Olive Beech diversified. Beech Aircraft factories made corn harvesters, cotton pickers, and washing machines, which sold well.

After the United States entered the Korean War (1950–53), aircraft sales rose again. Walter Beech died suddenly in 1950 of a heart attack. With a war on, Olive Beech had even more work than usual during this difficult time. She was named president, chairman of the board, and chief executive officer of the company. In 1951, the Women's National Aeronautical Association selected her as its Woman of the Year. Beech was now a single mother and an executive running a busy company, unusual for a woman of that era. She was determined that Beech Aircraft would continue to succeed and introduce outstanding new designs, so she supported a strong research and development department. At the office, she was known as a strict manager who expected employees to perform their jobs well.

During the 1950s and 1960s, the company was known for top-quality commercial and military aircraft. In 1955, Beech Aircraft produced the world's smallest jet, a military plane called the Model 73, and continued to produce its popular Bonanza. The twin-engine Queen Air series was brought out in 1960, along with lower-priced single-engine planes. Beech Aircraft also produced parts for other aircraft companies and set up a research and development facility to carry out special assignments for the National Aeronautics and Space Administration (NASA). Beechcraft cryogenic loading and transfer systems and gas storage systems were used for the Gemini, Apollo, and Lunar Module projects. Olive Beech also advised several U.S. presidents on aviation matters.

The year 1967 marked an all-time high in Beech Aircraft sales, and the future was promising. In 1968, Beech resigned as president and her nephew, Frank Hedrick, took over. She remained chairman of the board of directors of the company, which grew to include 10,000 employees, with annual sales of more than $900 million, in 1980. That year, at age 77, Beech sold Beech Aircraft to Raytheon Company but remained as chairman of the board for two more years, as well as a director on the board of Raytheon.

Olive Ann Beech died in Wichita on July 6, 1993. During her lifetime, Beech received many honors, both for her business achievements and civic contributions—to the arts, education, and youth programs. She received the Wright Brothers Memorial Trophy in 1980 and was inducted into the Aviation Hall of Fame (1981) and Kansas Aviation Hall of Fame (1986). Olive Beech was the first Kansan to be inducted into the National Business Hall of Fame (1983).

Further Reading

"Beech, Olive Ann—1981," National Aviation Hall of Fame. Available online. URL: http://www.nationalaviation.org/enshrinee/beecholive.htm. Downloaded on November 12, 2000.

"Kansas Aviation Hall of Fame Awards, Olive Ann Beech," November 14, 1986. Available online. URL: http://www.wingsoverkansas.com/archives/halloffame.htm/#olivebeech. Downloaded on November 4, 2001.

McDaniel, William H. *Beech: A Quarter Century of Aeronautical Achievement.* Wichita, Kansas: McCormick-Armstrong, 1947.

"Olive Ann (Mellor) Beech," Kansas Business Hall of Fame. Available online. URL: http://www.emporia.edu/kbhf/beech.html. Downloaded on November 5, 2000.

✾ BEERS, CHARLOTTE
(1935–   )   *Executive*

Once called "the most powerful woman in advertising," as of 2000 Charlotte Beers was the only person to have headed two of America's top

10 advertising agencies—Ogilvy & Mather and J. Walter Thompson. She was also the first woman to chair the American Association of Advertising Agencies. Her method of defining the relationship between consumers and brands, called "brand stewardship," has been used in college classes on advertising and is the basis of a well-known case study used at the Harvard Business School.

Beers was born on July 26, 1935, in Beaumont, Texas, where her father was in the oil business. She majored in math and physics at Baylor University, then taught algebra to engineering students after graduating in 1957. In 1959, she became a group product manager at Uncle Ben's, the rice company, in Houston. Ten years later, she left for Chicago to became an account executive at J. Walter Thompson, a prominent advertising firm, where she rose to become the first female vice president in that company's 106-year history.

Beers wanted to run an agency herself, so in 1979, she left Thompson for a smaller agency, Tatham-Laird & Kudner, where she was known for her enthusiasm and energy, often working 100 hours a week. Beers became chief executive officer (CEO) of the firm in 1982. Under her direction, the company's profits rose considerably as executives signed up major new brands and products to represent. Profit margins were double the industry average during the next decade, and client billings reached $325 million. A recognized leader in her field, Beers became the first woman elected as chair of the American Association of Advertising Agencies.

When Beers resigned from Tatham-Laird & Kudner in 1990, several companies tried to recruit her. She went to New York City, where she became president of Ogilvy & Mather Worldwide, one of the largest multinational ad agencies. For four years, during Beers's presidency, billings rose about 60 percent. When she went into semiretirement in 1996, another woman, SHELLY LAZARUS, took over the head job at Ogilvy.

Beers had planned to retire in Palm Beach, Florida, and do part-time consulting, but in 1999 she decided instead to assume the chairmanship at J. Walter Thompson, the agency where she had worked earlier in her career. WPP Group, a British advertising firm that has owned Thompson since 1987, acquired Young & Rubicam, another large multinational agency, in April 2000, creating the world's largest ad and marketing services company. Chris Jones, the CEO of J. Walter Thompson, said of Charlotte Beers, "She brings out the very best in people by understanding clients' brands sometimes better than they do."

In March 2001, President George W. Bush nominated Beers to the post of Under Secretary of State for Public Diplomacy, and she was sworn in on October 2, 2001. In this new role, Beers faced major challenges in the wake of the terrorist attacks on the United States on September 11. She said she would work to help "redefine who America is" to people around the world so they would understand America's values, such as freedom and tolerance. Beers, who is divorced, is the mother of a daughter.

Further Reading

"Charlotte Beers, Chairman, J. Walter Thompson Co., Age 64." *Crain's New York Business.* Available online. URL: http://www.crainsny.com/page.cms?pageId=7. Downloaded on March 4, 2001.

Cozens, Claire. "Profile: Charlotte Beers." MedicaGuardian.co.uk—Advertising. Available online. URL: http://www.media.guardian.co.uk/advertising/story/0,7492,46 4073,00.html. Downloaded on February 27, 2001.

Crain, Rance. "An Advertising Call to Arms," Available online. URL: http://www.adage.com/news.cms?newsId=33210. Downloaded on November 5, 2001.

Elliott, Stuart. "Charlotte Beers," *Texas Monthly,* September 1999, pp. 140–141.

Neuborne, Ellen. "Madison Ave: A Star Is Reborn," *Business Week,* July 26, 1999, p. 54ff.

BEGOUN, PAULA
(1953–) *Entrepreneur, Business Owner, Executive*

Paula Begoun, a consumer advocate who covers the cosmetics industry and founded a cosmetics business, is known around the world as the Cosmetics

Known as the "Cosmetics Cop," Paula Begoun provides consumers with up-to-date information about the contents and performance of various cosmetics and hair care products and offers her own line of products.
(Photo courtesy of Paula Begoun and Beginning Press)

Cop. Begoun once said that she began investigating cosmetics in order to give consumers more accurate information and "to get beyond the hype and chicanery of the cosmetics industry."

Begoun was born on November 14, 1953, in Skokie, Illinois. She attended Northern Illinois University, where she was a science major. However, she had always dreamed of a theatrical career and decided to become a freelance makeup artist and skin care consultant. She was especially interested in finding effective remedies for acne, a skin problem she had experienced firsthand.

During the late 1970s, she also began working part time at department store cosmetics counters. Begoun later said that her supervisors criticized her for showing customers less expensive products or alternatives to the product lines she was asked to promote. Her goal was to provide customers with products that would best suit their needs, regardless of brand.

By 1978, Begoun became increasingly critical of the way cosmetics were being promoted. She began studying cosmetics production and the advertising methods used by the multibillion-dollar beauty industry. Begoun later said, "I wasn't anti-makeup—just the opposite—but I was (and am) anti-hype and anti-misleading information." She was concerned about products that did not do what the makers said they would do or that even caused negative effects, such as irritating the skin.

Begoun decided to find out as much as possible about the cosmetics industry and the properties and effects of different ingredients and products. She believed that customers needed more accurate information in order to select the right products and obtain value for their money. Armed with more knowledge, they would know whether a product lived up to the claims manufacturers were making.

In 1981, she opened her own cosmetic stores, called Generic Makeup, in the Seattle area, and trained her salespeople to help customers make sensible choices. In addition, Begoun worked as a consumer reporter on television and was featured in the national and international media in her syndicated newspaper column.

Begoun self-published her first book, *Blue Eyeshadow Should Be Illegal*, in 1986, intending it to be a no-nonsense guide to cosmetics and beauty. After receiving numerous letters from appreciative readers, Begoun wrote two detailed guides listing items by brand name, one on cosmetics and skin care products—*Don't Go to the Cosmetics Counter Without Me*—and the other on hair care products—*Don't Go Shopping For Hair Care Products Without Me*. Begoun compared the claims companies made about their products to their actual ingredients and performance, while also considering costs. Later, she began publishing her Cosmetics Counter Update newsletter and ran a website to keep consumers informed about new products, research, and developments in the industry.

To obtain information about different products, Begoun and her assistants buy thousands of dollars' worth of cosmetics each year, watch numerous commercials, and study ads and makeup displays at stores. Begoun gains other information by talking with experts. She says, "I base all my comments on comprehensive interviews with dermatologists, oncologists, cosmetic chemists, and cosmetic industry magazines and medical journals." She also reads research abstracts and studies to learn more about various ingredients. Begoun welcomes feedback from consumers. Her newsletters address questions from consumers, who also share their experiences with different products, and include responses from companies whose products she has critiqued.

Begoun's best-selling books list thousands of different products, and she updates these reports in her syndicated newspaper column and newsletter, as well as on her website. Her company, Paula's Choice, offers a variety of skin care products and color cosmetics.

Further Reading

"About Paula." Available online. URL: http://www.cosmeticscop.com/meetpaula.htm. Downloaded on September 3, 2000.

Begoun, Paula. *The Beauty Bible.* Seattle: Beginning Press, 1997.

———. *Blue Eyeshadow Should Be Illegal.* Seattle: Beginning Press, 1986.

———. *Don't Go to the Cosmetics Counter Without Me: An Eye-Opening Guide to Brand-Name Cosmetics.* Seattle: Beginning Press, 1997.

———. *Don't Go Shopping for Hair Care Products Without Me.* Seattle: Beginning Press, 1998.

✳ BEHRMAN, BEATRICE ALEXANDER
(Bertha Alexander, Madame Alexander)
(1895–1990) *Entrepreneur, Business Owner, Executive*

Beatrice Alexander, founder of the Madame Alexander Doll Company, produced dolls that set international standards and have been prized as collectibles and playthings since the 1920s. The company became a leading manufacturer of hand-crafted dolls in America.

Bertha Alexander was born in Brooklyn, New York, on March 9, 1895, the daughter of Maurice (Max) and Hannah Pepper Alexander. Max Alexander, an expert at repairing antiques, had been born in Russia and educated in Germany before immigrating to America in 1885. In Brooklyn, he opened a porcelain repair shop and operated the first "doll hospital" in the United States. As a child, Bertha spent a lot of time around the dolls and helped out in the workrooms, as well as doing clerical work.

In 1912, Bertha, who changed her name to Beatrice, graduated from Washington Irving High School. That same year, she married Philip Behrman. The couple had one daughter, Mildred.

Beatrice Behrman continued to work in her father's business, which experienced sagging sales during World War I, when the United States and its allies were at war with Germany. Most dolls and doll parts had been imported from Germany but those imports were banned in wartime. In addition, the German dolls were made of porcelain, a material that can easily break and crack, which made them less popular.

To solve these problems, Behrman decided to make cloth dolls with lovely outfits and sell them in her father's shop. With her three sisters, she made Red Cross nurse dolls with three-dimensional features, then added dolls based on fictional characters in classic books and stores, including *Alice in Wonderland* and "The Three Little Pigs." She especially enjoyed designing their clothing.

With a small loan of $5,000, she founded her Alexander Doll Company in 1923. The bank officer who lent her the money told her he thought she was a poor risk, but her business thrived and she repaid the loan before the due date. Philip Behrman began working with her and later became general manager of the company. Beatrice Behrman played an active role in designing the dolls and sewing them and their costumes. She also promoted the dolls and sold them directly to stores during the 1920s.

Alexander dolls became known for their high-quality workmanship and realistic details, such as rooted hair, lifelike eyes, and movable limbs. As new materials became available, the dolls changed. During the 1930s, the company produced more cloth dolls as well as composition dolls, made from a type of plastic material, with painted-on features and eyes that closed and opened (sleep eyes). Hard plastic arrived in the 1940s, followed by vinyl, which became the most popular material for dolls. Alexander did not produce porcelain dolls. An employee later recalled, "[Madame] said a child shouldn't have a doll that will break." But the company found a way to give the doll's skin a satiny finish by tumbling the components in a mixture of olive oil and sawdust.

Since Behrman loved costume design, many of the dolls wore elaborate and distinctive outfits. Period dolls, such as the Little Women dolls (based on the 19th-century Louisa May Alcott novel) that were first produced in 1930, wore gowns that suited the era in which their character had been created. Despite the economic downturn of the Great Depression during the 1930s, the company continued to grow. In 1936, it was featured in *Fortune* magazine as one of America's three major doll manufacturers.

Operating out of its pink-and-blue factory in Harlem, a neighborhood of New York City, the Alexander company became the first to issue a doll based on a licensed character when it introduced its Scarlett O'Hara doll, based on the character in Margaret Mitchell's novel *Gone with the Wind,* in 1937. Different versions of Scarlett were issued in later years. Numerous firsts kept the company in the forefront of doll production. They included the first baby dolls with realistic features; the first composition dolls with sleep eyes; the use of distinctive face molds; the first dolls made in the likeness of famous living people (Queen Elizabeth, child actress Margaret O'Brien, the Dionne quintuplets); and the first full-figured fashion doll—Cissy—which came with fashionable outfits and accessories, in the late 1950s. Many Alexander dolls have been produced in series, including the International Dolls and the Baby Alexanders.

Through the years, the boxes, which are blue with pink floral designs, have borne the phrase, "It's a Madame Alexander—That's All You Need to Know." Another company slogan is "The Most Beautiful Dolls in the World Are by Madame Alexander."

During World War II, plastic and other materials were unavailable, so the company halted production. When the war ended in 1945, the Alexander company was among the first to make dolls from the new plastics that became available. Dolls were extremely popular during the Baby Boom years of the 1950s. Among the company's best-selling dolls were Cissy, Cissette (an 8-inch version of Cissy), Wendy, Elise, and Lissy, a fashion doll with jointed ankles that let her wear either high- or low-heeled shoes.

One of Behrman's most spectacular successes was a set of dolls she created in 1953 in honor of the coronation of Queen Elizabeth II. Abraham and Straus Department Store commissioned the project, which included 36 dolls, all beautifully costumed. They were displayed at the store and featured on television before the coronation, which was also televised in the United States. Behrman later donated the dolls to the Brooklyn Children's Museum.

The Alexander company has donated other dolls for charitable causes. In the early 1980s, 25 Portrait Dolls were given to the Children's Home Society of California for a benefit auction, where each fetched $2,900. Behrman also contributed money to the Cystic Fibrosis Foundation, the American Friends of Hebrew University, the Anti-Defamation League of B'nai Brith, and other causes.

In 1988, Behrman sold her company to private investors but remained as a design consultant. She died on October 3, 1990. The company was sold again in 1995.

Beatrice Behrman and her company won numerous awards, including the Fashion Academy Gold Medal Award for outstanding costuming in 1951, 1952, 1953, and 1954. She also received the first Lifetime Achievement Award given by *Doll Reader Magazine* (1986) and the F.A.O. Schwarz Lifetime Achievement Award as "First Lady of Dolls" (1986). Two Alexander dolls, Scarlett O'Hara and Madame Doll (from the American Revolution) were chosen for the Smithsonian Institution's historical doll collection.

Ten years after Alexander's death, she was inducted into the Toy Industry's Hall of Fame. As of 2001, most of the dolls were still being manufactured in the six-story Harlem plant that has been operating since the 1930s, and between 500,000 and 750,000 dolls were being sold each year.

Further Reading

Ilnytzky, Ula. "Madame Alexander's Work Endures at Harlem Doll Factory," *The Standard Times,* October 28, 1996. Available online. URL: http://www.s-t.com/daily/10-96/10-28-96/b011i036.htm. Downloaded October 11, 2001.

King, Constance Eileen. *The Collector's History of Dolls.* New York: Bonanza Books, 1981.

"Madame Beatrice Alexander Behrman," and "History of the Alexander Doll Company," Madame Alexander Doll Company. Available online. URL: http://www.alexanderdolls.com. Downloaded on February 7, 2001.

Uhl, Marjorie V. Sturges. *Madame Alexander Dolls on Review.* Dallas: Taylor Publishing Co., 1981.

�֎ BISHOP, HAZEL GLADYS

(1906–1998)   *Entrepreneur, Chemist, Executive*

Hazel Gladys Bishop, a chemist, founded a cosmetics company that featured her own lipstick formulas. Her Lasting Lipstick line was marketed as the world's first "kissproof lipstick." She later entered the financial field as a stockbroker and analyst.

Bishop was born on August 17, 1906, in Hoboken, New Jersey. In 1929, she graduated from Barnard College and planned to enter medical school. However, after the stock market crash in 1929, and the ensuing Great Depression, Bishop could not afford to pursue her education. She attended graduate school at night at Columbia University in New York City while working full time by day. From 1935 to 1942, she worked as an assistant in a dermatological (skin care) laboratory. From 1942 to 1945, while Bishop was working as a chemist with the Standard Oil Company, she developed high-altitude fuels for airplane engines. From 1945 to 1950, she worked as a chemist at the Socony Vacuum Oil Company.

During these years, Bishop had been experimenting with different cosmetic formulas in a laboratory she set up in her New York apartment. She devoted most of her time to finding a lipstick formula that would last longer than other commercial products yet would not dry out or irritate the sensitive skin on the lips. The formula she developed contained higher-than-normal amounts of colorant combined with a lanolin-based cream.

In 1950, she formed her company, Hazel Bishop, Inc., and began marketing Lasting Lipstick for one dollar a tube. The lipstick left a stain of color on the lips that lasted for hours. Ads for Bishop's lipstick called it "revolutionary" and proclaimed, "It stays on you . . . not on him." Women liked the fact that they did not have to keep reapplying their lipstick and that it even lasted overnight so they could wake up with color on their lips. Hazel Bishop, Inc., was a financial success, gaining a 25 percent share of the lipstick market with its Lasting Lipstick line. Other companies hastened to produce their own versions of this type of lipstick.

Bishop resigned as president of the company in 1951, during a dispute with the majority stockholder. Sales of her Lasting Lipstick continued to grow, especially after the company began advertising on television. Between 1950 and 1953, sales rose from $50,000 to $4.5 million. By 1954, sales were greater than $10 million annually; that year, Bishop sold her company.

Launching a new venture, Bishop created the Hazel Bishop Laboratories to develop new consumer products. During the 1950s and early 1960s, scientists in the lab developed a leather cleaner and various personal care products and cosmetics. In 1962, Bishop embarked on another career as a stockbroker at Bache and Company in New York City, and she later became a financial analyst for another New York firm, Evans and Company. She remained interested in the fashion and beauty industry and accepted a position as adjunct professor at the Fashion Institute of Technology.

Hazel Bishop, who was known for her wit as well as her inventiveness and business skills, died at the age of 92 on December 5, 1998.

Further Reading

McHenry, Robert, editor. *Her Heritage: A Biographical Encyclopedia of Famous American Women.* Cambridge: Pilgrim New Media, 1995.

Mulvey, Kate, and Melissa Richards. *Decades of Beauty: The Changing Image of Women, 1890s–1990s.* New York: Checkmark Books, 1998.

BISSELL, ANNA SUTHERLAND

(1846–1934) *Business Cofounder, Executive*

Anna Sutherland Bissell helped to found and then run the BISSELL Sweeper Company, making her one of the first women chief executive officers (CEOs) in America. While rearing five children and playing an active role in civic affairs, Bissell helped to build the largest corporation of its kind in the world.

Anna Sutherland was born in River John, Pictou County, Nova Scotia, Canada, on December 2, 1846. She grew up in De Pere, Wisconsin, where her family moved when she was three years old. At age 16, she became a schoolteacher. Three years later, she married Melville R. Bissell, whom she had met when he was visiting De Pere. The couple settled in Kalamazoo, Michigan, where they owned and operated a small crockery shop. In 1871, they moved their business to Grand Rapids, a larger city in Michigan.

While cleaning the shop each day, Anna Bissell found that the sweepers available at that time could not remove all the dirt embedded in the carpet fibers, including the bits of straw that were used to pack crates of china. Her husband, who suffered from chronic headaches and allergies, believed this dirt aggravated his health problems. Melville had good mechanical skills and he set out to solve the problem. He built a more compact sweeping device for cleaning floors. People who saw Bissell's sweeper wanted to buy one.

Bissell patented his first sweeper design in 1876, and the couple began building them for sale on the floor above their shop. Anna Bissell worked with her husband as a traveling salesperson, offering sweepers for $1.50 apiece. They often took a buggy full of sweepers door-to-door in residential sections of Grand Rapids. One of Anna Bissell's biggest sales successes was convincing New York department store owner John Wanamaker to stock the sweepers in his stores.

The first BISSELL manufacturing plant opened in Grand Rapids, Michigan, in 1880. Three years later, the corporation was organized, with Melville Bissell as president. Anna Bissell played a key role in the manufacturing and distribution of BISSELL sweepers. When a fire destroyed the manufacturing plant in 1884, she worked with local banks to obtain loans to maintain the business. In less than a month, production resumed. Profits from their business enabled the Bissells to expand and to buy real estate.

When Melville Bissell died of pneumonia in 1889, Anna Bissell took over as head of BISSELL to become one of America's first female corporate CEOs. She diligently studied all aspects of the company. Under her leadership, sales of BISSELL sweepers grew and the business expanded to other countries. She also oversaw the development of new and improved products.

From 1889 to 1919, she served as president, and from 1919 to 1934, she was chair of the board. Bissell was respected as a progressive executive who provided compensation insurance and pension plans and showed concern for her employees. Her grandson John Bissell recalled that during the Great Depression of the 1930s, when sales of all kinds of goods plummeted, she avoided laying off employees. Instead, she found ways to distribute work hours among the employees so that "everybody at least had something in their [pay] envelopes."

Despite her busy life as a mother and executive, Anna Bissell was active in her community, and she promoted opportunities for other women in business.
(Photo courtesy of BISSELL Company)

In addition to her busy schedule as an executive and mother, Bissell was actively involved in the community. A devoted Methodist, she became the first woman ever to be made a trustee of that church. She served on the executive committee of the Red Cross for her district and was a lifetime member of the Women's City Club. As a member of Zonta, an organization of business and professional women, she promoted opportunities for women in business. She also supported the work of the Union Benevolent Association, later the Blodgett Memorial Medical Center, and worked on behalf of the adoption of children as a board member for the Blodgett Home for Children.

In 1888, Anna Bissell joined the newly founded King's Daughters club, which carried

out charitable projects. When the group decided to build a settlement house in 1897, Bissell agreed to pay for the facility, which became the Bissell House. It offered training programs in homemaking, business skills, gardening, and the arts. The Bissell House also provided recreational opportunities for youth, such as sports, music, and drama. The house operated until 1912.

Bissell received numerous awards, including induction into the Michigan Hall of Fame and the local Business Hall of Fame. She was the first woman member of the National Hardware Men's Association and the only female member for many years. When she died in 1934, Bissell was eulogized as "a business executive without peer" and "respected and beloved philanthropist."

The company that Anna and Melville Bissell founded is still owned and operated by the family today. BISSELL produces various kinds of sweepers, carpet deep cleaners, vacuums, and cleaning products that are sold throughout the world.

Further Reading

BISSELL Company. "About Us: A History of Good Business Since 1876." Available online. URL: http://www.bissell.com/en/AboutUs/History/default.asp. Downloaded on May 23, 2001.

BISSELL, Inc. "Biography of Anna Bissell." Courtesy of BISSELL Inc., 2345 Walker Street NW, Grand Rapids, MI 49544.

Hallett, Anthony and Diane Hallett. *Entrepreneur Magazine's Encyclopedia of Entrepreneurs.* New York: John Wiley & Sons, 1997.

✸ BLACK, CATHLEEN
(1944–)   *Executive*

Cathleen Black has become a major force in American magazine publishing, where she has held executive positions no woman ever achieved before. As president of Hearst Magazines and director of Hearst Corporation, Black oversees the world's largest publisher of monthly magazines and has been ranked more than once in the top 50 of *Fortune* magazine's 100 most powerful American businesswomen.

Born in Chicago on April 26, 1944, Cathleen Black graduated from Trinity College in Washington, D.C., in 1966. After college, she sold advertising for magazines, including *Holiday* and *Travel & Leisure,* then left to join the staff of *New York* magazine in 1970.

Black continued to rise in the publishing world. In 1972, she became the advertising director at *Ms.,* the pioneer feminist magazine that was cofounded by Gloria Steinem. Black joined *New York* magazine in 1977 as associate publisher, then made history in 1979 by becoming the first woman publisher of a weekly consumer magazine when she attained that position at *New York.*

During the 1980s, Black joined Gannett Publications, first as president and, in 1983, as publisher of *USA Today,* a one-year-old national newspaper that featured color photos and other innovations. She later recalled that when the paper's founder recruited her for that job, "He persuaded me that this was a great opportunity to get in on the ground floor of a huge, new, groundbreaker in publishing. The biggest media launch of the decade, maybe the century. It would be an adventure, he said." Black continued as publisher of *USA Today* for eight years. At Gannett, Black served as executive vice president for marketing and became a member of the corporation's board of directors.

In 1991, Black was named president and chief executive officer (CEO) of the Newspaper Association of America. During her five-year tenure, six trade associations merged to become the newspaper industry's largest trade group.

Five years later, in 1996, Black became the first woman ever to be named president of Hearst Magazines Division, the world's largest publisher of monthly magazines. Hearst's publications include *Redbook, Good Housekeeping, Esquire, Harper's Bazaar,* and *Popular Mechanics.* Commenting on her appointment, the *New York Times* said that Black brought strong advertising skills to her new position. She has also been called a creative manager who looks for new ways to reach readers and advertisers. At Hearst, Black helped to launch a new magazine, Tina Brown's *Talk,* in 1999, and OPRAH WINFREY's *O* magazine in 2000. Circulation of *O* has grown steadily since its first issue.

Under her direction, Hearst has also extended the brand names of its titles into more than 3,500 products on the world market, and Black has promoted growth in licensing and the Internet. These products include the Good Housekeeping lines of kitchen appliances and other housewares. By 2001, Hearst was publishing 101 editions of its magazines in more than 41 countries.

Black has served on the boards of other companies, including Coca-Cola, where she became a director in 1993. She had previously served as a director there from April 1990 to May 1991. In addition, as of 2001, she was serving on the boards of iVillage and IBM, as well as on the boards of the United Way of America and the Points of Light Foundation, and she was also a trustee of the University of Notre Dame.

Fortune magazine ranked Cathleen Black as one of its top 30 Most Powerful Women in American Business in 1998, 1999, and 2000. In 2000, she was also honored by *Advertising Age* magazine as its Publishing Executive of the Year. Black lives with her husband and two children in New York City.

Further Reading

Black, Cathleen P. "Reflections on Leadership." Speech to the fall 1998 Fulbright Convocation, Institute of International Education, New York City, October 13, 1998. Available online. URL: http://www.iie.org/svcs/convocation/speech.htm. Downloaded on March 2, 2001.

"Business One Hundred: C. Black, D. M. Browne, B. P. Burns, J. Casey, M. M. Cashman . . ." *Irish America,* December 31, 1998, p. 40ff.

"Corporate Biographies: Cathleen Black, President, Hearst Magazines." The Hearst Corporation. Available online. URL: http://www.hearstcorp.com/biographies/corp_bio_black.html. Downloaded on May 15, 2001.

Gonser, Sarah. "The Incredible, Sellable O," *Folio,* February 1, 2001. Available online. URL: http://industryclick.com/magazinearticle.asp?magazineid=125&releaseid=4118&magazinearticleid=41344&siteid=2. Downloaded on May 13, 2001.

Rimm, Sylvia B., et al. *How Jane Won: 55 Successful Women Share How They Grew from Ordinary Girls to Extraordinary Women.* New York: Crown, 2001.

Saporta, Maria. "Transition at Coca-Cola." *The Atlanta Constitution,* December 7, 1999, p. D-7.

✖ BOEHM, HELEN (Elena Francesca Stefanie Franzolin, Helen Franzolin)
(1920–　) *Entrepreneur, Executive*

In 1950, Helen Boehm and her husband founded the Boehm porcelain company, which became one of the world's most prestigious makers of fine porcelain sculptures. When they began, Boehm was a two-person operation with very little capital, and the company faced tremendous competition from established firms. However, the couple decided to follow their dream. Helen Boehm says, "Life is a collection of risks. I am not afraid to take them. If you lose, you must work to win again."

She was born Elena Francesca Stefanie Franzolin on December 26, 1920, but later changed her name to Helen. Her parents had emigrated from Italy and settled in Brooklyn, a borough of New York City, where her father, Pietro, was a cabinetmaker, and her mother, Francesca, was a homemaker. When she was 13, her father died, and Helen and her six older siblings worked at part-time jobs to help support the family. Helen had learned to cook and sew, and she won awards in school for her sewing designs, so she made clothing for her classmates, charging them 50 cents a dress.

After Franzolin graduated from high school, she worked as a receptionist for the family optometrist while attending the Mechanical School of Optics in Brooklyn Heights at night. She became one of the first women in New York State to earn an optician's license, which meant that she was authorized to make the corrective lenses used in prescription eyeglasses.

At age 24, Franzolin met Edward Boehm, who was then working as a veterinary assistant. His hobby was sculpting animals from clay, an art he had taught himself, and he was a well-known aviculturist—a person who studies the biology and habits of birds. The couple were married on October 29, 1944. Edward Boehm continued working in the veterinary field, and Helen worked at a prestigious optical center. She especially enjoyed designing eyeglass frames and sometimes fitted celebrity clients, such as Clark Gable, a famous film actor.

Edward Boehm wanted to change his profession, and he and Helen decided he would turn his hobby into a business. In this way, he would combine his sculpting skills with his knowledge of animals. In 1949, the Boehms obtained a $500 loan from a veterinary colleague and a $1,000 bank loan. They opened a small one-room studio in Trenton, New Jersey, an important center of ceramic artwork, and called their company the Osso China Company. In 1952, they changed the name to Edward Marshall Boehm, Inc.

Edward Boehm had decided to work with hard-paste porcelain, and the Boehms knew they faced major competition from abroad, where this art had been developed over the centuries. Collectors regarded porcelains from Europe and Asia as superior to those made in the United States. The Boehms resolved to produce sculptures outstanding enough to attract collectors from around the world. While Edward worked on the artistic aspects of the business, Helen managed the financial affairs while continuing to work as an optician.

Their porcelain business received a major boost in 1951 when Helen Boehm sold to a Metropolitan Museum of Art curator two of Edward's animal sculptures, *Percheron Stallion* and *Hereford Bull.* A reviewer in the *New York Times* praised Edward Boehm's talent, and collectors and museums around the world began to buy his porcelain animals. Helen quit her job as an optician to devote more time to sales and marketing for the company. In 1953, they moved into a new and larger studio.

As Boehm produced new pieces, collectors and critics admired his designs and the realistic details he included in his flowers, birds, and animals. Britain's Prince Charles said, "All that is missing from a Boehm rose is the fragrance." Sales increased steadily. Helen Boehm's clever marketing ideas brought the company more recognition and

33

Since 1969, Helen Boehm, shown here with one of her company's creations, has headed one of the world's most famous makers of museum-quality porcelain sculptures.
(Photo courtesy of Boehm)

bigger sales. She suggested that President Dwight Eisenhower (1953–60) commission Boehm to make pieces he could present to visiting foreign dignitaries and he agreed. In 1959, the Boehms also gave several pieces to Pope John XXIII for the Vatican Museum art collection.

During these years, Edward continued to create new sculptures and oversee artistic production while Helen Boehm managed sales and marketing. By 1959, Boehm sculptures were fetching $1,000 apiece. The company continued to grow during the 1960s and added new staff members to help produce the sculptures and to work in the sales and marketing department.

In 1969, Edward Boehm died at age 55 of a heart attack. Helen Boehm resolved to carry on their business and she organized a new artistic staff

headed by Maurice Eyeington, who had been Edward's assistant. In 1970, she launched a second Boehm factory in Malvern, England, and, during the following years, she expanded the business in Trenton and Malvern. As Boehm hired more people, she worked hard to maintain the excellent quality that marked their products.

Collectors continued to seek Boehm figures. When President Richard Nixon visited the People's Republic of China in 1972, he presented Chairman Mao Tse-tung with a pair of Boehm swans known as the Bird of Peace sculpture. Helen Boehm was one of first businesswomen to visit China when she arrived there in 1974. The company received a challenging new assignment in 1977 when the Egyptian government commissioned it to reproduce 38 treasures from its King Tut exhibit for art collectors. Boehm had previously focused on birds, animals, and flowers, but their Egyptian sculptures were well received. The company also succeeded in new markets, including Saudi Arabia, and a major exhibit of Boehm sculptures was shown in Moscow in 1987. To commemorate this event, the Boehm *American Bald Eagle* sculpture was presented to the people of the Soviet Union.

Sales remained strong during the 1980s and the 1990s. In 1985, Boehm wrote her autobiography, called *With a Little Luck: An American Odyssey.* She and her staff designed a special trophy sculpture for a benefit polo match held in 1989 and sponsored by Britain's royal family. Boehm presented a life-sized Madonna and child to Pope John Paul II for the Vatican collection, which held a total of six Boehm pieces at that time. The two Boehm studios were consolidated in 1992.

As of 2000, some Boehm sculptures were selling at auction for prices ranging from $125,000 to $150,000. Pieces were being produced in limited editions numbering from 25 to 1,000. They could be found in 137 museums and institutions around the world, including the Smithsonian Institution, Buckingham Palace, the Metropolitan Museum of Art, and the Hermitage.

Boehm told author Patricia Harrison, "From the beginning we were dedicated to excellence and to mirroring nature with fidelity—we tried to improve every day. Our goal was to be the best and to provide the best." Toward that end, Helen Boehm, who makes her home in Palm Beach, Florida, continues to seek new ideas and learn new skills as she travels, observes, and studies the porcelain market.

Further Reading

Boehm, Helen. *With a Little Luck: An American Odyssey.* Trenton, N.J.: Edward Marshall Boehm, Inc., 1985.

Boehm Porcelain. "Boehm Profile." Available online. URL: http://www.boehmporcelain.com/profile.htm. Downloaded on February 4, 2001.

———. "In the Millennium The Boehm Porcelain Studio Celebrates 50 Years of Creating Beauty of Flora and Fauna, 1950–2000." Boehm Company, Trenton, NJ.

Harrison, Patricia. *America's New Women Entrepreneurs.* Washington, D.C.: Acropolis Books, 1986.

"Helen Boehm." Northwood University Distinguished Women. Available online. URL: http://northwood.edu/dw/1980/boehm.html. Downloaded on February 11, 2001.

BROWN, CLARA

(ca. 1800–1885) *Entrepreneur, Business Owner, Philanthropist*

Brown, who was born a slave in either Virginia or Tennessee, may have been the first African-American woman to cross the continent during the 19th-century California gold rush. She used her profits from several successful businesses to help other former slaves relocate to the West.

Clara's birthdate and birthplace are unknown. When Brown was nine years old, she and her mother were taken to Kentucky, where they worked on a farm. After her marriage at age 18, Brown gave birth to four children, one of whom died at birth. She was separated from her entire family when the farm owner sold her to another family in 1835. Over a period of about 20 years, her third master helped Brown look for her three surviving children, who apparently were taken to various states by new masters. Brown heard that one of her daughters had died and could not find any information about her son.

In 1859, after Brown's third owner granted her freedom, she decided to move to the West, where she hoped to find her surviving daughter, Eliza Jane. Brown arranged to pay for her transportation to Colorado by working as a cook on a wagon train. Five other women, all white, made the journey, which took eight weeks. Brown had to walk much of the 600 miles.

When she arrived, Brown lived briefly in Denver, then moved to Central City, a camp community

Pioneer and freed slave Clara Brown used the profits from her business and real estate enterprises to help other former slaves relocate to the West and to search for her children, who had been sold away from her.
(Photo courtesy of the Denver Public Library, Western History Collection)

for miners. The population of the region was growing, and people were going west in search of gold and silver. Brown founded the state's first commercial laundry service and also ran a business selling meals to the settlers. Within seven years, she managed to save $10,000 and invested some of that money in real estate and mines.

Determined to locate her family, she paid agents to search in the places they had lived. She found no trace of her son and continued the search for her surviving daughter, Eliza Jane. Brown personally traveled to Kentucky and Virginia looking for her daughter. She met numerous other freed slaves and helped them move to Colorado. When she returned from Kentucky and Virginia, she brought 16 former slaves with her, and 34 other family members whom she had located. Along with the former slaves she had met, she helped them find jobs and become self-sufficient. Some of them remained in Central City, while others moved to various towns in Colorado.

Besides running her businesses, Clara Brown promoted civic institutions that helped the camp community become a stable, law-abiding town. A religious woman, she founded a Sunday school, and her home was the birthplace of the St. James Methodist Church, the first church in the region. She offered rooms to travelers and sheltered poor and homeless people for free. It was said that "Aunt" Clara Brown never turned away a person in need.

By the 1880s, Brown still had not found her daughter, and members of the community launched a massive letter-writing campaign to help locate Eliza Jane, who was finally found in Iowa. Brown was reunited with Eliza Jane and with her granddaughter Cindy just before she died in 1885 in Denver.

In her adopted state, Clara Brown is honored as a member of the Society of Colorado Pioneers, and a memorial chair for Brown sits in the Central City Opera House. A stained-glass window in the Colorado State Capitol is dedicated to Brown. While eulogizing Brown, a member of the Colorado Pioneers Association said that she "[had risen] from the humble position of slave to the angelic type of noblewoman, won our sympathy and commanded our respect." The association buried her with honors.

Further Reading

Bolden, Tonya. *The Book of African-American Women: 150 Crusaders, Creators, and Uplifters.* Holbrook, Mass.: Adams Media Creations, 1996.
Colorado Women's Hall of Fame. "Historical Inductee: Clara Brown, Pioneer." Available online. URL: http://www.cogreatwomen.org/brown-clara.htm. Downloaded on May 11, 2001.

✳ BRUNSON, DOROTHY EDWARDS
(1938–)   *Executive, Business Owner*

In 1986, Dorothy Brunson became the first African-American woman to own a television station. Her company, Brunson Communications, owns and operates WGTW-Channel 48 in Philadelphia. Brunson, who claims that careful research and fact-based decision-making have played a major role in her success, says, "I read, I research, and I never do anything haphazardly. You can't make your judgments based on your own personality. You have to base them on facts."

Dorothy Edwards was born on March 13, 1938, in rural Georgia, but she spent most of her childhood in Harlem, a neighborhood of New York City. After Dorothy's father died in 1944, her mother worked in a laundry and as a domestic at United Airlines to support herself and her child. While Dorothy was growing up, her mother remarried and had three more children. The family was poor, but Brunson later said that they always had enough food and clothing. Her mother encouraged her to get a good education and took her to the library each week. In the book *On Our Own Terms,* Brunson recalled, "Every Saturday we went to the branch a few blocks from where we lived. When I was older, I went by myself. I brought home stacks of books and read them all." However, she kept her passion for reading a secret, because her peers teased people who read a lot.

Determined to succeed, she attended Empire State College in New York State and earned a degree in accounting and finance. She entered the field of broadcasting in 1964 when she became a bookkeeper at WWRL radio station in New York City. She worked her way to the position of controller at the station. During those years, she married, and her two sons were born in 1967 and 1968. The marriage ended after 12 years.

In 1971, Brunson, who had taken her husband's last name, briefly left broadcasting. However, she returned to that field in 1973 when Inner City Broadcasting asked her to take charge of a small music station that was not making enough money. Brunson raised $300,000 to save WLIB, then became the general manager. By raising advertising revenues and cutting unnecessary costs, Brunson revived the station. She then bought its FM sister station, which enabled the company to sell ad time for both stations at once. In addition, she conducted market research to develop a plan for the radio station. They changed their sound from mostly rock and roll to more rhythm and blues and "mellow jazz"—what Brunson calls "a softer, more adult sound . . . 'urban contemporary.'"

The station attracted so many listeners it became number one in the world, according to Nielsen ratings, and it influenced other stations. Pleased with her success, Brunson continued using research to determine what audiences wanted to hear. When she left WLIB in 1979, revenues were $22 million. The company owned seven stations, and its estimated value was greater than $60 million.

Nonetheless, Brunson left her high-paying job and comfortable Manhattan apartment for new challenges. Using some of her own money, as well as investment capital, she bought three floundering radio stations—in Baltimore, Maryland; Atlanta, Georgia; and Wilmington, South Carolina—and proceeded to turn them around. She was the first black woman ever to own a radio station in Baltimore when she moved there to take over WEBB-AM. The station became highly profitable, adding to Brunson's career successes.

She decided to tackle television next and discovered a station in Pennsylvania that had been off the air for 10 years, which meant that its license had reverted back to the Federal Communications Commission (FCC). The cutoff date for applying to the FCC to revive the license was January 4, 1984. When she applied, Brunson owned three radio stations and had a strong track record in the broadcasting business. To put together the financing she needed, Brunson sold the radio stations and some personal assets, so that she was investing $1.2 million of her own money in this venture.

After the FCC granted her the license for what became WGTW-TV (which stood for "Good Television to Watch") in Philadelphia in 1986, she devoted tremendous time, energy, and talent to reviving it. The station had sold off its equipment, so Brunson had to buy a transmitter and managed to find a used one for $50,000. She went with the trucks that picked up the equipment from Florida and then helped to supervise the repair process. At times, Brunson put on a hard hat and boots to help the workers with some of the physical labor.

When the station first went back on the air, she broadcast series reruns and movies that did not cost too much money, choosing the programs she thought would appeal to its audience. As the station's ratings and advertising increased, she added original programming, such as a talk show for senior citizens. Revenues grew from zero in 1992 to $2 million in 1993 to more than $4 million in 1994.

As of 1995, Brunson was the only black woman and one of only eight African Americans to own a television station in the United States. Brunson has called herself a demanding boss who helps her employees grow. She says that in addition to working hard to understand the audience, it is important for television executives to hire "the best people you can find," people who will work well together and carry out their responsibilities, which, in television, includes the ability to think and act quickly. She was still serving as president and general manager of station WGTW-TV 48 in late 2001. That September, Brunson was a panelist at the Black Broadcasters Alliance 2nd Annual Fall Media Conference.

Brunson devotes a considerable amount of her time to social causes, including programs to empower women and minorities. She is active in the African Methodist Episcopal (AME) Zion church and, in conjunction with her church, visits West Africa several times a year to work with women to improve their status, education, and economic condition. The AME church has started a bank, schools, clinics, and other programs in West Africa. Of her financial success, Brunson has said, "Doing a good job and winning are a huge 'high' for me, and money is the barometer that indicates you have done a job well."

Further Reading

Enkelis, Liane, and Karen Olsen. *On Our Own Terms: Portraits of Women Business Leaders.* San Francisco: Berrett-Koehler Publishers, 1995.

Helgesen, Sally. *The Female Advantage: Women's Ways of Leadership.* New York: Doubleday, 1995.

Taylor, Russel. *Exceptional Entrepreneurial Women: Strategies for Success.* Westport, Conn.: Praeger, 1988.

C

CARSEY, MARCY (Marcia Lee Peterson)
(1944–   ) *Executive*

Called the most powerful woman in television during the late 1970s, Marcy Carsey played a key role in making ABC the top-rated network for several years, then went on to cofound a successful independent TV production company, Carsey-Werner.

Marcia Lee Peterson was born on November 21, 1944, in Weymouth, outside Boston, Massachusetts. In 1966, she graduated with honors from the University of New Hampshire with a degree in English. Her first job after college was as a tour guide in NBC's Rockefeller Center complex in New York City, followed by a job as a gofer with *The Tonight Show.* In 1968, she joined William Esty Company, an advertising agency, to work in the programming department.

Peterson married John Jay Carsey in 1969, and they headed for the West Coast, where Marcy Carsey read television scripts and acted in commercials. In 1974, Carsey accepted a job at ABC as a program executive in the comedy department. Pregnant at the time, Carsey was pleased to see that ABC had other women

employees and that "you didn't have to wear a suit," as she later said. Within two years, she was promoted to vice president of prime-time comedy development, then to vice president of prime-time comedy and variety programs. Working with Tom Werner, she set out to improve ABC's ratings, which were then the lowest of the three major networks (CBS, NBC, and ABC). The duo introduced shows that became hits, including *Happy Days, Taxi, Mork and Mindy,* and *Laverne and Shirley,* that made ABC the top-rated network in the late 1970s.

Carsey decided to leave ABC in 1980 to develop her own productions. After Tom Werner left the network the following year, they formed an independent company, Carsey-Werner Productions, to create comedy series they could sell to the networks. Their first situation comedy was canceled in midseason, but their next project was a breakthrough hit. Working with actor-comedian Bill Cosby, they came up with the idea for a series about an upper-middle-class African-American family called the Huxtables. This turned into the top-rated *Cosby Show,* which premiered in 1984. During that decade, it often captured a 40-to-50-

percent share of the viewing audience and may have been watched by more people than any TV show in history. *Cosby* was widely praised for promoting family values and avoiding stereotypes. A spin-off, *A Different World,* premiered in 1987 and ran for six years.

In 1988, Carsey-Werner decided to produce a show about a blue-collar family with a working mother—*Roseanne,* starring comedian Roseanne Barr. This show was another hit, and during the first week of November that year, all three of the top-rated shows on television were Carsey-Werner productions. Along with some less well-received programs, Carsey-Werner had more hits in the 1990s with *Grace Under Fire, Cybill,* and *Third Rock From the Sun.* Carsey and Werner were both elected into the Broadcasting and Cable Hall of Fame in 1996. They have also won numerous awards, including the Emmy, the Golden Globe, the People's Choice, the NAACP Image Award, and the Peabody.

In 1999, Carsey was awarded the highest honor of the University of New Hampshire Alumnae Assocation. In conferring the award, Paul Caswell, first vice president of the association, said, "Marcy's accomplishments as a television producer, businesswoman, role model for other women in business, and philanthropist are legion. . . . She has brought a sense of quality, substance, and integrity to television."

In 2000, Carsey, Werner, and another partner, Caryn Mandabach, teamed with former Nickelodeon head GERALDINE LAYBOURNE and OPRAH WINFREY on a new multimedia venture called Oxygen. They announced that the venture, which is geared toward women, planned to operate an Internet site and new cable television channel, which were operating in 2001.

Having been called a role model for working mothers, Carsey, the mother of two, has noted the challenges of her various roles. She told journalist Eric Schmuckler, "Of course you can have it all, if you want it. And it won't be perfect, but it won't be perfect anyway, so you might as well do what you want."

Further Reading

Marc, David, and Robert J. Thompson. *Prime Time Prime Movers.* Boston: Little Brown, 1992.

Paine, Maggie. "T.V. Producer Marcy Carsey Garners UNH Alumni Honor," University of New Hampshire News, June 22, 1999. Available online. URL: http://www.unh.edu/news/Jun99/mp_19990622carsey.html. Downloaded on May 17, 2001.

Schmuckler, Eric. "The Top 50 Women Business Owners," *Working Woman,* May 1996, pp. 31–47.

Zoglin, Richard. "Midas Touch," *Time,* September 23, 1996, pp. 68–70.

CHIN, LEEANN

(1933–)   *Chef, Restaurant Chain Owner, Executive, Teacher, Author*

As founder of a successful restaurant chain, Leeann Chin relied on hard work and talent, along with the capacity to look beyond the customary women's roles that prevailed in her Chinese culture. She said, "The way I was brought up, women don't work. You are taught to be a good wife and mother and to obey your husband and mother-in-law." In that tradition, notes Chin, women are taught that "men have the authority and men are smarter and men have ability and men can do this and men can do that."

She was born in Canton, China, on February 13, 1933. By age 11, the future restaurateur was working in her father's retail and wholesale market. Although her family did not praise Leeann's work, customers commented on her skill with the abacus, a counting device that many Chinese used at that time.

At age 18, she met Tony Chin in Hong Kong and they were married. In 1956, the Chins immigrated to the United States with their daughter and moved to Minneapolis, Minnesota, where Tony began working in a restaurant. Later, he became a technician in a photo laboratory at the University of Minnesota. Leeann Chin did alterations in a clothing store and gradually developed her own successful tailoring and dressmaking business at home. This business helped the Chins to support their family, which grew to include four daughters and one son, all of whom would eventually attend college and graduate school.

During the early 1970s, Chin began making special Chinese luncheons for her sewing customers, and they urged her to teach cooking classes so they could duplicate the dishes at home. Besides teaching from her home, Chin began teaching Chinese cooking in the evenings at the local high school and community education center. She added a professional catering business that grew steadily, as people hired her to cook for important parties, receptions, and banquets.

In 1979, with the help of a $165,000 loan from the Federal Small Business Administration, Chin opened a restaurant—Leeann Chin—that featured authentic Cantonese and Szechuan food. Individual investors, including celebrities who patronized her restaurant, each invested $25,000 in Chin's business. The restaurant, which seated 80 people, was opened in a Minnetonka shopping center in 1980. The elegant decor included Chinese art objects from Chin's collection. That first year, the restaurant enjoyed sales in excess of $1.5 million. Recognizing Chin as an expert in Chinese cookery, the General Mills Corporation asked her to write a Chinese cookbook for its popular Betty Crocker series.

Chin expanded her restaurant, doubling the seating, in 1983. The next year, she opened another restaurant, this time in St. Paul. It featured a gourmet Chinese carry-out service, which drew, on average, 500 customers a day.

In 1985, Chin sold her business to General Mills but decided to buy it back three years later. The two parties remained on good terms, and, five years later, Chin authored a second cookbook for General Mills. Leeann Chin, Inc., continued to expand. By the end of 1994, with three restaurants and 19 carry-outs, the company employed more than 700 people and had annual sales of $25 million. Chin's daughter Laura was an executive vice president in charge of marketing and advertising, and one of Chin's sisters also worked at the company.

Chin continued to look for new opportunities. In 1995 she opened the moderately priced Asia Grille restaurant in St. Paul, Minnesota, which combined Japanese, Vietnamese, Korean, Thai, and Chinese cuisines. She later added another Asia Grille in Seattle and two Asia Grille Express takeouts in Minnesota, but decided to sell that concept in 1998 in order to focus on her Chinese cuisine. As of 1999, there were 46 Leeann Chin units, including restaurants, carry-outs, and outlets at grocery stores. The company operated stores in Detroit and Kansas City, as well as in the Minneapolis–St. Paul area. People could buy Leeann Chin's bottled Peking sauce, imperial sauce, and Asian salad dressing in grocery stores.

Describing her role as an executive, Chin has said that her managerial policies may differ from those of many other companies. For example, she tries to provide continuing learning opportunities for employees. She hires enough people so that the restaurant managers do not have to work seven days a week or 15 hours a day. She says, "Sure, it cuts into our profitability now. But it's one of the reasons my business is successful. . . . We are training people and promoting them. I travel, in this country and in China, to develop new recipes and learn about new foods and changes in customer taste. I take our people on some of those trips with me. You can't just tell people things and expect them to learn, you have to show them." Chin also takes groups of people on eating tours of China.

Leeann Chin has served on the boards of numerous organizations in Minnesota including the Minnesota Vikings Advisory Board and the board of the Boy Scouts of America. She supports the YMCA and public television, among other causes, and has worked to improve relations between the United States and China. The National Association of Women Business Owners named her Woman Business Owner of the Year in 1988. She is a member of the Minnesota Business Hall of Fame and was chosen as one of Minnesota's Ten Best Entrepreneurs in 1993. Chin has appeared as a guest chef on the Food Network with her daughter Katie, now an entertaining-marketing consultant. Together they wrote a new cookbook, *Everyday Chinese Cooking,* which was published in 2000.

Further Reading

Chin, Leeann, and Katie Chin. *Everyday Chinese Cooking: Quick and Delicious Recipes from the Leeann Chin Restaurants.* Clarkson Potter, 2000.

CityBusiness: The Business Journal. "Leeann Chin Expands Into New Markets." Available online. URL: http://twincities.bcentral.com/twincities/stories/1999/05/03/story2.html. Downloaded on February 3, 2001.

Godfrey, Joline. *Our Wildest Dreams: Women Entrepreneurs Making Money, Having Fun, Doing Good.* New York: Harperbusiness, 1993.

Michalski, Patty. "Leeann Chin, An Asian Dining Dynasty True To Its Roots," *Minneapolis-St. Paul Magazine,* May 1999. Available online. URL: http://www.mspmag.com/feature.asp?featureid=792. Downloaded on February 4, 2001.

✺ CLAIBORNE, LIZ (Liz Ortenberg)
(1929–) *Entrepreneur, Designer, Executive*

Fashion designer Liz Claiborne founded Liz Claiborne, Inc., a clothing, shoe, and fragrance company listed on the Fortune 500. She has served as president, chairman, and chief executive officer (CEO) of this successful business.

Elizabeth Claiborne was born in Brussels, Belgium, on March 31, 1929. Her father, an American, was a bank manager. In 1939, the family left Europe to avoid the Nazi threat, but Claiborne returned to Europe after the war ended in 1945 to study art. When she was 21 years old, Claiborne won a fashion design contest sponsored by *Harper's Bazaar,* a top fashion magazine. In New York City, she entered the fashion business as a design assistant to a manufacturer, then joined the Jonathan Logan Company as chief designer for junior dresses.

In 1976, she founded Liz Claiborne, Inc., with her husband Arthur Ortenberg (a former consulting-business owner) and their partners Leonard Boxer and Jerome Chazen. Their focus was on producing moderately priced, good-quality sportswear, to be sold in major department and specialty stores.

Claiborne had definite ideas about what kinds of garments busy women needed and wanted, for both work and leisure, and her business thrived. To increase sales, the company also came up with a trademarked retailing technique called Claiboards—pictures and explanations showing salespeople how to organize the clothing in groups so that customers could easily see how to mix and match the garments.

Just four years after she started her company, in 1980 Claiborne was named Entrepreneurial Woman of the Year. It was the first time a fashion designer had won this honor.

In 1981, the company went public with a stock offering. Net sales were up again that year, reaching $116.8 million. Claiborne, who served as company president, expanded her business in the eighties, adding a petite line that became very successful, as well as shoes, handbags, belts, jewelry, and fragrances for both men and women.

Liz Claiborne, Inc., was listed on the Fortune 500 for the first time in 1986. In 1987, Claiborne became chair and chief executive officer as well as company president. Two years later, she retired from actively running the company. She has continued to lecture at the Parsons School of Design and the Fashion Institute of Technology (FIT), both located in New York City.

Sales at Liz Claiborne, Inc., rose to $3.1 billion in 2000. More than 7,000 people are employed at the company worldwide.

Further Reading

"FAQs." Liz Claiborne, Inc. Available online. URL: http://www.lizclaiborne.com/faqs.asp. Downloaded on April 23, 2001.

✺ CRAIG, JENNY
(Genevieve "Jenny" Guidroz)
(1932–) *Entrepreneur, Executive*

Jenny Craig pioneered the combination of a nutrition-based formula and active lifestyle to build a multimillion-dollar international weight-loss empire.

Genevieve "Jenny" Guidroz was born on August 7, 1932, in New Orleans, Louisiana, where her parents worked hard to support their family of six children during the Great Depression. Her father, James, was a carpenter and boat captain who provided crews and supplies to oil rigs in the Gulf of Mexico. Jenny, the youngest child, worked as a dental assistant during summer vacations from school. She planned to become a dental hygienist after graduation, but her mother, Gertrude, suffered three strokes and was left paralyzed. Jenny was the only unmarried child at that time, so she chose to care for her mother.

Gertrude Guidroz died at age 49, and four of Jenny's five brothers and sisters also died before they were 50 years old. All of them were overweight. This was an important reason that Jenny was drawn to a career in health and fitness. She later recalled that her family had eaten rich Creole foods: "Everything we ate involved butter and fat, with lots of starches. I just figured that was the way to eat."

In 1954, she married her first husband, Robert Bourcq, with whom she had two daughters. She joined a fitness center in 1959 to lose the 45 extra pounds she had gained during her second pregnancy. She began exercising and changed her diet to limit portions and eliminate desserts. Impressed by her interpersonal skills and fit appearance, the owners offered her a job at the gym, which was called Silhouette/American Health. She worked hard and studied the ways people lost weight and improved their fitness levels, and was eventually promoted to manage several fitness centers in the chain. After mortgaging her house to raise capital, she and a partner opened their own fitness center, Healthletic, which they sold to Silhouette in 1968. She continued to work there for more than a year.

In 1970, she was looking for a franchise to operate when she saw an ad in the paper placed by Sid Craig, a former dance school owner and child performer. He was part of a group of investors who owned Body Contour, Inc., a chain of women's figure salons in California. The group was expanding, and Sid Craig was looking for people to staff a center in New Orleans. He hired

Jenny, and she rose to the rank of manager. As the chain spread across the southern states, she supervised all of the centers. Eventually, she became national director of operations.

After both she and Craig were divorced from their first spouses, the two began dating and were married in 1979. By then, Sid Craig had started more than 160 Body Contour centers nationwide. Jenny Craig proposed a new program that would focus on a nutritional plan for attaining and maintaining one's ideal weight. The partners in Body Contour did not want to change their system, and the chain was sold to Nutri/System in 1982 for $15 million.

Jenny and Sid Craig were determined to set up a company that embodied her weight loss philosophy and plan. Using the $3.5 million that Sid Craig had received for his share of Body Contour, they set up Jenny Craig Weight Loss Centres in Australia, a difficult market in which the Gloria Marshall Figure Control Salons were already operating successfully.

Craig later summed up the formula that became her company's trademark: "a weight-loss program that involves nutritional guidance, prepackaged food, exercise and behavior modification." Counselors worked with clients to develop the most effective program for each person and to provide ongoing support. The program showed people exactly what to eat, based on menus approved by a dietitian, so they did not have to make daily decisions about food as they were changing their eating habits. Clients attended lifestyle classes designed by a psychologist with a specialization in eating disorders, and watched videos that covered various topics, including exercise and nutrition. Each week, they practiced an assignment to change their behavior regarding food and exercise. Gradually, as clients reached their weight loss goals, they began to plan their own meals at home.

Sid Craig devised the marketing campaign, which included TV advertising on Australia's top talent show. Soon, people throughout the country recognized the Jenny Craig name, and the business

Jenny Craig built her successful business around a weight loss program based on nutritional guidance, preplanned menus, exercise, and behavioral change.
(Photo courtesy of Jenny Craig)

grew rapidly. By 1985, the centers were grossing $50 million a year.

Then the Craigs proceeded to set up new Jenny Craig Centres in the United States, beginning with 12 centers in the Los Angeles area. They knew they faced stiff competition, and, as Craig recalls, "We realized that we had to do something different." They believed customers would prefer to have frozen planned meals available on the premises. No other weight loss company offered frozen dinners as part of its program, so the Craigs developed a line of frozen dinners that have become basic to the program.

Craig also believed that obesity was a growing problem in America, and statistics showed this to be true. Between 1980 and 1997, the number of obese American adults grew by 10 percent, to reach 35 percent of the population. Within five years, Jenny Craig, Inc., based in Del Mar, California, was the sixth-fastest growing private company in America. In 1991, the company went public with a stock offering that raised $66 million and repaid bank loans the Craigs had used for the business. By 1999, there were 780 Jenny Craig Centres, with revenues exceeding $350 million, and it was the largest chain of weight loss centers in the world. About 20 percent of the centers were franchises; the company owned the rest. The weight loss industry as a whole experienced a decline during the 1990s, and the Craigs worked to adapt and restructure their company. In 1997, they launched a new, easier-to-use program with a shorter guidebook and more flexible meal plans. That allowed users to select foods from different categories without calculating fat grams or calories.

In 1999, Jenny Craig, Inc., took on a leading role in the Federal Trade Commission's Partnership for Health Weight Management, which is working to promote standards in the weight loss industry.

Jenny and Sid Craig have contributed time and money to numerous philanthropic causes and were named 1991 Humanitarians of the Year by the San Diego Hospice. They have also supported Easter Seals, the United Way, and the Susan G. Komen Breast Cancer Foundation. In 1992, the Craigs gave California State University in Fresno $10 million for the Sid Craig Business School. Jenny Craig served on the board of the University of San Diego (USD) from 1990 to 1996. In 1996, the Craigs donated $10 million to USD. The university allocated $7 million of that money to build a multiuse student activities facility called the Jenny Craig Pavilion. President Alice B. Hayes said, "She has captured many hearts on this campus. Thanks to this gift, her name will continue to inspire our students as they learn and grow."

After injuring her jaw during an accident in 1996, Jenny Craig required surgery and physical therapy and was not able to speak easily enough to continue as company spokesperson. Her family and friends praised her courage and determination to recover from her injuries.

Further Reading

Craig, Jenny. *Jenny Craig's What Have You Got to Lose?* New York: Villard Books, 1992.

Ericksen, Gregory K. *Women Entrepreneurs Only: 12 Women Entrepreneurs Tell the Stories of Their Success.* New York: John Wiley & Sons, 1999.

Press Release, University of San Diego: "Sid and Jenny Craig Donate $7 Million to the University of San Diego for Pavilion." Available online. URL: http://www.acusd.edu/president/craig. Downloaded on October 4, 2000.

Silver, A. David. *Enterprising Women.* New York: AMACOM, 1994.

D

DACHÉ, LILLY
(1904–1989) *Entrepreneur, Designer, Executive*

One of the most successful hat designers in history, Lilly Daché founded a world-famous millinery company in New York City that expanded to sell fashions, accessories, and beauty products to provide what Daché called "head-to-toe glamour." Known for her wit as well as her designing skills, Daché once said, "Glamour is what makes a man ask for your telephone number. But it is also what makes a woman ask for the name of your dressmaker."

Daché was born in the south of France in 1904. At age 14, she went to work for an aunt in Bordeaux who taught her to design and make hats. After her apprenticeship ended, she moved to Paris and worked for a well-known hat designer. At age 18, Daché immigrated to the United States, first to New Jersey, and then to New York City where she worked as a salesperson at Macy's department store. However, Daché soon left the store because she preferred to spend her time selling hats to customers and was impatient with the process of writing up sales receipts.

While working in a small millinery shop, Daché began building her own custom-made hat business. During the first half of the 20th century, hats were regarded as an essential accessory, and women wore various kinds of headgear for shopping, church, visiting friends, dining out, and other occasions. With no savings of her own, Daché used the small deposits customers gave her when they ordered a new hat to buy materials, then worked on the hats after work each night. Her artistry and sewing skills brought Daché many new customers by word-of-mouth, and, within a few years, she had saved enough money to buy the shop where she worked.

Daché went on to become a top designer, creating new hats in the form of the cloche, turban, "swagger hat," and other popular styles. Women clamored for the swagger hat when actress Marlene Dietrich was seen wearing this design or when numerous other celebrities, including Greta Garbo and Bette Davis, were photographed in Daché creations. Lilly Daché also began designing women's clothing, lingerie, and jewelry.

During the late 1940s and 1950s, she added cosmetics, including a face cream made with jelly that came from queen honeybees. Offering clients what she called "head-to-toe glamour," Daché operated salons where women could receive hairstyling, skin care treatments, cosmetics services, and fashion assistance in the same building. A number of famous people began their careers with Daché, including hairstylist Kenneth and designer Halston.

Married in 1952 to Jacques Despres, an executive at Coty, Inc., a cosmetics and fragrance company, Daché divided her time between a New York City apartment and a house in the country. She wrote two books: *Talking Through My Hats* (1946) and *Lilly Daché's Glamour Book* (1956). Dache retired in 1968 but continued to appear at fashion industry functions. She died in 1989. In 2000, she was one of 46 top American designers nominated for inclusion in New York City's Fashion Walk of Fame.

Further Reading

Daché, Lilly. *Talking Through My Hats.* New York: Coward-McCann, 1946.

———. *Lilly Daché's Glamour Book.* Philadelphia: Lippincott, 1956.

�֎ DAVIDSON, JAN
(1944–)   *Entrepreneur, Teacher, Executive*

As the founder and president of Davidson & Associates, Jan Davidson has found innovative ways to help children learn basic skills and is a pioneer in the educational software publishing industry. Davidson is also a forceful advocate for making technology available as a learning tool for all American students. During a speech in 1993, she pointed out, "Anyone who's seen what a kid can do when let loose on a well-designed computer tool has seen the future."

Born in February 1944 in Fort Knox, Kentucky, Jan Davidson earned a B.A. from Purdue University in 1966, her master's in communications from the University of Maryland, and her doctorate in American studies from the University of Maryland. She embarked on a 15-year career as a teacher of high school and college students. While teaching high school in California in the late 1970s, she developed a nonprofit learning center called Upward Bound to

offer supplemental after-school courses to college-bound students. As Davidson looked for new ways to work with her Upward Bound students, she realized they could benefit from computer learning games that made learning more interactive and fun. Davidson had noticed how much her three children and their friends enjoyed playing games on their Apple computer. She later said, "These computer games completely captured the kids' attention, a task that as a teacher I knew was no small feat."

She set out to learn about computers herself and to figure out how to program a computer to help her students. Since she could not find the kinds of games she needed, Davidson created her own teaching tools, starting with a game to increase reading speed called Speed Reader. She hired a programmer, who developed the program according to her suggestions. After Speed Reader, she created her Word Attack and MathBlaster games.

When Apple Computer heard about Davidson's programs, it began listing them in its mail-order catalog. After that catalog was discontinued the next year, Davidson considered marketing her products through a software publisher, then decided to publish the software herself. Although she knew she would miss the teaching profession if she went into business, she realized that the educational software business would give her the opportunity to reach many students. She founded her business in Torrance, California, in 1982. It launched its successful MathBlaster game in a version that ran on an Apple II with 48K of memory.

One of Davidson's earliest challenges was getting dealers to devote shelf space to her educational software, which was designed for use in both schools and homes. Davidson later said, "For example, to get people to realize the value of computers for learning, we started Computer Learning Month which evolved into the Computer Learning Foundation."

Davidson & Associates went on to develop new math, science, history, reading, and writing titles and games for children from preschool through 12th grade. As the company grew, Jan Davidson saw the need for more professional business management. Her husband, Bob, agreed to join the company in

1989, taking over the managerial responsibilities, while Jan Davidson focused on developing new products based on her knowledge of the school curriculum and sound teaching techniques.

In 1986, she became a board member of the Software Publishers Association in Washington, D.C. She became president of the association in 1993. That year, her company's stock began trading on the NASDAQ. In 1994, company sales reached $88 million, with an annual growth rate of 73 percent.

Although competition was keen, the company's creative products and skillful marketing and distribution brought it continuing success. Davidson introduced more than 30 products and the company sold millions of copies of the games. Educators praised the products, which won awards for excellence from educational organizations.

In 1997, Jan and Bob Davidson left the company to focus on philanthropy and investments, as well as new projects to promote education through their Davidson Foundation. That year, Jan Davidson served on the President's Committee of Advisors on Science and Technology, Panel on Educational Technology. She is a popular public speaker who especially enjoys meeting with young people.

Davidson continues to be an active educational advocate. In 1999, she and her husband, Bob, founded the Davidson Institute for Talent Development, a nonprofit organization, to recognize, nurture, and support profoundly gifted young people. "All children should have an opportunity to learn at a level and a rate according to their abilities," she insists, "and the opportunity to develop their talents in positive ways to create value for themselves and others." Through the Davidson Institute's scholarships and talent development programs, she is actively attempting to turn her beliefs into reality.

Looking back on the years she spent building her company, Jan Davidson said, "We proved that you can run a good business, you can make money, you can create a great environment for your employees, and you can create something your customers value, all in a way that helps society."

Further Reading

"A Conversation with Jan Davidson." *Children's Software Review,* June/July 1997, p. 25.

Guglielmo, Connie. "Class Leader." Wired Digital, Inc. Available online. URL: http:www.wired.com/wired/archive/2.02/davidson.html. Posted February 1994. Downloaded on May 7, 2001.

Leisey, Donald E., and Charles W. Lavaroni. *The Educational Entrepreneur: Making a Difference.* Los Angeles, Calif.: EduPreneur Press, 2000.

Silver, A. David. *Enterprising Women.* New York: AMACOM, 1994.

✳ DEMOREST, ELLEN LOUISE CURTIS
(1824–1898) *Entrepreneur, Business Owner*

Demorest developed mass-produced and accurate paper patterns for home dressmaking and helped to found a company that made and distributed patterns featured in her fashion magazine.

The daughter of a prosperous milliner, Ellen Louise Curtis was born on November 15, 1824, in Schuylerville, New York, and grew up in Saratoga, a fashionable resort community. At age 18, she opened her own millinery shop and developed several successful millinery businesses before she married William Jennings Demorest in New York City in 1858.

The couple lived in Philadelphia briefly before returning to New York in 1860. Demorest opened Madame Demorest's Emporium of Fashions on Broadway, and she and her husband published a quarterly magazine, *Mme. Demorest's Mirror of Fashions,* which was later expanded to *Demorest's Illustrated Monthly Magazine and Mme. Demorest's Mirror of Fashions.* The magazine contained several innovations, including the nation's first personal-advice column.

During that era, factory-produced fabrics and sewing machines for home use were becoming widely available. Ellen Demorest later said that one day, when she saw her maid cutting out a pattern for a dress from wrapping paper, it occurred to her that there was a need for well-designed commercial patterns. She and her husband decided to mass produce paper patterns in standard sizes so that homemakers could create their own clothing more easily. Ellen Demorest's sister helped her to develop a mathematical method for calculating standardized sizes to fit a range of figures, and they developed patterns with instructions showing people how to cut fabric and put together fashions in various popular designs.

Their fashion magazine contained a garment pattern in each issue, and the Demorests also began selling their patterns through a nationwide sales network. Sales were excellent from the start and soon numbered in the millions, as the business expanded to include 30 distribution agencies and more than 200 saleswomen. Three million patterns were sold in the peak year, 1876. They greatly influenced fashion in America by making the latest French styles available to dressmakers around the country and to home seamstresses.

In addition, the Demorests sold sewing aids and other items by mail order. Ellen Demorest continued to operate her Broadway store, and she developed an inexpensive hoopskirt and various cosmetics and other products for sale.

A devoted feminist and abolitionist, she was committed to hiring women, including African Americans, in her various businesses, and she offered equal opportunities to her employees. In 1868, she joined other businesswomen and women journalists to found Sorosis, the first women's professional club, in response to an incident in which women were excluded from the New York Press Club when author Charles Dickens visited the city. She also worked to promote the New York Medical College for Women.

The Demorests neglected to file a legal patent for their pattern idea, which enabled competitors, primarily Ebenezer Butterick, to enter the pattern-making field. They sold their business in 1887. Widowed in 1895, Ellen Demorest died in New York on August 10, 1898.

Further Reading

Museum of American Heritage. "Sewing Machines." Available online. URL: http://www.moah.org/exhibits/virtual/sewing.html. Downloaded on May 4, 2001.

Ross, Ishbel. *Crusaders and Crinolines.* New York: Harper & Row, 1963.

DE WOLFE, ELSIE (Ella Anderson de Wolfe; Lady Mendl)
(1865–1950)   *Entrepreneur, Interior Designer*

Elsie De Wolfe is regarded as America's first woman professional decorator and an influential authority on domestic taste. An article that appeared in *House & Garden* magazine during her lifetime declared, "Elsie De Wolfe is a woman who has imposed her taste on one generation and lived to see it taken for granted by another."

Ella Anderson De Wolfe was born in New York City on December 20, 1865, and was educated in exclusive private schools in New York and Edinburgh, Scotland, where her maternal relatives lived. In 1883, she was presented at court to Queen Victoria and spent a year taking part in the social activities of London society, after which she returned to New York.

Although her family was socially prominent, their financial situation was unstable, depending on the state of her father's various business ventures and investments. De Wolfe later said that she felt physically ugly as a child and that this motivated her to focus on health and fitness. She looked for beauty in her surroundings and developed a strong interest in fine clothing, architecture, and furnishings. As De Wolfe reached her twenties, she gained more self-confidence and found that she enjoyed attending parties, balls, and other events that made up the social season for prominent New Yorkers. De Wolfe wanted to remain a part of this select world.

When she returned to New York in 1884, De Wolfe, who loved the theater, enjoyed putting on amateur theatrical performances for charity. After her father died in 1890, the family was short of money, so she became a professional actress. From 1891 to 1894, she toured with Charles Frohman's famous theatrical company. De Wolfe did not consider herself a great acting talent and knew that many people came to see her primarily because of her style and the fashionable clothing she wore onstage. Couturiers who wanted to promote their

Interior designer Elsie De Wolfe, shown here in 1896, lived in this New York apartment
at 122 East 17th Street from 1887 to 1911.
(Photo courtesy of the Museum of the City of New York–Byron Collection)

creations sold them to De Wolfe at a discount so
she would wear them during her performances. In
1900, *Harper's Bazaar* named her "the best-dressed
woman of the American stage." She formed her
own theater company in 1901 and presented a
play on Broadway, after which the company
toured for two years. In 1905, she retired from acting and producing.

During her years in the theater, friends had
noticed her talent for set design. They encouraged
De Wolfe to enter the field of interior design,
which was then dominated by men. People were
surprised and impressed when she redecorated Irving House, the home she shared with her longtime

companion ELISABETH MARBURY, a wealthy
socialite and literary and theatrical agent. De Wolfe
had the walls painted in pale colors and avoided
the thick velvet curtains, dark-painted walls and
heavy, dark wood furniture that had prevailed during the Victorian era, which she considered
gloomy. Irving House became a gathering place for
a unique blend of people in the arts, literature,
politics, and society.

In 1905 De Wolfe decided to open her own
decorating business and sent out printed cards featuring her trademark—a wolf with a flower in its
mouth. The well-known society architect Stanford
White helped De Wolfe land an important com-

mission, designing the interior of New York's first social club for women, the Colony Club. Once again, De Wolfe created a light, uncluttered look.

Her business grew as clients hired De Wolfe to decorate their homes with pale wall colors and delicate 18th-century furniture. For curtains and upholstery, she often used floral-patterned chintz, a lightweight, glazed cotton fabric, and she was especially fond of the colors beige and ivory. De Wolfe once said, "I believe in plenty of optimism and white paint, comfortable chairs with lights beside them, open fires on the hearth and flowers wherever they 'belong,' mirrors and sunshine in all rooms." She promoted her ideas by writing articles for *Good Housekeeping.*

De Wolfe's style of decorating became more popular than the Victorian look. Clients came from San Francisco, Chicago, and other cities, as well as New York, and they paid De Wolfe high fees. She also added a 30 percent fee to the cost of antiques she found for her clients. Her best-paying job came from the steel millionaire Henry Clay Frick, who asked her to design his new mansion on Fifth Avenue in New York. In addition to designing interiors, she also came up with ideas for practical furnishings, such as a vanity dressing table with drawers, upholstered bed rests with arms, and several other items.

In 1906, De Wolfe and Marbury bought the Villa Trianon in Versailles, France, outside Paris, and began restoring it, after which they used the villa for entertaining. When World War I broke out in 1914, the mansion was used as a storage facility and, throughout the war, De Wolfe helped to nurse the troops. De Wolfe began working on a book, *The House in Good Taste,* which was published in 1913. The book, which is considered a classic, was beauti-

fully designed and included photographs of De Wolfe's own rooms, as well as many practical and creative ideas. It set a new tone for books on decorating. Her successful cookbook, *Elsie De Wolfe's Recipes for Successful Dining,* which included suggestions on entertaining and etiquette as well as menus and recipes, was published in 1934. In addition, she negotiated endorsement fees for promoting Pontiac cars, Gulistan carpets, and skin care products.

During World War I (1914–18 in Europe) De Wolfe was awarded the Croix de Guerre and Legion of Honor for her hospital relief work for injured soldiers. In 1926, she married Sir Charles Mendl, a British diplomat on assignment in France. As Lady Mendl, Elsie De Wolfe entertained on a grand scale and gained fame as a society hostess.

When World War II broke out, the Mendls moved to California and bought a lavish home in Beverly Hills, which De Wolfe renovated and furnished. Mendl regained her U.S. citizenship, which had been lost when she married. After the war ended, De Wolfe moved back to Villa Trianon, where she enjoyed visits from monarchs and celebrities during her final years. She died there on July 12, 1950. She continued to influence interior design in the decades that followed. Biographer Jane Smith says that De Wolfe was a key force in making interior design a major industry and that she oversaw the "professionalism of taste" in the 20th century.

Further Reading

Smith, Jane S. *Elsie de Wolfe: A Life in High Style.* New York: Simon and Schuster, 1982.

Smith, Meredith Etherington. *Elsie de Wolfe: A Decorative Life.* New York: Random House, 1988.

Tapert, Annette, and Diana Edkins. *The Power of Style.* New York: Crown, 1994.

E

EVANS, LETTIE PATE WHITEHEAD
(Letitia Pate)
(1872–1953) *Executive, Philanthropist*

Lettie Pate Whitehead Evans was one of the first women to serve as director of a major U.S. corporation, Coca-Cola, and she oversaw the expansion of this thriving business during the early 1900s, a time when few women worked in the corporate world.

Born in Thaxton in Bedford County, Virginia, in 1872, Letitia Pate attended private schools in Bedford and Lynchburg, Virginia. At age 23, she married attorney Joseph Brown Whitehead, and the couple settled in Chattanooga, Tennessee, where their two sons were born in 1895 and 1898.

In 1899, Joseph Whitehead and a partner contracted with Asa Candler, founder of the Coca-Cola Company, to bottle his soft drink, which was then sold at soda fountains in the southern United States. They obtained the exclusive right to bottle and sell Coca-Cola throughout most of the country. The family relocated to Atlanta, where the bottling company was founded. At that time, Lettie Whitehead was a homemaker raising the couple's children, Joseph B. Jr. and Conkey Pate. White-head's company grew steadily more successful, and the Whiteheads both devoted time to civic work in their community and to the Episcopal Church.

After her husband died of pneumonia in 1906, Lettie Whitehead took charge of the family's business affairs, which also included various investments, and she served as chairman of the Whitehead Holding Company and president of the Whitehead Realty Company. As an executive, she displayed keen insights about the product and a practical understanding of finances, as well as a desire to learn from others working at the Coca-Cola Company, which expanded greatly under her direction. She became one of the first women to serve on the board of directors of a major U.S. corporation when she began serving as a director of the company in 1934, a position she held until 1953.

In 1913, Whitehead remarried, to Colonel Arthur Kelly Evans, a retired Canadian army officer. They entertained prominent people from around the world at their main home in Hot Springs, Virginia. Known for her charm and generosity, Lettie Whitehead Evans continued to devote much of her time to the community, supporting the arts and civic organizations. During her lifetime, she

Lettie Pate Whitehead Evans was one of the first women to serve as a director of a major American corporation, the Coca-Cola Company, when she was appointed to the board in 1934.
(Photo courtesy of the Lettie Pate Evans Foundation)

donated millions of dollars to various educational institutions, including Agnes Scott College, Emory University, the Georgia Institute of Technology, the College of William and Mary, Washington and Lee University, Episcopal Theological Seminary, and Episcopal High School.

Evans also supported numerous medical institutions and programs to benefit young people. During World War II, she assisted air raid victims in Europe and provided ambulances to the French military. Concerned about the plight of women, especially elderly women, she provided help to several nursing and retirement homes.

Two foundations continue to support the causes that were important to Lettie Pate Whitehead Evans. They are the Lettie Pate Whitehead Foundation, which was created by her son Conkey Pate Whitehead, and the Lettie Pate Evans Foundation, which she established herself before her death on November 14, 1953. The foundations support various religious, charitable, and educational causes, including scholarships, especially for women pursuing careers in the medical, nursing, and allied health professions. In 1998, the administration building at Georgia Tech was renamed the Lettie Pate Whitehead Evans Building in recognition of the contributions, totaling more than $327 million, that the institution had received over the years from her foundation. The College of William and Mary, which has received more than $10 million through the years, named the Lettie Pate Whitehead Evans Graduate Residence Hall in her honor.

Her attorney, Hughes Spalding, said of Lettie Whitehead Evans, "Mrs. Evans made it her business to go about the world doing good. She believed in seeing the result of her material benefactions and in feeling the pulsations of the intangible ones."

She was selected as a Georgia Woman of Achievement in 1998. Her foundations continue to operate from offices in Georgia.

Further Reading

"Georgia Women of Achievement: 1998 Inductee Lettie Pate Evans." Available online. URL: http://www.gawomen.org/honorees/long/evans_long.htm. Downloaded on September 20, 2000.

"Lettie Pate Whitehead Foundation." Available online. URL: http://www.geocities.com/HotSprings/2021/whitehead.html. Downloaded on September 20, 2000.

F

FARMER, FANNIE MERRITT

(1857–1915)   *Entrepreneur, Cooking School Founder, Author*

Farmer, a self-published cookbook author and founder of cookery schools, standardized cooking methods in America and promoted healthy, well-balanced menus.

Fannie Merritt Farmer was born on March 23, 1857, in Boston, where her father owned a printing business. She had to leave high school before graduation because she suffered a stroke, which left her with a permanent limp. By her late twenties, Farmer was feeling well enough to take a job as a mother's helper, and her wages helped to boost the family income, which had declined when her father's business failed.

While working for her host family, Farmer learned to cook. For generations, people had used recipes with measurements that usually were not precise. Sometimes, cooks were told to add "a glass of" something or a "nut-size lump" of something else. Farmer began to measure ingredients more accurately and she wrote down the results. At age 30, she enrolled in the Boston Cooking School and completed two years of training. The school offered her the position of assistant principal, and in 1894, she became the director. She said that her students learned by doing: "They do the work themselves, prepare lunch, take turns serving it, and eat it."

She had been writing down recipes with ingredients measured as level cups, tablespoons, and teaspoons, and she tested them over and over in the school's kitchen. In 1896, she tried to have the recipes published as a revised and improved version of the *Boston Cooking-School Cookbook,* but the publishing companies, all headed by men, did not think the book would be profitable. They said she would have to finance the project herself, so Farmer self-published the 700-page collection of recipes. Using level measurements, said Farmer, would provide consistent results. The book contained step-by-step instructions that allowed even an inexperienced cook to succeed.

Farmer was also interested in nutrition and urged homemakers to think about healthful meals. She wrote, "The time is not too far distant when a knowledge of the principles of diet will be an essential part of one's education." She told readers how to select different cuts of meat, fresh poultry and game, and fresh eggs. According to Marion

Cunningham, who wrote the preface for the 1996 edition of the *Fannie Farmer Cookbook,* Farmer would always encourage students to do better and would say, "I have no patience with cooks who just boil their vegetables, instead of putting heart and soul into cooking so that it becomes enjoyable instead of drudgery."

The recipes in the book were for traditional home cooking, mostly from the New England region, but included such French classics as soufflés and hollandaise sauce. Some critics said the recipes were too plain and unsophisticated and concentrated too much on regional cuisine. Yet the book sold millions of copies, and new editions were printed in the years that followed. It became known as the bible of cookery for American women.

Farmer opened her own cooking school, Miss Farmer's School of Cookery, in 1902, and the school attracted housewives as well as people who aspired to become professional cooks. She traveled throughout the United States performing cooking demonstrations for interested audiences. In addition, she developed diet plans for people who were ill or disabled and presented these ideas to students at the Harvard Medical School.

In 1908, Farmer suffered a second stroke and was confined to a wheelchair. She continued to lecture on cooking and nutrition and to perform cooking demonstrations until just 10 days before she died of kidney disease on January 15, 1915.

Further Reading

Forbes, Malcolm. *Women Who Made a Difference.* New York: Simon and Schuster, 1990.

Jones, Evan. *American Food: The Gastronomic Story.* Woodstock, N.Y.: Overlook Press, 1990.

✳ FERTEL, RUTH (Ruth Udstad)
(1927–) *Entrepreneur, Restaurant Chain Owner*

Called the First Lady of American Restaurants, Ruth Fertel founded and chairs the nation's largest upscale restaurant company and the world's largest steak house chain, Ruth's Chris Steak Houses, which sells more than 13,500 steaks a day.

Ruth Udstad was born on February 5, 1927, in the fishing village of Happy Jack in rural Louisiana, outside New Orleans. Although times were difficult for the family during the Great Depression years of the 1930s, her parents conveyed a positive attitude and her father, a hardworking salesman, inspired Ruth and her older brother to strive for excellence. She later said, "I grew up in the country in a neighborhood of many boys, no girls. I was trying to keep up with the boys or beat them at their own games. . . . I'm very competitive."

She worked her way through college and earned a degree in chemistry, with a minor in physics, from Louisiana State University (LSU) at age 19. For a while, she taught at Lake Charles (now McNeese) Junior College in Lake Charles, Louisiana, then left in 1951 to marry and raise a family in New Orleans.

Divorced in 1965, Ruth Fertel needed a job to supplement the small child-support payments she was receiving. She found a job sewing draperies at home, then worked as a lab technician at Tulane University Medical School in New Orleans but neither job paid enough for her to raise and educate her two young sons. Despite warnings from her friends and attorney, Fertel, who was interested in the food business but had no restaurant experience, decided to mortgage her home to buy the 60-seat Chris Steak House in New Orleans. With a loan of $22,000, she paid for the business and had $4,000 left to buy foods and supplies.

From the beginning, she tried to create a warm family atmosphere in the restaurant and worked long hours, performing different jobs, among them mixing drinks and washing dishes. She later said, "I used to butcher the meat, wait on the tables, run the register, and do the books. I was there from 9 A.M. till closing, which was usually around midnight to 1:00 A.M."

After a fire in 1976 forced her to relocate, she added her name to make the restaurant Ruth's Chris Steak House. She moved to a location down the street and had a new restaurant constructed, large enough to seat 160 people. The next year, she had a special broiler built so the restaurant could cook steaks at 1,700–1,800 degrees to sear the meat and keep the insides juicy. The steaks were served immediately on prewarmed plates.

A patron had approached her in 1975 about opening a franchise steak house in Baton Rouge. It was the first of dozens of new Ruth's Chris restaurants, some franchises and some company-owned, each one designed to suit its locale. The steak houses continue to specialize in steaks and baked potatoes, serving portions that range from 12 to 22 ounces of prime, corn-fed Midwestern beef. Menus offer meats and seafoods, several kinds of potatoes and other vegetables, salads with fresh dressings, and homemade desserts. Customers can select from a large list of wines, both domestic and imported.

By the early 1990s, the chain had grown to 39 restaurants bringing in gross annual sales of about $100 million. As of January 2001, the chain had 78 locations in the United States and Puerto Rico and seven other international locations, including the Caribbean and Far East. Gross revenues were more than $325 million at the end of 2000.

Fertel, who is a popular motivational speaker, has received numerous awards. In 2001, she won the LSU Hall of Distinction Award, the Restaurant Business High Performance Leadership Award, and the Ella Brennan Savoir Faire Award. In the 1990s she counted among her honors the Executive of the Year Award from *Restaurants and Institutions* magazine (1997); the Golden Plate Award from the International Association of Foodservice Equipment Manufacturers; the Horatio Alger Award (1995); one of the top 50 entrepreneurs among women business owners by the National Foundation of Women Business Owners, Chicago Chapter (1993); Women of Achievement from the National Foundation of Women Business Owners (1993); and the Golden Chain Award (first woman recipient) from *Nation's Restaurant News* (1992).

Further Reading

Ruth's Chris Steak House. "Company Biographies: Ruth Fertel, Founder." Available online. URL: www.ruthschris. com. Downloaded on June 22, 2001.

Fotter, Marsha. "Food & Wine: New Kids on the Block," *Sarasota Magazine,* November 1999, pp. 222–26.
Polvay, Marina. "A Winning Combination," *Smoke Affair,* spring 1998. Available online. URL: http://www. ruthschris.com/news pr/fsmkaffairSpr98.htm. Downloaded on May 21, 2001.
Sanders, Adrienne. "Success Secrets of the Successful," *Forbes,* November 2, 1998, p. 22.

✳ FIELDS, DEBBI (Debra Jane Sivyer, Debra Fields Rose)
(1956–) *Entrepreneur, Executive*

Debbi Fields founded Mrs. Fields Cookies, a multimillion-dollar company with more than 1,000 outlets in 12 countries. Fields has described her recipe for success: "I use nothing but the best ingredients, like real butter, pure vanilla, and lots of rich chocolate. My cookies are always freshly baked. I price cookies so that you cannot make them at home for any less."

Debra Jane Sivyer was born on September 18, 1956, in East Oakland, California, where she was the youngest of five daughters. Her father was a welder and her mother was a homemaker. The family lived in a modest two-bedroom home. She enjoyed baking and later said that she began making chocolate chip cookies for her family and friends when she was 13 years old. By that age, she was already working at her first job, as foul ball girl for the Oakland A's baseball team. In high school, she worked as a store clerk, and at age 17, she became the official Miss Marine World, appearing in a water-skiing show. She was not particularly interested in academics.

At age 19, she married Randy Fields, an economist with whom she eventually had five daughters. While raising her family and attending junior college, Debbi Fields enjoyed trying new cookie recipes. People often told her that her chocolate chip cookies were the best they had ever tasted.

In 1977, at age 20, Fields decided to sell her cookies to the public and, after numerous rejections, managed to get a $50,000 loan. She was determined to succeed despite pessimistic predictions from some of her acquaintances who said a cookie business would not survive. She later said that she realized she had several disadvantages: "I was young, had no college credentials, came from little means. I was blond and people figured I had no brains."

Fields set up shop in Palo Alto, California. When no customers came into her store on opening day, she took a tray outside and offered samples. People came into the store to buy more, and her first day's sales reached $75. Her company, Mrs. Fields' Chocolate Chippery, soon attracted many regular customers along with new business. As a manager, Fields learned to predict customer count and revenues so that she could determine how many staff she needed throughout the day. She later said, "It's all tied to a very simple principle that's called hour-by-hour management and today colleges use it as a case study in business efficiency."

The company placed stores in business centers, shopping malls, and free-standing locations. She changed the name to Mrs. Fields Cookies as she began offering a wider selection of products. Fields, who emphasizes friendliness and good customer relations, has said, "Without superior customer service, it doesn't matter how good your product is, you are not going to keep that customer." In addition, Fields aimed to sell only fresh cookies, made from high-quality ingredients, so customers could enjoy large, chewy cookies still warm from the oven. This made Fields's cookies much different from commercially packaged cookies in grocery stores, which might remain on the shelf for long periods of time. Mrs. Fields's cookies that were not sold within two hours were donated to food banks.

By 1980, there were 15 Mrs. Fields stores, and Randy Fields had joined the business as a partner. Other companies began to introduce their versions of larger, chewier cookies. Fields expanded and actively managed her company, overseeing operations, developing new products, and conducting public relations. The Fields family built a new home in Woodland, Utah, near Salt Lake City, where they located their headquarters. The nine-bedroom, 16,000-square-foot house featured an indoor swimming pool, and the grounds included a 23-stall horse barn and a tennis court.

In 1984, *Esquire* magazine named Debbi Fields one of its Men and Women Under 40 Who Are Changing America. She has received numerous other awards, including Woman of the Year (1986) by the Young Women's Christian Association. Fields has also written some best-selling cookbooks, including *100 Recipes From the Kitchen of Debbi Fields* (1992), *I Love Chocolate* (1994), and *Great American Desserts* (1996). She hosted a daily television program called *The Dessert Show* for public television and overcame an admitted fear of public speaking to become a popular speaker. She often tells audiences, "Never chase money, but chase the passion to bring quality products to the people."

Fields has devoted time and money to charitable causes. In 1986, she founded Mrs. Fields Children's Health Foundation, which provides grants to medical organizations that benefit children. She has served on the boards of the Primary Children's Medical Foundation in Utah, the Outback Steakhouse company, and the *America 3* Women's Sailing Team. Fields also initiated her One Smart Cookie program, which rewards schoolchildren who attain goals—for example in attendance, reading, or citizenship—with free cookies.

In 1989, Mrs. Fields became the first company in the food industry to use state-of-the-art computer technology to plan operations and production schedules. After Fields sold her company to a group of private investors in 1993 and retired as chairman, she continued to act as a consultant and to serve on the board of directors. Fields was able to spend more time at home while still traveling several days each month to meetings, book signings, and public appearances.

Debbi and Randy Fields were divorced in 1997, and she moved to Tennessee after marrying her second husband, Michael Rose, retired chairman of the Promus Hotel Corporation, which is based in Memphis, Tennessee. The company she founded is still thriving. By 2000, there were more than 1,000 Mrs. Fields stores in 12 countries, and annual sales topped $250 million.

In an interview for *Career World Magazine,* Fields said, "The important thing is not being afraid to take a chance. Remember, the greatest failure is not to try. Once you find something you love to do, be the best at doing it."

Further Reading

About.com. "Investing for Women: Debbi Fields." Available online. URL: http://womensinvest.about.com/money/womensinvest/blfields.htm. Downloaded on May 3, 2000.

Fields, Debbi, and Alan Furst. *"One Smart Cookie": How One Housewife's Chocolate Chip Cookie Recipe Turned into a Multi-Million Dollar Business.* New York: Simon and Schuster, 1987.

Frank, Christina. "Oops! The Biggest Career Goof I Ever Made," *Redbook,* November 1995, p. 120ff.

Petrone, Gina. "A Special Hobby," Centercourt. Available online. URL: http://www.centercourt.com/www.centercourt.com/use/petrone3.html. Downloaded on May 23, 2000.

Sabljak, Mark. "This Public Speaker Isn't Half-baked," *The Business Journal of Milwaukee,* March 29, 1999. Available online. URL: http://milwaukee.bcentral.com/milwaukee/stories/1999/03/29/newscolumn3.html. Downloaded on May 20, 2000.

Sadler, Marilyn. "Baking a Name for Herself," *Memphis Magazine,* June 1999. Available online. URL: htp://www.memphismagazine.com/backissues/june1999/feature.htm. Downloaded on May 20, 2000.

✷ FIORINA, CARLY (Cara Carleton Sneed)
(1954–) *Executive*

Carly Fiorina is the chief executive officer (CEO), president, and chairman of Hewlett-Packard, the second-largest computer manufacturer in the world. She was the first woman to become a CEO of one of America's 20 largest corporations, as well as the first woman to head a Dow 30 company (30 companies that make up the Dow Jones Industrial Averages, or DJIA).

She was born on September 6, 1954, in Austin, Texas, and named Cara Carleton Sneed, in keeping with a family tradition. During the Civil War, the Sneed family had lost all the men named Carleton,

so each succeeding generation named a son Carleton or a daughter Cara Carleton. Carly's mother, Madelon, was an artist who painted portraits and vivid abstracts in oils. Her father, Joseph, was a law professor and judge. Fiorina later said that her mother "had an unquenchable zest for life" and that "she taught me the power of keeping a positive attitude." Of her father, she once said, "His guidance and example have always meant the world to me."

The Sneeds moved frequently while Carly was growing up, so she attended five different high schools, while the family was living in California, North Carolina, London, and Ghana. After high school, she attended Stanford University, in Palo Alto, California, and majored in medieval history and philosophy. While she was at Stanford, Sneed worked as a summer intern at Hewlett-Packard, the company she would later lead. She worked in the shipping department, typing bills of lading. After she received her bachelor of arts (B.A.) degree, Sneed taught English in Bologna, Italy, then enrolled in law school at the University of California, Los Angeles. She enjoyed the intellectual stimulation of her studies but did not think she would enjoy practicing law. After one semester, she made the very difficult decision to leave law school. She later called this an "important life lesson," which she expressed in these words: "Love what you do, or don't do it. Don't make a choice of any kind, whether in career or in life, just because it pleases others or because it ranks high on someone else's scale of achievement. . . . Make the choice because it engages all of you."

Sneed then studied at the Robert H. Smith School of Business at the University of Maryland, where she earned a master's degree in business administration (M.B.A.). Beginning in 1980, Sneed embarked on a career at the telecommunications giant AT&T and its Lucent Technologies division that would last nearly 20 years. She started as an account executive in the long-distance division, then moved to the network systems division, where she assumed positions of increasing responsibility. Sneed showed great skills in marketing and customer relations.

As CEO of Hewlett Packard Corporation, Carly Fiorina is one of the most prominent executives in the United States and the first woman to head one of America's 20 largest corporations.
(Photo courtesy of Hewlett-Packard)

At AT&T, she met Frank Fiorina, who was a vice president at the company. They were married in 1985. Carly Fiorina had been married briefly in her early twenties, then divorced.

At age 35, Carly Fiorina became the first female officer in AT&T's history. Five years later, she was chosen to head the company's North American operations. In 1989, Fiorina also earned her master of science (M.S.) degree from the Massachusetts Institute of Technology (MIT). She was named one of *Business Week* magazine's top 50 women in business in 1992.

Fiorina played a key role in AT&T's spinoff of Lucent Technologies in 1996. She led the initial public offering (IPO) in 1996 when Lucent went public and the stock began trading on the New York Stock Exchange. It was one of the most successful IPOs in history. In 1998, she became president of Lucent's $19 billion global service provider division, which sells equipment to the largest telephone companies in the world. Fiorina launched a $90 million brand-building campaign and led the marketing effort that made Lucent a major Internet supplier. Under her leadership, the growth rate increased tremendously. All of Lucent's products gained a market share in every region. She was known as a tireless worker who took time to personally thank and compliment her staff members for their achievements. A securities analyst for Paine Webber later said of Fiorina, "She understood the telecommunications business and how customers' needs would evolve in a changing environment." By 1998, Lucent had sales of more than $30 billion.

In 1999, Fiorina was recruited from her position as group president at Lucent Technologies to become CEO of Hewlett-Packard (HP), the world's second-largest computer company (after IBM). HP is a provider of computing, Internet, and intranet services and communications products.

Fiorina was named president and CEO of HP on July 19, 1999. She described her vision for the company: "In this new world we must always remember that technology is only as valuable as the use to which it is put. In the end, technology is ultimately about people." She said that she aimed to improve growth and revenues at the company and develop new and more innovative products, as well as to maintain excellent customer relations. In addition, Fiorina said HP would develop useful new products and strive to sell customers the combination of products and services that best suits their needs. Observers said Fiorina was a dynamic leader who had the expertise to position HP for the future.

Evidently, the observers were right. Carly Fiorina made *Fortune* magazine's list of the 50 Most Powerful Women in business in 1998, 1999, 2000, and 2001. She has served on the boards of directors for Merck & Company, Kellogg Company, Goldstar Information & Communications, the USA–Republic of China Economic Council, and the U.S.-China Board of Trade and presently sits on the board of Cisco Systems. She is also a member of the board of PowerUp, a gathering of business, government, and nonprofit organizations devoted to providing access to technology and technology education to underserved youth. A popular public speaker, Fiorina delivered the 2000 commencement address at MIT, one of her three alma maters. She often rises at 4 A.M. to exercise and feed the wild birds on her property and begin the day's work. She and her husband, who is now retired, enjoy boating.

Further Reading

Burrows, Peter. "The Radical: Carly Fiorina's Bold Management Experiment at HP," *Business Week,* February 19, 2001, pp. 70–80.

Burrows, Peter, and Peter Elstrom. "HP's Carly Fiorina: The Boss," *Business Week,* Available online. URL: http://www.businessweek.com:/1999/99_31/b364000 1.htm?scriptFramed. Posted on August 2, 1999. Downloaded on January 6, 2001.

"50 Most Powerful Women: Carly Fiorina," *Fortune.* Available online. URL: http://www.fortune.com/fortune/ mostpowerful/1.html. Downloaded on August 17, 2000.

Fiorina, Carly. "Commencement Address, Massachusetts Institute of Technology, Cambridge, Mass., June 2, 2000," Hewlett-Packard Company Information. Available online. URL: http://www.hp.com/hpinfo/ceo/ speeches/ceo_mit_commence.htm. Downloaded on January 5, 2001.

Gallagher, Carol. *Going to the Top.* New York: Viking, 2000.

"The *Ladies' Home Journal* 100, Business and Finance: Carleton Fiorina," *Ladies' Home Journal,* November 1999, p. 162.

Sellars, Patricia. "The 50 Most Powerful Women in Business," *Fortune,* October 16, 2000, pp. 131ff.

✺ FORD, EILEEN (Eileen Otte)
    (1922–   ) *Entrepreneur, Modeling Agency Co-owner*

Eileen Ford cofounded and became the director of the Ford Modeling Agency, one of the world's foremost agencies.

Eileen Otte was born in New York City on March 25, 1922, and grew up in Great Neck, New York, with her three brothers. Her parents made a comfortable living operating a business that conducted credit ratings of large corporations.

Although Otte had no particular plans to pursue a career, her parents encouraged her to attend college and become a lawyer. In 1939, she enrolled at Barnard College in New York City. Her mother had been a fashion model, and Eileen also began modeling during her summer vacations from school. When she graduated in 1943 with a psychology degree, she planned to enroll in law school, but she had become increasingly interested in different aspects of the fashion industry as she took jobs as a photographer's stylist and as a fashion reporter.

At age 22, Eileen Otte met a college football player named Jerry Ford. They eloped three months later, on November 20, 1944. Within two years, they welcomed their daughter Jamie. Although Jerry was working in Eileen's parents' company, they needed extra money for their growing family. Eileen Ford decided to handle bookings for two friends who worked as models, so she acted as their agent, something that was uncommon in the modeling field at that time. Ford negotiated better fees for the jobs her models performed, and soon they recommended her services to other models. She collected a percentage of the models' payments for handling their bookings and other business matters.

By 1947, she was representing eight models, and within another year, the total had risen to 34. Her husband, Jerry, had been attending business school and working, but they decided to develop the modeling business together. During the next decade, the Fords had three more children—Bill, Katie, and Lacie—while working long hours on their business, called the Ford Modeling Agency. The photographers, advertising agencies, and stores that hired Ford models paid the agency 10 percent of the fee for a given job, and the models also paid 10 percent, so that the agency received a total commission of 20 percent.

The Fords set new standards in the modeling business and personally helped their models with many facets of their lives and careers. They offered advice regarding housing, diet, skin care, and wardrobe, among other things, and helped them to develop as models in the fashion and entertainment industries. Ford models were respected for their professional behavior and were not permitted to take assignments the Fords considered inappropriate. Models who came to New York from other places were welcomed at the Fords' home, where they could adjust to their new way of life under the Fords' supervision.

Through the years, Ford models have included some of the most famous names in the world, such as Jean Patchett, Jean Shrimpton, Carmen Dell' Orefice, Jerry Hall, Christie Brinkley, Rene Simonsen, Rachel Hunter, Vendela, Christy Turlington, and Patricia Velasquez. Some well-known actresses who began as Ford Models include Lauren Hutton, Kim Basinger, Brooke Shields, Shari Belafonte, Sharon Stone, and Rene Russo. The agency also began to sign male models during the 1980s.

As the head of this successful business, Eileen Ford was respected by her peers and became known as a beauty and fashion expert. She has been a judge at beauty pageants, including the Miss Universe Pageant in 1980. Ford also authored five books about beauty.

In 1995, the Fords' daughter Katie Ford took charge of the business as the chief executive officer (CEO). She said, "My long-term goal is to turn Ford into a company that is a total management company and to build the brand into Ford products." As of 2000, the company included 12 offices around the world, some 200 employees, and thousands of models. Eileen Ford continues to help evaluate the thousands of potential models who contact the agency each year.

Nina Blanchard, head of her own modeling agency, once said of Ford, "Eileen was the first to start everything that was helpful to models and their agents. That was really groundbreaking. People sat back and waited to see. If she did it, you'd almost go ahead with it."

Further Reading

"A Classic Ford: Modeling Still Suits Agency's Boss to a 'T,'" *St. Louis Post Dispatch,* September 9, 1993, p. 7.

Ford, Eileen. *The Ford Models Crash Course in Looking Great.* New York: Simon and Schuster, 1985.

———. *Secrets of the Model's World.* New York: Trident, 1970.

Strailey, Jennifer. "A Model Company." MyPrimeTime. Available online. URL: http://www.myprimetime.com/ work/entrepreneur toolkit/content/pm ford/index.shtml. Downloaded on May 1, 2001.

Wilson, Craig. "The Ford Factor," *USA Today,* April 8, 1997, p. 1-D.

✳ FRANKLIN, ANN SMITH
(1696–1763)   *Printer, Publisher, Business Operator*

Ann Smith Franklin was the first woman printer in New England and probably the longest-operating and most successful of the women printers in colonial America.

Born on October 2, 1696, the daughter of Samuel and Anna Smith, Ann Smith grew up in Boston, where she met and married James Franklin, a printer and the brother of statesman Benjamin Franklin, in 1723. The couple had three children. James Franklin went on to found the first commercial printing business in Newport, Rhode Island, and Ann and her two older children assisted him. After James died in 1735, Ann Franklin carried on the business with the help of her two daughters, who were "correct and quick compositors." When he was old enough, her son James, whom she had trained, worked in the business until he died in 1762.

Franklin became the official printer in Rhode Island colony in 1736, and her business produced numerous legal documents, government publications, and pamphlets, as well as the colony's paper money and ballots for the election of 1744. Between 1728 and 1735, Franklin published a series of almanacs written by Joseph Stafford. For the next five years, she published a set of almanacs she had written herself. In 1745, Franklin began printing an edition of the laws of the General

Assembly, which eventually numbered 340 pages, for the government of Rhode Island.

Franklin retired in 1757 but decided to return to the business in 1762, at which time she published a newspaper called the Newport *Mercury,* which had debuted in the fall of 1758 and came out on Mondays. She tried to revive a paper called the *Rhode Island Gazette,* which her husband had printed in 1732 and 1733, but it did not succeed.

A Massachusetts-born printer named Samuel Hall married Ann Franklin's daughter, also named Ann, and Franklin formed a partnership with Hall in 1763. After she died on April 19, 1763, Samuel Hall operated the business under his own name. Franklin was eulogized as a woman who "by her Economy and Industry in carrying on the Printing Business supported herself and Family." Two centuries later, Franklin became the first woman inducted into the Journalism Hall of Fame at the University of Rhode Island.

Further Reading

Hudak, Leona. *Early American Women Printers and Publishers, 1639–1820.* Metuchen, N.J.: Scarecrow Press, 1978.

Sherr, Lyn, and Jurate Kazickas, *Susan B. Anthony Slept Here: A Guide to American Women's Landmarks.* New York: Random House, 1994.

Thomas, Isaiah. *The History of Printing in America.* New York: Weathervane, 1970.

✳ FUDGE, ANN M. (Ann Marie Brown)
(1951–)   *Executive*

As president of Maxwell House Coffee, a division of Philip Morris's Kraft Foods division, Ann Marie Fudge became one of the top-ranking women in American industry. She also helped to set monetary policies as a director of the Federal Reserve Bank of New York. Fudge says, "The core values needed for managing a business are leadership, strategies, flexibility and understanding the issues. Women are equipped for these jobs—we have been managing households for years."

Ann Marie Brown was born on April 23, 1951, in Washington, D.C., where her father was a U.S. Postal Service administrator. She earned her bachelor of arts (B.A.) degree with honors from Simmons College and married Richard Fudge Sr., an educational consultant to businesses, in 1970. Their first son was born while Fudge was still pursuing her degree. After graduating in 1973, Fudge worked in human resources at General Electric before entering Harvard University, from which she received her master's degree in business administration (M.B.A.) in 1977. By the time she enrolled at Harvard, Fudge had given birth to her second son.

Returning to corporate life, Fudge became a marketing assistant at General Mills, Inc., where she rose to the position of product manager in 1980 and marketing director in 1983. Three years later, Fudge accepted a position as associate director of strategic planning at General Foods Corporation, which later merged with Kraft Foods. She steadily rose to higher positions in the company. By 1987, she was marketing director of the beverage division and, in 1989, she became marketing director of the Kraft General Foods dinners and enhancers division. She was promoted to brand manager of that division in 1991. That year, *Black Enterprise* magazine named her one of the country's "21 Women of Power and Influence."

Fudge was promoted again in 1993 when she was named vice president of the division, which was a $600-million-a-year business. Her responsibilities included managing the production and promotion of various products, including Stove Top Stuffing Mix and Minute Rice. She improved sales in a highly competitive market and was known for her ability to build brand dominance for various food products. Coworkers praised Fudge for her energy, strong leadership skills, and ability to understand consumers' needs and interests. For example, her team developed the "Why Fry?" slogan for Shake 'n Bake, a coating for oven-baked chicken, when more people became concerned about dietary fat and health.

In 1994, Fudge was named executive vice president of General Foods USA and president of the Maxwell House Coffee division, which included the brand names Sanka, Yuban, International Coffees, and General Foods' foodservice business. As president of Maxwell House, a $1.4-billion business, 44-year-old Fudge took charge of 2,400 employees and three coffee processing plants, located in Jacksonville, Florida; Houston, Texas; and San Leandro, California. One of her major goals was to ensure a quality product, so Fudge worked closely with the teams that selected coffee beans. Robert S. Morrison, president of General Foods USA and Fudge's boss, said, "As a business leader, Ann combines a very forceful personality with a great sensitivity to people. She relies heavily on a team approach to achieving business goals. Ann has positively affected every area she's been in." Maxwell House doubled its earning under her leadership.

In 1997, Fudge was named president of Kraft's Maxwell House Coffee and Post Cereal division, located in Tarrytown, New York. The division had revenues of $2.7 billion in 1998 and 1999, making Fudge the only African American in charge of a billion-dollar industry at that time. Fudge once said that when she was moving up in business, "I didn't stop and say, 'Oh, there aren't a lot of black women. I just thought about the opportunities.'"

As a wife, the mother of two sons, and a grandmother, Fudge has juggled several roles during her busy career and also found time for community work, supporting Habitat for Humanity, Boys and Girls Clubs of America, and other organizations.

As of 2000, Fudge had also served on the boards of General Electric, AlliedSignal, Honeywell International, and LIZ CLAIBORNE, Inc. Fudge has said that these positions enable her to help increase the number of qualified minorities in executive positions and to advocate for equal opportunity in employment. Fudge has also served

as vice president and president of the Executive Leadership Council, a nonprofit group of African Americans in senior management and directorship positions that works to promote leadership qualities and expand opportunities for minorities.

During her career, Fudge has won numerous honors, including Advertising Woman of the Year, given by the Advertising Women of New York in 1995. She has been named to Who's Who of American Women, is one of *Ebony* Magazine's top 100 black people in corporate America, and is one of the top 50 female executives named by *Executive Female* magazine. She was on *Fortune* magazine's list of the 50 most powerful women in American business in 1999 and 2000. Madelyn Condit of Korn/Ferry International, an executive search firm, said of Fudge, "She has shown she can take a product and reposition it and increase the bottom line."

In February 2001, Fudge resigned from Kraft. She has been a featured guest speaker and panelist at conferences for business leaders and also now serves on the Board of Trustees of the Brookings Institution, a think tank in Washington, D.C.

Further Reading

Executive Leadership Council. "Achievement Award: Ann M. Fudge." Available online. URL: http://www.elcinfo.com/achv_2000.html. Downloaded on March 29, 2001.

"50 Most Powerful Women," *Fortune,* August 1998.

New York Times News Service. "The Workplace: At the Top at Maxwell House," *Minneapolis Star Tribune,* June 4, 1995, p. 5-D.

Reynolds, Rhonda. "Ann M. Fudge Brewing Success: The Newest Chief Executive at General," *Black Enterprise,* August 31, 1994, p. 68.

Washington, Huel. "Ann M. Fudge Named President of GF's Maxwell House Division," *The Sun Reporter,* March 23, 1994, pp. PG.

G

GIBBS, KATHARINE RYAN

(1863–1934) *Entrepreneur, Business School Founder*

With her sister Mary Ryan, Katharine Gibbs founded a nationwide chain of schools to teach secretarial and business skills to women.

Katharine Ryan was born on January 10, 1863, in Galena, Illinois, where her father was a meat packer and she was educated at a small private school. When Ryan's husband, William Gibbs, a gold prospector, died in a boating accident in 1906, she found herself without enough money to support their two sons and her younger sister Mary. She and Mary tried to build a dressmaking business but were not successful, and Gibbs had to sell her jewelry to pay their living expenses.

In 1910, Mary Ryan set out to become self-supporting, so she enrolled in a secretarial school in Providence, Rhode Island, where she became an instructor after graduation that same year. A year later, the owner decided to sell the school. Ryan and Gibbs combined their small savings and borrowed $1,000 so they could buy the business.

Determined to prepare women for broader careers in the business world, Katharine Gibbs became the administrator and Mary Ryan the instructor of a new school that offered the traditional secretarial curriculum—typing, shorthand, filing, and bookkeeping—along with classes in English, liberal arts, and business law. In 1915, they also launched a new method of shorthand they had developed because they saw ways to improve the existing systems. The sisters also worked with college professors to strengthen the curriculum at the school.

Gibbs and Ryan resolved that Gibbs graduates would be first-rate secretaries with a reputation for "background and intelligence." Students were required to dress neatly, with hats and white gloves. Many Gibbs students had already earned degrees from prestigious eastern colleges, including Vassar, Wellesley, and Mount Holyoke, which enhanced the school's status.

Another early goal was to expand into other areas of the country. A new Katharine Gibbs school opened in Boston in 1917, and another school opened in New York City the next year. The business filled a major need during those years, as men, who had filled most clerical and secretarial jobs in America, left to serve in the military during World War I. To attract more students, the Gibbs schools welcomed both college graduates and promising young women without a college education. The latter group was encouraged to enter the Gibbs Secretarial Arts program, which combined liberal arts courses with business courses. Teachers for this two-year program came from Columbia College in New York.

Katharine Gibbs died in 1934, but the business continued and it remained in the family. Her son Gordon and his wife took charge of the schools, which continued to expand into more states. There were four schools—in Providence, Rhode Island; Boston, Massachusetts; New York, New York; and Montclair, New Jersey—when Gordon Gibbs sold the business to Macmillan, Inc., a publisher that focused on educational books at that time. In 1997, Career Education Corporation bought the business, which was operating with 24 campuses in 13 states and two provinces in Canada as of 2000.

Further Reading

Brownlee, W. Elliott, and Mary Brownlee. *Women in the American Economy: A Documentary History.* New Haven: Yale University Press, 1976.

Gray, Sonja F. "Making a Difference: Katharine Ryan Gibbs (1863–1934)—A Radical Idea—Women Can Work." *Providence Journal.* Available online. URL: http://www.projo.com/special/women/94root13.htm. Downloaded on June 30, 2000.

�֎ GLEASON, KATE

(1865–1930)   *Executive, Engineer, Bank President, Contractor, Philanthropist*

Kate Gleason broke new ground when she studied engineering and became the first woman president of a national bank and the first woman ever elected to the American Society of Engineers, as well as director of a successful machine-tool company. Her achievements were particularly impressive in an era when few women ventured into these arenas.

Gleason later commented that her gender had been both an advantage and disadvantage during her career. She said, "In those early days, I was a freak; I talked of gears when a woman was not supposed to know what a gear was. It did me much good. For, no matter how much men disapproved of me, they were at least interested in seeing me, one distinct advantage I had over the ordinary salesman." She also commented, "It pays to be the first in any field, if you can."

Gleason was born on November 25, 1865, in Rochester, New York. She became interested in tools as a child. Her Irish-born father, William Gleason, was a mechanical designer who owned a small toolmaking business, the Machine Tool Manufacturing Works, and her mother was a feminist and suffragist. Kate began working at her father's company when she was only 11, shortly after her older brother Tom died. By age 14, she was the company bookkeeper and made increasingly important contributions to the business.

In 1884, Gleason became the first woman engineering student at Cornell University, where she was classified as a special student. She was disappointed to leave her studies after only a year when her father asked her to come back to work. She studied at Cornell again briefly in 1888. In addition, she studied at the Sibley College of Engraving and Mechanics Institute (now the Rochester Institute of Technology). However, she did not receive a degree.

In 1887, Gleason made her first sales trip for her father's company when she traveled to Ohio to sell machines. She was so effective that she became the company's chief sales representative by the age of 25. In 1890, she also became the secretary and treasurer of the company, giving her father more time to design and test a gear-planing machine that made beveled gears faster and less expensively than other machines of its type. This gear-planer enabled the Gleason company to produce more gears for the rapidly growing automotive industry. The company, which changed its name to the Gleason Works, became the leading producer of gear-cutting machinery.

As the chief sales representative, Kate Gleason opened new markets for Gleason products both

As head of the Gleason Works, the company her father founded, former engineering student
Kate Gleason was so effective that a local bankruptcy court later asked her to take charge of a machine tool
company that had failed.
(Photo courtesy of Gleason Foundation and Rochester Institute of Technology)

inside and outside the United States. Customers were impressed with her technical knowledge about the equipment and her personality. The well-read Gleason was regarded as a good conversationalist with a quick wit. She enjoyed the outdoors, especially horseback riding. Although she had numerous suitors, she never married.

Gleason went abroad in 1893 after her doctors encouraged her to take a vacation for health reasons. She visited England, Scotland, Germany, and France. Instead of traveling in luxury, Gleason took a cattle steamer to Europe and brought along a single good dress, a simple black one. Unlike other young women from wealthy families, Gleason traveled alone, not with a chaperone. She took advantage of her trip to market and sell Gleason tools. At that time, few American products had large markets overseas, so she achieved a breakthrough in this area. Gleason returned to Europe on other occasions. In 1900, she organized the Gleason Works exhibit at the Paris Exposition.

She also became more interested in fashion after her European trip. She later said that her mother's friend, suffragist leader Susan B. Anthony, had encouraged her to pay more attention to her appearance. Gleason, who wore plain clothing and a rather short hairstyle, began wearing what she called "soft, frivolous gowns" and often carried a spray of violets. She had her hair styled in a more fashionable manner.

In 1914, she left the family business, possibly due to growing conflicts with her brother Andrew and some other family members. A bankruptcy court asked her to take on the job of revitalizing a machine-tool company that had failed. In just over a year, Gleason had turned the Ingle Machine Company around so that it was making a profit again, and she managed to repay the company's $140,000 in debts.

Three years later, she ventured into banking. When the president of the First National Bank of East Rochester left to serve in World War I, the board unaminously elected Kate Gleason to take over his job. It was the first time a woman had served as president of a national bank. Gleason

took a strong interest in the large-scale development of low-cost housing in East Rochester to provide much-needed jobs as well as housing. In addition, Gleason foresaw that residential areas outside cities would grow as more people moved there. She envisioned communities that contained affordable housing, factories, shops, and recreational facilities.

When she left the bank after the war, she had helped eight new businesses to open and the bank's balance sheet showed higher profits than when she had arrived. However, Gleason modestly said that this was "due mainly to circumstances." One of the businesses she fostered built low-cost block style houses in East Rochester. These six-room homes were made of poured concrete and mass-produced, using a method Gleason helped to develop. Other suburban areas later used this method in their own housing developments. As a result of this work, Gleason became the first woman member of the American Concrete Institute.

Next, Gleason went to northern California, where officials in Berkeley had requested her help in rebuilding the city after a fire. Gleason also began building and selling low-cost homes in Sausalito, a business venture that increased her personal fortune. However, the state government took over some of the land she planned to use in order to build the Golden Gate Bridge.

In 1920, she bought land in Beaufort County, off the coast of South Carolina, with plans to build a resort for artists and writers that would include a golf course and beach clubhouse. (Her younger sister Eleanor would complete this project after Kate Gleason's death.) Gleason thought Beaufort would become a tourist attraction. She later moved to a home in downtown Beaufort and also maintained homes in her native Rochester and in France, where she helped to restore the French castle village of Septmonts, which had been badly damaged during the war.

The American Society of Mechanical Engineers (ASME) had already recognized Gleason's accomplishments by electing her in 1918 as its first full woman member. In 1930, she was the society's representative to the World Power Conference, which was held in Germany that year. Gleason had been elected to the German Engineering Society (Verein, Deutscher Ingenieure) in 1913 and may have been the first woman member of that organization as well. She was also the first woman inducted into the Rochester Engineering Society and Rochester Chamber of Commerce.

Gleason died from complications of pneumonia on January 9, 1933. During her lifetime, she had contributed significant amounts of money to schools, orphanages, and other charities, sometimes anonymously. In her will she bequeathed $25,000 to the Rochester Engineering Society. A large portion of her $1.4 million estate was used to set up the Kate Gleason Fund for charitable and educational programs. The Gleason Foundation had assets of about $139 million as of 1998. One beneficiary was the Rochester Institute of Technology (RIT), which named its Kate Gleason College of Engineering in her honor and established the Kate Gleason Scholarship for female engineering students.

Gleason Corporation continues to operate out of Rochester and is a leading producer of gears used in power equipment and in the automotive, aircraft, aerospace, truck, and recreational vehicle industries.

Further Reading

Bartels, Nancy. "The First Lady of Gearing," *Gear Technology Magazine,* September/October 1997. Available online. URL: http://www.geartechnology.com/mag/gt-g.htm. Downloaded on February 21, 2001.

Fitzroy, Nancy Deloye, "It's Time to Recognize the Contributions of Women Inventors," *USA Today Magazine,* January 1, 1999, p. 57.

The Foundation Center. "Rochester Institute of Technology Receives $10 Million to Recruit Minorities," *Philanthropy News Digest,* July 1, 1998, p. 1.

"Kate Gleason Took on Male Domain as Bank President; Businesswoman Made a Name for Herself." *Coin World,* August 16, 1999. Available online. URL: http://www.swe-bws.org/newslettr/oct99.html. Downloaded on December 8, 2000.

McHenry, Robert, editor. *Her Heritage: A Biographical Encyclopedia of Famous American Women.* Cambridge, Mass.: Pilgrim New Media, 1995.

Rochester Engineering Society. "SWE and RES Plan the Kate Gleason Award." Available online. URL: http://www.roceng.org/KatGleAw.html. Downloaded on March 1, 2001.

Wentzel, Michael. "Foundation Announces $10 Million Gift to RIT," *Democrat and Chronicle (Rochester),* June 28, 1998, pp. 1-A, 6-A.

GODDARD, MARY KATHERINE
(1738–1816)   *Printer, Publisher, Business Owner*

Mary Katherine Goddard operated a successful colonial printing business and published a prestigious newspaper before and during the American Revolution. The daughter of a doctor and homemaker, Goddard was born in either Groton or New London, Connecticut, on June 16, 1738. She grew up in New London where her father, Dr. Giles Goddard, was the postmaster.

After her father died in 1762, Goddard and her mother, Sarah Updike Goddard, moved to Providence, Rhode Island, where her elder brother William had established a printing business with money from their father's estate. He was the first printer in Providence. The two women took over the business in 1765 after William Goddard moved to Philadelphia where, once again, he started a printing shop and newspaper. They began to publish and edit a weekly newspaper, the *Providence Gazette,* and also issued an almanac each year. Goddard sold the Providence printing shop in 1768, and she and her mother moved to Philadelphia in order to help William run his business there. Together they published the *Pennsylvania Chronicle.* They repeated this process a third time, when William moved to Baltimore and founded the *Maryland Journal* in 1773, then asked Mary to move there and run the business in 1774. She operated both the *Journal* and the *Baltimore Advertiser.* They tried to inform and entertain at the same time, in keeping with their motto, from the Latin writer Horace: "He carries every point who blends the useful with the agreeable, amusing the reader while he instructs them."

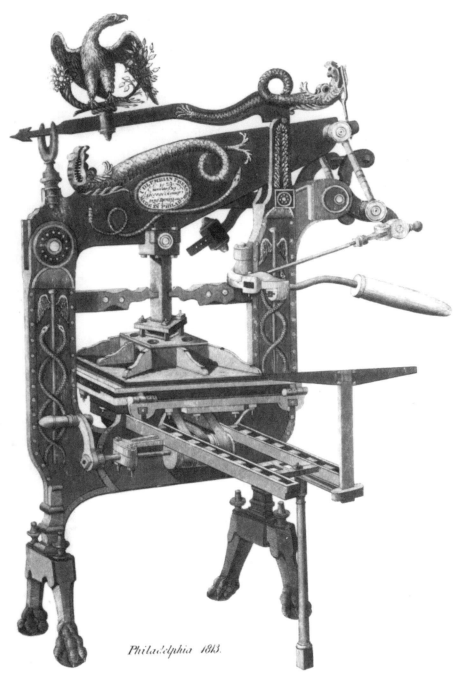

Philadelphia 1813.

This lithograph, made in 1813, shows a printing press similar to the one
Mary Katherine Goddard used in her Philadelphia shop.
(Photo courtesy of Library of Congress)

Mary Goddard's name appeared on the masthead of the *Journal* as editor and publisher beginning in May 1775. She not only managed the shop but was also an expert at typesetting and knew how to operate the presses.

In 1775, impressed by her speed and efficiency, Benjamin Franklin appointed Goddard the postmaster of Baltimore, and she served in that position until 1789. Historians believe she is the first woman to have ever held a federal office.

She continued to publish her highly respected paper during the American Revolution and was among the first to publish an account of the Battle of Bunker Hill, printing a three-column description of the event that marked the onset of the Revolutionary War less than a month after the battle took place. Despite the challenges posed by the war, she managed to keep publishing the paper and it was said that the *Journal* was "a journal second to none in the colonies in interest." Her paper contained numerous patriotic articles, and when pro-British readers objected, Goddard, who supported freedom of speech and the press, complained to the Baltimore Committee of Safety that some of these readers had threatened her. The committee supported her.

In December 1776, the Continental Congress came to Baltimore, where Goddard ran the only print shop. A month later, the Congress hired her to print the first official version of the Declaration of Independence, which they had written and approved the previous July. The version that appeared in Goddard's paper was the first to list the names of all the signers. On January 18, 1777, the Congress, which was then sitting in Baltimore, Maryland, ordered signed copies of the Declaration of Independence to be printed by Goddard's company and distributed. After printing the Declaration, Goddard hired post riders to deliver it to the various colonies.

In 1784, Goddard had a dispute with her brother after William insisted that she sell her shares of the *Maryland Journal* back to him. Mary Goddard retired from the printing business that year. In 1789, President George Washington replaced her as postmaster with a male political appointee, and the citizens of Baltimore protested. More than 200 people signed a petition on her behalf. The reason given for replacing Goddard was that the duties might entail travel and other activities more difficult "than a woman could undertake." Goddard ran her own bookstore until 1809 or 1810. When she died in 1816 or 1814 at approximately age 78, she willed her small estate to the African-American woman who had been her servant.

Further Reading

Read, Phyllis J., and Bernard L. Witlieb. *The Book of Women's Firsts.* New York: Random House, 1992.

Sherr, Lynn, and Jurate Kazickas, *Susan B. Anthony Slept Here: A Guide to American Women's Landmarks.* New York: Random House, 1994.

Thomas, Isaiah. *The History of Printing in America.* New York: Crown, 1970.

GORDON, ELLEN RUBIN
(1931–) *Executive*

Ellen Rubin Gordon is president of Tootsie Roll Industries, a company that produces 50 million lollipops, 15 million Junior Mints, and 14 million Dots every day. Describing her management style, Gordon has said, "One of the things about managing is that you really don't know all the answers. . . . I prefer that there be leadership and some consensus, rather than just dictating from above."

Ellen Rubin was born in New York City on May 29, 1931. Her grandfather had supplied paper to the Sweets Company of America, a small candy company that began making a chewy chocolate confection called Tootsie Rolls in 1896. Around the time Ellen was born, her parents began buying stock in the company, which was first listed on the New York Stock Exchange in 1922, and other family members followed suit. During the 1930s, the Rubins acquired a major share of the company. Ellen's father, William B. Rubin, became a board member in 1948; in 1949, he was named president. During the postwar

As president and chief operating officer of Tootsie Roll Industries, Ellen Gordon leads one of the world's most famous and profitable candy companies.
(Photo courtesy of Ellen Gordon and Tootsie Roll Industries)

years, sales of both Tootsie Rolls and Tootsie Roll Pops were strong. Ellen, who was then a teenager, sometimes went to the Sweets Company office with her father.

At age 18, she married Melvin J. Gordon, a textile company executive from Boston. In 1950, Ellen Rubin was majoring in mathematics at Vassar College. That summer, she returned home to work in the advertising department at the candy company, and she modeled in Tootsie Roll ads that appeared in *Life* magazine. Ellen Gordon continued her education and received her bachelor of arts (B.A.) degree from Brandeis University in 1965, then went on to major in Indo-European linguistics at the Graduate School of Arts and Sciences at Harvard University. Between 1951 and 1969, she and Melvin Gordon had four daughters: Virginia, Karen, Wendy, and Lisa.

In 1968, Ellen Gordon formally joined the company where her father had worked, which had changed its name to Tootsie Roll Industries, and became a director overseeing its pension plan and certain investments. Her husband had become chief executive officer (CEO) of the company in 1962 after William Rubin's death. There were not many women executives at that time, and Ellen Gordon later recalled, "I can remember the days when I had to go in a back door to chair the board of directors' meeting because they weren't allowing women in the front door."

In her role as the financial and investment expert in the company, Gordon believed the family should buy a larger percentage of the stock to prevent others from taking control of the company. She also played a key role in helping the company make profitable acquisitions. In 1972, the company bought Mason Company, manufacturers of Dots and Crows candies, and Bonomo, which made Turkish Taffy. Between 1969 and 1971, the company also expanded its operations into the Philippines, Canada, and Mexico.

Gordon advanced to new positions at Tootsie Roll Industries, becoming vice president of product development and quality assurance in 1974, then senior vice president and director of HDI Investment Corporation in 1977. The next year, Gordon became president and chief operating officer of Tootsie Roll, making her the second woman elected president of a company listed on the New York Stock Exchange. While running the company, Gordon also worked to improve business opportunities for other women. In 1982, she helped to found the Committee of 200, a group of top women executives and entrepreneurs. She would later serve as president of that organization in 1987.

One of Gordon's main goals was to find ways to modernize the plants and use technology to improve production. She has said, "Our manufacturing facilities are beyond state-of-the-art. We feel it is very important to reinvest in our company." Describing her vision, Gordon says, "Our mission is to make a very fine product, high quality at a good price value, and to increase our business over the years." The company remained quite profitable throughout the second half of the 20th century.

Ellen and Melvin Gordon, who serves as CEO and chairman of the company, continued to seek acquisition opportunities. In 1985, they bought Cella's Confections, a chocolate-covered-cherry maker. That same year, Gordon became the first woman and the 40th person to win the confectionery industry's top award, the Kettle Award. In 1993, the company acquired the caramel and chocolate brands of Warner-Lambert Company, including Junior Mints (which debuted in 1949), Sugar Daddy, Sugar Babies, and Charleston Chew. New acquisitions in 2000 included O'TEC Industries, (maker of Fluffy Stuff Cotton Candy), and Andes Candies, maker of Andes Créme de Menthe Thins, Cherry Jubilee Thins, Toffee Crunch Thins, and a brand of mint patties.

By 1998, sales had reached a record $388 million. The company surpassed this figure the very next year, when sales hit $396.7 million. The company's two divisions were Charms and Tootsie Roll, which were manufactured at the Chicago plant, and their products were sold in North and South America, the Far East, the Middle East, and eastern Europe. As of 2000, the company was the world's largest lollipop manufacturer.

Tootsie Roll Industries has introduced new products about twice a year and tries to ensure that acquisitions fit with the company's image of selling distinctive candies. Along with new products, the company strengthens its core brand candies and continues to sell Tootsie Rolls in the original red, white, and brown packaging that most customers remember from their childhood.

Ellen Gordon has been involved in numerous professional and civic associations. She has served as a member of the Board of Fellows of the Faculty of Medicine of the Harvard Medical School; the Harvard College Overseers Committee on University Resources; the Kellogg Graduate School of Management of Northwestern University; and the Board of Advisors of WomenIncorporated. She is also a director of the National Confectioners Association and has been director of the Bestfoods cor-

poration, a trustee of the Committee for Economic Development, and a member of the President's Export Council. The Gordons have homes in Chicago and in New England.

Further Reading

Eig, Jonathan. "Ellen Gordon: Success Is So Sweet," *Priorities, the Journal of Professional and Personal Success,* Vol. 1, Issue 3. Reprint from Tootsie Roll Industries.

Kelly, Katy. "Tootsies—Still on a Roll," *USA Today,* March 28, 1996, p. 1-D.

"Roll Model," *Forbes,* January 12, 1998, p. 168.

"Tootsie Roll: Company History 1896–2000." Available online. URL: http://www.tootsie-roll.com/history.html. Downloaded on June 20, 2001.

Wilkinson, Stephan. "The Practical Genius of Penny Candy," *Working Woman,* April 1989, p. 98.

GRAHAM, BETTE MCMURRY NESMITH
(1924–1980)   *Inventor, Entrepreneur, Executive*

Creative problem-solving led Bette McMurry Nesmith Graham to develop the popular product that became known as Liquid Paper, which is used to conceal typing mistakes.

Bette McMurry was born in Dallas, Texas, on March 23, 1924. Growing up, she did not care much for school and planned to become an artist. She left high school at age 17 to work in an office, but she could not type, so the company sent her to secretarial school to study typing and shorthand. McMurry completed her high school degree in night school.

At age 19, she married Warren Nesmith. Shortly after her husband left for military duty in World War II, she gave birth to their son, Michael. When Warren Nesmith returned a year later, the couple was divorced. With a young son to support, Bette Nesmith remained in the secretarial field. By 1951, she had worked her way up to the position of executive secretary to W. W. Overton, the chairman of the board of the Texas Bank & Trust.

During the 1950s, companies began using electric typewriters with new carbon-film ribbons that made it more difficult to erase typing mistakes. Since she was not a great typist, Nesmith tried to figure out a solution. Knowing that artists can paint over their mistakes, she came up with the idea of using a watercolor paintbrush dipped in white paint to cover typing mistakes. She came up with a mixture made from a base of white tempera paint. At work, she began using it secretly, but when other secretaries saw it, they wanted some too. She distributed samples in bottles labeled Mistake Out.

Nesmith decided to sell her product and began making batches of a new and improved form of Mistake Out in her kitchen. Her son, Michael, and his friends bottled the product in the garage. In 1956, she changed the name of her product to Liquid Paper and applied for a trademark, then studied business methods to learn how to market and promote her product. By the end of 1957, sales averaged 100 bottles a month. In October of 1958, a well-known business magazine, *The Office*, mentioned Liquid Paper, and hundreds of additional orders were received.

As sales increased, Nesmith spent evenings and weekends working on her business, but she did not have enough time to really promote her product until she was fired from her bank job for typing the wrong address on a business letter. After she began working on Liquid Paper full time, the business grew more rapidly. She was able to hire a chemist to help her develop a formula that dried faster. By 1962, she had hired two employees. That year, she also married Bob Graham, a man who shared her interest in the company and helped her to promote her product.

During the 1960s, Liquid Paper became popular with secretaries and office workers around the world. These were also exciting days for Graham's son, Michael Nesmith, who became a rock musician in 1966 and gained fame as a member of the Monkees, a band created for its own television series that also played concerts.

Bette Graham's business kept expanding and, in 1968, she moved the business into a large building where machines made 60 bottles of Liquid Paper a minute. She sold 1 million bottles that year, and

three years later reached 5 million. In 1975, the company moved into its remodeled 35,000-square-foot international headquarters in Dallas that Graham helped to design and had a total of 200 employees. In this plant, with machines that could turn out 500 bottles per minute, they produced 25 million bottles in 1975. Increased production enabled the Liquid Paper Corporation to achieve net earnings of $1.5 million in 1976. That year, Graham resigned as chairman of the board of the Liquid Paper Corporation to spend more time on her religious and charitable activities.

In 1979, Graham sold her company to Gillette Corporation for $47.5 million. Gillette also agreed to pay Graham royalties on every bottle sold until the year 2000. Graham died in May 1980. In her will, she left half of her multimillion-dollar estate to her son, Michael, and the other half to charitable foundations. She particularly supported organizations designed to help women gain employment skills that would enable them to support themselves.

Further Reading

Massachusetts Institute of Technology (MIT). Lemelson-MIT Prize Program: "Bette Nesmith Graham (1924–1980)." Available online. URL: http://web.mit.edu/invent/www/inventorsA-H/nesmith.html. Downloaded on February 2, 2001.

Stuber, Irene. "'Liquid Paper' and Other Female Cover-Ups," TSBJ.com, The Small Business Journal. Available online.URL: http://www.tsbj.com/editorial/0207113htm. Downloaded on January 24, 2001.

Vare, Ethlie Ann, and Greg Ptacek. *Mothers of Invention: From the Bra to the Bomb: Forgotten Women & Their Unforgettable Ideas.* New York: William Morrow and Company, 1988.

GRAHAM, KATHARINE MEYER
(1917–2001)   *Executive, Publisher*

As president and publisher of the Washington Post Company, a business empire that includes *Newsweek* and cable TV stations around the United States, Katharine Meyer Graham became one of the world's most influential women.

Katharine Meyer was born June 16, 1917, in New York City. Her father, Eugene Meyer, was a successful businessman who owned an investment firm; her mother, Agnes Ernst Meyer, was an intellectual and an art collector. Katharine was the fourth of their five children.

In 1933, Eugene Meyer bought the *Washington Post,* which had gone bankrupt during the Great Depression, for $825,000. Meyer was a Republican at that time but said he wanted the paper to be nonpartisan, and its masthead read, An Independent Newspaper. In addition to running the newspaper, Eugene Meyer served in various government posts, including governor of the Federal Reserve Bank.

During high school, Katharine began working at the paper as a copy girl. She attended Vassar College for two years, then finished her education at the University of Chicago, where she received her bachelor of arts degree in 1938. After graduation, she spent a year at the *San Francisco News* working as a reporter, then rejoined the *Washington Post* in the editorial department.

After she married Philip L. Graham, an attorney and Supreme Court law clerk, in June 1940, he went to work at the *Post.* When Eugene Meyer retired in 1945, he gave Phil Graham the job of publisher, and in 1948, the Grahams bought the *Post* from Meyer. For 17 years, Katharine Graham did not work as a journalist but spent her time managing their home, raising four children, and handling numerous social obligations that came with her husband's job in the nation's capital. She later wrote that she regarded herself as something of a "doormat" during these years and did not have much self-confidence.

In 1963, Phil Graham, who had been suffering from clinical depression and mood swings, committed suicide. By that time, the Washington Post Company included *Newsweek* magazine and some radio and television stations, but the newspaper was not particularly distinguished and had only a modest circulation.

Despite her lack of experience and uncertainty about her abilities, Graham surprised many people by announcing that she would take over the paper's presidency herself. Although some board members expressed skepticism, she resolved to learn what she needed to know in order to perform the job and keep the business in the family. In her 1997 autobiography, Graham said, "What I essentially did was to put one foot in front of the other, shut my eyes, and step off the ledge. The surprise was that I landed on my feet."

Graham proceeded to serve as president for nearly 30 years while also serving as publisher from 1969 to 1979. During these years, the *Post* was at the center of dramatic political events. In 1971, Graham made the courageous decision to have the *Post* publish the Pentagon Papers, top secret documents that detailed the role of the United States during the Vietnam War. The government had filed a lawsuit against the *New York Times* when it published parts of the Pentagon Papers in June of that year, and the *Post* risked similar problems. Graham knew her decision would also threaten her relationships with the White House and certain government officials, as well as exposing the company to possible costly lawsuits.

President Nixon and his staff sharply criticized the *Post* in 1972 when it began publishing a series of articles by reporters Carl Bernstein and Bob Woodward, investigating the Watergate coverup. Graham supported her editor-in-chief, Ben Bradlee, whom she had hired herself, and the *Post*'s journalists during that time, not censoring their articles but directing them to be accurate and fair. The paper suffered economic consequences, and its stock fell when the Nixon administration refused to renew some of the company's television licenses. Graham received anonymous death threats and stood up to courts that threatened to put her in jail if she did not hand over notes made by *Post* reporters. Eventually, the Watergate investigation showed that top White House officials had been involved in a cover-up, which led to Nixon's resignation in 1974 and to the criminal prosecutions of numerous staff members. Graham later said, "I have been credited with courage [during] Watergate. I never felt there was much choice."

In 1991, Graham retired but remained chairman of the executive committee of the Washington Post Company. Her son Donald E. Graham, publisher of the *Post,* was expected to control the company in the future. Her daughter, Lally Weymouth, writes for the *Post.*

Graham wrote her autobiography, *Personal History,* which was published in 1997 and became a best-seller. The book won the 1998 Pulitzer Prize for biography. The *Post* had earned 17 Pulitzers for various stories during Graham's first 28 years as head of the company.

During a 1998 interview with Bob Levey, Graham was asked how she felt about being called "the most powerful woman in the world." She replied, "I don't think what I have is power. I have responsibility for seeing to it that the company is run well."

Graham died at age 84 on July 17, 2001, after sustaining head injuries during a fall.

Further Reading

Berger, Marilyn. "Katharine Graham of *Washington Post* Dies at 84," *The New York Times,* July 18, 2001, pp. A-1, C-20.

Graham, Katharine. *Personal History.* New York: Knopf, 1997.

Levey, Bob. "Levey Live: Q & A With Katharine Graham." Washington Post.com Available online. URL: http://discuss.washingtonpost.com/wp-srv/zforum/98/bob0721.htm. Downloaded on April 11, 2001.

✳ GRAY, MARIE HERMANN (Marie St. John)
(ca. 1936–) *Entrepreneur, Executive*

Marie Gray helped to found St. John Knits, an upscale fashion design business. Marie Hermann was born in Yugoslavia in about 1936. Her family immigrated to the United States after World War II, and Marie worked as a model and television performer under the professional name Marie St. John. As a model in Los Angeles, she decided to knit herself an attractive dress like one she had worn on a runway but could not afford to buy.

One day, while working as a hostess on the television show *Queen for a Day,* Gray wheeled a knitting machine onto the set and realized that this device would enable her to make knit dresses more quickly and easily. She later said "I didn't really set out to knit. . . . the best I can tell you is that I saw something that I wanted and, trying to economize, I tried to make it."

Her fiancé, an air force veteran and clothing salesman named Robert Gray, showed the dresses she had made to some buyers in Los Angeles department stores and boutiques. They ordered several dozen, and the couple was in business. They founded St. John Knits in 1962. For several years, they used large amounts of their earnings and took out loans to expand the company. The Grays lived in Irvine, California, where they were active in the social scene and enjoyed boating in their free time. In 1966, their daughter, Kelly, was born, and Marie designed special knitted baby clothes for her.

Marie Gray focused on the design end of the business and created conservative, durable knit suits in classic styles similar to those made by the famous French designer Coco Chanel and the Italian designer Adolfo. In marketing the garments, Gray emphasized that the knits pack well and do not wrinkle. St. John clothing became renowned for its top-quality fabrics and its guarantee to repair any defects, free of charge, during the life of the garment.

St. John garments are relatively expensive, but company ads praise them as investments because the styles are classic and garments are designed to last. During the 1990s, prices for suits and dresses began at about $800 and evening gowns cost up to $8,200. Wool for St. John garments comes from seven farms in Australia where sheep are raised to produce the finest wool. A St. John signature is gold-plated buttons hand-decorated in enamel.

In the decades after founding the company, Marie Gray added perfume and accessories, such as shoes and handbags, to her product line. In 1989, the first St. John Knits boutique opened, in Palm Desert, California.

That same year, the Grays sold 80 percent of their company to Escada, a German clothing firm, and they expected this move would help them expand into European markets. Four years later, Escada took the company public, and shares of its stock were traded on the New York Stock Exchange. As of 1996, *Forbes* magazine had listed St. John Knits among its 200 Best Small Companies three times. During those years, the company introduced a shoe division and a sportswear division, St. John Sport, as well as a line of faux-fur coats. By 1999, there were 17 boutiques around the United States.

Robert Gray's son, Michael, worked for the company for 25 years and served as president for five years, starting in 1986. In 1991, he left to open a food products business. In 1996, the Grays' daughter, Kelly, was named president and creative director of the company. Kelly had begun working at the company, answering phones and wrapping boxes, when she was 12 years old, and she began modeling for St. John Knits at age 15. She became the company's signature model for print ad campaigns when she was 18.

St. John Knits have been among the best-selling high-end clothing lines at Saks Fifth Avenue and other upscale stores since the 1960s. Prominent and affluent customers have worn the designs. Gray designed suits that First Lady Hillary Clinton wore to the 1996 Democratic National Convention. Catherine Kangas, a host on the Home Shopping Network, claims to own more than 250 St. John items, including dresses, jackets, skirts, pants, faux-fur coats, and accessories. Kangas says, "You can mix and match styles, and you always look well-coordinated."

After Kelly Gray became president, Marie Gray remained St. John's vice chairman and chief designer. During the 1990s, Kelly Gray oversaw product development, promotions, advertising, and retail. Robert Gray served as chairman and chief executive officer (CEO). The year 2000 brought a new high in the company's sales. In January 2001, H. W. Mullins succeeded Gray as CEO; Marie Gray continued to serve as the chief designer, while Kelly Gray remained president and creative director.

Further Reading

Baron, Kelly. "One Size Too Big?" *Forbes,* June 14, 1999, pp. 160ff.

Earnest, Leslie. "Ex-Neiman Marcus Exec Is Tapped to Head St. John Knits," *Los Angeles Times,* January 5, 2001, Business Section, p. 1.

Fryer, Bronwyn. "Too Closely Knit?" *Equity,* September 1999.

Servin, James. "Gray Dynasty," *Harper's Bazaar,* July 1997, pp. 122ff.

Townsel, Lisa Jones. "St. John Knits Founder Here," *St. Louis Post-Dispatch,* May 3, 2001, p. 6.

GRISWOLD, DENNY (Denny Griswold Sullivan, Denora Prager)
(1908–2001)   *Executive, Entrepreneur, Publisher*

Called the First Lady of public relations (PR) and the Grande Dame of PR, Denny Griswold founded and published the world's first public relations weekly, *Public Relations News,* and served as its editor for nearly 40 years.

Denora Prager was born on March 23, 1908, and raised in New York City, where she earned her bachelor of arts (B.A.) degree at Hunter College. At Radcliffe College in Massachusetts, she earned her M.A. degree. Later, she took postgraduate courses in music at Columbia University, in New York. After college, she worked in various jobs in advertising and public relations, including positions at Condé Nast Publishing, National and Mutual Broadcasting, the J. Walter Thompson ad agency, the Edward L. Bernays ad agency, and *Forbes* and *Business Week* magazines. She married Glenn Griswold, the editor and publisher of *Business Week* magazine, in 1930.

Eager to improve opportunities for women in her field, in 1946 Denny Griswold helped to found the organization Women Executives in Public Relations, now called Foundation of Women Executives in Public Relations (WEPR). The organization brought together women in the public relations field for the first time, and they gained more recognition for their achievements.

Griswold had long dreamed of starting a weekly newsletter about her profession, and she achieved that goal in 1944 when she cofounded *Public Relations News,* the first public relations weekly in the world. The newsletter reported on key developments in the PR field and contained case histories that showed how to handle various public relations situations. As the owner of the publication, Griswold also sponsored annual awards for people who made major contributions to the profession and hosted an annual banquet to recognize people who had been promoted to major PR positions. She defined PR as "the management function which evaluates public attitudes, identifies policies and procedures of an organization with the public interest, and plans and executes a program of action to earn public understanding and acceptance."

Her first husband died in 1950, and the next year Griswold married J. Langdon Sullivan, head of an investment management firm. She served on the boards of the USO, New York World's Fair, Public Relations Society of America, and Newsletter Association. In addition, she belonged to the advisory committees of the U.S. Chamber of Commerce, the Camp Fire Girls of America, the International Public Relations Association, the Joint Council on Economic Education, and Pace College. In 1986, Griswold was the lecturer at Ball State University in Muncie, Indiana, for its Vernon C. Schranz Distinguished Lectureship in Public Relations. During her career, she accumulated more than 130 awards for her achievements.

Griswold died on February 8, 2001, at a nursing home in Connecticut. In her honor, the WEPR has established a fund to assist college students seeking careers in public relations.

Further Reading

Business Wire. "Women Executives in Public Relations," Business Wire online. Available online. URL: http://biz.yahoo.com/bw/010502/2195.html. Posted on May 2, 2001.

"Denny Griswold Is Dead At 92," *O'Dwyer's PR Daily.* March 6, 2001. Available online. URL: http://www.odwyerpr.com/archived_stories_2001/march/0306grisdied.htm. Downloaded on November 11, 2001.

Griswold, Glenn, and Denny Griswold. *Your Public Relations.* New York: Funk & Wagnalls, 1948.

Hu, Winnie. "A Private End for a Public Relations Star," *The New York Times,* May 3, 2001.

Northwood University Distinguished Women. "Denny Griswold." Available online. URL: http://www.northwood.edu/dw/1987/griswold.html. Downloaded on May 31, 2001.

Pederson, Wes. "Denny Griswold Dies at the Age of 92," The Matrix (Association of Women in Communications) on the Web. Available online. URL: http://www.womcom.org.SpringMatrix2001/griswold.html. Downloaded on June 4, 2001.

PR Canada. "Memorial Service for Denny Griswold." PR Canada on the Web. Available online. URL: http://www.fastmpr.com/GRIST.HTM. Downloaded on June 3, 2001.

GROSSINGER, JENNIE
(1892–1972)   *Executive, Author, Philanthropist*

Jennie Grossinger spearheaded the growth of a small family farm into one of the most successful resorts in the world.

Grossinger was born on June 16, 1892, in a small village in Austria, into an Orthodox Jewish household. Her mother, Malka, was the daughter of an innkeeper; her father, Asher, worked as an overseer on an estate. The Grossingers saved their money so they could move to the United States, and in 1910 they settled in New York City's Lower East Side. They operated a small kosher restaurant. (A kosher restaurant observes Jewish dietary laws.)

As a child, Jennie had attended school for several years, and in New York she worked in a garment factory making buttonholes. She earned about two dollars a week, working about 11 hours a day. In 1912, she married a cousin, Harry Grossinger, and the couple lived next door to her father's restaurant, where Jennie Grossinger worked as a waitress. Two years later, in order to improve Asher's weakening health, the family moved to the country. They chose a farm in Ferndale, New York, which had a strong Orthodox Jewish community.

The land on their small farm had poor soil, but it was located in a scenic area of the Catskill Mountains, so the family decided to earn extra money by taking in boarders during the summers. Nine guests joined them during the first year. They enjoyed the traditional kosher foods Malka Grossinger cooked, as well as the peaceful surroundings. While Jennie Grossinger worked as the hostess, chambermaid, and bookkeeper, her father and husband did maintenance work on the buildings and grounds.

The next year, more guests asked to stay at the farm, but the Grossingers did not have enough room to accommodate them all. They moved to a larger piece of land in Liberty, New York. Known as Nicolas Farm, the property included a hotel and a barn for cows, which the family kept for fresh milk. Jennie Grossinger became increasingly busy running the hotel and raising her two children: Paul, born in 1915, and Elaine, born in 1927.

To attract more guests, the Grossingers added other buildings and high-quality recreational facilities, including tennis courts, bridle paths, and a theater. They also operated a children's camp so parents would be free to enjoy activities on their own. A social director organized numerous activities, and a theater group presented plays and musical performances. The resort continued to grow and drew thousands of guests each year. Many celebrities began their careers at Grossinger's or returned to perform after they became famous. Well-known actors, athletes, politicians, and others stayed at the resort. Guests appreciated Jennie Grossinger's warm personality and her efforts to make them comfortable.

By the 1940s, Grossinger's was one of the most famous resort hotels in the world. Besides running the resort, Jennie Grossinger worked for various civic and patriotic causes. During World War II, she raised millions of dollars in war bonds by selling them to people at the hotel. In honor of her efforts, the U.S. Army Air Force named one of its combat planes Grossinger's. She contributed to numerous other causes and helped to fund a health clinic and convalescent home in Israel after the war. Grossinger's continued to expand; it grew so large that it became a town in itself, with its own airport and post office address. In response to many requests, Grossinger wrote a popular cookbook called *The Art of Jewish Cooking* in 1956.

Jennie Grossinger retired from the business in 1964. At that time, the resort she had worked so hard to expand and promote consisted of 35 buildings on 1,200 acres. About 150,000 guests patronized Grossinger's each year, and famous entertainers appeared regularly. In 1972, Jennie Grossinger died of a stroke at a cottage where she lived on the grounds of the resort. Her descendants continued to operate Grossinger's. Business declined during the 1970s and 1980s, because fewer people vacationed in the Catskills. Grossinger's eventually closed its resort in the late 1980s, but the golf course remained open. The property was sold during the 1990s.

Further Reading

Brody, Seymour. *Jewish Heroes & Heroines of America*. Hollywood, Fla.: Lifetime Books, 1996.

Catskills Institute Hotel News. "Jennie Grossinger Day June 16, 2000." Available online. URL: http://brown.edu/Research/Catskills_Institute/hotelnews/grossinger4.html. Downloaded on October 25, 2001.

CatskillOnline.Com—History—Town of Liberty/Village of Liberty. "Grossinger's Hotel." Available online. URL: http://www.catskillonline.com/history/liberty/. Downloaded on January 5, 2001.

Grossinger, Jennie. *The Art of Jewish Cooking*. New York: Random House, 1971.

H

HANDLER, RUTH MOSKO
(1916–) *Entrepreneur, Executive*

Ruth Handler and her husband, Elliot, cofounded the business that became Mattel Toys, the world's largest toy company, and she introduced the Barbie doll, which became the best-selling doll of all time, bringing the company billions of dollars annually. Elliot, an artist and designer, focused on the creative end of their company, while Ruth thrived on the business and marketing aspects.

Ruth Mosko was born in Denver, Colorado, on November 4, 1916, the youngest of 10 children born to Polish immigrants. Her father, Jacob, was a blacksmith and her mother, Ida, was a homemaker. When Ruth was just a baby, her mother became ill and never totally regained her health, so Ruth was sent to live with her 20-year-old sister Sarah and her husband, Louis, who owned a drugstore. Starting at age 10, Ruth began helping out in the store after school and during vacations. Her brother Joe became a lawyer, and Ruth also worked as a secretary in his office.

At age 16, Ruth met Elliot Handler, an aspiring artist who was also 16, and they began dating.

When Ruth graduated from high school, she enrolled at the University of Denver as a prelaw major, while Elliot went to an art school in the same city. Two years later, while visiting Los Angeles, California, she decided to leave school and move there, so she got a job working as a secretary at the Paramount movie studios. Elliot also moved to Los Angeles, where he found work designing lighting fixtures and enrolled in a local art school.

The couple married in June 1938 in Denver, then returned to Los Angeles where Ruth resumed her job. Elliot Handler continued to design lighting fixtures and went to art school studying industrial design. He designed giftware from Lucite and Plexiglas, a new kind of plastic material, in those days. Ruth thought his lamps, tables, trays, bookends, and other items would sell, and this sparked their first business venture together. Ruth carried samples of his work to merchants and worked to gain orders. As the business grew, they hired four people to help make the items. They also sold the jewelry Elliott made from leftover plastic, as well as Plexiglas picture frames.

In 1941, Ruth left her job at Paramount when their daughter, Barbara, was born; a son, Ken,

Ruth Handler cofounded the Mattel Company and developed "Barbie," the best-selling doll of all time.
(Courtesy of Ruth Handler)

arrived in 1944. Elliott formed a company called Elzac with some other men and he ran that business while Ruth stayed home rearing their children. In 1944 Ruth and Elliott formed a company with their former foreman, Harold Matson, combining the names Matson and Elliot naming it Mattel. Ruth later enrolled in business classes at the University of California in Los Angeles. She was the only woman in the program.

In 1945, after the Handlers started making doll furniture in their garage, Ruth played the major role in selling it, as well as the toy ukeleles and toy pianos they made. By 1947, Mattel had grown from a small business to become a major toy manufacturer. Matson sold his share of the company to Ruth's sister and her husband, who joined the Handlers in the business. Elliot was president and Ruth was vice president. The rapidly expanding company moved to a larger plant and hired hundreds of new employees during the early 1950s, when it introduced a successful line of musical toys and books. Millions of Mattel music boxes were sold.

Ruth Handler saw the potential benefits of advertising on television, a medium that was becoming more popular in the early 1950s. In 1955, Mattel became the first toy maker to run TV ads, which boosted toy sales. It was also the first toy company to advertise year-round instead of focusing on the Christmas season. Their first giant venture in TV advertising was to sponsor Disney's *Mickey Mouse Club* show 52 weeks a year.

Another brainstorm came to Handler as she watched her daughter, Barbara, and her friends spend hours playing with paper dolls that were made to resemble teenagers and adults. Handler envisioned a three-dimensional plastic "young lady" doll they could dress in beautiful clothes and play with in different ways. During those years, most dolls were baby- or childlike. There were a few adult dolls in the marketplace, but they were not mature in their build and their clothes were made for childlike dolls. Handler also envisioned well-made clothing with lovely designs.

At first, executives at Mattel rejected her idea, claiming the dolls would cost too much to produce and might not sell well. While traveling in Europe, Handler saw a German doll named Lilli, and she brought some samples home to show to Mattel's production staff. The company purchased the legal rights to Lilli and altered her appearance to create a more American-looking doll.

In 1959, Mattel introduced Barbie, the Teen-Age Fashion Model, named after the Handlers' daughter. Ruth Handler said that Barbie was "created to project every little girl's dream of the future" and that girls could play with the doll in many ways, making her whatever they wanted her to be. Barbie's shapely figure and worldly appearance, complete with made-up eyes and lips, were controversial. Sears Roebuck & Company said the $11^1/_2$-inch doll was "too sexy" and did not buy the first Barbies. Many other stores also showed little interest in the doll, but whenever stores did stock the dolls, they sold quickly.

Sales increased dramatically after Barbie was advertised on *The Mickey Mouse Club,* a popular weekday children's television show. Children loved Barbie and her wardrobe, inspired by high-fashion designs, complete with jewelry, high-heeled shoes, hats, and other accessories. That first year, Barbie set new records when 351,000 dolls were sold. Within a few years, millions of children throughout the world owned and played with one or more Barbie dolls. As new versions of the doll were created each year, collectors bought the dolls.

Barbie's facial features, hairdos, fashions, and accessories have changed through the years, reflecting changing fashions and women's changing roles in American society. The 1960 version had rounder, blue eyes, smoother brows, and darker, more natural-looking skin. The 1961 Barbie came with either a ponytail or "bubble cut" resembling the popular bouffant hairstyle. A new red-haired Barbie was called Titian.

More than 6 million Barbie dolls were produced each year during the early sixties. Mattel added Ken, a boyfriend for Barbie, in 1961. His molded hair was originally styled in a crewcut, but Ken's looks also changed through the years. In 1962 he had a short, tough-looking hairstyle, and was sold with a stick of wax for grooming. During the 1970s, Now Look Ken dolls had stylishly long hair.

Barbie's activities and professions changed greatly over the years. In the mid-sixties, Fashion Queen Barbie was sold with three wigs: a redheaded flip, platinum bubble cut, and brunette pageboy. Midge and Francie dolls were created as friends for Barbie. In 1967, Mattel added the slimmer-figured Francie doll. The next year, Christie, a new black doll with a distinctive personality, was introduced. Curtis was Christie's boyfriend, and black Ken dolls were also available. Japanese Barbie and Ken dolls also came out during the 1960s, with more youthful faces than those sold in America.

While Elliot Handler, chairman of the board and chief executive officer (CEO), focused on product design and development, Ruth Handler became president of Mattel and cochairman of the board of directors. The company produced many other successful products, including Hot Wheels cars, See 'N Say toys, and the Chatty Cathy doll, as well as new versions of Barbie and Barbie makeup, clothing, accessories, houses, cars, pools, boats, camping equipment, children's sleeping bags, and other related products.

In 1970, Ruth Handler underwent radical mastectomy surgery for breast cancer. During this difficult period, Mattel Toy Company was also experiencing financial and legal problems. The Handlers decided to retire from the company in 1975. Meanwhile, Ruth Handler launched another business called Nearly Me to produce more realistic breast prostheses for women who had undergone mastectomies. Beginning in 1976, the company produced lightweight and comfortable prostheses, the first that had ever been made, and also made the first left- and right-sided artificial breasts. Handler sold this company in 1991.

The Handlers were honored guests at the Toy Industry Hall of Fame inaugural ceremonies in 1984, and they were inducted into the hall in 1989. They also received the Lifetime Achievement Award from *Doll Reader* magazine in 1987.

Further Reading

BillyBoy. *Barbie: Her Life and Times.* New York: Crown, 1987.

Cavuto, Neil, and Karen Gibbs, "Mattel Cofounder—Interview," *The Cavuto Business Report,* Fox News Network transcript, March 9, 1999.

Handler, Ruth, with Jacqueline Shannon. *Dream Doll: The Ruth Handler Story.* Stamford, Conn.: Longmeadow Press, 1994.

Manos, Paris, and Susan Manos. *The World of Barbie Dolls.* Paducah, Ky.: Collector Books, 1983.

Stern, Sydney Ladensohn, and Ted Schoenhaus. *Toyland: The High-Stakes Game of the Toy Industry.* Chicago: Contemporary Books, 1990.

HARITON, LORRAINE

(1954–) *Executive*

Lorraine Hariton achieved a high position in technology as senior vice president of development and marketing for Network Computing Devices, Inc. a strategic partner of IBM, which provides computer network software and hardware to companies that include IBM, SunSoft, and Novell. More recently, Hariton became chief executive officer (CEO) of Beatnik, Inc., which makes software to play music online.

Hariton was born on November 7, 1954, in New York City and grew up in Syosset, New York. She has said that her mother was an important role model for her while she was growing up. When Hariton was 10 years old, her mother returned to college, earned her Ph.D. in psychology, and then set up a successful private practice. Said Hariton, "She combined her personal achievements with raising three capable children. Through her, I had a role model that told me I could achieve my career dreams as well as being able to successfully combine that career with marriage and raising my children." During her early school years, Hariton also faced the challenge of dyslexia, a learning disability, and became an excellent student.

Before embarking on her career in the high-tech industry, Hariton earned a bachelor of science (B.S.) degree in 1976 in mathematical sciences from Stanford University, having studied computer science, operations research, math, and statistics. She received her master's of business administration (M.B.A.) degree from Harvard Business School in 1982. After finishing college, she worked as a scientific programmer in the operations research department at American Airlines. During that time, she lived in an apartment in Manhattan and enjoyed the air travel benefits that came with her job. She later said, "I took advantage of the travel privileges and flew on standby for free. In the course of a year, I visited Europe (three times), Brazil, Mexico, Canada, Bermuda, and the Far East."

Hariton found that her analytical work did not allow her to spend as much time as she liked working with other people. She left American Airlines the next year to become a sales representative at IBM and embarked on a year-long training program at that company. For 15 years, Hariton worked in a number of sales and marketing positions at IBM. She had married Stephen Weyl in 1979 and their two children were born in 1985 and 1988. After leaving IBM, Hariton moved to Verifone Corporation, a top supplier of electronic payment systems, where she became director of marketing strategy and programs.

In 1993, Hariton joined Network Computing Devices, Inc. (NCD) as vice president of marketing. NCD promoted her to head of business

Lorraine Hariton became one of the top women in the network computer industry, which was once dominated by men.
(Photo courtesy of Lorraine Hariton and Beatnik.com)

development and engineering in 1997, and in 1998, she took over sales as well. In this position, she was in charge of marketing, sales, and product management. She negotiated sales agreements with clients such as Sun Microsystems, IBM, AT&T, and Novell. Hariton said that she enjoyed the diversity of her job and the challenge of constantly inventing and reinventing strategy.

In 1998, Hariton was elected to the Women in Technology International (WITI) Hall of Fame. During an interview, she said "My work is tremendously diverse and that is the essence of what keeps me interested. I do a lot of work with customers, partners, press and analysts. I love representing my company, NCD, to the world. I work with a strong group of people comprised of both my direct team and my peers. . . . Our industry is very

dynamic. There is a constant need to reinvent strategy and it is very exciting."

In mid-1999, Hariton left NCD for another challenging position, as president and CEO of Beatnik, Inc., a company in the business of interactive audio technologies and content for the World Wide Web and digital devices. With Mixman, it markets Mixman Software, a line of remixing and performance music software and consumer audio products.

Under Hariton, the Beatnik company has worked with Texas Instruments, Intel, and Nokia to develop new products. In 2000, the company's managers made a strategic decision to shift from marketing its software directly to consumers and licensing it to makers of Internet net devices and mobile phones.

Hariton, who has said that she strives for a balance between personal and professional life, enjoys distance running for physical fitness and recreation. In 2001, she trained for a triathlon.

Further Reading

"NCD Promotes Hariton," Daily Edition: The Business Journal. Available online. URL: http://www.bizjournals. com/sanjose/stories/1997/03/10/daily13.html. Downloaded on August 17, 2000.
WITI. "WITI Campus-Lorraine Hariton." Available online. URL: http://www.witi.com/center/witimuseum/ womeninsciencet/1998/061198.shtml. Downloaded on August 14, 2000.

✳ HARPER, MARTHA MATILDA
(1847–1950)   *Entrepreneur, Executive*

Called the Mother of Modern Franchising, Harper founded a chain of successful hairdressing salons during the late 1800s and enabled thousands of working women to become independent business owners. She popularized the idea that "health is beauty."

Born in Ontario, Canada, in 1847, she was bound as a servant at age seven. Her work was sold to a master for a certain number of years in return for a sum of money and room and board. She continued to work as a domestic for 25 years. During that time, she discovered ways to use herbs to beautify the hair and skin. In one household, she learned an effective formula for improving the health of the hair.

In 1882, Harper left Ontario for Rochester, New York, because that seemed to be a promising city in which she could launch a beauty salon business. In Rochester, she joined the Christian Science Church, which promoted equality of women and men, as well as the virtue of good health.

Six years later, Harper took her life savings of $360 and founded her first salon. A hair salon was an unusual concept in Victorian days because at the time hair care was a private matter attended to in the home. To draw customers, Harper decided to rent space in the city's most prestigious building, and she hired tutors to advance her own education and teach her to speak in a cultured way. Women who were visiting from other places were among her first customers. These affluent women urged her to build salons in their communities, and Harper agreed to do so—but only after they gave her a list of people who pledged to patronize the new salons.

Within three years, she had devised a way to develop a chain of Harper Hair Dressing Salons and beauty schools. At its peak in 1928, the chain boasted 500 units worldwide. Harper called them branches and she recruited working-class women, particularly former servants, to run the salons, which could be found in New York City, San Francisco, Detroit, Edinburgh, and Berlin, among other places. Harper knew that women who had been servants understood the importance of pleasing their customers, and she believed that they would also be loyal. Branch owners bought their supplies from Harper but kept their profits.

In addition to hiring capable employees, Harper set certain standards for the operation of all her salons. Employees, known as Harperites, attended her training schools, sold Harper products, and used the same tools and techniques (called the Harper Method) from one salon to another. This meant that customers could depend on consistent service in any Harper salon, as well as immaculate surroundings. Advertising was also

uniform, and Harper's logo featured a horn of plenty, which symbolized the idea that a poor woman could aspire to become a successful business owner. The petite (under five feet tall) Harper had striking, floor-length chestnut hair. Photos of her appeared in ads to promote the salons and the products she developed.

Harper promoted the use of safe treatments using simple ingredients. She said women were naturally beautiful and did not need elaborate treatments or complicated products, so her skin and scalp treatments were designed to improve the health of the hair and skin and bring out their natural beauty. Harper criticized potentially dangerous beauty products and processes and insisted on organic ingredients for her line. Harper said, "When a [person] is healthy, [she] is beautiful."

Customers, who included both women and men, were encouraged to relax during their visits, and head, neck, and shoulder massages were among the treatments. Patrons enjoyed using the reclining shampoo chair that Harper developed, but neglected to patent, and sinks with a cutout neck rest. In 1919, while in Paris negotiating the postwar Treaty of Versailles, President Woodrow Wilson went to a Harper salon for scalp massages. Other well-known customers included suffragist leader Susan B. Anthony, first ladies Grace Coolidge and Eleanor Roosevelt, playwright George Bernard Shaw, actress Helen Hayes, and members of the wealthy Hearst and DuPont families.

As a business owner, Harper encouraged franchise managers to accommodate both employees and customers and to take an active role in community service. She urged them to set up child care centers and to hold regular meetings with staff where they would be able to discuss their needs. She often said that one of her greatest achievements was helping thousands of women to become self-sufficient and productive.

At age 63, Harper married Captain Robert McBrain, a native of Iowa, who was 39. In her seventies, Harper retired from actively running her business and gave that responsibility to McBain. Martha Matilda Harper died in 1950 when she was nearly 93; her husband died in 1965. The Harper Method chain operated until 1972, when a competitor bought out the business, but two Harper salons still remained open as of 2000, including the Harper Method Founder's Shop, in Rochester, New York.

Further Reading

Lopez, Kathryn Jean. "Equality in the Mailbox," *National Review.* Available online. URL: http://www.nationalreview.com/nrcomment/nrcomment082100b.shtml. Posted on August 21, 2000. Downloaded on October 20, 2000.

Parker, Sally. "Martha Matilda Harper and the American Dream," *Rochester Review,* fall 2000. Available online. URL: http://www.rochester.edu/pr/Review/V63N1/feature2.html. Downloaded on October 22, 2000.

Plitt, Jane R. *Martha Matilda Harper and the American Dream: How One Woman Changed the Face of Modern Business.* Syracuse, N.Y.: Syracuse University Press, 2000.

✳ HAUGHERY, MARGARET O'ROURKE GAFFNEY

(ca. 1813–1882) *Entrepreneur, Business Owner, Philanthropist*

Called the Mother of the Orphans, Haughery overcame poverty and personal tragedy to become an entrepreneur who founded businesses in order to support her orphanages and other charities.

Margaret O'Rourke Gaffney was born in about 1813 in County Cavan, Ireland. The family left for the United States when Margaret was five and moved to Baltimore, Maryland, where her parents both died during an epidemic in 1822. A kind Welsh-American neighbor invited nine-year-old Margaret to live with her.

After her marriage in 1835, she became Margaret Gaffney Haughery, and she and her husband moved to New Orleans, Louisiana, with their baby daughter. In less than a year, epidemics of cholera and yellow fever swept through the city, and her husband and daughter both died, along with 10,000 other victims. Thousands of children and widows were left homeless.

Haughery resolved to find useful work serving others, and she took a job at a local orphanage that was struggling to make ends meet during the crisis. She began buying milk for the children with her own limited funds but realized that much more needed to be done. Working as a laundress at the St. Charles Hotel and as a milk deliverer, she saved as much money as possible, planning to start her own orphanage with the help of the nuns in the local Sisters of Charity.

Although she was uneducated and had no business experience, Haughery managed to establish the Female Orphan Asylum, locating it in a house that was unoccupied because people thought it was haunted. She worked with Sister Francis Regis Barret, a nun in the order of the a Sisters of Charity, and other concerned people to make the house livable. When the owner threatened to evict them from the improved residence, Haughery appealed to his sense of philanthropy and he agreed they could stay in the house rent-free.

The need for orphanages increased as more epidemics swept through the region during the 1850s. The 1853 yellow fever epidemic took another 11,000 lives. Haughery nursed the sick, sometimes going door to door, and helped anyone in need, regardless of race or religion. To shelter the large number of infants who needed homes, Haughery and Sister Francis Regis Barret founded the St. Vincent de Paul Infant Asylum. Haughery took a job at a bakery to finance the project, and she asked customers to contribute money to help build a new orphanage.

In 1859, Haughery used her own savings and borrowed money to buy another new enterprise, a failed bakery. Named Margaret's Bakery, it may have been the first steam bakery in the South. The store sold Margaret's Bread, leading many people in town to call her the Bread Woman. The bakery became a thriving business that employed a number of citizens. To those who could not afford her bread, Haughery distributed free flour and loaves.

Haughery also bought cows—eventually her herd numbered 40—and ran a dairy business.

Through the milk business and bakery, she was able to invest money, keep her orphanages running, and expand her enterprises. She gave most of her money away, both to existing institutions that helped the poor and for new projects, such as building the chapel that became St. Theresa of Avila Church.

She also helped imprisoned soldiers during the Civil War. During those years, she negotiated with military officials to transport the flour she needed for her orphans across the battle lines. By 1880, she had organized four orphanages and several homes for the aged.

When Margaret Haughery died in February 1882, an archbishop paid tribute to her generosity, and former governors and mayors were among her pallbearers. Mourners stretched for a block outside the doors of the church and stores, businesses, and city offices were closed on the day of her funeral. In her will, Haughery bequeathed $600,000 to the city's orphanages. Haughery was a devout Roman Catholic, but she specified that her charities were to serve people of all religions. The New Orleans press noted that despite the wealth she had accumulated, "She never had upon her hand a kid glove, and she never wore a silk dress."

Two years later, Haughery became probably the first woman in America to have a statue erected in her honor, after local citizens raised money for this tribute. The statue, by sculptor George François Mugnier, shows a woman dressed in a plain cotton dress with her arm around a child. This public monument stands on the corner of Prytania and Camp Streets in New Orleans in a park named Margaret Place.

Further Reading

Gehman, Mary and Nancy Ries. *Women and New Orleans: A History.* New Orleans, La.: Margaret Media, Inc., 1996.

King, Grace. *New Orleans: The Place and the People.* New York: Macmillan, 1899.

Randolph, Regina. "Margaret Haughery." In *The Catholic Encyclopedia.* Volume IX. Edited by Charles G. Herbermann, et. al. New York: Robert Appleton, 1910.

Widmer, Mary L. Margaret, *Friend of the Orphans.* New York: Pelican, 1996.

❈ HOFFMAN, CLAIRE GIANNINI
(1904–1997)   *Banker, Executive, Philanthropist*

Claire Giannini Hoffman was the first woman director of the world's largest bank, as well as the first woman to serve on the board of Sears Roebuck & Company and the first to serve on the board of trustees of the Sears Roebuck Savings and Profit Sharing Fund.

Claire Giannini was born on December 30, 1904, the year her father began building the banking business that would turn into the largest bank in the world. A. P. Giannini, an Italian immigrant, founded the Bank of America in San Francisco, California, and it became a multimillion-dollar business. Claire Giannini, who was educated in private schools, attended Bryn Mawr College in Pennsylvania but returned home to attend Mills College in Oakland during the 1925–1926 academic year. She married Clifford Pierson "Biff" Hoffman; Hoffman died in 1954.

During her lifetime, Hoffman was actively involved in numerous business and charitable organizations. She was the first woman appointed to the Board of Regents of St. Mary's College of California, as well as trustee of the Margaret Chase Smith Library; vice chairman of the board of trustees of the National Library of Sports in Santa Clara, California; a member of the board of trustees of the National Small Business Administration; part of the board of directors of Affiliate Artists; and member of the board of directors of Junior Achievement. Hoffman was also named a member of the first Federal Executive Board, a committee that initiated the first Federal Employee of the Year award. She was also the only honorary member of the American Institute of Banking. During World War II, she was active in the United Service Organizations (USO) and later became a member of its board of governors.

After her father died in 1949, Hoffman was appointed to his seat on the board of directors of the Bank of America and continued in that position until 1966. In 1952, her brother L. M.

Giannini died, and Hoffman became a member of the general executive committee of the bank. She also became vice chairman of the board of trustees of the Bank of America–Giannini Foundation. Hoffman showed herself to be an astute business executive, not just the heir to a business empire.

From 1963 to 1970, she served on the board of Sears Roebuck & Company. She was a delegate to the United Nations Conference on Trade in Geneva, Switzerland, in 1964. In 1970, President Richard Nixon and Arthur F. Burns, chairman of the Board of Governors, asked Hoffman to serve as governor of the Federal Reserve Board of the United States, and she became the first woman to hold that post.

Hoffman, who received an honorary doctor of humane letters degree from Mills College in 1965, was known for her keen interest in international affairs and her support for understanding among the peoples of different nations. She supported the Pacific Council on International Policy and other organizations. She once said that "it's critical for women in business today to go beyond local women's professional organizations and to become active and recognized in the national and international business organizations still dominated by men."

After her death in San Mateo, California, on December 20, 1997, the Claire Giannini Hoffman Foundation continued to contribute to the various causes she supported during her lifetime, including libraries and educational institutions.

Further Reading

Associated Press. "Claire Hoffman, Daughter of Bank Founder," Obituary. *Detroit News.* Available online. URL: http://detnews.com/1997/obits/9712/23/12230032. htm. Posted December 23, 1997. Downloaded on August 29, 2000.

Northwood University. "Claire Giannini Hoffman," Northwood University Distinguished Women. Available online. URL: http://www.northwood.edu/dw/1977/hoffman. html. Downloaded on September 2, 2000.

Popofsky, Linda. "Mills Women Who Made History," *At Mills,* July–September 1985, p. 6.

✳ HOPKINS, DEBORAH C.
(Debby Hopkins)
(1955–)   *Corporate Executive*

Deborah Hopkins, who has served as senior vice president and chief financial officer (CFO) at the Boeing Company and as executive vice president and as CFO Lucent Technologies, frequently ranks in the top 10 on *Fortune* magazine's list of the 50 most powerful women in business.

Born in 1955, Hopkins, who is known as Debby, received her bachelor's degree from Walsh College, in Troy, Michigan, and attended an executive development program at the Wharton School of Business at the University of Pennsylvania. She worked as a finance executive at the National Bank of Detroit and the Ford Motor Company, then spent 13 years at Unisys Corporation. From 1991 to 1993, she was vice president of Corporate Business Analysis, where she helped to develop a new strategy that made the company more profitable. She then served as vice president, corporate controller, and chief accounting officer at Unisys until 1995. As part of the program management team, Hopkins helped the company to launch its imaging systems products in world markets.

Hopkins then became vice president of finance and CFO for General Motors Europe, based in Zurich, Switzerland. From 1995 to 1997, she was the general auditor for General Motors.

Her next job was with the Boeing Company, a leading aircraft-manufacturing corporation, where she rose to the position of senior vice president and CFO. She also served as chairman of Boeing Capital Corporation, which provides financing and leasing services for aerospace products. Hopkins led Boeing's Investor Relations and Corporate Development programs.

In 2000, she accepted the position of CFO at Lucent Technologies, a leading telecommunication firm. Chief executive officer Rich McGinn, who hired Hopkins, said of his choice, "I wanted someone with broad leadership skills and passion—a strong desire to have an impact." One of her major roles at Lucent was to help design a turnaround plan and put the financing together to execute that plan.

In a 2000 interview for *Fortune* magazine, Hopkins described herself as "a relentlessly executing, no-holds-barred, take-no-prisoners, be-in-front-with-the-shield-and-sword, go-to-war, stay-in-the-ditch-with-you executive." She is also a member of the board of directors at Dupont, the Foundation for the Malcolm Baldrige National Quality Award, and the Private Export Funding Corporation.

In May 2001, Hopkins announced that she was leaving Lucent to pursue other opportunities now that the company's turnaround plan was well in place. She said that she planned to take some time off to spend with her children before deciding what position she would take next.

Further Reading

"Lucent Technologies Announces Chief Financial Officer Deborah Hopkins to Leave the Company." Lucent Technologies, Inc. Press release, May 6, 2001.

Sellars, Patricia. "The 50 Most Powerful Women in Business: Secrets of the Fastest Rising Stars," *Fortune,* October 16, 2000, pp. 131–134.

HUSTED, MARJORIE CHILD
(Betty Crocker)
(ca. 1892–1986)   *Executive*

Behind the famous trademark name Betty Crocker was a real woman named Marjorie Child Husted, an advertising and marketing expert with special knowledge in the field of food products.

Marjorie Child was born in Minneapolis, Minnesota, about 1892, and attended public schools. In 1913, she graduated from the University of Minnesota, where she studied for an additional year to earn a degree in education. She served as secretary of the Infant Welfare Society of Minneapolis, then joined the Red Cross during World War I.

From 1918 to 1923, Child worked with the Women's Cooperative Alliance, then became supervisor of promotional advertising and merchandising for a food products business, the Creamette Company of Minneapolis. In 1924, she became a field representative in home economics for the Washburn-Crosby Company, a flour-milling and sales firm.

She continued to work with this firm after her marriage to K. Wallace Husted in October 1925. The next year, Husted organized a home service department for Washburn-Crosby. Its staff answered letters containing questions from homemakers, and they signed their replies Betty Crocker, a name the company had begun using in 1921.

In 1928, Washburn-Crosby merged with several other firms to become General Mills. The new parent company sold its Gold Medal flour and continued to operate the home-service department, which was renamed the Betty Crocker Homemaking Service in 1929. Husted served as director and promoted the use of the Betty Crocker trademark on various food products and related consumer goods, such as the best-selling Betty Crocker cookbooks. In addition, Husted appeared on radio shows as Betty Crocker.

In 1946, Husted became a consultant to the officers and executives of the company, and two years later, she was named consultant in advertising, public relations, and home service. In 1948, she also served the U.S. Department of Agriculture as a consultant on food conservation.

Husted left General Mills in 1950 to form her own consulting firm, Marjorie Child Husted and Associates. Among other things, she consulted with restaurants and endorsed products, including cookbooks from the famous Brown Derby Restaurant in Hollywood, California. Husted died in Minneapolis on December 23, 1986.

Further Reading

"Betty Crocker Picture Cook Book Edition History." Available online. URL: http://www.cookbkjj.com/college/betty crocker.htm. Downloaded on October 23, 2000.

"A History of Innovation." (General Mills Company History) Available online. URL: http://www.generalmills.com/explore/history/. Downloaded on September 28, 2000.

McHenry, Robert, editor. *Her Heritage: A Encyclopedia of Famous American Women.* Cambridge, Mass.: Pilgrim New Media, 1995.

I

✷ INMAN, ELIZABETH MURRAY CAMPBELL SMITH

(1726–1785)   *Business Owner, Business Operator*

Elizabeth Murray owned and operated a successful millinery, cloth, and sewing supply business in 18th-century Boston and helped other women to start and operate their own businesses.

Murray was born in Scotland in 1726, where at 22 she established a dry-goods business with money from her brother James. She was already a successful merchant when she married Thomas Campbell, also a Boston merchant, in 1755, but she did not continue running her business during the brief time they were married before his death. However, she thought that women should have the means to support themselves and encouraged her five nieces to engage in business, as she had done.

When Elizabeth Campbell remarried in 1760, she negotiated a premarital contract with her new husband, James Smith, giving her control over her own property. She also retained the right to make a will bequeathing her assets to whomever she chose. Although Smith was a wealthy man, she returned to her work as a shopkeeper because she enjoyed the business world. After James Smith died in 1769, leaving her a widow once again, she stopped running the store in order to manage the sizeable estate he had left her. She then left America to visit relatives in Scotland and England.

After Smith returned from her travels, she was distressed to find that her brother had mismanaged her business affairs, leaving her with only 1,000 pounds. She said, "I found things in a Situation that was very disagreeable to me." When she married for a third time, she was pleased that her husband, Ralph Inman, was an industrious and sensible businessman. Once again, she arranged for a premarital contract that preserved the property she had earned and inherited. During their marriage, she actively helped to run Inman's farms in Cambridge, Massachusetts. During the American Revolution, she raised large hay crops, knowing they would be in demand by the army.

Throughout her life, Elizabeth Inman encouraged other women to become self-sufficient and often provided money to get them started. She helped Janette Day, an unwed mother, to open a sewing school and financed a shop that was run by two orphaned sisters. She also provided funds for two of her nieces and Janette Day's daughter to open a millinery shop in Boston.

Some of Smith's friends also tried to operate businesses and found it difficult. They realized that it took far more than just the money to buy goods to run a store successfully. A friend who began running a store in Massachusetts during her husband's absence wrote to Smith in 1770 about some of the new challenges she faced—purchasing insurance, managing credit, securing transportation, and handing bills.

For various reasons, Inman thought people should devote more time to work than to leisure. In 1770, Inman wrote to a friend that she disliked "young people being brought up in idleness and entering the world with all its gaietys, triffling away the most active part of their life." She said they should improve their minds and cultivate the habit of industriousness. Inman also contended that women would make wiser choices in marriage if they became more independent and learned to take care of themselves. One of her friends said of Inman that she was "above the little fears and weaknesses which are the inseparable companions of our sex." When she died in 1785, Inman had accumulated a fortune.

Further Reading

Berkin, Carol Ruth, and Mary Beth Norton. *Women of America, a History.* Boston: Houghton Mifflin, 1979.

Cleary, Patricia. *Elizabeth Murray: A Woman's Pursuit of Independence in Eighteenth-Century America.* Amherst: University of Massachusetts Press, 2000.

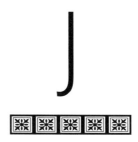

JAMES, BETTY (Elizabeth James)
(1918–   )   *Entrepreneur, Executive*

Betty James helped to cofound the company that makes Slinky, one of America's classic toys. As the head of James Industries for nearly 40 years, she expanded the company and promoted Slinky and other toys. When asked to explain Slinky's popularity, James says, "I think it's the simplicity. It's not a sophisticated toy, but it's fun and has a nice sound. There's nothing to wind up or put chips in or anything else."

Born in Altoona, Pennsylvania, on February 13, 1918, Betty James was busy as a wife, homemaker, and mother of six when the idea for Slinky was born in 1943. Her husband, Richard James, was working as a mechanical engineer in a naval shipyard. One day, while he was working to make a set of springs that could be used to support delicate instruments onboard ships in rough seas, James saw a torsion spring fall onto the floor. He was fascinated by the way it bounced, making a series of arclike movements. James wondered about other ways to use this bouncing spring, and he showed it to Betty. They agreed it might make a good toy.

While Richard James searched for a type of steel that could be used to create a wiggling, walking spring, he asked Betty James to name the toy. She combed the dictionary for ideas about a name and decided on "slinky," which means "stealthy, silky, sleek, sinuous." She later recalled that for two years, her husband "kept testing and testing until he got what he wanted" in terms of materials.

In 1945, the couple borrowed $500 and founded James Industries in Philadelphia to produce their new toy, which was made from 80 feet of coiled, bluish-black steel wire on machines Richard had designed. The machines were able to make each Slinky in about 10 seconds. Friends who saw the toy were unimpressed, but the couple pursued their idea, even though, as Betty James recalls, "It was very difficult. We started trying to sell them, and it was right after the war."

As Christmas 1945 drew near, they convinced Gimbel's department store in Philadelphia to let them display the Slinky, which they priced at one dollar. A display with steps was set up to demonstrate to shoppers how Slinky could "walk" down by itself. Within 90 minutes, all of the Slinkys they had—400—were sold. After they exhibited

Slinky at the American Toy Fair in 1946, sales increased dramatically.

During the 1940s and 1950s, Richard James, who had quit his engineering job, served as head of the company. The company brought out a new toy, Junior Slinky, in 1950, and earnings remained solid, although they slumped slightly in the mid-1950s. The family was living in a large home in suburban Philadelphia when Betty James's life changed dramatically in 1960. Richard James had become increasingly involved in a religious group and had donated large sums of money to the sect, creating large debts for both the couple and the company. That year, he left his family and the business to move to Bolivia to pursue religious activities with members of the group.

Determined to continue running the business and pay off millions of dollars in debts, Betty James became the head of James Industries. In 1961, James moved the factory to Blair County, Pennsylvania, where it operated in Hollidaysburg, near James's hometown of Altoona. She also convinced the company's creditors to give her a chance to turn the business around. Through Betty James's leadership, profits rose higher than ever, and she repaid the debts within four years. She proceeded to expand the company and launch products that extended the Slinky brand name. A snappy jingle was part of Slinky's new ad campaign, which included spots on children's television shows. New products included Slinky pull-toys, plastic versions, and even a gold-plated collectible Slinky. The regular Slinkys had gone from dark wire to silvery wire, then to colored plastic. In 1971, for safety reasons, the company changed the Slinky design so that the wire ends of the Slinky were crimped. In 1974, James and her children received news that Richard James had died in Bolivia of a heart attack.

During the 1980s and 1990s, the company moved in still other directions, making pinwheels, batons, pom-poms, and toys for infants and toddlers. Betty James retired in 1998 and sold the company to Poof Products, which is based in Detroit, Michigan. As part of their agreement, the factory in Hollidaysburg continues to make Slinkys and other toys.

By 2000, more than 250 million Slinkys had been sold around the world. The wire used to make them amounted to about 50,000 tons—enough to circle the globe 126 times. Betty James, mother of six and grandmother of 16, received many honors for her achievements. In 1995, she received the Douglas D. Danforth Award for Quality in Manufacturing from the L. C. Smith College of Engineering and Computer Science. The next year, she was honored as one of Pennsylvania's Best 50 Women in Business. In November 2000, the Toy Manufacturing Association of America (TMA) announced that James would be inducted into the Toy Industry Hall of Fame, becoming its 40th inductee and the sole inductee for 2001. TMA president David A. Miller said, "We are proud to honor Betty for her commitment and perseverance, which has allowed children

Betty James, shown here in a recent photo, helped to found James Industries, maker of the famous Slinky toy, then became head of the company in 1960.
(Photo courtesy of *Betty James*)

In this 2001 photo, Betty James holds the toy that made her family company famous.
(Photo courtesy of *Altoona Mirror*)

the world over the opportunity to relish the ingenuity and the pure fun of a Slinky."

The Slinky, which regularly appears on lists of children's favorite toys, has been used for a variety of other purposes—to hold mail, as military antennae strung over trees in Vietnam, in physical therapy treatments, and as drapery holders and other decorative objects. The National Aeronautics and Space Administration (NASA) has used Slinkys in several space shuttle experiments, and the toy can also be found in elementary and secondary school classrooms, where students use it to study principles of physics. In 1999, the U.S. Postal Service released a new 33-cent Slinky stamp. Slinky has also appeared in several movies. A Slinky dog was featured in the popular animated film *Toy Story 2*, released in 2000.

Further Reading

Asakawa, Gil, and Leland Rucker. *The Toy Book*. New York: Knopf, 1991.

Baum, Michele Dula. "It's Slinky, It's Slinky," CNN.com. Available online. URL: http://www.cnn.com/2001/US/02/10/slinky/story. Posted on February 11, 2001. Downloaded on May 2, 2001.

Shaw, Tiffany. "A Marvelous Thing," *Altoona Mirror*, Feb. 19, 1999, p. 1.

Thomas, Karen. "A Favorite Toy Sees 50 Years and a Renewal," *USA Today*, December 1, 1995, p. D-1.

Toy Manufacturers of America. "Press Release: Betty James to be Inducted into Toy Industry Hall of Fame at The First Annual T.O.T.Y. Awards," TMA on the Web. Available online. URL: http://www.toy-tma.org/industry/news/press/2000/bettyjames.html. Posted on November 16, 2000. Downloaded on January 4, 2001.

Weiss, Michael J. "Zing Went the Spring," *Discovery*. Available online. URL: http://discovery.com/stories/history/toys/SLINKY/shoulda.html. Downloaded on June 4, 2001.

JONES, AMANDA THEODOSIA
(1835–1914)   *Entrepreneur, Inventor, Author*

After inventing a patented vacuum canning process that changed the food production industry, Amanda Jones founded the U.S. Women's Pure Food Vacuum Preserving Company, a canning company that employed only women. The versatile Jones was also an author.

Amanda Theodosia Jones was born on October 19, 1835 in the small town of Bloomfield in Ontario County in New York State. She was an imaginative child and an excellent reader and student. During her childhood, her older brother Lester died unexpectedly while they were both at school, a shock that seems to have caused Amanda to have an emotional breakdown in her late teens. She also developed an interest in spiritualism and attended séances in attempts to contact her dead brother. In 1850, while she was still a high school student, she began a teaching career that lasted four years. In 1854, she also sold several of her poems to a publication called the *Ladies' Repository*. She continued to write and sell poetry while studying spiritualism and experimenting with treatments to bolster her frail health.

During her thirties, Jones experimented with different methods of canning, later saying that her brother had spoken to her from the "other side" with an idea for a new canning process. With the help of a distant relative, Leroy Cooley, who had technical expertise, she finally discovered an effective method of vacuum canning in 1872 and obtained several different food-related patents during the 1870s. Older methods of canning required the food to be cooked so long that it lost both flavor and nutritional value. Using her methods, foods including fresh foods, could be canned and preserved more quickly and safely, then shipped from place to place. Jones's method became the standard way to can food after she patented the "Jones process" in 1873.

By 1880, Amanda Jones had moved into new areas. Claiming that she had been spiritually moved to help Pennsylvania's oil drillers, she went to the oil fields. Accidents had been occurring when people burned crude oil for heat. Jones studied the equipment they were using and came up with the idea of adding a safety valve that would control the rate at which oil was released from either the pipe or oil container. On March 23, 1880, Jones proceeded to patent the oil burner, but she did not succeed when she tried to go into the oil burner business. However, the safety valve that reduced the accident rates was adopted by the U.S. Navy, and the burner was featured in *Steam Engineering* magazine.

In 1890 Jones decided to open the Women's Canning and Preserving Company in Chicago, Illinois, hiring only women to work as managers and in the factory. Jones envisioned her new business as a place where women would learn business management skills and take charge of their own lives. She said, "This is a woman's industry. No men will vote our stock, transact our business, pronounce on women's wages, supervise our factory. Give men whatever is suitable, but keep the governing power. This is a business training school for working women." Ads for the company appeared in national magazines and described the company as "makers of choice puddings, lunch tongues, fruit preserves and general canned goods." However, within three years, Jones was forced out of the business after she agreed to allow male investors to help run the company.

Although Amanda Jones had succeeded as an inventor and entrepreneur, she was probably better known as a poet and author, writing about a variety of subjects, including wildflowers, wildlife, and spirituality. She also supported women's suffrage and other rights for women. Jones used some of her earnings from the canning business to build a home for working women. She published a collection of her work, *Poems 1854–1906,* in 1906. In 1910, she published her life story, entitled *A Psychic Autobiography.*

Further Reading

About Entrepreneurs. "Amanda Jones." The Inventors Museum on the Web. Available online. URL: http://www.inventorsmuseum.com/AmandaJones.htm. Downloaded on October 20, 2000.

Altman, Linda Jacobs. *Women Inventors.* New York: Facts On File, 1997.

IEEE Fort Worth Section Newsletter. "Mothers of Invention: Women Engineers." Signals, November 1998. Available online. URL: http://www.ewh.ieee.org/r5/fort_worth/sig1198.html. Downloaded on October 18, 2000.

Jones, Amanda T. *A Psychic Autobiography.* New York: Greaves, 1910.

✳ JOYNER, MARJORIE STEWART
(1896–1994)   *Executive, Inventor*

Called the Grande Dame of Black Beauty, Joyner was a successful business executive who served as national supervisor of Walker Beauty Schools and assumed leadership roles in business, politics, journalism, and education.

One of 13 children, Marjorie Stewart was born on October 24, 1896, in Monterey, Virginia, in the Blue Ridge Mountains. Her father, George Stewart, was a teacher, and her mother, Annie Dougherty Stewart, was a domestic. In 1912, after her parents divorced, Marjorie moved to Chicago, Illinois, with her mother and became the first African

American to graduate from the A. B. Molar Beauty School, in 1916.

She married Dr. Robert E. Joyner that same year and opened her own beauty salon. Marjorie Joyner also became a sales agent for MADAM C. J. WALKER's famous beauty products company and was eventually named national supervisor of all Walker Beauty Schools. She recruited thousands of other sales agents for the Walker company. In 1924, she also helped to write Illinois's first beauty culture law.

As a cosmetologist and hairstylist, Joyner knew that women became discouraged when their hair did not retain its style for long after a salon appointment. She invented the permanent-wave machine to solve this problem and then received a patent for her design on November 27, 1928, becoming the first African-American woman to obtain a U.S. patent. Her domelike machine sent an electrical current to one-inch sections of a woman's hair, pressing them in place so that customers could retain their wavy or curled styles for weeks after they had a salon permanent. Joyner did not profit from the invention, which became the property of her employer, the Walker company. She was later named the director of Madam Walker's nationwide chain of beauty schools.

During the Great Depression of the 1930s, Joyner, who was raising her two daughters, continued to travel and teach and became part of several New Deal programs that helped young African Americans find jobs and housing. In the years that followed, Joyner devoted most of her time to politics and civic affairs. A strong supporter of education, she worked with educator Mary McLeod Bethune and others to found the United Beauty School Owners and Teachers Association in 1945. The association operated a program called Pay While You Learn that helped thousands of people begin new careers in the beauty business. Joyner herself continued to pursue more education and received her bachelor's degree in psychology from Bethune-Cookman College in 1973.

Joyner also worked for civil rights and served as chairwoman of the *Chicago Defender* Charities for more than 50 years. The *Defender,* a newspaper,

supports charitable outreach activities in the community. Joyner also helped to found the National Council of Negro Women. In addition, she served on the Democratic National Committee and worked to elect candidates she supported, including Mayor Harold Washington of Chicago. Her many friends included prominent people of all races.

Joyner's philanthropic activities included fundraising for Bethune-Cookman College and other schools that served African Americans. She advised young people: "Get all the learning or education you can get, stand on your two feet and hold your head up high. And know that you have the understanding anybody else has."

Marjorie Stewart Joyner died in December 1994.

Further Reading

Amram, Fred B., Stanley P. Jones, and Susan K. Henderson. *African American Inventors.* Mankato, Minn.: Capstone Press, 1996.

Bundles, A'Lelia. *On Her Own Ground: The Life and Times of Madam C. J. Walker.* New York: Scribner, 1999.

Macdonald, Anne L. *Feminine Ingenuity: How Women Inventors Changed America.* New York: Ballantine, 1992.

Inventors Museum, "Marjorie Joyner: First African American Female Patent Holder," Inventors Online Museum. Available online. URL: http://www.inventorsmuseum. com/MarjorieJoyner.htm. Downloaded on May 24, 2001.

Salem, Dorothy C. *African American Women: A Biographical Dictionary.* New York: Garland, 1993.

Worley, Kelli. "Joyner Marks a Century of Black Progress," *The Chicago Reporter.* Available online. URL: http://www.chicagoreporter.com/1993/1293/1293Joyner MarksaCenturyofBlackProgress.htm. Posted December 1993. Downloaded on May 3, 2001.

✴ JULIBER, LOIS D.
(1949–) *Executive*

As executive vice president and chief operating officer of Colgate-Palmolive, Lois D. Juliber has helped to expand markets for one of the world's largest personal care and household products companies.

Lois Juliber received a bachelor of science (B.S.) degree from Wellesley College in Massachusetts in

1972 and earned her master's degree in business administration (M.B.A.) from Harvard University. At General Foods Corporation, she worked in product management, rising to the position of product group manager in charge of children's cereals in 1978, then to the rank of vice president of the company.

In 1988, Juliber joined Colgate-Palmolive as general manager. Colgate-Palmolive is one of the world's leading producers of personal care and household products, including toothpastes, soaps, deodorants, and detergents. Brands they own include Colgate toothpaste, Ajax cleanser, and Mennen deodorant. Juliber became president of the company's $800 million Far East/Canada division. The division grew rapidly in Asia and the Indian subcontinent to become the most profitable of Colgate-Palmolive's regional operations.

Juliber was elected a corporate officer in 1992 and was promoted to chief technological officer, which meant she was in charge of directing Colgate-Palmolive world research and development. Juliber spearheaded the development of new products at the company and oversaw major developments, including global Colgate's efforts to consolidate its manufacturing operations and facilities. During these years, she also played a key role as Colgate expanded its information technology network and addressed consumers' concerns regarding environmental affairs, health, and safety.

Juliber was promoted again, in May 1994, when she became president of Colgate North America, in charge of businesses in the United States, Canada, and Puerto Rico. Under her direction, profit growth increased greatly and new products were successfully launched. In 1997, for the first time in 35 years, Colgate regained its position as the worldwide leader in toothpaste sales and the company also saw increasing sales of its Palmolive dishwashing liquid and Softsoap products.

In 1995, Juliber, who is married with no children, was ranked as 15th on *Working Woman* magazine's list of the 20 highest-paid women in corporate America. Two years later, she was promoted to executive vice president and chief of operations, developed markets, in charge of all Colgate operations in North America and Europe. That year, her salary rose to $450,000, with a bonus of $607,500. In 2000, she was promoted again, this time to chief operating officer of the company, with responsibility for the company's operations in Europe, Asia, Latin America, Africa, and the South Pacific.

During her successful corporate career, Juliber says she has sometimes had to meet a higher standard than male coworkers, commenting, "I really do believe that day in and day out you have to deliver performance more strongly and more consistently to make it through."

Juliber also serves on the boards of Wellesley College, the Brookdale Foundation, and DuPont Corporation.

Further Reading

Morris, Betsy, and Ann Harrington. "Tales of the Trailblazers: Fortune Revisits Harvard's Women MBAs of 1973," *Fortune,* October 12, 1998, pp. 106ff.

Williams, Jeannie. "USA's Highest-Paid Women: Magazine Tallies Top Compensation for '95," *USA Today,* December 17, 1996, p. 2-B.

✳ JUNG, ANDREA
(1959–)   *Executive*

As the president and chief operating officer (COO) of Avon Products, Andrea Jung is one of the top female executives in the world. The daughter of immigrants, Jung was born in Toronto on and grew up in Wellesley, Massachusetts. Her father, a native of Hong Kong, was an architect who received his master's degree from the Massachusetts Institute of Technology. Her mother, who was born in Shanghai, was a chemical engineer and an accomplished pianist who encouraged Andrea's lifelong love of music. Jung began taking piano lessons as a child and continues to play as an adult. She also studied Mandarin and became fluent in that Chinese dialect.

Her parents stressed the value of education and self-discipline and urged both Jung and her brother to have careers. Jung later recalled, "They told me I could do everything my brother could."

Jung attended Princeton University where she earned her degree, with great honors, in English literature in 1979. When she chose to work in the retail field, her parents expressed dismay. Jung later said, "No one in my family had a retail or marketing background. They were professionals. They didn't understand just what I was doing by going into retailing. After I started, though, it got into my blood. I knew this was what I wanted."

Jung began her career as a management trainee at Bloomingdale's, then worked at the upscale department store I. Magnin, where she became second in command while still in her twenties. At Neiman Marcus in Dallas, Texas, Jung was promoted to head the entire women's apparel division at age 32.

When Jung joined Avon Products, Inc., in 1994, the company had experienced disappointing sales the previous year. Jung expressed enthusiasm about the opportunity to improve the company's performance. She helped Avon to grow, expanding its international markets and developing new marketing strategies. The company gained more exposure as a sponsor of the 1996 Olympics, and the website Avon.com was launched in 1997.

In 1998, Avon set up kiosks around the country, the first time they had sold their products retail. (Avon had previously sold only via personal representatives.) That year, Jung was inducted into the Advertising Hall of Fame by the American Advertising Federation. She was also ranked number 14 on *Forbes* magazine's annual list of the 50 most powerful women in business in America.

Late in 1999, Jung was named CEO of the entire Avon operation, with responsibility for overseeing marketing, advertising, and product development for the United States. She was one of four women named as a chief executive officer (CEO) of a Fortune 500 company (the 500 largest corporations in America) during 1999. Jung said that her vision for Avon was an organization that would offer women all the products and services they needed, available online, in a store, or from a door-to-door salesperson. Jung also spearheaded a program called Beauty

Advisor, which trains sales representatives to serve as personal advisers to their customers, recommending effective products for individual needs. The company adopted a multilevel marketing program, giving representatives a percentage of the sales earned by people they recruit.

Under Jung's leadership, Avon has taken an increasingly active role in promoting women's health through its Avon Worldwide Fund for Women's Health. The fund supports programs in more than 30 countries. By the end of 2000, the fund had reached the $100 million mark and Jung said they were committed to surpass $200 million by the end of 2002. The fund donated millions of dollars to research centers, including gifts of $2 million and $10 million to Columbia Presbyterian Hospital's Herbert Irving Comprehensive Cancer Center. This money will be used to advance breast cancer research and to provide care to women with breast cancer who lack sufficient resources to pay for their treatment. In November 1999, Jung was chosen to receive Columbia Presbyterian's Award for Distinguished Service. Jung said, "Corporations can have dreams, and at Avon our dream is to see the eradication of breast cancer."

As 2001 arrived, Avon was selling about $5.3 billion of beauty goods in 137 countries each year with its network of 3 million direct sales representatives, who were producing about 98 percent of Avon's revenue. Jung planned to boost sales on the Avon.com website and to promote a new line of products at boutiques in J. C. Penney, and other retail stores.

In 2001, Jung was working to improve the website and to make Avon representatives available online. Avon representatives can pay $15 a month to become "e-representatives" and sell online, earning commissions on these sales. The company sought feedback from its representatives, asking them to suggest ways to operate and improve the website.

Jung, who also serves on the board of the Fashion Institute of Technology and the American Management Association, is the mother of a son and daughter. The family lives in New York City. After seeing her children off to school, Jung typically walks to her office in midtown Manhattan, arriving by 8 A.M. She plans her day so that she can arrive home by 7:30 P.M. for dinner.

Further Reading

"Avon CEO Andrea Jung to Receive Award for Distinguished Service from Columbia Presbyterian Hospital," Columbia Presbyterian Medical Center/New York Presbyterian Hospital Press Release. Available online. URL: http://www.nyp.org/news/nov 9 avon.html. Posted November 9, 1999.

"Executive Sweet," Goldsea: Asian American Wonder Women. Available online. URL: http:goldsea.com/WW/ Jungandrea/jungadnrea.html. Downloaded on January 6, 2001.

Byrnes, Nanette, "Avon: The New Calling," *Business Week,* September 18, 2000, pp. 136–148.

K

KAMALI, NORMA
(1945–) *Designer, Entrepreneur, Business Owner*

A fashion designer, Kamali founded a design firm based in New York City that produces sportswear for women and children, furniture, fabrics, bridal wear, and a fragrance line.

Born on June 27, 1945, Norma Kamali graduated from Washington Irving High School and the Fashion Institute of Technology (FIT), both located in New York City. After receiving her bachelor of fine arts degree (BFA) in fashion illustration from FIT in 1964, she worked briefly as a transatlantic flight attendant before she went into business. In 1968, she opened her own shop to market the creative and sometimes offbeat fashions that were then being made, such as the Carnaby Street look that emerged in England. She began selling her own designs, including sleek separates made from soft, stretchy fabrics. Some of her most popular pieces were T-shirts studded with rhinestones and clothes with leather patches or ornate appliqués. Kamali also liked to use snakeskin, patchwork, and animal prints in her designs and became especially well known for her leisure wear and unexpected uses for fleece.

Her shop was a success, and Kamali also made headlines as a costume designer when she created costumes for the cast of the 1978 film *The Wiz* and for dancers in productions by choreographer Twyla Tharp. That year, she reorganized her company, calling it Norma Kamali OMO ("on my own"). She won the Coty Fashion Award in both 1981 (for design innovation) and in 1982 (for women's fashion design). She won the Coty Hall of Fame Award in 1983.

Kamali continued to introduce new ideas, such as clothing made from parachute silk, the "pull bikini," and a group of jersey knit separates that could be rolled up in a suitcase and remain wrinkle-free, as well as her trademark "sleeping bag coat," which she began making in 1975. She launched her fragrance line in 1985.

During the 1990s, Kamali branched out in still other areas. She designed eyewear, bridal fashions, skin care products, cosmetics, and a new line of athletic clothing. In 1995, she presented the commencement speech to graduates of the Fashion

Institute of Technology. Her new line of jersey essential pieces, designed to be worn in all seasons, were advertised as an ideal solution for carefree, lightweight travel.

Norma Kamali has also been involved in projects to benefit the community, especially young people and schools. In 1997, she worked with the staff at her former high school to help students form a business so they could earn money while they learned new skills. The students began operating a clothing design and retail business. Since then, she has continued to spearhead projects to connect businesspeople with public schools, and she sponsors internships and part-time jobs for students. She launched a website that presents the creative work of public school students and lists things people can donate to help the schools. Kamali said, "There's lots you can do once you know what a school needs."

In 1998, Kamali developed an innovative personal shopper service on her website to give customers help in selecting products. Her Shop Like a Celebrity service gives women a chance to preview her designs and work with a personal shopper who knows their size, measurements, tastes, and special needs. A client can select items and have them sent. Kamali has said that she especially enjoys feedback from customers who visit her website. Her 1998 collection featured a group of wrinkle-proof jersey separates and dresses trimmed in ostrich feathers, as well as comfortable fleece sportswear and a black denim Edwardian jacket.

Further Reading

Capalaci, Sylvi. "Shop Like a Celebrity at Kamali," *Toronto Sun,* December 1, 1998, p. 49.

Healy, Michelle. "Principal Players Go Back to School: Talented Adults, 1,100 Strong, Donate Time to NYC Pupils," *USA Today,* April 28, 1999, p. D-9.

Scully, James. "Jersey Girl," *Harper's Bazaar,* February 2001, p. 264.

White, Constance R. "Fashion's New Order: Female Designers Prove They're a Cut Above with Clothes that Stress Comfort, Function." *Denver Rocky Mountain News,* August 17, 1997, p. 3.

✳ KARAN, DONNA FASKE
(1948–) *Designer, Entrepreneur, Executive*

Sometimes called the Queen of Seventh Avenue, Donna Karan is a prominent fashion designer and the owner and chief executive officer (CEO) of her own company. Her designs are known and appreciated around the world.

She was born Donna Faske on October 2, 1948, in Forest Hills, New York. Her mother was a showroom fashion model and sales representative, and her father, who died when she was three, was a haberdasher, so fashion was part of her life from the beginning. As a high school student, she worked during the summers as an intern for designer LIZ CLAIBORNE. After graduation, she attended the Parsons School of Design in New York City and began working with ANNE KLEIN, a well-known designer. She left briefly to work for another sportswear designer and then returned to Anne Klein in 1968.

Three years later, Karan, who married boutique owner Mark Karan, was made an associate designer and rose to the position of head designer after founder Klein became ill. Her friend Louis Dell' Olio agreed to join her as codesigner of the Anne Klein Collection. Together, they developed classic sportswear with stylish details that suited the lifestyles of modern women. Karan's Anne Klein II line was a success after it debuted in 1982. The next year, Karan, who had divorced Mark Karan, married sculptor Stephen Weiss.

In 1984, Karan decided to develop her own company, which was launched in 1985. She created a high-end clothing line that featured interchangeable pieces geared for stylish women with busy lives. Karan's first collection, based on the color black, was called The Essentials—a group of seven pieces that included a bodysuit women could combine with slacks, skirts of different lengths, and blouses. Karan noted the virtues of black: "It goes day-into-evening. It packs. It's city friendly. And you never have to worry about how to dress the leg." The fabrics draped easily and subtly revealed the body. Critics raved about her designs, saying they were stylish, luxurious, and comfortable and suitable for various occasions. In 1985, the Council of Fashion Designers of America named Karan Designer of the Year, an honor that was repeated in 1990.

In her collections, Karan also popularized the sarong skirt and bold jewelry as an accessory for her basic pieces, often made from stretch fabrics in neutral colors. She noted that her clothes were designed to fit a rounded body, since most women were not pencil-thin but rather had curves. She said, "I am a woman with a rounded figure. . . . I won't design clothes that can't be worn by a woman who is a size 12 or 14." She introduced new lines, including her less expensive DKNY line in 1988, which was inspired by a desire to create fashions for her teenage daughter Gabby and other young adults. Her designs for men were also well received, and Karan was named Menswear Designer of the Year in 1992.

In 1996, Karan took her company public with a stock offering. That year, she stepped down as CEO of Donna Karan International but remained as board chair and chief designer. As of 2000, the company was producing lines of clothing for women and men, intimate apparel, stockings, shoes, handbags, jewelry, home products, and beauty products. She was involved in many aspects of the business, including marketing as well as design. The company had nearly 2,000 employees and annual revenues of more than $622 million.

A mother of three, Karan was widowed when Stephan Weiss died in 2001. She resides in New York City and East Hampton, New York. Karan has actively worked on behalf of AIDS awareness programs and fund-raising activities for people with AIDS, including the Pediatric AIDS Foundation. She is also the author of a book, *Modern Souls,* with photography by Herb Ritts.

Further Reading

"Biography of Donna Karan." *Vogue.* Available online. URL: http://www.angelfire.com/mi2/llennium3/donnakaran.html. Downloaded on February 18, 2001.

Rudolph, Barbara. "Business: Donna, Inc.," *Time,* December 12, 1992, p. 54.

Singer, Sally. "Love Story," *Vogue,* August 2001, pp. 280–85.

KATEN, KAREN L.
(1949–)   *Executive*

Karen L. Katen is president of Pfizer Pharmaceuticals Group and executive vice president of Pfizer, Inc., overseeing its global pharmaceuticals organization. When Chief Executive Officer (CEO) Henry A. McKinnell Jr. announced Katen's promotion in 2001, he said, "Karen's U.S. organization built an outstanding sales force, which for the sixth straight year has been acknowledged as the best in the U.S. She now brings this record of accomplishment to our worldwide pharmaceutical operation, where she will be instrumental in bringing to global markets the exciting near- and longer-term pharmaceutical products in our pipeline."

Katen, who received both her bachelor of arts (B.A., 1970) and master's of business administration (M.B.A., 1974) from the University of Chicago, began her career with Pfizer in 1974 and has remained there for more than two decades, explaining, "I've never been bored." She rose to progressively higher positions in the marketing department before being named president of Pfizer U.S. Pharmaceuticals in 1995. This division had revenues of about $7 billion when Katen took charge. In 1997, she arranged a profitable comarketing plan with Warner-Lambert to launch the prescription drug Lipitor, which lowers cholesterol. Pfizer went on to buy Warner-Lambert in 2000.

After she became president, Pfizer launched several highly successful prescription products, including Zyrtec (for allergies), Trovan (an antibiotic), and Viagra (for impotence). Katen increased the sales force by 750 people between 1995 and 1999 and also served as a member of the corporate management team at Pfizer.

In 1998, *Business Week* magazine named her one of the top executives in America for 1998, on a list that included Apple Computer's Steve Jobs and Cisco Systems's John Chambers. That same year, Katen was elected to the University of Chicago Board of Trustees, and the American Diabetes Association (ADA) honored her for her commitment to diabetes research and education with its inaugural Women of Valor award. The award recognizes women who have made civic and human service contributions to combat diabetes and who promote programs that help people with the disease. In 2001, her alma mater, Barnard College, honored her with the Iphigene Ochs Sulzberger Award. Katen has served on the boards of General Motors and the Harris Corporation, as well as the National Pharmaceutical Council, the National Alliance for Hispanic Health, and the American Bureau for Medical Advancement in China.

Further Reading

"Karen L. Katen: Pfizer's Pep Pill," *Business Week,* February 1999.

"Pfizer to Name Katen as World Pharmaceuticals Head," *Reuters Business Report,* March 5, 2001.

"Tribute to Valor," *Pharmaceutical Executive,* June 8, 1998, p. 144.

KECKLEY, ELIZABETH HOBBS (Elizabeth Hobbs Keckly)

(1818–1907) *Entrepreneur, Business Owner, Author*

Elizabeth Hobbs Keckley, a former slave, operated a successful dressmaking business with a clientele that included first lady Mary Todd Lincoln. She later wrote a book describing her experiences as a slave and as a free woman, including firsthand accounts of life in the Lincoln White House.

Elizabeth was born in Dinwiddie County, Virginia, in 1818, a slave in the household of George and Agnes Hobbs. At age 13, she was sold away from her mother to another slaveowner, Robert Burwell, in North Carolina. She later described the abuse and harsh treatment she suffered in that setting. In 1839, she gave birth to a son, after being raped numerous times by a male friend of the Burwells.

The next year, she was sent to live with Burwell's sister, who lived near Dinwiddie. Her son, George, and her mother, Agnes, joined her there in 1844, but in 1845, Elizabeth and her son were sent away again, this time to a new owner in St. Louis, Missouri. Since childhood, Hobbs had shown a strong talent for dressmaking, and she started a business that supported herself and her son as well as her owner's family. In 1852, she married James Keckley, who had misrepresented himself to her as a free man but who turned out to be a slave and an alcoholic. The marriage was not a happy one, and she left him eight years later.

Keckley was determined to be free, and she knew that slaves could sometimes buy their freedom from their owners. In 1854, loyal customers loaned her enough money to pay her owners $1,200, enough to purchase freedom for herself and her son. Keckley stayed in St. Louis for five more years, working to pay back the loans.

In 1859, she moved to Baltimore, Maryland, where she opened a new dressmaking business. Within a year, she had relocated to the nation's capital and started yet another business. One of her first important customers was Varina Howell Davis, the wife of Senator Jefferson Davis from Mississippi. Keckley's expertise attracted other prominent women in Washington, D.C., including Mrs. Stephen Douglas, wife of the senator from Illinois. Also in 1859, Keckley's son, George, entered Wilberforce University in Xenia, Ohio. However, he left school in 1861 to join the Union army, where he was assumed to be white because of his light skin color.

First Lady Mary Todd Lincoln noticed Keckley's work and requested her dressmaking services in 1861. By this time, Keckley was so busy she employed 20 assistant seamstresses. As their acquaintance grew, Keckley became Mrs. Lincoln's personal dressmaker, companion, and trusted confidante. She moved into the White House, where she took care of the First Lady's wardrobe and accessories and styled her hair for important occasions. She continued to design beautiful gowns for Mrs. Lincoln.

During these years, Keckley actively tried to help the abolitionist effort and worked with abolitionist Frederick Douglass to help former slaves. She created a fund, made up of donations from prominent people, to support her First Black Contraband Relief Organization. The organization first aided former slaves who had moved to

Washington, and, later, African-American soldiers. Keckley also helped to found the Home for Destitute Women and Children and a school for young black girls. She spoke out on behalf of civil rights for African Americans.

Keckley remained at the White House until Abraham Lincoln was assassinated in 1865. For the next three years, she continued to make garments for Mrs. Lincoln. Eager to share her life story, Keckley wrote a book with James Redpath called *Behind the Scenes; or, Thirty Years as a Slave, and Four Years in the White House.* She discussed the mistreatment she had suffered during her years of bondage. The book also revealed private details of life at the White House and discussed members of the Lincoln family.

Former slave Elizabeth Hobbs Keckley ran a prestigious dressmaking business that served prominent women in the nation's capital, including First Lady Mary Todd Lincoln.
(Photo courtesy of the Lincoln Museum, Fort Wayne, Indiana)

Mary Lincoln resented these disclosures and broke off their relationship after the book was published in 1868. Her son Robert Lincoln used his connections to have the book removed from shelves and also halt its publication. Critics said that Keckley was presumptuous to write such a book, and Mrs. Lincoln's friends called it a betrayal. Historians have since praised the book as a source of valuable and accurate information. Keckley once said philosophically, "As one of the victims of slavery I drank of the bitter water; but then, since destiny willed it so, and since I aided in bringing solemn truth to the surface as a truth, perhaps I have no right to complain."

Keckley continued to run her business until 1892, when she left Washington for Ohio to work as a sewing instructor in the Department of Domestic Science Arts at Wilberforce University. In 1893, she represented the university at the Columbian World's Exhibition in Chicago.

Keckley returned to Washington in 1898. Her son, George, had died while fighting with the Union army, so she received a small pension of $12 a month, which helped to support her during her final years. She moved into the rest home that she had helped to found and died there, in her sleep, of a stroke on May 26, 1907.

Further Reading

Brown, Hallie Q. *Homespun Heroines and Other Women of Distinction.* New York: Oxford University Press, 1988.

Foster, Frances Smith. *Written By Herself: Literary Production By African American Women, 1746–1892.* Bloomington: Indiana University Press, 1993.

Keckley, Elizabeth. *Behind the Scenes; or, Thirty Years as a Slave, and Four Years in the White House.* 1868. Reprint, New York: Oxford University Press, 1988.

KEENE, LAURA (Mary Frances Moss)
(1820–1873)   *Actress, Theatrical Producer, Theater Proprietor*

Actress and businessperson Laura Keene is believed to be the first woman in America to manage a theater. She was known for her fine artistic and busi-

Laura Keene's theatrical company, shown here in an 1856 performance of "Varieties," attracted large audiences in New York, Washington, D.C., and other eastern cities.
(Photo courtesy of Library of Congress)

ness judgment, prompting actor Joseph Smith to write, "Her plays were produced with an artistic and financial splendor practically unknown at any other theater of her day." An actress who worked in her theatrical company said, "She was prompt, precise, punctilious and exacting to the very letter of the law."

Laura Keene was born Mary Frances Moss in 1820 in Westminster, England. Her father died

when she was 14, and young Mary looked for work in order to help the family. She married Henry Wellington Taylor in 1844 and gave birth to two children but had to raise them alone after Taylor abandoned his family. Her aunt Elizabeth Yates, an actress, encouraged her to pursue a career on the stage, saying that her striking red hair and good looks would help her to succeed in this profession. She adopted the professional name of Laura Keene and, after her debut with the company of Madame Vestris in 1851, became a successful actress.

In 1852, Keene moved to America and began building a successful stage career there as well, beginning at Wallack's Lyceum in New York City. She earned excellent reviews in New York and also in Baltimore, Maryland, and San Francisco, California, where she appeared under her own management. She briefly toured in Australia, where she was not as successful. After returning to San Francisco, Keene produced several lavish plays, managing her own troupe of actors.

In 1855, she settled in New York, and her mother and two daughters joined her there. That year, she became the manager of Laura Keene's Varieties Theater, formerly the Metropolitan Theatre, in New York City. She reconstructed it and reopened it as Laura Keene's Theatre, which later became the Olympic Theater, in 1856. For the next eight years, she produced and performed in a variety of American and foreign plays, featuring such prominent actors as Joseph Jefferson and Edward A. Sothern. One of her most popular plays was the satirical comedy *Our American Cousin,* by Tom Taylor, which premiered in America in 1858 and ran longer than any play had ever before run in New York. Her efforts helped the city become known as a center of the American theater.

In 1862, a reviewer for the *New York Sun* newspaper called her "an excellent judge of artists and plays." She also distinguished herself from other managers by spending large amounts of money on advertising.

Our American Cousin was revived in 1865. Keene had performed in the play more than 1,000 times when her troupe presented a benefit performance at the Ford Theater in Washington, D.C., on the evening of Friday, April 14, 1865. President and Mrs. Abraham Lincoln arrived late, during the second act, and Keene called a halt in the play while the musicians played "Hail to the Chief," and the Lincolns were seated in their box. At about 10:15 that night, Lincoln was assassinated as he sat watching the play. His assassin, John Wilkes Booth, managed to get to the box and

shoot Lincoln at close range. Afterward, Booth fled and nearly toppled Keene as he dashed across the stage to make his escape. Keene urged the audience to remain calm. It was also reported that she went to the box to comfort Mrs. Lincoln.

Keene, who had given up her own theater in May 1863, performed less often in the years after the assassination. In 1867, she became the first to offer prize money—$1,000—for the best-written play by an American author. Although she briefly managed a theater in Philadelphia, she bought a farm in Acushnet, Massachusetts, where she lived during her final years. Keene died on November 4, 1873, at age 53.

Further Reading

Creahan, John. *The Life of Laura Keene: Actress, Artist, Manager, and Scholar.* Philadelphia: Rodgers Publishing, 1897.

Johnson, Claudia. *American Actress.* Chicago: Nelson-Hall, 1984.

Turner, Mary. *Forgotten Leading Ladies of the American Theatre.* Jefferson, N.C.: McFarland and Co., 1990.

✳ KELLOGG, ELLA EATON
(1853–1920) *Entrepreneur, Home Economist, Author*

Ella Kellogg helped her husband, Dr. John Harvey Kellogg, develop products that enabled him and his brother, William Keith Kellogg, to launch a successful cereal company that became Kellogg's Cereals. Dr. Kellogg said of his wife, "Without the help derived from this fertile incubator of ideas, the great food industries of Battle Creek would never have existed."

Ella Eaton was born on April 7, 1853, the oldest of four children, and raised in the Seventh Day Baptist Church. Her parents recognized her intelligence and enrolled her in school at age three. After she graduated from Alfred Academy at age 16, Eaton attended Alfred University and received her degree just three years later, making her the youngest woman who had ever graduated. Some of her companions believed that young women did

Ella Kellogg's skills in dietetics and food preparation were an asset to the family's health resort and helped to launch her brother-in-law's cereal products business.
(Photo courtesy of Willard Library)

not need so much education. She later wrote, "But I looked on it differently. It seemed to me life is intended for progress, constant and continuous toward higher and better things, and I wanted to get just as high as I could."

After teaching school for several years, she accompanied her sister Jennie on a trip to visit an aunt in Battle Creek, Michigan. A typhoid epidemic was raging in the region at that time, and Jennie caught the disease. Because there were not enough nurses to care for all the typhoid victims, Ella Eaton nursed her sister. During that time, she met Dr. John Harvey Kellogg and decided to take classes in his new hygiene school. When Kellogg saw she was also a talented writer, he asked her to become an editor for his *Good Health* magazine.

Eaton married Kellogg in 1879. Although they did not have children of their own, during the course of their marriage they raised more than 40 adopted or foster children and sometimes had 12 to 19 children in the house at one time. Ella Kellogg also helped to found and manage the Haskell Home, an orphanage that held up to 200 children.

In 1883, Ella Kellogg set up an experimental kitchen at the sanitarium. Her husband's brother, William Keith Kellogg, had been selling brooms, but he also came to work at the Battle Creek Sanitarium, which resembled today's health spas and was affiliated with the Seventh-Day Adventist Church. As a devout Seventh-Day Adventist, John Kellogg did not use alcohol or tobacco or eat meat. He advocated exercise and a healthy diet based on grains and vegetables and hoped Ella would devise some nutritious and tasty vegetarian recipes for the patients at the facility. In 1892, Ella Kellogg published her first cookbook describing this experimental work. It was called *Science in the Kitchen: A Scientific Treatise on Food Substances and Their Dietetic Properties Together with a Practical Explanation of the Principles of Healthful Cookery, and a large number of Original, Palatable, and Wholesome Recipes.* Her work concentrated on legumes and grains, and these foods became more popular as a result of her work.

Ella Kellogg worked long hours, often into the night, with her husband and brother-in-law. In

1894, they came up with a method of rolling out mashed wheat, cooking it, and then flaking the dough. The patients liked this toasted cereal, and most people gave Dr. Kellogg the credit for it, but he said that Ella played the key role. The Kellogg brothers and Ella continued working on new recipes, and they found a way to make the first flaked corn cereal in 1898. The next year, William K. Kellogg became general manager of the Sanitas Nut Food Company, which marketed cereal products to former Battle Creek Sanitarium patients. The Kelloggs sold their cereal by mail order.

Although cereal was rarely eaten for breakfast at that time, Will Kellogg believed their corn flake cereal would appeal to many Americans. In 1906, he founded the Battle Creek Toasted Corn Flake Company, which was later renamed the W. K. Kellogg Company. Will Kellogg promoted the cereal vigorously in a national ad campaign that emphasized the virtues of this new breakfast food: healthful, tasty, and convenient for people of all ages. Within just a year, he sold 175,000 cases of corn flakes. Next, the company began selling wheat flakes, followed by other products.

Meanwhile, C. W. Post, a former sanitarium patient who had enjoyed the cereals the Kelloggs served there, had also formed a cereal company. The cereal industry proliferated in Battle Creek, which became known as Cereal City. Within 10 years, 40 different companies were making cereal products. During the early 1900s, Kellogg's was the most successful. It eventually grew into a global company.

While the cereal business was developing, Ella Kellogg continued to experiment with new grain recipes. She founded the School of Home Economics at the Battle Creek College in 1906 and completed more writing, including a treatise entitled "Studies in Character Building." Shortly after Ella Kellogg died in 1920, her husband gave her credit for the advancement in dietetics and the growth of the cereal industry.

Further Reading

Kellogg, Ella Eaton. "Autobiography." From the Archives of the Historical Society of Battle Creek, n.d.

Neumeyer, Elizabeth. "'Mother' Ella Eaton Kellogg," *Heritage Battle Creek,* fall 1997, pp. 58–65.

South, Amy. "Ella Eaton Kellogg—author, dietician, cereal developer," *Enquirer and News,* Battle Creek, Mich., September 1976.

✱ KING, HENRIETTA CHAMBERLAIN
(Henrietta Maria Morse Chamberlain)
(1832–1925) *Entrepreneur, Land Developer*

Henrietta King helped to build a multimillion-dollar ranching business in Texas and used innovative livestock breeding and shipping methods. She helped to develop the agricultural and oil-producing town of Kingsville along a railroad right-of-way.

She was born Henrietta Maria Morse Chamberlain on July 21, 1832, in Boonville, Missouri. Her mother died when she was three years old, and her father, a Presbyterian missionary, traveled frequently. Beginning at age 14, she attended the Female Institute of Holly Springs in Mississippi.

In 1849 she moved to Brownsville, Texas, where Reverend Chamberlain was organizing a mission. In December 1854, she married Richard King, a former steamboat captain on the Rio Grande, who began buying land in the area from the Spanish in 1853, when he was 19 years old. During the next decade, he built dams in order to water livestock and began buying herds of cattle and horses. Henrietta gave birth to their five children and managed their home while also supervising housing and education for the families of Mexican-American workers on the ranch. After the Civil War ended, King began sending the herds on long cattle drives through Kansas and Missouri to markets in Chicago and was able to purchase more land with his profits. By the 1870s, King owned about 600,000 acres of land in Texas.

After her husband died in 1885, Henrietta King ran the ranch and appointed her son-in-law Robert Justus Kleberg, who had married her daughter Alice in 1886, as ranch manager. He reduced the ranch's debts, which were about $500,000 when Richard King died, and together they expanded it in profitable ways. At the turn of the century, they also worked to bring a railroad to the area so goods could be transported more easily. In 1904, the first train of the St. Louis, Brownsville, and Mexico Railway passed about three miles from the main house of the ranch. King and Kleberg had formed the Kleberg Town and Improvement Company the previous year, which installed waterworks and other essential services, including a power company and ice factory. The community of Kingsville grew up around the ranch. Henrietta King constructed the First Presbyterian Church and donated land for other churches and various community buildings.

In 1906, King paid nearly $700,000 for an additional 170,000 acres of land. It grew to about 825,000 acres of cattle-ranching and oil-producing land, with the largest beef cattle operation in the United States. King devoted some of her time to finding ways to breed heartier cattle and horses.

When the King ranch burned down in 1912, the family built a new home that cost $350,000 and took two years to construct. Although the home had lavish spaces for entertaining, Henrietta King made sure that no alcohol was served, in keeping with her religious beliefs.

Henrietta King died in 1925 and left an estate worth about $5 million. Her assets included 94,347 head of cattle, 3,782 horses, 802 mules, 355 goats, 595 sheep, and nearly 1 million acres of land.

Further Reading

"King, Henrietta Chamberlain." The Handbook of Texas Online. URL: http://www.tshassutexas.edu/handbook/online/articles/view/kk/fkille.html. Downloaded on August 12, 2001.

Led, Tom. *The King Ranch.* 2 vols. Boston, Little Brown, 1957.

✱ KLEIN, ANNE (Hannah Golofsky)
(1923–1974) *Fashion Designer, Entrepreneur*

Fashion designer Anne Klein revolutionized the fashion industry by her treatment of "juniors"-sized clothing and her collections of coordinated separates and upscale sportswear.

Born Hannah Golofsky in Brooklyn, New York, on August 3, 1923, she began working in fashion as a teenager when a wholesale fashion house hired her as a sketcher in 1938. She studied at the Trophagen School of Fashion. Golofsky, who used the first name Anne, married Ben Klein in 1939 and joined Varden Petites as the designer of its junior clothing lines. Shortly thereafter, she left to form her own company, Junior Sophisticates, with her husband. Her lines of upscale clothing for young women filled a gap between children's clothing and women's clothing and became quite popular during the late 1940s and the 1950s. She transformed the junior fashion industry.

In 1968, Klein formed another firm, Anne Klein & Company, which specialized in fashions for youthful women, including sophisticated sportswear that was praised for suiting the lifestyle of American women, many of whom were now looking for clothing they could wear to work. Klein's jersey dresses and jackets and her slim-waisted dresses were regarded as both fashionable and practical. They were sold in fine department stores. Her logo included a lion's head, which appeared on metal belt buckles, among other items. Klein also designed earrings featuring this design.

Anne Klein was one of the first designers to be given floor space within department stores expressly to display and sell her lines. She won the Coty American Fashion Critics' Award, the National Cotton Council Award, and other honors. In 1971, she was elected to the Coty American Fashion Awards Hall of Fame.

After Klein died of cancer in 1974, designer DONNA KARAN and Louis Dell'Olio created clothing for the Anne Klein label. During the 1990s, Richard Tyler was the head designer of Anne Klein, followed by Ken Kaufman and Isaac Franco.

Further Reading

Coleridge, Nicholas. *The Fashion Conspiracy: A Remarkable Journey Through the Empires of Fashion.* New York: Harper & Row, 1988.

Martin, Richard, editor. *Contemporary Fashion.* Farmington Hills, Mich.: Gale Group, 1995.

———. *The St. James Encyclopedia: A Survey of Style from 1945 to the Present.* Mt. Kisco, N.Y.: Visible Ink Press, 1996.

Peacock, John. *20th Century Fashion: The Complete Sourcebook.* London: Thames & Hudson, 1993.

Stegemeyer, Anne. *Who's Who in Fashion.* Fairchild Publications, 1995.

KNOX, ROSE MARKWARD
(1857–1950)   *Entrepreneur, Business Executive*

Once known as the grand old lady of American business, Knox ran a successful food products business that became the premier producer of gelatin, and she instituted progressive management policies.

Rose Markward was born on November 18, 1857, in Mansfield, Ohio, where her father, David, was a druggist and her mother, Amanda, was a homemaker. During the 1870s, the family moved to Gloverville, New York. After high school, she found a job sewing gloves. In 1883, she married Charles Briggs Knox, a salesman at the knit goods company. Knox was born in New York but had lived in Michigan and Texas, where he worked in the logging business and sheep business, respectively. His family had moved to Johnstown, New York, in 1876.

The couple, who settled in Newark, New Jersey, decided to save their money in order to start a business. Charles Knox had watched his wife carry out the tedious process of making gelatin and came up with the idea of making pregranulated gelatin so that people could simply add water, then use it in recipes. With $5,000, the couple opened a prepared gelatin business in Johnstown, New York, in 1890. The town was located near a rail line, and the region contained power sources they would need to manufacture gelatin, as well as the raw material Knox needed—collagen, a protein that comes from cattle and pigs.

In the early days, gelatin was considered a delicacy because it was so time-consuming to make at home. It was used to make foods for invalids who could not eat solids or to make elegant dishes like cold bouillon. The Knox product made gelatin much more convenient and easy to make. Still, during the early years, sales came slowly. Rose Knox later told a reporter, "In order that we might continue to eat three times a day, Mr. Knox went on the road selling gloves. And in his off hours, he would sell his own product."

The Knoxes set out to publicize powdered gelatin and help people learn more ways to use it. Charles Knox devised innovative and dramatic ways to promote his company and earned the nickname the Napoleon of Advertising. He put Knox Gelatine banners on the first motor car in New York State and on a hot-air balloon. During the presidential campaign of 1900, he had a banner strung across Herald Square in New York City that said "Bryan Wants to Win, McKinley Wants to Win, Knox Gelatine *Always* Wins!"

Rose Knox focused on providing information to homemakers, who were most likely to buy their product. She wrote a recipe book, *Dainty Desserts,* that showed numerous ways to use gelatin. A million copies circulated in 1896 when the booklet was first published, and the company continued to distribute millions of copies year after year. By 1900, the business had become quite successful and the family had built "Rose Hill," one of the most elegant homes in Johnstown.

After Charles Knox died of heart disease in 1908, Rose Knox, age 50 and the mother of two teenage sons, (a daughter had died in infancy) decided to take over as director. In a 1949 interview she said, "I either had to run the business myself or employ a manager. If I did the latter, I figured that by the time my boys came of age the business would belong to the manager." She sold off several other business ventures her husband had owned and focused squarely on the gelatin division and the homemakers who bought and used the product. To develop more gelatin recipes, she set up an experimental laboratory and publicized recipes on the package, as well as in leaflets and cookbooks.

As head of Knox Gelatine Company, one of the first changes Rose Knox made was to lock the back door of the building. She decreed that all employ-

As head of Knox Gelatine, the company she and her husband cofounded, Rose M. Knox tripled the company's profits between 1908 and 1915. (Photo courtesy of Kraft Foods; KNOX is a registered trademark of KF Holdings. Used with permission.)

ees, from top executives to janitors, would use the same door, saying, "We are all ladies and gentlemen working together here, and we'll all come in through the front door." She also asked for the resignation of a top administrative executive who had announced that he would not be willing to work for a woman.

Within a few years, Knox instituted new policies that included a five-day workweek, two weeks of annual vacation, and sick leave, all of which were rare in those years. As an executive, she was considered efficient and stern but fair, and her company experienced a low turnover of employees. Each morning, Knox herself arrived for work promptly at 9:30 A.M.

Under Rose Knox's direction, the company grew and prospered, and in 1911 it was moved into a larger plant. Knox's second book, *Food Economy*, published in 1917, contained new recipes. In addition, she wrote a newspaper column of recipes and household hints called "Mrs. Knox Says." The company's profits tripled by 1915, at which time it was a multimillion-dollar firm. A year later, Knox purchased a half-interest in Kind and Landesmann, a New Jersey company that sold Knox the ingredients for its product.

By 1925, the Knox Gelatine Company had a capitalization of $1 million. Rose Knox was named vice president of the combined company, Kind and Knox Gelatine Company, in 1936. The Knox company also managed to get through the Great Depression of the 1930s without laying off any employees. It was the leading distributor of gelatin and sold about 60 percent of its product to home and institutional consumers. The other 40 percent was sold for industrial and medical use.

One of the foremost businesswomen in the country, she became the first woman to attend a meeting of the Specialty Manufacturer's Association (forerunner of the American Grocery Manufacturers' Association [AGMA]) in 1911. At her first meeting, Knox chose to wear a plain black velvet dress with a high neck to show the association that she was a no-nonsense person. She also wore her trademark hat, something she wore to the office and even while testing recipes in the lab kitchen. It took 12 years before she was invited to become the association's first female member, and, in 1929, she was elected as the first female director of the AGMA as a member of the board. *Collier's Weekly* magazine called Knox "American's foremost woman industrialist," and in 1937 the New York State Federation of Business and Professional Women voted her the woman who had contributed most to American business. In an interview with a writer for the New York *World Telegram*, she said, "All I've had to guide me is just plain common sense in dealing with people. I've always tried to remember that molasses catches more flies than vinegar." She also said, "Every woman, if forced to, can do more than she ever thought she could."

Knox made time for civic affairs and philanthropic activities. She bought a mansion in Johnstown and gave it to the Presbyterian Church to be used as a home for elderly women, and she also donated money to the African Methodist Episcopal Church so they could build a Sunday school room. In addition, she donated money to the YMCA, the local board of education, and the city of Johnstown for the construction of the Knox Athletic Field. She belonged to the Business and Professional Women's Club and the Johnstown Historical Society. Knox also enjoyed raising flowers, especially exotic orchids, and had about 2,000 orchid plants in her greenhouse. She gave orchids to the women of her acquaintance for their wedding bouquets. Knox built this hobby into a successful business, too, growing plants for sale.

Knox was active in her later years, both as a businessperson and in her personal life. At age 80, she traveled alone on a 30-day cruise to South America. In 1946, 88-year-old Rose Markward Knox resigned as president of the company, although she remained chairperson of the board. By then, arthritis had confined her to working from home. Her son Charles had died in his mid-twenties and her other son, James, took over the presidency but said that his mother was still in charge and that she was writing ads and recipes and signing all checks. When employees gave her a party on her 90th birthday, Knox said, "My life has been made up of sunshine and shadows, but the glory of work in the home and out of the home has had a very interesting side and has helped to keep me young."

Knox died in Johnstown on September 27, 1950. She was survived by her son James, four grandchildren, and six great-grandchildren. James Knox became chairman of the board of directors; at his death in 1958, his son John took over the presidency of Knox Gelatine.

As of 1998, the plant near Sergeant Bluff, Iowa, that produces gelatin for the Knox company was the largest in the world, producing 24 million to 25 million pounds of dry granular gelatin each year. The gelatin is used not only in food products such as marshmallows, spices, candy, and apple juice, but also to make camera film, medical X rays, and pharmaceutical capsules, and to coat the paper used in ink-jet printers. In 1994, the Knox Gelatine Company became a division of Nabisco, now part of Kraft Foods, Inc., North America's largest food company.

Further Reading

Bowman, J. S., editor. *The Cambridge Dictionary of American Biography.* New York: Cambridge University Press, 1995.

Forbes, Malcolm. *Women Who Made a Difference.* New York: Simon and Schuster, 1990.

"Knox Gelatine Marks Its 100-Year Anniversary." Courtesy of Knox Gelatine Company, a division of Kraft Foods, 1990.

"Mrs. Rose M. Knox, Pioneer Businesswoman." Knox Gelatine, Inc., Diamond Jubilee Publication, 1965.

"Rose M. Knox: The Businesswoman, Her Civic Pride, Many Honors Bestowed Upon Her." Available online. URL: http://www.johnstown.com/city/knoxbsns.html. Downloaded on May 1, 2001.

The Gelita Companies. "History of Kind and Knox Gelatine." Available online. URL: http://www.gelita.com/kind&knox/history.htm. Downloaded on November 4, 2001.

✳ KOPLOVITZ, KAY SMITH
(1945–) *Executive, Business Owner*

Kay Koplovitz became the first female network president in television history and made significant contributions to the growth of mass media.

Kay Smith was born on April 11, 1945, in Milwaukee, Wisconsin. She was already interested in television when she enrolled at the University of Wisconsin, where she received a bachelor of science degree (B.S.) in psychology and communications in 1967. In 1968, she received her master's degree (M.S.) in communications from Michigan State University and married William C. Koplovitz Jr., an attorney and corporate executive. Along the way, she worked in various radio and television jobs, learning different aspects of these businesses. After receiving her master's degree, she gained experience in producing and directing,

worked as a broadcast analyst, and helped to start a public relations firm.

When her boss asked Koplovitz to find a new way to broadcast sports events via satellite, she became the first to negotiate national cable rights with the National Hockey League (NHL), National Basketball Association (NBA), and Major League Baseball. Her independent cable network, MSG Sports, became USA Cable Network in 1977 and she became both chairman and chief executive officer (CEO), making her the first woman to become a network president. The USA network was TV's first advertiser-supported basic cable network.

In 1980, she resolved to draw more viewers and build the network, so Koplovitz considered what segments of the population were likely to watch at various times of the day. She then acquired popular off-network series and theatrical movie packages geared for those viewers. USA also began airing its own original movies and miniseries. Her strategy, and the growing financial success of the USA network, attracted investors, including Dow Jones, Time Inc., Paramount Pictures, and MCA. Koplovitz went on to found the Sci-Fi Channel in 1992. She launched USA International two years later and by 1998 it was operating in Latin America, Europe, and Southern Africa. By the end of the 1990s, the USA network was the largest provider of original programming among the basic cable networks. About 74 percent of all households subscribed to USA in 1998.

Kay Koplovitz is also known for her public-interest activities. In 1990, together with the Partnership for a Drug-Free America, she led an industry-wide antidrug inititiative. Four years later, she launched a program called Erase the Hate, which aims to combat racism and other types of bigotry. USA Networks has continued this public affairs initiative, which received an Emmy Award and praise from the U.S. Senate. With support from the national YMCA and the Anti-Defamation League (ADL), April 30 has been designated as National Erase the Hate and Eliminate Racism Day. In 1997, the network presented its National Hate Test to help viewers identify their own biases regarding people of other races, religions, sexual orientations, and disabilities. In an interview with Karen Gibbs, Koplovitz said, "I can help because people have a voice, because we have television networks. We do reach the public. We're a platform." In recognition of her contributions, the ADL gave Koplovitz its Champion of Liberty Award in 1998. Her other honors include the Action for Children's Television award in 1979 and the Matrix Women in Communications award in 1983.

In June 1998, Koplovitz was sworn in as chair of the National Women's Business Council. President Bill Clinton appointed her to serve a four-year term. Koplovitz noted that in 1998, women-owned businesses received only 2 percent of all venture-capital money, and said that she aimed to make sure women entrepreneurs had more access: "It's very important that women don't miss out on another major round of financing. As chair of the council, I've started a series of venture-capital forums for women entrepreneurs. . . . We have to take down a few barriers and open the doors."

That year, Koplovitz retired from the USA network. Describing her achievements, media mogul Barry Diller, who had bought the network, praised "her consistency of management" and said that "her style and substance all underscore just how first rate an executive, and person, she is." Koplovitz said, "I've had a wonderful twenty years building USA Network into the top-rated cable network, and launching Sci-Fi channel into nearly 50 million homes."

Koplovitz embarked on new business ventures. In 1999, she founded Koplovitz & Co., a firm that invests in high-growth new media companies. In 2001, she became CEO of the Working Woman Network, which publishes *Working Woman* and *Working Mother* magazines and provides goods and services for millions of entrepreneurial, corporate, and professional women around the world.

Koplovitz has served on the board of Nabisco Holdings Corp., Inc.; Liz Claiborne, Inc.; and Oracle. She is a member of the board of trustees for the Museum of Television and Radio, Junior Achievement, and the Tennis Hall of Fame.

Further Reading

Bushey, Christine. USA Network CEO Interview. MSNBC Business Video. November 25, 1997.

Cooper, Jim. "The USA According to Kay," *Brandweek*, May 4, 1998, pp. 4–6.

Gibbs, Karen. "USA Networks Chairwoman and CEO—Interview." *The Cavuto Business Report*, Fox News Network transcript. April 30, 1998.

Griffin, Cynthia E. "Girls Just Wanna Have Funds," *Entrepreneur*, March 2000. Available online. URL: http://www.entrepreneur.com/Magazines/Copy of MA SegArticle/0,4453,233153----1-,00.html. Downloaded on June 5, 2001.

Richard, Ray. "Koplovitz Waves a Steady Flag for USA," *Variety*, October 27, 1997, pp. 60–61.

Rosenberg, Jill. "Giving Back." *Fast Company*. December 12, 1999, p. 109.

Sander, Jennifer Basye. "On Your Own." *USA Today*, May 30, 2000. Available online. URL: http://www.usatoday.com/small/on/on049.htm. Downloaded on November 20, 2001.

KURTZIG, SANDRA
(1947–) *Entrepreneur, Executive*

Sandra Kurtzig is a pioneer entrepreneur whose software company—ASK Computer Systems, Inc.—became the largest publicly owned company founded and run by a woman.

Born in Chicago in 1947, Sandra Kurtzig is the daughter of a real-estate developer father and author mother. In 1958, the family moved to California, and Kurtzig attended the University of California at Los Angeles, where she earned a bachelor's degree in both chemistry and math. She then attended Stanford University, where she earned her master's degree in aeronautical engineering.

After graduation, she worked in marketing and technical positions at General Electric and TRW corporations. As a newlywed living in Atherton, California, in 1972, Kurtzig decided to start a small business working from home. Her starting capital was the $2,000 severance check from her previous job. She expected to work part time while raising her children.

With some knowledge of computer programming and software applications, she decided to develop software programs for businesses, including minicomputer programs and information systems that could help manufacturers with quality control. Her new company, ASK Computer, was born. Kurtzig's first assignment was to automate the circulation department of a suburban newspaper that had 1,200 delivery people. Realizing that other companies could use similar software, Kurtzig worked with some talented engineering and computer graduates to create these kinds of programs. To fund her company, Kurtzig sought help from venture capital firms, but they declined to invest in her company. Since her staff needed to work on minicomputers, she was able to obtain permission from executives at Hewlett-Packard (HP) to let them use HP's machines after hours, during the night. By 1978, ASK was able to offer its first products, a set of programs called Manman (for "manufacturing management").

Kurtzig also began working with several small firms and expanded her work with computer giant Hewlett-Packard. As her business grew, Kurtzig worked hard to remain debt-free in the process. Sales rose rapidly, growing from $2.8 million in 1979 to $39 million in 1983. Shares of ASK went public in 1981, and Kurtzig's holdings were worth about $65 million in 1983.

In 1985, she resigned as chief executive officer (CEO) of the company, which was then called the ASK Group, Inc., in order to spend more time with her growing sons. She was persuaded to return, however, in 1989 when the board asked her to help them reposition and expand the company. Back at ASK, Kurtzig refined the management team and helped the company reengineer its software to run on various computers. Revenues increased dramatically, reaching $450 million in sales for 1992. The next year, once again, Kurtzig retired from the business.

In 1994, the company was purchased by Computer Associates International, Inc. In 1997, ASK Computer reported $100 million in annual sales. Kurtzig is now chairman of the board of E-benefits, an insurance and human resources service provider she founded with her son Andrew in 1996. She lives in San Francisco.

Further Reading

Deutschman, Alan. "Fortune People: Why Sandy Returned to Her Baby," *Fortune,* November 6, 1989, p. 195.

Kurtzig, Sandra. *CEO: How to Build a $400 Million Company from the Ground Up.* Cambridge, Mass.: Harvard Business Press, 1994.

Schumacher, Mary Louise. "Sandra Kurtzig: Multiple Success: Establishing Company, Raising Two Sons," Mercury Center, *San Jose Mercury News* on the Web. Available online. URL: http://www0.mercurycenter.com/archives/womenhistory/skurtzig12.htm. Downloaded on December 14, 2000.

Wawro, Thaddeus. "Hero Worship: Sandra Kurtzig, Founder of ASK Computer Systems, Inc.," *Entrepreneur,* March 2000.

L

LA FORGE, MARGARET SWAIN GETCHELL

(1841–1880)   *Executive*

Getchell rose from the position of bookkeeper to become superintendent of Macy's, the famous New York City department store. Under Getchell, the store tripled in size. She often said that much of her business success came from following these principles: "Be everywhere, do everything, and never fail to astonish the customer."

Born on Nantucket, an island off the coast of Massachusetts, in 1841, Margaret Getchell became a schoolteacher while still in her teens. However, because of a childhood accident, she lost the sight in one eye and had to start wearing a glass eye at that time. She decided to leave her teaching job for New York City, where she went to work for her distant cousin, Rowland Hussey Macy. In 1858, Macy had opened a new, fancy dry-goods, one-entrance store on Sixth Avenue.

Getchell rented a room on Sixth Avenue in 1860 and worked as a cashier at Macy's store, which then sold laces, ribbons, and other accessories. Often, she stayed in the evening to help her cousin with the bookkeeping and to discuss the operation of the store. Getchell suggested new ways to promote merchandise, and she advised Macy to expand the store's inventory, adding clothing, toiletries, hats, and jewelry.

In 1864, Getchell, who had moved into the Macy family home, was named bookkeeper. It was the third-highest position at the store, after the superintendent and Rowland Macy himself. Getchell continued to make suggestions to expand and improve the store. As a result, Macy's began to offer its growing number of customers groceries, toiletries, jewelry, furs, toys, and household goods.

In 1866, Getchell was promoted to the rank of superintendent, which made her the first woman in New York—possibly in the nation—to head a major retail store. Ralph M. Hower, who interviewed people who had worked with her, said that they "still speak of her remarkable executive ability and attractive personality." Getchell supported plans to further expand Macy's, which soon occupied the entire blockfront between Thirteenth and Fourteenth Streets. By 1869, sales topped $1 million and Macy's employed 200 people. Within a few years, the store was also selling books, candy,

At age 25, Margaret Getchell La Forge became superintendent of Macy's store in 1866, making her America's first female retailing executive.
(Photo courtesy of Macy's)

and more home furnishings, such as silver, glassware, and china. By 1875, they had added sewing machines, rugs, art objects, luggage, shoes, and more ready-to-wear items for adults and children.

Getchell was known for her innovative and colorful window displays and other advertising techniques. One of her most successful ideas was installing a soda fountain deep inside the store so customers would pass by numerous displays of merchandise as they made their way to this refreshment area.

In 1869, Getchell married Abiel La Forge, a former Civil War captain and a friend of Rowland Macy's son. La Forge became a buyer at Macy's,

and the couple lived in a five-room apartment located on a floor above the store. In a letter to his sister, La Forge wrote proudly of his wife, "She is the Superintendent, having full charge of the entire business; as we sell a million dollars worth of goods a year and have nearly two hundred employees, her position is a very responsible one."

After her marriage, Margaret Getchell La Forge bore six children, including a set of twins. She became less active at the store but still worked there during the busy holiday season and inventory time and took full charge three months each year when Macy and Abiel La Forge, who was made a partner in 1871, went on buying trips to Europe.

When Rowland Macy died in 1877, he left one of his nephews and Abiel La Forge in charge. However, Abiel died of tuberculosis the next year, and Macy's nephew bought Margaret La Forge's share of the store for $82,500.

In 1880, when she was only 38 years old, Margaret Getchell La Forge died of heart disease and other health problems.

Further Reading

Hower, Ralph M. *History of Macy's of New York, 1858–1919.* Cambridge, Mass.: Harvard University Press, 1946.

Hungerford, Edward. *The Romance of a Great Store.* New York: Robert M. McBride & Co., 1922.

Johnson, Curtiss S. *Macy's Founding Geniuses, Book II: America's First Lady Boss.* Ellinwood, Kans.: Macy's of Ellinwood, 1985.

Reilly, Philip J. *Old Masters of Retailing: A History of Merchant Pioneers and the Industry They Built.* New York: Fairchild Publications, 1966.

✳ LANSING, SHERRY LEE HEIMANN
(1944–) *Executive*

As chairman and chief executive officer (CEO) of the Paramount Motion Picture Group, Sherry Lansing has been called the most powerful woman in Hollywood. In May 2000, Lansing was ranked as the seventh most powerful person in Hollywood for the second consecutive year.

Sherry Lee Heimann was born on July 31, 1944, and grew up in Chicago, Illinois. After her father died of a heart attack when Sherry was nine, her mother, Margot, who had escaped from Nazi Germany at age 17, had to support herself and two daughters. Margot Heimann went into the real estate business, even though she had no previous experience, and Sherry was impressed by the way her mother learned the business and acquired financial independence. Her mother later married Norton Lansing, whose last name Sherry adopted. A gifted student, Sherry Lansing attended the University of Chicago Laboratory High School.

Sherry Lansing majored in theater at Northwestern University, where she was married before graduation. Since childhood, she had loved movies, and her strong interest in filmmaking led the couple to move to Los Angeles, California, after she received her bachelor's degree in 1966. There, she taught math, English, and drama at a Los Angeles high school in Watts for four years, then became a model for Max Factor cosmetics and Alberto-Culver hair products and acted briefly on television and in a film. She was divorced in 1970.

Lansing, who thought she was a poor actress, decided to focus on nonacting aspects of the film industry and became a script reader, working at night for five dollars an hour, then learning other skills as a script editor for Metro-Goldwyn-Mayer (MGM). She took film courses at UCLA and the University of Southern California and rose to the position of vice-president of creative affairs at MGM. After going to Columbia Pictures in 1979, Lansing was promoted to increasingly higher positions in the film industry and eventually produced such well-received films as *The China Syndrome* (1979) and *Kramer vs. Kramer* (1979).

In 1980, at age 35, Lansing became the first woman to head production at a major studio, 20th-Century Fox. After three years, Lansing left Fox to become an independent film producer. She and Stanley Jaffe formed Jaffe-Lansing Productions in 1983, and their company produced several hit films, including *Fatal Attraction* (1987) and *The Accused* (1989).

In 1991, Lansing remarried. She has commented that since her husband, director William

Friedkin, is in the movie business he understands her work.

In 1992, Lansing was named the head of Paramount Motion Pictures—the first time a woman had ever chaired a movie studio. At Paramount, she produced *Indecent Proposal* (1993), *The Firm* (1993), and *Forrest Gump* (1994). Paramount also coproduced the blockbuster film *Titanic* with Fox (1997). During the late 1990s–2001, Lansing had more film hits with *Double Jeopardy* (1999), *Mission Impossible* (2000), *Tomb Raider* (2001), and *The Original Kings of Comedy* (2001). She was widely regarded as one of the top producers in her industry and the most influential woman in the film business.

In an article for *Premiere* magazine in November 2000, She told Anne Thompson, "My days are all about getting movies made, making sure while they're shooting that they're realizing everything we want, then [overseeing] their marketing and distribution."

Further Reading

Abramowitz, Rachel. *Is That a Gun in Your Pocket? Women's Experience of Power in Hollywood.* New York: Random House, 2000.

Hall, Carla. "Sherry Lansing, Living On Hollywood's Front Lines," *Newsday,* September 23, 1992, p. 49.

Jennet, Conant. "Sherry Lansing (Chairwoman of Paramount Pictures' Motion Picture Group)," *Harper's Bazaar,* January 1994, pp. 112–14.

Seger, Linda. *When Women Call the Shots.* New York: Henry Holt, 1996.

Thompson, Anne. "Sherry Lansing," in Women of Hollywood, *Premiere,* November 2000, p. 83.

Wechsler, Pat. "Succeeding Tartikoff in Top Spot," *Newsday,* November 5, 1992, p. 79.

✳ LAUDER, ESTÉE
(Josephine Esther Mentzer)
(1909–) *Entrepreneur, Business Owner, Executive*

Estée Lauder cofounded the world-famous prestige beauty products company that bears her name in

Beauty industry gaint Estēe Lauder, shown here sampling fragrances in her New York office, has taken an active role in developing products.
(Photo courtesy of Estēe Lauder)

1946. By the 1990s, Estēe Lauder brands controlled 45 percent of the cosmetics market in U.S. department stores, and they were the top-selling department store beauty products in the world.

She was born Josephine Esther Mentzer on July 1, 1908, in Corona (Queens), New York, to a Hungarian-born mother and Czech-born father. Although her family always called her Esty, she later became known as Estēe. As a child, Estēe took an interest in beauty routines and hairstyling and enjoyed watching her mother apply makeup. Her mother's brother, John Schotz, was a chemist who had moved to the United States, where he made and sold his skin preparations, including face cream, cleansers, and skin fresheners. People often praised teenage Estēe's complexion, and she credited her uncle's products and treatment techniques. Later she

helped him sell these products and gained additional business experience by working in her father's hardware store.

In 1930, she married Joseph Lauder, and the couple moved to Manhattan. During the early 1930s, Estēe Lauder briefly studied acting then opened a beauty concession in a hair salon in Manhattan and also sold the products she had developed in hotels on Long Island. The Lauders were divorced in 1939. For several years, Estēe Lauder lived in Florida and sold her uncle's skin care products in resorts and hotels. After she remarried Joseph in 1943, the couple began selling these products together and formed a company bearing her name in 1946. The initial product line included four skin care products. Their family grew to include two sons: Leonard, who was born in 1933 and Ronald, who arrived in 1944.

Lauder enthusiastically promoted her products and worked hard to gain counter space in department stores. She had decided to offer her cosmetics in department and specialty stores rather than the less prestigious drugstore market. In 1948, the company obtained its first department store account, at Saks Fifth Avenue in New York. Others soon followed. Stanley Marcus, former president of Neiman Marcus, later recalled his meeting with Lauder in 1950: "She came to see me late one afternoon . . . and she introduced herself. 'I'm Estée Lauder and I have the most wonderful beauty products in the world and they must be in your store.'" She had brought along her own merchandise and set it up the next day, making personal contact with customers who came into the department.

Working with a limited advertising budget, she decided to spend that money on samples, mailing customers invitations asking them to stop by an Estée Lauder counter for a free gift. Customers who bought Lauder products also received free samples of other products, or "gifts-with-purchase." These methods worked, and sales grew steadily. While Estée Lauder focused on product development and marketing, Joseph Lauder became the director of factory production and oversaw the company's finances.

Lauder achieved a major success in 1953 when she introduced her famous Youth-Dew fragrance. Youth-Dew earned about $50,000 for the company and remains popular. Another winning product was Re-Nutriv cream, introduced in 1957, priced at $115 a pound and advertised as a "creme of creams" that contained "rare ingredients" and "youth-giving agents."

In 1957, Estée Lauder employed five people and grossed $850,000 in sales; in 1960, the company posted $1 million in sales for the first time, a figure that grew to $100 million in 1972. The company moved into larger headquarters at the General Motors Building in Manhattan, and Lauder conducted business from a spacious office where she could also visit with family and friends. Carol Phillips, who later helped to launch the Clinique product line, once described the com-

fortable atmosphere in Lauder's office, saying that it contained "all the pleasant things that go with running a household."

During the 1960s, the company became international. Lauder continued to introduce new products, including a men's line, Aramis, in 1965. Four years later, the company also created its Clinique line of hypoallergenic lotions, cleansers, and toners as part of a total skin care program. Clinique salespeople wore white coats that resembled those worn in a laboratory and offered customers a "skin care analysis." Later, Clinique added color cosmetics and fragrances.

Throughout the 1960s and 1970s, Lauder was actively involved in various aspects of the business, including ad campaigns. Lauder ads have featured classically beautiful models in elegant settings. In 1962, the company began choosing a model as the "face of Estée Lauder" to represent its products in media campaigns. These top models have included Karen Graham, Willow Bay, Paulina Porizkova, and Elizabeth Hurley. Lauder also paid close attention to product design. For instance, she chose a particular shade of blue for Estée Lauder packages because she thought that color would work with the decor of most bathrooms and bedrooms.

Estée Lauder retired as head of the company in 1995. Her son Leonard, who had officially joined the company in 1958, served as president from 1972 to 1995 and as chief executive officer from 1982 to 1999. He has been chairman since 1995. Ronald Lauder serves as chairman of Clinique Laboratories, Inc., and chairman of Estée Lauder International, Inc. Lauder's daughter-in-law and grandchildren have also worked in the company, which went public in 1995. Estée Lauder continued to make personal visits to department store counters until her health declined in the 1990s.

By 2001, the Estée Lauder Companies had grown into a nearly $5 billion cosmetics empire with 16 brands. Lauder products are sold in more than 120 countries and territories around the world. The lines include Estée Lauder, Clinique,

Aramis, Prescriptives, Bobbi Brown, *jane* (a line of cosmetics aimed at teenagers), Aveda (distributed in thousands of beauty salons), and Origins botanical products. Three lines—Aramis, Clinique, and Lauder for Men—offer men's products. Aramis also developed the Tommy Hilfiger franchise, which includes men's fragrances. New Lauder products are launched regularly, including fragrances such as Alliage (1972), Private Collection (1973), White Linen (1978), Beautiful (1985) and Estée Lauder *Pleasures* (1995). Men's fragrances include Aramis, Aramis 900, and JHL.

Lauder has received numerous honors through the years. In 1967, the American Business Women's Association (ABWA) named her one of 10 outstanding women in business in the United States. She also received the Cosmetic Executive Women's President's Award for excellence in her field in 1989 and the Neiman Marcus Award for Distinguished Service in the Field of Fashion in 1962 and 1992. The American Society of Perfumers gave her its first Living Legend award in 1994. She has contributed generously to various charitable causes, including many civic and cultural programs. The Lauder Foundation built several children's playgrounds in New York City's Central Park. The family also donated money to the French government for the restoration of the palace at Versailles.

Leonard Lauder once said that the word *ambition* best explains his mother's great success and that she "was determined to give women the opportunity to feel beautiful."

Further Reading

La Ferla, Ruth. "The Young Woman Most Invited," *The New York Times,* March 28, 1999, Section 9, p. 1, 7.

Lauder, Estée. *Estée: A Success Story.* New York: Random House, 1994.

Munk, Nina. "Why Women Find Lauder Mesmerizing," *Fortune,* May 25, 1998.

Roth, Gil Y. "Aramis Takes U-Turn in Men's Market," *Happi,* February 1998. Available online. URL: http://www.happi.com.special/feb982.html. Downloaded on April 2, 2000.

Salmans, Sandra. "Estee Lauder: The Scents of Success," *The New York Times,* April 18, 1982.

✻ LAWRENCE, MARY WELLS
(Mary Georgene Berg)
(1928–)   *Executive, Business Owner*

During the 1960s, Mary Wells Lawrence rose to the top of the male-dominated advertising business and cofounded an agency known for its creative and dynamic campaigns. She once said of the advertising profession that "you have to be learning all the time. . . . you have to see, hear, and read everything."

The only child of a furniture salesman and homemaker, Mary Georgene Berg was born in Youngstown, Ohio, on May 25, 1928. As a child, she was shy, so her parents enrolled her in drama and dance lessons, and she considered becoming an actress. At age 17, she went to New York and studied at the Neighborhood Playhouse School of the Theater. Berg then spent two years at the Carnegie Institute of Technology in Pittsburgh, Pennsylvania. In 1949, she married Burt Wells, an industrial design student at the institute who later became art director for the advertising firm of Ogilvy & Mather. They lived in Youngstown where Mary Wells was hired to write advertising copy at McKelvey's Department Store.

The couple moved to New York City in 1952, and Mary Wells became the fashion advertising manager at Macy's department store. A year later, she landed a job as writer and copy group head at the advertising agency of McCann-Erickson, Inc. She remained there until 1956, then worked briefly for Lennen & Newell Advertising before accepting a job at the famous ad agency of Doyle Dane Bernbach (DDB), where she advanced to the position of chief copywriter. In 1963, she was named vice president of the company. While at DDB, she worked on the Avis and Volkswagen accounts. One of her most famous ad lines was for the Warner's girdle: "Slip into something comfortable and take two inches off your waistline." She became known as a brilliant and creative force in the business.

In 1964, Wells, now divorced, left DDB to become senior partner at Jack Tinker & Partners, an agency known for its creative and innovative advertising. Her salary was $60,000, a first for a woman in advertising and more than six times the average salary for American men at that time. Moreover, the vast majority of executives on Madison Avenue were men, so her advancement was even more remarkable.

At DDB, Wells often worked with copywriter Richard Rich and artist Steward Greene, and this team developed some memorable and popular ads, known particularly for their humor. Among their creations were television commercials for Alka-Seltzer, Benson & Hedges cigarettes, and Braniff International Airlines, which was struggling to survive during that time. For Alka-Seltzer, makers of products for indigestion, she and her partners came up with a humorous television ad that showed the abdomens of various people, including a heavyset man operating a jackhammer. The ad was accompanied by a jingle with the famous line: "No matter what shape your stomach's in." Wells drew attention to her client American Motors by commissioning two trendy designers, Emilio Pucci and Pierre Cardin, to design interiors for the cars.

For Braniff, she had bold designs painted on the outsides of their planes, as well as adding colorful designer interiors. Wells hired designer Alexander Girard to spruce up Braniff's terminals, and she had Emilio Pucci design vibrant new uniforms for the flight attendants. They featured short skirts and jersey prints in shades of pink, melon, turquoise, and green.

In 1966, Wells and her two colleagues left DDB to form their own advertising firm, Wells, Rich, Greene, Inc. They signed Braniff and other large accounts and became one of the most prominent ad agencies in the country. Mary Wells became Mary Wells Lawrence when she married the chairman of Braniff Airlines, Harding L. Lawrence, in 1967.

In an interview with *Newsweek* magazine in 1966, Wells said, "People are very sophisticated about advertising now. You have to entertain them. You have to present a product honestly and with a tremendous amount of pizzazz and flair, the way it's done in a James Bond movie. But you can't run the same ad over and over again. You have to change your approach constantly to keep

on getting their attention." Her new company specialized in television ads and came up with some classic lines, such as "I can't believe I ate the whole thing" for Alka-Seltzer during the early 1970s. They also developed these well-known lines: "At Ford, Quality is Job 1," "Trust the Midas touch," and "Raise your hand if you're Sure" (for Sure deodorant). Their Benson & Hedges ad showed the "disadvantages" of smoking an extra-long cigarette—for example, getting them stuck in car windows. These ads conveyed the message that such things were minor inconveniences, because the cigarettes were so good and long-lasting. Between 1966 and 1970, sales of Benson & Hedges rose from 1.6 billion units to 14.4 billion.

Mary Wells Lawrence served as president, chairman of the board, and chief executive officer (CEO) of the company; by 1969, her annual salary had risen to $250,000. That year, she became the youngest member of the Copywriter's Hall of Fame. Wells, Rich, Greene, Inc. boasted the fastest growth any ad agency had ever experienced, when it reached $100 million in billings just five years after it opened. In 1971, the American Advertising Federation named Lawrence advertising woman of the year. She served on the boards of May Company Department Stores and the American Film Institute.

During its 32-year history, her agency's other major clients included Cadbury Schweppes, International Business Machines (IBM), MCI Communications, the New York State Board of Tourism, Pan American World Airways, Procter & Gamble, the Ralston Purina Company, Royal Crown Cola, TWA, and Sheraton Hotels. The company did lose one big account in 1972 when American Motors took its $22 million annual advertising budget to another agency.

Feminist leaders who thought she should speak out more about feminist issues and promote more women to top positions at her firm sometimes criticized Wells. In 1976, she said, "I'm not a feminist, not in the serious, activist sense, but I have a very strong feminist feeling about things like the

Equal Rights Amendment and salaries. I feel strongly about the unfairness that exists. A lot is changing, though."

Some women who pursued business careers in later decades have called Lawrence their role model. At age 25, Ann Tynion, now president and CEO Unicorn Financial Services, Inc., worked on a "think tank" advertising project with Lawrence. Tynion later said, "She had a tremendous amount of capabilities, but also the ability to be a woman. I learned from her to be smart, have a presence about you, be loyal to clients and know your business."

In 1990, Wells retired from the advertising business, and Wells, Rich, Greene was sold to the French advertising giant Boulet Dru Dupuy Petit (BDDP). During the next few years, the firm experienced management problems and lost major accounts, including Procter and Gamble. It was finally closed in 1998.

After her retirement, Mary Wells Lawrence and her husband, Harding Lawrence, spent their time at various homes in the United States and Europe. In 2000, she was inducted into the American Advertising Federation's Advertising Hall of Fame. Harding Lawrence died in January 2002. Mary Wells Lawrence had been writing her autobiography, which was to be published in spring 2002.

Further Reading

Braniff International. "Mary Wells—Wells, Rich, Greene." Available online. URL: http://www.braniffinternational. org/people/mary_wells.htm. Downloaded on January 5, 2001.

Fox, Stephen. *The Mirror Makers: A History of American Advertising and Its Creators.* New York: William Morrow, 1984.

Lawrence, Mary Wells. *A Big Life in Advertising.* New York: Knopf, 2002.

Lazarus, George. "All's Still Well for Ad Pioneer Mary Wells," *Chicago Tribune,* March 22, 2000, p. 3.

Meyers, William. *The Image Makers: Power and Persuasion on Madison Avenue.* New York: Times Books, 1984.

Northwood University Distinguished Women. "Mary Wells Lawrence." Available online. URL: http:www. northwood.edu/dw/1971/lawrence.html. Downloaded on December 20, 2000.

LAYBOURNE, GERRY (Geraldine Bond)
(1947–) *Executive*

Gerry Laybourne has held several key positions in television, including president of Nickelodeon/Nick at Nite, vice chair of MTV Networks (the parent division of Nickelodeon), and president of Disney/ABC Cable Networks.

Born on May 19, 1947, in Plainfield, New Jersey, Geraldine Bond was most interested in math and science as a child. Later, she found her interests changing, and she received her bachelor of arts (B.A.) degree in art history from Vassar College and her master of science (M.S.) degree in elementary education from the University of Pennsylvania. She married Kit Laybourne, a professional animator, in 1970, and their daughter Emmy was born in 1971.

During the 1970s, Laybourne held a variety of jobs in education and in the media. She taught at Concord Academy in Massachusetts from 1972 to 1973 and worked as festival coordinator for the American Film Festival in New York from 1974 to 1976. Next, Laybourne helped to found the Media Center for Children, where she worked from 1974 to 1977. She and her husband then worked on independent productions for children's television, including a new cable network called Nickelodeon.

In 1980, Laybourne joined Nickelodeon as program manager. As a mother of two children, she had ideas about what children would like to watch. Over the next 13 years, she steadily rose to higher positions at the network. At Laybourne's suggestion, the network involved young people in the process of developing ideas. Nickelodeon's team of young advisers came up with *Clarissa Explains It All* and other popular shows. In an interview with Jonathan Sapers, Laybourne said, "I built a team of people and we got into the hearts and minds of kids in a very short time."

To expand into evening hours, Laybourne programmed "Nick at Nite," beginning in 1985. It offered family entertainment in the form of reruns of classic television series, including *I Love Lucy, The Andy Griffith Show, The Dick Van Dyke Show,*

123

and *Dragnet*. The following year, Laybourne was named president of Nickelodeon/Nick at Nite. Six years later, she was named vice chairman of MTV Networks, owned by Viacom.

During her 16 years at Nickolodeon, Laybourne developed innovative and popular shows such as *You Can't Do That on Television* and *Double Dare*. Nickelodeon reportedly grew to $355 million in annual earnings, including ad revenues, monthly subscriber fees, and licensing and merchandising of related products, including toys and *Nickelodeon* magazine. By the 1990s, Nickelodeon had its own production studio, located at Universal Studios in Orlando, Florida, and was drawing a larger audience of child viewers than ABC, CBS, NBC, and FOX combined. Laybourne was elected to the Broadcasting and Cable Hall of Fame in 1995.

In 1996, Gerry Laybourne became president of Disney/ABC Cable Networks, which gave her the responsibility for programming the Disney Channel, Lifetime, A & E, the History Channel, and E! Entertainment. That year, *Time* magazine called Laybourne one of the 25 most influential people in America. In 1999, the *Hollywood Reporter* called her one of the 50 most influential women in the entertainment industry.

In 2000, Laybourne took on yet another new position in media as the chief executive officer (CEO) of Oxygen Media, the multimedia company with offices in New York, Chicago, Los Angeles, San Francisco, and Seattle. Laybourne called this venture, which includes a cable station and cluster of websites, "a new way of connecting with modern women" and delivering practical information for women's lives. Her husband, Kit, is creative director.

Laybourne also sits on a number of committees: the National Endowment for Children's Television, the National Council for Families and Television, New York Women in Film & Television, Cable in the Classroom, Children Now, Cable Positive, Children Affected by AIDS Foundation, the Annual Family Life Awards, the American Center for Children's Television, Bank of America's Women's Banking Initiative Advisory Council, and the Creative Coalition.

Further Reading

Business/Finance: The LHJ 100. *Ladies' Home Journal.* November 1999, p. 170.

Sapers, Jonathan. "Geraldine 'Gerry' Laybourne," Women to Watch—women's wire on the Web. Available online. URL: http://www.womenswire.com/watch/laybourne. html. Downloaded on March 17, 2001.

Shortt, Denise, Emma Smith, and JoAnn Napier. *Technology with Curves: Women Reshaping the Digital Landscape.* New York: HarperCollins, 2001.

✳ LAZARUS, SHELLY (Rochelle Braff)
(1947–) *Executive*

As chairman and chief executive officer (CEO) of Ogilvy & Mather Worldwide, the world's sixth-largest advertising agency, Shelly Lazarus is one of the most prominent executives in the advertising industry, overseeing a company that has annual billings of about $7.6 billion.

Rochelle Braff was born and raised in Oceanside, New York, the oldest of three children. Her father was an accountant and her mother was a homemaker. Shelly was an excellent student who enjoyed writing for and editing the school newspaper. In 1960, the family moved to Brooklyn, where Shelly attended Midwood High School. At Smith College in Northampton, Massachusetts, she majored in psychology and earned her bachelor of science (B.S.) degree in 1968. She later recalled that her interest in the advertising business was sparked in her senior year when she heard a lecture sponsored by the Advertising Women of New York.

She married George Lazarus, whom she had met while he was attending Yale University. While he studied medicine, Shelly Lazarus pursued her master of business administration (M.B.A.) degree at Columbia University in New York City. She received it in 1970 and became assistant product manager at Clairol. When she sought a position in advertising, she was rejected for reasons of gender. In a 1995 interview with *USA Today*, Lazarus recalled that one interviewer told her, "We'd love to give you a job, but what would our account executives' wives say when you had to work late with their husbands?"

In 1971, Ogilvy & Mather hired her as a junior account executive. At that time, she was the only woman among 100 account managers. Lazarus recalled, "We'd be talking about what women would buy, and then suddenly everyone would look at me." In 1973, when she was expecting her first child, Lazarus became the first female account supervisor at Ogilvy. She left the firm for two years in 1974 while her husband served an air force commitment, then returned to become account executive for major accounts, including Avon, Campbell Soup, and Ralston Purina. She managed the Clairol account again in 1977; three years later, she took on the American Express account.

Lazarus continued to advance in the company and was promoted to general manager of the direct marketing branch in 1987. She was known for her willingness to take on difficult assignments, such as building up the direct marketing branch. Lazarus recalled that "the worst moment of my professional career" was losing the American Express account in 1991. The company returned to Ogilvy a year later. Lazarus went back to the advertising side of the business when she was named president of Ogilvy & Mather New York, then became president of Ogilvy North America in April 1994. That year, Advertising Women of New York named Lazarus Woman of the Year. The following year, she was honored by New York Women in Communications.

Other successes folowed. One of her biggest coups was landing IBM's worldwide advertising account, worth between $400 and $500 million. Other accounts as of 1997 were Kodak, Shell, Mattel, and GTE.

Lazarus became chief executive officer (CEO) of Ogilvy in September 1996, succeeding CHARLOTTE BEERS, who was the first woman to run a top international ad agency. With offices on four continents, Lazarus does a great deal of traveling. In 2001, she told an interviewer for CBS News, "I feel the influence of women in the companies I deal with much more. They're at the tables for the big decisions, and they occupy jobs now of enormous influence."

Married to a pediatrician, Dr. George Lazarus, Shelly Lazarus is the mother of three children. The family lives in New York City.

Further Reading

McDonough, John. "Shelly Lazarus Talks About the Challenges and Satisfactions of Her Role as CEO of Ogilvy & Mather," *Advertising Age,* 1998, pp. 42–55.

Moreno, Katarzyna. "Executive Moms," *Forbes,* July 6, 1998, p. 20.

Rather, Dan, and Anthony Mason. "More Female Executives Tasting Sweet Success," *CBS Evening News With Dan Rather.* Broadcast February 21, 2001.

Sellers, Patricia, with Cora Daniels. "Women, Sex & Power. We'll Get Right to the Point," *Fortune,* August 5, 1996, pp. 42ff.

Sellers, Patricia, with Eryn Brown and Tim Carvell. "The 50 Most Powerful Women in American Business: In an Age of Celebrity, It May Surprise You That Our No. 1 Woman Is Someone You've Never Heard Of," *Fortune,* October 12, 1998, pp. 76ff.

Yancey, Kitty Bean. "Shelly Lazarus," *USA Today,* June 11, 1995. Available online. URL: http//:wwws.elibrary.com/getdoc.cgi?id=196914229×127y46316....:US;EL&dtype=0~0&dinst=. Downloaded on May 6, 2001.

LEWENT, JUDY
(1950–) *Executive*

Judy Lewent became one of the first women to serve as chief financial officer (CFO) of a Fortune 500 company (America's 500 largest corporations) when she rose to that position at Merck & Co., Inc., a leading pharmaceutical manufacturer.

Lewent, the daughter of an importer and homemaker, was born in 1950 and raised in New York City. She received her bachelor's degree in economics from Goucher College in 1970, then earned her master's degree in management from the Massachusetts Institute of Technology (MIT) Sloan School of Management in 1972.

Lewent first worked in investment banking at E. F. Hutton and Bankers Trust. After a few years, she became interested in the pharmaceutical industry both because of its products and the global nature of this business. After working at Pfizer for three years as a division controller, she joined Merck in 1980.

At Merck, Lewent rose in the finance department to become vice president and treasurer in 1987, vice president for finance and chief financial officer in 1990, and then senior vice president and chief officer (CFO) in 1992. As CFO, Lewent worked with a 500-member finance team, which faced the special requirements of the high-risk pharmaceutical industry. Because the costs of developing and marketing new drugs is very high (averaging $359 million per drug) and product development averages about 10 years, pharmaceutical companies operate in a challenging environment. In 1994, Lewent said, "Everywhere I look in the pharmaceutical industry today, I see increasing complexity and uncertainty. Whether I am considering health care reform, the emergence of the generic drug market, therapeutic substitution, or even currency fluctuations, I see both volatility and risk."

In 2001, Lewent was named executive vice president and chief financial officer of Merck. Among other things, Lewent evaluates whether to invest in certain types of research for new products. She says, "We know that scientists will probe an idea they feel has merit for as long as they possibly can, which is great. . . . The challenge from the point of view of the finance department is to put parameters around that curiosity and determine what is and what is not productive."

The Judy Lewent Scholarships for Women in Science were established to aid students at Goucher, Lewent's alma mater. Lewent, who is married and has no children, enjoys swimming, tennis, and running in her spare time.

Further Reading

Herper, Mathew. "America's Top Businesswomen," *Forbes.com.* Available online. URL: http://www.forbes.com/2001/03/28/0327/women_print.html. Downloaded on August 28, 2001.

Luehrman, Timothy A. "Scientific Management at Merck: An Interview with Judy Lewent," *Harvard Business Review,* January 1994, pp. 88ff.

MIT Sloan School of Management. "Who's Who After Sloan: Judy Lewent." Available online. URL: http://mitsloan.mit.edu/akem/whoswho/profiles/lewent.html. Downloaded on November 9, 2001.

✵ LEWIS, TILLIE
(1901–1978)   *Entrepreneur, Business Owner*

Tillie Lewis—known as the Tomato Queen—brought a new agricultural crop to the United States and pioneered the processing of the pomodoro tomato in her successful food products business, which grew to include other types of foods as well.

A native of Brooklyn, New York, Lewis became interested in agriculture during trips to Europe, particularly Italy. She believed that the pear-shaped tomato, called the pomodoro, could be grown commercially in California because the climate there was similar to conditions in the Mediterranean. During the 1930s, she began growing these tomatoes, which she brought from Italy, in San Joaquin County. Lewis implemented new methods of growing the crop in the fertile soil of the region. Canners used the plum tomatoes to make concentrated canned tomato paste, and that industry boomed as people around the country bought canned tomatoes for sauces and other uses.

Lewis took over the Western California Canners, which became known as Tillie Lewis Foods. The plant was located on a waterfront on the west side of Antioch, California. Foods were shipped out to various parts of the country via the Santa Fe Railroad.

Lewis added other items to her food products business, which grew to include three canneries. During the 1950s, she became a pioneer in the diet food industry. She introduced canned foods artificially sweetened with saccharin and developed weight-loss menus and recipes. Her Tasti-Diet line of peaches, puddings, jellies, and chocolate sauces debuted in 1951. The company also printed diet booklets for consumers describing its Tasti-Diet foods and eating plans. By the 1950s, Lewis was a multimillionaire.

In 1951, Lewis was voted Businesswoman of the Year, and this honor was made part of the Congressional Record in March 1952. The New York Institute of Dietetics named her Outstanding Woman in Food in 1952. She served as port commissioner of Stockton, California, in 1968. That year, she was also a delegate to the World Food Conference, which was held in Rome, Italy.

The tomato processing business continued to grow during the 1960s, especially after new labor-saving machines came onto the market. The mechanical tomato harvester was developed at the University of California, Davis, then manufactured in Solano County.

When Lewis died in 1978, she left an estate valued at $11.5 million. A street in Stockton is named in her honor and a theater she endowed in that city has also been named after her.

Further Reading

"Tillie Lewis Foods Collection." City of Stockton, CA—History. Excerpts available online. URL: http://www.stocktongov.com/clerk/hstry-pg.htm. Downloaded on June 2, 2001.

Treleven, Mike. "SJ County Farms Celebrate More Than 100 Years in Business," *San Joaquin Farm Bureau News,* January 2000. Available online. URL: http://www.sjfb.org/jan2000/100yrs.html. Downloaded on June 1, 2001.

�֎ LOPKER, PAMELA (Pam Meyer)

(1954–)   *Mathematician, Entrepreneur, Software Engineer*

Mathematician Pamela Meyer Lopker is the founder of QAD, a worldwide leader of integrated and distribution software for manufacturing plants and e-commerce. QAD has a reputation for software that performs well and is user-friendly. Lopker has said, "Software needs to be intuitive, easy to implement, and highly reliable. It needs to provide immediate value at a low cost."

The daughter of a U.S. Navy aircraft-electronics engineer, Pamela Meyer was born in Japan in 1954, and attended eight different schools in 12 years as her family moved, depending on her father's assignments. She and her sister and brother grew up discussing new developments in technology and learning how appliances worked. Pam Meyer became the first girl at Cupertino High School in California to enroll in the auto shop course, then became the first student ever to earn an A in the course, when she took apart and rebuilt an old Austin-Healy automobile.

In 1977, she earned a degree in mathematics and economics at the University of California at Santa Barbara, where she also took computer programming courses. Her first jobs were as a programmer for software companies in California. She recognized a gap in the software market when she was helping her friend Karl Lopker, who would become her husband, try to locate software that could be used in operating a shoe and leather-goods factory. Lopker, an electrical engineer, had begun running the factory in college and needed software that would "tie together manufacturing with distribution, finance and other activities."

Pam Lopker decided to go into business, creating software that targeted midsize manufacturing companies. In 1975, she founded QAD—the letters stand for quality, application, and delivery—in Carpinteria, California. Her goal was to make enterprise resource planning (ERP) software to help companies track and control various aspects of their business. Husband Karl Lopker joined her at QAD in 1981 after selling his interest in the leather-goods factory.

In the beginning, the Lopkers worked with two programmers to develop software that ran on Hewlett-Packard computers. Later, they developed software that was compatible with Unix and DOS operating systems. In order to develop cutting-edge products, Lopker spent months studying the manufacturing industry carefully so she would understand what managers needed to run their companies.

QAD launched its first business application to run on Unix in 1987. The MFG/PRO (for manufacturing professional) was praised for its large capability, relative ease of use, and the speed at which it could be implemented. The program has been updated through the years and can be found at numerous corporations and about 20 Fortune 500 companies (America's 500 largest corporations), including Colgate-Palmolive and Merck, a global pharmaceuticals company. Users have noted that QAD software took into account that companies might need to implement different versions of the program to run various operations, such as filling orders or making products. By focusing on manufacturing instead of trying to design programs that suited numerous types of businesses, QAD found an important niche. Lopker says, "My premise is that you can't be all things to all people because it will get too complicated and is too difficult to implement."

The company became a financial success. In 1996, *Forbes* magazine called Pamela Lopker "the richest self-made woman on the Forbes 400," a list of the wealthiest Americans. It noted that QAD was one of the 30 largest companies led by a woman. A working mother (she had a child in 1988 and in 1989), Lopker and her husband also made sure to make time for family life and do not have a business office in their California home.

As president and chair of QAD, Pam Lopker focuses on research and software development, while Karl Lopker, the chief executive officer (CEO), handles sales and marketing. Early on, the Lopkers decided to think globally, and the MFG/PRO was designed to accommodate the methods of invoicing, accounting, and amortization that are used in different countries. By 2000, about 65 percent of their clients were outside the United States, and MFG/PRO supported 24 languages. The Lopkers also saw the need for software that helped manufacturers complete transactions between plants and their suppliers and customers—what is known as the supply chain.

By 2000, the company had revenues of $239 million and employed 1,600 people. An employee stock program, launched in 1993, gives employees the chance to buy stock in the company. About 5,000 manufacturing plants around the United States were using QAD software as the 21st century began. During the late 1990s, QAD also invested

time and money developing its eQ system to help companies in the growing e-commerce market.

Pamela Lopker has received numerous awards for her achievements, including being named Entrepreneur of the Year in 1998 by the Lloyd Greif Center for Entrepreneurial Studies at USC's Marshall School of Business and induction into the Women In Technology International (WITI) Hall of Fame in 1997. *Working Woman* magazine named her one of the country's top 50 women-owned-business leaders in 1997, calling Lopker "an entrepreneur, software visionary and business leader." To educate young people in the Santa Barbara South Coast area about the Internet, in 1995 she launched QAD's 2006 Project. Upper-grade students from the elementary schools take part in the project, which offers them an introduction to the Internet.

Further Reading

Bylinsky, Gene. "Heroes of U.S. Manufacturing," *Fortune,* March 2001, Lloyd Greif Center for Entrepreneurial Studies. "Pamela Lopker: Entrepreneur of the Year, 1998." Available online. URL: http://www.marshall. usc.edu/entrepreneur/events/PamelaMeyerLopker.htm. Downloaded on May 4, 2001.

Women In Technology International (WITI). "Pamela Meyer Lopker." Available online. URL: http://www.witi.com/ center/witimuseum/halloffame/1997/plopker.shtml. Downloaded on May 4, 2001.

LUKENS, REBECCA WEBB PENNOCK
(1794–1854)   *Executive, Manager, Owner*

As manager and owner of an iron mill in the 19th century, Rebecca Pennock Lukens has sometimes been called the nation's first woman chief executive officer (CEO).

The oldest of Isaac and Martha Pennock's seven children, Rebecca Webb Pennock was born on January 6, 1794. The roots of her devout Quaker family (members of the Society of Friends were called Quakers) stretched back to the founding of Pennsylvania colony in the 1680s. The family lived in a rural area, and Rebecca spent many hours outdoors playing with her siblings and three cousins who lived nearby.

In 1792, two years before Rebecca was born, Isaac Pennock had opened the Federal Slitting Mill iron works, about four miles from the town that would become Coatesville. Pennsylvania was then the center of the iron industry, and Pennock realized that the newly independent United States would prefer to develop its own industry instead of purchasing goods from England. In 1810, he formed a partnership with Jesse Kersey, who wanted to develop a community nearby (later called Coatesville) that would attract residents and industry. They purchased 110 acres of land owned by Kersey's father-in-law, and Pennock converted a sawmill on that property into the Brandywine Iron Works and Nail Factory. Within seven years, he was the sole proprietor.

At age 12, Rebecca Pennock was sent to a boarding school, and the next year, she entered another school. She was an enthusiastic learner who later recalled her school years as a time of great personal growth. When Rebecca returned home at age 16, she missed school and spent much of her free time reading. Soon, she resumed her education, this time attending school in Wilmington, Delaware, where she especially liked to study French and chemistry.

In 1813, at age 19, she married Dr. Charles Lloyd Lukens, who practiced medicine in Abingdon, Pennsylvania. After the wedding, Charles Lukens went to work in Isaac Pennock's iron business. Within a few years, the business expanded as the nation relied on steam power, especially for steamboats. Steam power required iron plate, which was used to make the boilers and hulls of ships. The Brandywine Iron Works became one of the world's foremost makers of rolled iron and steel.

When Charles Lukens died at the early age of 39 in 1825, Rebecca Lukens had three children and was expecting a fourth. Before her husband died, he made it clear that he wanted his widow to continue running the business, even though it faced some critical problems. The company was then in debt, and its facilities were in need of repair.

Despite criticism from her family and the community as a whole, she agreed to become sole manager and owner. Her brother Solomon supervised day-to-day operations. During the 1830s, new opportunities arrived, as railway steam locomotives began running. Lukens decided that Brandywine would make manufacturing iron for locomotives and rails. She managed to pay off the factory's debts, and the company became more profitable.

As an executive, Lukens showed a great deal of loyalty to her employees. In 1837, an economic depression that would last six years settled over the country, but Lukens did not lay off any workers. Instead, she had them repair the ironworks or work on her farm, paying them in produce when she lacked enough cash. During the mid-1840s, the company sustained a strong financial position and reputation. Lukens would later say that she

Rebecca Pennock Lukens became one of the first American women to run a factory when she became the manager of the Lukens Ironworks in 1825.
(Photo courtesy of Bethlehem Steel)

The Brandywine Iron Works was the first mill in the United States to roll iron boiler plate, and it became one of the world's foremost makers of rolled iron and steel, used in steamboats and locomotives.
(Photo courtesy of Bethlehem Steel)

had "built a very superior mill, though a plain one, and our character for making boiler iron stood first in the market." In 1849, Lukens decided to retire as manager of the firm, and she transferred her duties to two sons-in-law.

Rebecca Pennock Lukens died on December 10, 1854. The company has continued to operate, first as Lukens Steel, and then as Bethlehem Steel. In 1994, Lukens was inducted into the National Business Hall of Fame.

Further Reading

Gustaitis, Joseph. "Woman of Iron," *American History,* April 1995, p. 32. "History: Bethlehem Lukens Plate." Available online. URL: http://www.bethsteel.com/divisions/beth-lukens/history. Downloaded on November 26, 2000.

U.S. Department of Transportation. "Women's History in Transportation." Available online. URL: http://www.fhwa.dot.gov/wit/page1.htm. Downloaded on November 24, 2000.

M

⁂ MALONE, ANNIE TURNBO
(1869–1957)   *Business Owner, Executive*

Annie Turnbo Malone built a financial empire and provided opportunities for thousands of people to learn and earn a living through her hair products business and philanthropy.

Born in Metropolis, in southern Illinois, on August 9, 1869, Annie Turnbo grew up as an orphan and overcame childhood poverty and racial discrimination to make her way in the world. In the 1890s, she began making hair products based on ingredients she had learned about from an aunt who was a traditional herbal healer. Turnbo was especially interested in products that would keep the scalp healthy, encourage hair growth, and beautify the hair of African Americans. One of her first products contained egg and sage.

After she and her sister moved to Lovejoy, Illinois, they sold their product, Wonderful Hair Grower, door-to-door because local retail drugstores objected to doing business with African-American women. Malone later said that she showed customers how to use her product so they would see for themselves how it improved their hair. She also discussed hair care and hygiene with the women she visited. Orders steadily increased, and the Turnbo sisters hired assistants to help them produce and sell their hair products.

In 1902, Turnbo relocated to St. Louis, Missouri, which had a much larger population. Business grew steadily, especially after the 1904 World's Fair brought thousands of visitors to that city. Turnbo trained more and more agents who then sold her products throughout the Midwest, then in the South and Northeast, under the trademark name Poro, which she registered in 1906. Poro agents, who continued to sell door-to-door, attended special training programs to improve their sales skills and ability to demonstrate the product. One young agent, Sarah Breedlove (later MADAM C. J. WALKER), later created her own very successful hair products business.

In 1914, Annie Turnbo married Aaron Malone, who took an active interest in the business. By then, Poro products were so popular that white-owned businesses also wanted to stock them. Malone advertised in newspapers and various periodicals written for the black community, which brought still more business.

In 1918, she opened Poro College, a factory and beauty-training school she had built in St. Louis. The complex contained offices, sales operations, and a factory, as well as educational facilities, a chapel, gym, and theater. Students and employees could attend musical performances and lectures at the center, which also served as a gathering place for events in the black community. By 1926, about 75,000 agents had graduated from the school.

Malone continued to expand her operations and added skin care products and face powder to her product line in 1922. She gave speeches and demonstrations in churches and women's clubs, where she also recruited women to become hairdressers and sales agents for Poro products. Her business provided job opportunities for thousands of African-American women, who had few opportunities for well-paid jobs in those days.

By the 1920s, Malone had become wealthy. As she continued to promote her products, she shared her wealth with the community and contributed both time and money to churches, schools, and other organizations. It was reported that at one time Malone had a net worth of about $14 million, which would make her the nation's first black woman millionaire (although some historians think Madam C. J. Walker was the first). Annie Malone continued to donate large sums of money to charitable causes and built the St. Louis Colored Orphan's Home (now the Annie Malone Children and Family Service Center). She gave $25,000 to Howard University and supported numerous individual students through the years.

In 1927, Annie and Aaron Malone were divorced, and they fought for legal control over the Poro Company. Annie Malone finally won that battle in the early 1930s, but by then, the company was experiencing financial problems, a process that was exacerbated by the Great Depression. Competitors were outselling Poro. When Malone died, in 1957, her estate was valued at about $100,000.

Further Reading

Green, Lorenzo, Gary R. Kramer, and Antonio F. Holland. *Missouri's Black Heritage.* Revised edition. St. Louis: University of Missouri Press, 1993.

Majors, M. A. *Noted Negro Women.* Freeport, N.Y.: Books for Libraries Press, 1971.

Peiss, Kathy. *Hope in a Jar: The Making of America's Beauty Culture.* New York: Metropolitan Books, 1998.

Smith, Jessie Carney, editor. "Annie Turnbo Malone," in *Notable Black American Women.* Detroit: Gale Research, 1992.

✳ MARBURY, ELISABETH
(1856–1933)   *Business Agent, Theatrical Manager, Author*

Elisabeth Marbury was a theatrical and literary agent during the late 19th and early 20th centuries and was the first woman to succeed in these professions. She found effective new ways to promote her clients' careers.

Born in New York City on June 19, 1856, Marbury grew up in a well-to-do family and received a private education. Her interest in the arts led her to organize theatrical performances for charity during her twenties. At that time, live theater was the foremost entertainment in the world. Her productions were so successful that she decided to manage a theater herself. In 1888, she negotiated with Frances Hodgson Burnett, the author of *The Secret Garden* (1909) and other popular novels, to let her produce her best-selling book *Little Lord Fauntleroy* (1886) for the stage. Working as Burnett's agent, Marbury found ways to promote her work.

Marbury then opened an office in New York to manage her growing agency business, and she worked for both American and European clients. From 1891 until about 1906, Marbury represented prominent foreign authors in U.S. markets, including the French playwrights Jean Richepin, Edmond Rostand, and Victorien Sardou. She negotiated lucrative royalty contracts to have their works published in English and then performed as plays for English-speaking audiences in the United States and Britain. Marbury also promoted the careers of British authors George Bernard Shaw and James M. Barrie, author of *Peter Pan,* whom she persuaded to rewrite *The Little Minister* as a theatrical vehicle for the popular actress Maude Adams. Marbury's American clients included authors Clyde Fitch and Rachel Crothers.

In 1913, Marbury began promoting the ballroom dance team of Vernon and Irene Castle, whom she had seen and admired in Paris. She helped the Castles enjoy unprecedented success in the United States by introducing them to members of New York society, including the Vanderbilts and Astors. To promote their name, she encouraged them to found a dancing school in New York and write how-to articles about dancing and dance etiquette for popular magazines, as well as a book that promoted their style of dancing. Marbury also promoted dance itself, saying, "Dancing is first and foremost a healthful exercise; it is pleasure; and it is an art that brings to the front courtesy, ease of manner, grace of body and happiness of mind." Soon, Marbury arranged for the Castles to perform in Broadway shows. For several years, they were the world's most famous dance team.

American theatrical producers, including Charles Frohman and the Shubert Brothers, who operated rival theatrical syndicates, both worked with Marbury. In 1914, Marbury and several other agents formed the American Play Company.

In addition to her profitable businesses, Marbury was involved in civic affairs and philanthropic activities. She helped to found the Colony Club, the first social club for women in New York City, where Marbury and her longtime companion ELSIE DE WOLFE entertained prominent politicians, literary figures, artists, and socialites at their apartment near Gramercy Park. She was also actively involved with the Democratic Party. During World War I, Marbury spent months in Europe working on relief programs, and she later made many visits to U.S. military hospitals. For this work, she received honors from both the French and Belgian governments. She was the author of two books, *Manners: A Handbook of Social Customs* (1888) and *My Crystal Ball,* an autobiography (1923).

Further Reading

Lewis, Alfred Allan. *Ladies and Not-So-Gentle Women.* New York: Viking, 2000.

Tapert, Annette, and Diana Edkins. *The Power of Style.* New York: Crown, 1994.

⚜ **MASON, BRIDGET** (Biddy Mason)
(1818–1891)   *Entrepreneur, Real Estate Investor*

Bridget "Biddy" Mason, a former slave, built a real estate fortune in California during the mid-1800s. She used her wealth and position to improve conditions for the growing African-American community in her state and to help people of all colors who were in need. Mason liked to say, "The open hand is blessed, for it gives in abundance even as it receives."

Mason was born a slave in Hancock County, Georgia, on August 15, 1818. As a young child, she was taken from her mother and sent to a different slave-owning family in Mississippi. In 1836, she became the property of Robert Marion Smith and his wife Rebecca, owners of a plantation in Logtown, Mississippi. It was later rumored that Mason's three daughters, Ellen, Ann, and Harriet, were fathered by Smith.

In 1847, Robert Smith converted to the Mormon religion, and the next year he moved his entire household to a Mormon settlement in Utah. During the 2,000-mile journey west across the wilderness, Mason had to herd cattle, prepare meals, care for the children, and serve as a midwife. She also knew how to care for the sick and prepare plant and herbal remedies for various medical conditions.

Four years later, Smith moved again, this time to join a new community that Mormon leader Brigham Young was founding in San Bernardino, California. California had been admitted to the Union in 1850 as a free state, so slavery was banned there, but these laws were not always enforced. However, as the antislavery movement gained support during the 1850s, the Smiths decided to leave for Texas, where slavery was still permitted.

133

Before they could leave, Biddy Mason petitioned the courts for her freedom. Robert C. Owens Sr., a prosperous businessman whose son later married one of Mason's daughters, was one of two free African Americans who advised Mason during her legal battle. In 1856, Benjamin Hayes, the district court judge, ruled in Mason's favor, granting her and her daughters their freedom. Judge Hayes declared that they were "entitled to their freedom" and could "go work for themselves—in peace and without fear." It was at that time that Mason chose "Mason" as her last name, possibly having met someone by that name during her journey west.

An accomplished nurse and midwife, Mason found work in Los Angeles, in the office of Dr. John S. Griffin, who knew both Judge Hayes and Robert Owens. Mason earned $2.50 a day, which was a good wage in those days. People of different classes sought her expertise and she walked miles every day, visiting sick people around the city. Now able to support herself, she rented a house on San Pedro Street near her daughter Ellen, who had married Charles Owens. Sadly, her daughter Ann died in 1857 during a terrible smallpox epidemic that raged throughout the city that year. Despite the risks of catching the disease, Mason visited people's homes to help those who were stricken.

By working hard and saving as much money as she could, Mason became financially independent, and, by 1866, she had accumulated $250. She decided to invest her savings in real estate and purchased two lots on Third and Fourth Streets, between what are now Broadway and Spring Streets, which made Mason one of the first women of color to own land in California. After she saved another $375, Mason bought more land, this time around Sixth and Olive Streets.

The city was growing rapidly as new shops, hotels, schools, and residences were built, and Mason became increasingly involved in community organizations. In 1872, she held a meeting at her home on San Pedro Street to organize the Los Angeles First African Methodist Episcopal Church, the first black church in the city. (This congregation later held services in several other locations before moving to 8 Town Avenue in 1903.) Throughout the 1870s, Mason continued her work as a midwife and delivered hundreds of babies.

In 1884, Mason sold part of her land for $2,800 and built a commercial building with rental spaces on the remaining parcel. Her family occupied rooms on the top floor. After she sold another small parcel of land, she invested those profits in more real estate and engaged in profitable business transactions. In 1885, Mason helped two of her grandsons open a livery stable and a livestock feed business on part of her homestead, which was located in what was becoming the city's financial center. By 1890, she had amassed a fortune estimated at about $300,000.

Mason contributed to charities that benefited people of all races, and she gave direct help to the needy, who often lined up outside her home. In 1884, she paid a local grocery store to provide food for people who had been made homeless by seasonal floods. She also founded an orphanage, a day-care center, and a school in her neighborhood. With her son-in-law Charles Owens, she continued to support the First African Methodist Episcopal Church and paid the bills and the minister's salary when the congregation lacked enough money.

Upon her death, her fortune passed to her children and grandchildren. Her grandson Robert Curry Owens was one of the wealthiest men in Los Angeles during his lifetime and became a politician as well as a real-estate developer. When Mason died on January 15, 1891, she was buried in an unmarked plot at Evergreen Cemetery in Los Angeles. Nearly a century later, on March 27, 1988, Los Angeles Mayor Tom Bradley, Mason's descendants, and 3,000 members of the First African Methodist Episcopal Church gathered to see the unveiling of a new tombstone in her honor. November 16, 1989, was declared Biddy Mason Day in Los Angeles, and a memorial to her achievements was displayed downtown at the Broadway Spring Center.

Further Reading

Bolden, Tonya. *The Book of African American Women: 150 Crusaders, Creators and Uplifters.* Holbrook, Mass.: Adams Media Corporation, 1996.

"California Inventory of Historic Sources," Sacramento: State of California Dept. of Parks and Recreation, 1976.

Christian, Charles M., and Sari J. Bennett. *Black Saga: The African American Experience, A Chronology.* Washington, D.C.: Counterpoint Press, 1998.

Mungen, Donna. *Life and Times of Biddy Mason.* Sacramento: California Arts Council, MC Printing Co., 1976.

Sims, Oscar L. "Biddy Mason." In *Epic Lives: One Hundred Black Women Who Made a Difference,* edited by Jessie Carney Smith. Mt. Kisco, N.Y.: Visible Ink Press, 1993.

✺ ## McCARDELL, CLAIRE
(1905–1958) *Entrepreneur, Designer, Author*

Known as the groundbreaking designer who developed "the American look," Claire McCardell claimed that her success came because "I have always designed things I needed myself."

Born in Frederick, Maryland, in 1905, she was interested in fashion as a child and spent hours poring over her mother's fashion magazines and creating paper dolls and their wardrobes. She studied design at the Parsons School in New York and then in Paris before returning to New York to work in a dress shop. The well-known New York designer Robert Turk recognized her talent, and in 1929 he hired McCardell as a model and designer at Townley Frocks, where he headed the design department. When Turk died in 1931, McCardell, who had become Turk's assistant, became chief designer at the company. In 1940, she began producing designs under her own name.

At a time when designers around the world were imitating French styles, McCardell offered women something new. She became known for designing practical, relaxed clothing with clean lines. Often, she cut fabric on the bias, which made it more flexible, and it skimmed over the curves of the body in a natural way. She created simple, loose dresses without darts that could be tied at the waist with wraparound sashes and harem-style pants, pedal pushers, and hooded sweaters. Other McCardell trademarks were large pockets with top-stitching, spaghetti straps, small puffed sleeves, and new uses for denim and wool jersey fabrics. With her mix-and-match separates, such as dirndl skirts and leotards, women could combine pieces in various ways to expand their wardrobes. Her easy-to-pack separates worked well for travel.

Women found that McCardell's designs suited their increasingly active lives during the 1930s and 1940s as they moved into the workplace and participated in more areas of life. She also designed practical clothing for women working in the home, such as her famous Popover, a wraparound denim dress with a matching oven mitt that retailed for $6.95.

Critics used words like "flattering," "sophisticated," and "modern yet feminine" to describe her work, which they said offered a new American way of dressing. To avoid being influenced by foreign designers, McCardell made it her policy after 1940 not to even look at the French couture collections.

During World War II, when fabric was in short supply, McCardell showed her patriotism by making designs from government surplus cotton weather balloons and blue-and-white-striped mattress ticking. She popularized the use of cotton fabrics for various items of clothing and found a way to make cotton plaid evening dresses in designs that used all the fabric, including the scraps left over after cutting the main pieces.

McCardell became even more popular in the 1950s when many of her clothes were mass-produced and marketed through the Fuller Brush catalogs. McCardell also influenced changes in women's accessories. In the early 1950s, she asked shoemaker Capezio to add hard soles to its ballet slippers to make a flat shoe that would be comfortable and also complement her sportswear designs. Ballet flats became popular with teenagers as well as older women.

During the 1950s, Claire McCardell lectured at the Parsons School of Design, where she influenced another generation of designers. Her career was cut short by her death in 1958.

Claire McCardell once described her work: "It looks and feels like America, its freedom, its democracy, its casualness, its good health. Clothes can say all that."

Further Reading

McCardell, Claire. *What Shall I Wear?* New York: Simon and Schuster, 1956.
Yohannan, Kohle, and Nancy Nolf. *Claire McCardell: Redefining Modernism.* New York: Harry M. Abrams, 1998.

✳ McCORMICK, NETTIE
(Nancy Maria Fowler)
(1835–1923)   *Executive, Philanthropist*

Nettie McCormick helped to expand the International Harvester Company with her husband, Cyrus, the inventor of a mechanical reaper, and she served as the company's president beginning in 1886.

Nancy Maria Fowler, later called Nettie, was born on February 8, 1835, in Brownsville, a small town near Clayton, New York. Her father, a shop owner, was killed by a horse when Nancy was a baby, and her mother died from an illness when she was only seven. After she was orphaned, her grandmother Maria Fowler took care of her and her brother Eldridge. During her youth, Nancy was a devoted student and quite active in the Methodist Episcopal Church.

At age 15, she left to pursue more education at three different seminaries, attending them for one year each. Her studies included courses in geography, algebra, astronomy, meteorology, botany, chemistry, electricity, theology, philosophy, logic, music, painting, French, and the classics, and she earned high marks. She was fascinated by a course in hydraulics and showed a strong aptitude for writing. During these years, she remained active in church activities, including the Methodist Mission Society.

In 1856, at age 21, Fowler went to Chicago, Illinois, to visit some relatives. There she met 48-year-old Cyrus McCormick, the son of a farmer and blacksmith, who had invented the mechanical reaper to cut grain in 1831. This invention significantly reduced the amount of time and labor needed to produce grain. McCormick courted Fowler and impressed her as a mature and considerate man. They were married in Chicago in 1858.

Between 1858 and 1884, Nettie McCormick was busy with homemaking responsibilities and rearing their four children. The family lived in different cities, spending the years from 1858 to 1860 in Washington, D.C. Cyrus was often gone on business trips in America and abroad, as well as on trips related to his church activities. In 1862, they traveled to Europe, where Nettie McCormick stayed with the children until late in 1864 when the family moved to New York City.

A practical woman known for her intelligence and strong character, Nettie McCormick began to take a strong interest in the business during the 1870s. In 1871, the reaper factory was destroyed in the Chicago fire, and Cyrus McCormick decided to retire. His wife urged him to rebuild and then expand the business. During the rebuilding, she helped to select building materials, consulted with the architects, and visited the construction site. As a result of her influence, a new McCormick Harvesting Machine Company factory was erected on Blue Island Avenue, and she urged her husband to return to full production as soon as possible. She told him that a year's delay would cause the company to lose its supremacy in the reaper business. The new plant opened in February 1873.

Once the plant was running, Nettie McCormick became closely involved in the business, advising her husband, accompanying him on business trips, and handling correspondence. The business prospered, and in 1880 the McCormicks moved into a lavish new home they had planned before leaving for Europe in 1878 on a business and pleasure trip. The couple was also very active in the Democratic Party and Presbyterian church.

During the early 1880s, Cyrus McCormick's health declined, and Nettie McCormick became even more active in the business. He died in 1884, and she was named president of the company in 1886.

Beginning in the 1890s, Nettie McCormick devoted herself increasingly to philanthropic efforts, funding programs at her Presbyterian church and donating money to local and national YMCAs and YWCAs and to schools and academies, especially those that helped people learn useful work skills. Some of these programs were located in the Appalachian region. She also supported an orphanage in South Carolina and foreign missions.

In 1902, the McCormick Harvesting Company joined some other related companies to form International Harvester. Cyrus McCormick Jr. was the first president of this new company. Nettie McCormick died in 1923.

Further Reading

Burgess, Charles O. *Nettie Fowler McCormick, Profile of an American Philanthropist.* Madison: The State Historical Society of Wisconsin for the Department of History, University of Wisconsin, 1962.

Casson, Herbert Newton. *Cyrus Hall McCormick: His Life and Work.* Philadelphia: Ayer Company Publishers, 1977.

�֍ McGRATH, JUDITH (Judy McGrath)
(1952–   ) *Executive*

As president of MTV, the preeminent music television network, Judy McGrath has a global audience of more than 265 million viewers in 75 nations and territories on five continents and runs a media group that holds the attention of young people around the world.

She was born on July 2, 1952, in Scranton, Pennsylvania. Growing up, she was interested in both pop music and writing and thought she might like to write for *Rolling Stone* magazine after college. McGrath earned her bachelor of arts (B.A.) degree in English from Cedar Crest College in Allentown, Pennsylvania, then went to work as a copywriter for a Scranton radio station. In the late 1970s, she moved to New York City to write for popular women's magazines, including *Glamour* and *Mademoiselle.* Her columns for *Glamour* included the fashion "Do's and Don'ts."

McGrath left journalistic writing for copywriting in 1981 when she joined the newly formed Warner Amex Satellite Entertainment Company (WASEC), which later became MTV, to write on-air promotions. She rose to new positions at MTV, becoming creative director, then executive vice president, and finally copresident in the 1990s. During those years, her team developed such series as *The Real World, MTV's House of Style,* and the *Choose or Lose* program during the 1992 presidential campaign. They also launched the MTV Movie Awards, Music Video awards, and *Total Request Live.* The MTV series called *Fight For Your Rights: Take A Stand Against Violence* won an Emmy Award.

With Sara Levinson, McGrath shared the job of MTV president; after Levinson left to become head of NFL Properties, McGrath was sole president of MTV. In June 2000, McGrath was named president of MTV Group and chairperson of Interactive Media, in charge of a media group that includes shows, movies, music videos, books, and Internet operations.

McGrath says that as head of MTV she has to keep her own taste separate from the music business and does not always agree with the content of every video or the lyrics of every song the network presents. She says the network presents educational programs along with entertainment and tries to encourage viewers to discuss social issues, including sexism and racism in music.

McGrath has been praised for promoting minority artists and women. The American Civil Liberties Union (ACLU) Foundation of Southern California gave her its Torch of Liberty Award, for "leadership and individual contributions to preserving civil liberties and promoting human rights," and in 2001 McGrath received the Rock the Vote Patrick Lippert Award for MTV's contributions, which totaled about $10 million in on-air time and donations, to 2000's Rock the Vote campaign. Rock the Vote aims to educate young people about the political process and encourage them to participate. McGrath sits on the board of Rock the Vote, as well as those of The Music Industry Fights AIDS, People for the American Way, and the New York City Ballet.

In March 2001, Judy McGrath became the first woman to present the keynote address to the National Association of Recording Merchandisers (NARM), which was holding its 43rd convention. NARM spokesperson Pamela Horovitz said, "MTV is a powerhouse in our industry and in our culture in large part because of Judy McGrath's vision. Because MTV is celebrating its 20th anniversary this year, I think the timing is perfect for Judy to come to NARM and talk about life in the music biz, past, present, and future."

Further Reading

Bauder, David. "MTV Celebrates Its 20th Birthday with—What Else? A Party." Miami Herald, 2001. Available online. URL: http://www.miami.com/c/family_and_kids/teens/digdocs/056342.htm. Downloaded on November 5, 2001.

Crain's New York Business. "New York's 100 Most Influential Women in Business." Available online. URL: http://www.crainsny.com/page.cms?pageId=13. Downloaded on June 1, 2001.

"50 Most Powerful Women in Business." *Fortune,*

"MTV President Judy McGrath to Keynote NARM Convention." Press release from NARM. Available online. URL: http://www.narm.com/news/Press%20Releases/Jan2001/mcgrath.htm. Downloaded on May 30, 2001.

Sapers, Jonathan. "MTV Honcho Judy McGrath," Women's Wire, July 1996. Available online: URL: http://www.womenswire.com/watch/mcgrath.html. Downloaded on May 29, 2001.

METOYER, MARIE-THERESE (Coincoin) (1742–1816) *Plantation Owner, Entrepreneur*

Marie-Therese Metoyer was one of the most successful entrepreneurs in colonial America. As a planter and landowner, she founded a prosperous community of free blacks and Creoles (American-born people, often of mixed race) in the Louisiana Province. Historian François Mignon wrote that she "was endowed with unusual energy and intelligence."

She was born in Natchitoches in the French colony of Louisiana in 1742 and baptized Marie-Therese, but was called Coincoin (Ko Kwe in the Glidzi dialect), a name traditionally given to the second-born daughter in a family born to the Ewe people of Togo in western Africa, her parents' homeland. Because Louisiana was governed by French law, slaves were allowed to legally marry, as her parents, François and Françoise, did.

Her family was owned by a French military officer, Louis Juchereau de Saint-Denis. After his death, Coincoin was given first to his widow, then his son. She was then sent to live with Claude Thomas Pierre Metoyer, a merchant living in the Red River Valley. The two apparently fell in love and Coincoin gave birth to 10 of his children. In the French colony, mixed-race relationships were not uncommon, and most French colonists did not share the prejudice toward Africans that prevailed among other white European settlers during that era. Metoyer purchased Coincoin from her mistress and granted her freedom when she was pregnant with their fifth child, so that the remaining children were born free.

Coincoin and Metoyer ended their relationship in 1786, and he married a young Frenchwoman two years later. To protect his Franco-African family with Coincoin, Metoyer had his future wife sign an agreement that gave him sole ownership of his slaves. He eventually freed the children born to Coincoin.

Metoyer gave Coincoin a small plot of land and annual payments of 120 piastres to support herself and the children. She began building a ranch on the land and resorted to buying slaves herself in order to operate the ranch and various businesses. Coincoin provided her slaves, who eventually numbered 16, with better food, clothing, and accommodations than was customary in the region. Sources of labor were scarce, and the fact that she owned slaves protected Coincoin and her family from being suspected of participating in slave insurrections themselves. On her property, she raised and sold indigo and tobacco, as well as cattle and turkeys. Her workers trapped bears, which yielded hides and grease.

During the years when she was a slave in the home of Louise Juchereau de Saint-Denis, Coincoin, who took the name of Marie-Therese Metoyer, had given birth to five children, all of whom had been sold away from her and were living in Louisiana and eastern Texas. As she earned money from her businesses, she bought their freedom, one at a time, throughout the 1780s and 1790s. She was not able to secure freedom for one daughter, Françoise, but did manage to buy Françoise's children. Her family members joined her on her land and helped to expand her businesses.

Yucca Plantation (renamed Melrose in the 1880s) was the first plantation to be owned and run by a free black woman. The family's holdings increased substantially in the 1790s. By 1794, Metoyer had achieved a respected position in the region and was known as an industrious and astute business operator. Either she or her son Louis Metoyer obtained a grant of 640 acres of land on Isle Brevelle, where they built a two-story building of brick and wood that reflected African architecture. The family began planting crops and raising cattle there as well. In 1814, she told Claude Thomas Pierre Metoyer that she no longer needed the annuity he had been paying her to support her and the children. By this time, she had fulfilled her long-standing dream to free her family from slavery.

By the time Metoyer died in 1816, her family owned thousands of acres of land and was cultivating profitable indigo, corn, cotton, and tobacco crops, as well as continuing to raise cattle. Her descendants built a lavish plantation home surrounded by the original buildings. The estate on Isle Brevelle has been declared a national historic landmark.

Further Reading

Berlin, Ira. *Slaves Without Masters: A Free Negro in the Antebellum South.* New York: Pantheon, 1974.

Melrose Plantation Association. "Melrose Plantation—Association for the Preservation of Historic Natchitoches." Available online. URL: http://www.natchitoches.net/melrose/melrose.htm. Downloaded on July 23, 2000.

Mills, Gary B. *The Forgotten People.* Baton Rouge: Louisiana State University Press, 1974.

Nardini, Louis R., Sr. "Legends About Marie Therese Disputed," *Natchitoches Times,* October 2, 1972, p. 8-A.

MILLER, HEIDI
(1953–)   *Executive*

As the chief financial officer (CFO) of Citigroup, the world's largest financial company, Heidi Miller has been called one of the most powerful female executives on Wall Street and one of the foremost American women in finance. *Fortune* magazine consistently ranked her as one of its Top 50 American Women in Business during the late 1990s.

Miller grew up in Queens, a borough of New York City, and earned her bachelor's degree at Princeton University, where she majored in history with a focus on Latin American studies. Miller went on to earn her Ph.D. in history at Yale University and taught for two years at the University of Rhode Island. She then went to work at Chemical Bank as a Latin American specialist and rose to the position of marketing director of the emerging markets structured finance group.

In 1992, she went to work at Travelers Group, Inc., an insurance and securities firm, as an assistant to Jamie Dimon. Miller's responsibilities steadily grew through the years as she became the CFO at Travelers Group Inc., which became Primerica in 1995. In 1998, the company merged with Citicorp to become Citigroup, a financial services company that offers a full range of banking and brokerage services to individuals and businesses. At Citigroup, Miller administered more than $700 billion in assets and served as the chief risk officer for the firm's investment banking unit, Salomon Smith Barney.

In 1999, she was ranked second on *Fortune* magazine's list of the top 50 most powerful women in American business. Recognized as one of the preeminent people in her field, Miller continued to expand her knowledge and skills. During the 1990s, she completed studies in international finance at New York University's Leonard Stern School of Business.

In March 2000, Miller left Citigroup for a job in the rapidly expanding e-commerce arena. She accepted the position of CFO at Priceline.com, an online bidding service that allows consumers to shop for the best prices for airline tickets and other goods and services. In addition to her position as CFO, Miller was senior executive vice president in charge of strategic planning and administration. Richard Braddock, Priceline.com's chief executive officer (CEO), said of Miller: "She has a unique combination of experience and skills that will help us to accelerate the growth of the business."

Miller left Priceline.com that November and returned to a more traditional type of business in January 2001 when she joined Marsh and McLennan, Inc. as vice chairman of its insurance brokerage division, which ranks as the largest in the world. In a statement published by Bloomberg News, Miller said she was pleased to be joining the company and to be in "an industry that I know and enjoy." For their part, Marsh and McLennan said that Miller's previous jobs had given her an outstanding combination of skills and experiences. In her new position, Miller had responsibility for administration, strategy, finance, e-commerce, human resources, and technology.

In a 1999 address to students at Princeton University, Miller discussed the qualities of a good leader. She said, "Act like a leader in all things you do." She also told students that it was more important to be a team player than to lead with "arrogance and entitlement."

The mother of two boys, Miller serves on the boards of General Mills, Inc., Merck & Co., the Mead Corporation, and Bank One Corporation. She is a trustee of Princeton University and the New York University School of Medicine Foundation.

Further Reading

Bloomberg News, "Female Exec to Join Marsh & McLennan," *Newsday,* January 10, 2001, p. A55.

Hofstetter, Sara. "Citigroup CFO Miller advises Princeton Students Seeking Careers in Finance," University Wire, November 19, 1999. Available online. URL: www.businesswire.com. Downloaded on May 3, 2001.

Woodyard, Chris. "Priceline.com Lures Citigroup CFO Called Second-Most-Powerful Female Exec," *USA Today,* February 24, 2000, p. 6B.

�֍ MILLER, SYDELL L.

(1939–)   *Entrepreneur, Executive, Philanthropist*

Sydell Miller cofounded Matrix Essentials, then served as the president of the company. She led its expansion into the color cosmetics and skin care field, and while she was at the helm, Matrix grew into the world's largest manufacturer of hair products for the salon industry.

As the owners of a beauty salon in Cleveland, Ohio, Sydell and her husband, Arnold Miller, saw the need for a complete line of top-quality hair products, including shampoo, conditioners, styling lotions, hair color, and permanent solutions for professional use. In 1980, they founded Matrix Essentials, using the basement of their salon as the first office for the business.

Believing they must do more than just produce hair care products, the Millers emphasized education and professionalism for the people who bought, sold, or used those products—employees, distributors, and salon owners. They began sponsoring events in salons and classrooms, first in the United States and then in other countries where the Matrix line is sold, to show people how to use the products to best advantage.

Sydell Miller also was one of the first salon owners to offer a complete array of beauty services, an idea that developed during the 1980s as more salons adopted the "day spa" concept. Clients at her salon could receive hair care, skin care, nail services, and body care, as well as cosmetic application. They could even browse in a clothing boutique.

After Arnold Miller died in 1992, Sydell Miller ran the business herself and continued to develop new products and markets. She strengthened the company's already strong distribution network. Revenues at Matrix Essentials grew to $300 million in 1994, up from $150 million in 1992. That year, Miller decided to sell Matrix Essentials to the

Bristol-Meyers Squibb Company. Miller remained chairperson of the board of Matrix Essentials until she retired in 1998 to reside in her home in Palm Beach, Florida.

Sydell Miller is considered a leader in the cosmetology field and was named one of the top 50 women business owners in America. She was inducted into the National Cosmetology Hall of Fame in 1993. She has supported medical research, children's charities, and the arts. Miller played a key role in organizing the salon industry's antidrug program, S.T.A.N.D. (Salons Tell America No to Drugs). The Arnold and Sydell Miller Family Foundation grants money to various causes, including education, to which Sydell Miller has a strong commitment. In 2000, Case Western Reserve University received $10 million from the foundation to create the Arnold and Sydell Miller Center for Entrepreneurship, scheduled to open in 2002, at its Weatherhead School of Management.

Matrix Essentials remains a leader in the salon hair products market, with sales exceeding $340 million in 1999. As of 2000, the company estimated that 7 million people used Matrix products at least once a week. The products are sold in 85,000 salons in North America, as well as in Italy, the United Kingdom, Europe, Scandinavia, and the Pacific Rim.

Further Reading

Bendix, Jeff. "Miller family gift creates entrepreneurship center," Case Western Reserve on the Web. Available online. URL: http://www.cwru.edu/2828000/pubs/cnews/s000/6-1/miller.htm. Posted on June 1, 2000. Downloaded on December 31, 2000.

MINYARD, LIZ (Liz Minyard Lokey) (1954–) *Executive* and GRETCHEN MINYARD WILLIAMS (1956–) *Executive*

Liz Minyard and Gretchen Minyard Williams are the cochairs and co-chief executive officers (CEOs) of Minyard Food Stores, Inc., a large food store chain based in Coppell, Texas. During the 1990s, this food store chain was the eighth-largest privately held company in the United States being run by women.

Liz Minyard was born on January 23, 1954, and Gretchen was born on December 18, 1956, when the family business was expanding rapidly. Although both sisters worked in the business while they were growing up, their father did not insist that they continue. Gretchen Minyard later recalled that he told them, "You can do anything you want when you grow up."

The company dates back to the 1930s, when the first Minyard Food Store was opened during the Great Depression. In 1932, A. W. "Eck" Minyard bought a grocery store in East Dallas for $1,200 and hired his three brothers, who had just graduated from high school, to work there. Minyard hoped the store would enable the family to make a living during a time when jobs were scarce. With their sister, Fay Minyard, the four brothers were able to operate the store profitably and they opened another grocery, as well as a convenience store, during the 1930s. However, during World War II, all four brothers left to serve in the military and the family kept only one store open, the original grocery on Lindsley Avenue. When the Minyard brothers returned after the war, they opened three new stores within two years. The chain grew quickly during the 1950s, and six new stores were built by 1957. The family built the largest Minyard store to that date, as well as a new grocery store in Lancaster. The family also entered the shopping center business in 1959, founding Minyard Properties, Inc.

After their mother died when Liz was 13 and Gretchen was 10, their father often took them to the office. There, they observed family members, both men and women, working at the company. As the Minyard sisters held jobs in various departments, they saw how a food business was run. They learned how to make decisions, manage finances, select and purchase products, hire and promote employees, organize meetings, and arrange merchandise.

Both Liz and Gretchen Minyard attended Texas Christian College, where each earned a bachelor of arts (B.A.) degree in business. Liz Minyard went to work for Minyard Food Stores in 1976 and was charged with setting up and running a consumer affairs/community relations department. She later described her job: "I deal with philanthropic requests, serve on many outside boards, and participate in industry groups, conferences, and trade shows." She later was chosen as a member of the Food Marketing Institute Board, a prestigious national association for the food industry. Throughout 1986, Liz and Gretchen Minyard worked with their father to make the company's largest and most ambitious acquisition, the purchase of 27 Safeway stores in 1987. When their father died in 1987 the sisters became cochairmen of Minyard Food Stores. They worked hard for a smooth transition, meeting with store managers and supervisors and carving out complementary roles for themselves.

Some of their responsibilities overlap, although Liz Minyard focuses on community relations, while Gretchen Minyard Williams handles facilities management and employee relations. They seek to maintain an informal family atmosphere at the company while still maintaining professionalism. During the 1990s, they added stores in African-American and Hispanic communities and launched Carnival Food Stores, a moderately priced chain. By the late 1990s, the company included 44 Minyard, 20 Sack n' Save, and 20 Carnival Food stores, as well as eight gas stations, and it had more than 6,500 employees. In 1998, the Minyard Company earned more than $1 billion in sales.

The Minyards are involved in many community activities and philanthropic endeavors, including the Urban League, Goodwill Industries, and the food bank program Second Harvest, for which Liz Minyard serves on the board of directors. In 1996, Liz Minyard became the first woman chairman of the Dallas Chamber of Commerce. Both sisters are also active church members.

Further Reading

"Company History. Minyard Food Stores, Inc." Available online. URL: www.minyards.com/Company%20 History/company_history.html. Downloaded on March 19, 2000.

Enkelis, Liane, and Karen Olsen. *On Our Own Terms*. San Francisco: Berrett-Koehler, 1995.

"Sisters Doing It On Own," *Waikato Times* (New Zealand), February 3, 1998, p. 12.

✷ MOODY, PATRICIA ELLEN
(1947–) *Manufacturing Management Consultant*

Patricia Ellen Moody is a manufacturing management consultant to major corporations, as well as the author of eight books about the manufacturing business. A certified management consultant (CMC), she is president of her own consulting firm, Patricia E. Moody, Inc., based in Manchester, Massachusetts.

Moody, called Tricia by her friends, was born on October 7, 1946. She grew up in Pepperell, a town located near Lowell, Massachusetts, a city with a long history of manufacturing dating back to the well-known textile mills which began operating there during the Industrial Revolution. Her ancestors included factory workers, engineers, entrepreneurs, and managers; one of them, Paul Moody, cocredited with designing machinery that launched the Lowell system of textile production in the late 1700s. Moody's father was a power plant engineer who took her to visit factories, including a paper mill, while she was a child. During that time, Moody also overcame dyslexia, a learning disability, which went undiagnosed during her school years.

In college, Moody majored in French at the University of Massachusetts, where she received her bachelor's degree. In 1967, she cofounded an underground newspaper called *The Mother of Voices*. She and the small staff were involved in selling ads, writing and editing, and the printing process.

In the early 1970s, Moody applied for a purchasing job at a manufacturing company but was told she could not perform the job because

Tricia Moody has broken new ground as a woman providing expert consultation services to the management of large manufacturing companies.
(Courtesy of Patricia Moody)

"women can't go on the road." Instead, she went to work for a private company, Simplex, that made hardware for security systems. When she took charge of purchasing, she became the first woman the company had ever promoted to a middle-management position.

By that time, Moody was interested in manufacturing as a career but did not think she would have the opportunity to advance quickly if she remained at Simplex. She applied for a job at Dig-ital Equipment Corporation, and waited nine months for an opening in manufacturing. During that time, she took a job at a plant in Westminster, Massachusetts, that made minicomputers. After working at Digital, Moody's next job was at Data General, where she worked in management and business planning. She especially enjoyed spending time on the shop floor and participating in business planning activities that involved memory planning for high volume.

143

In 1978, Moody became the first woman consultant ever hired at Rath & Strong in Lexington, Massachusetts. In that job, she worked with companies that wanted expert help to develop business plans or solve special problems, such as developing production schedules. They included steel companies, aircraft companies, computer companies, printing companies, manufacturers, and others. She married Douglas Paul Glasson in 1982.

When she first entered the manufacturing profession, Moody was one of the first women in the field. She later said that she and the other women had "to be the smartest, be five steps ahead, clear away objections, and prove capabilities." Nonetheless, she demonstrated her abilities and built a career that included such clients as Johnson & Johnson, Motorola, Honda, Schering-Plough, and Mead Corporation, representing a range of industries. Moody also served as the editor of *Target,* the journal of the Association for Manufacturing Excellence.

Moody is a member of the Institute of Management Consultants (IMC) and the IMC New England (IMC/NE). She has written numerous magazine articles for professional journals, and trade publications, and her books include *Powered by Honda, The Kaizen Blitz, The Technology Machine, The Perfect Engine,* and *The Purchasing Machine: How the Top Ten Companies Use Best Practices to Manage Their Supply Chains.* She advises women who want to succeed in the manufacturing field to develop strong math skills and to learn to communicate with engineers using sketches. The mother of a daughter born in 1985, Patricia Moody lives in Massachusetts with her husband, a naval architect and aerospace engineer. In 2000, *Fortune* magazine named her as one of "10 Women Heroes" of manufacturing.

Further Reading

Bylinsky, Gene, and Alicia Hills Moore. "Women Move Up In Manufacturing," *Fortune,* May 15, 2000, pp. 1372ff.

Moody, Patricia E. *Breakthrough Partnering.* New York: Wiley, 1993.

———. *Leading Manufacturing Excellence.* New York: Wiley, 1997.

———. "The Path to More, Better, Faster," *MIT Sloan Management Review,* spring 2001, pp. 13ff.

Moody, Patricia E., and Anand Sharma. *The Perfect Engine.* New York: Free Press, 2001.

Moody, Patricia E., and Dick Morley. *The Technology Machine.* New York: Free Press, 1999.

Moody, Patricia E., Dave Nelson, and Jonathan Stegner. *The Purchasing Machine: How the Top Ten Companies Use Best Practices to Manage Their Supply Chains.* New York: Free Press, 2001.

✳ MOORE, ANN S.
(1950–) *Executive*

As president of AOL Time Warner's *People* Magazine Group, Ann S. Moore oversees the business operations for what may be the world's most profitable magazine and a group of publications that also includes *Teen People, InStyle, People en Español,* and *Real Simple,* launched in 2000. Moore also helps to develop new businesses within the *People* group.

Moore was born in 1950. She grew up in McLean, Virginia, and entered the publishing industry after graduating from Harvard Business School in 1978. At Time, Inc., she worked as a financial analyst. From 1978 to 1991, she held positions in management at several magazines that are part of Time, Inc., including *Sports Illustrated, Fortune, Money,* and *Discover.* She was also the founding publisher of *Sports Illustrated for Kids* in 1989. Moore believed that there was a ready audience of young readers who would enjoy a version of the adult sports magazine that was geared to their interests. The new magazine became a success, gaining institutional subscribers, such as schools and libraries, as well as individual subscribers.

In July 1991, Moore became the publisher of *People* magazine, then rose to the rank of president of that magazine in September 1993. Moore said, "We're preparing to celebrate the 25th anniversary of *People,* the most successful brand in magazine publishing. After a quarter of a century, in print and also on the Web, *People* magazine is the world's definitive resource for factual personality journalism."

People magazine continued to attract new subscribers during the 1990s. In 1999, it had a circulation of 3.25 million, and about 36 million people read *People* every week. *InStyle* also increased its readership, from 900,000 subscribers at its June 1994 introduction to 1.1 million in January 1999. *Teen People,* which debuted in 1998, also has more than 1 million subscribers.

In January 1999, Time, Inc. announced that Moore had been named president of the People Magazine Group. That year, *Fortune* magazine ranked Moore 24th on its list of the 50 most powerful women in business. In 2000, she was 21st. When *min* magazine named her its 1999 Consumer Player of the Year, journalist Jack Feuer wrote, "Her publishing track record is extraordinary, especially when it comes to new magazine introductions. Counting *WHO Weekly,* the Australian version of *People,* she has developed and launched five magazines in a little over 10 years and each one has been, at worst, successful and at best, explosive."

Although *People* focuses on celebrities and its covers feature a well-known person who is the subject of one of that issue's main articles, the magazine also presents the stories of interesting and accomplished people who are not famous. Moore notes that the magazine's loyal fans enjoy reading about these people, too, and declares, "People buy us for celebrity news but they love us for the non-celebrity news."

Moore, who has strongly supported programs that improve the lives of young people, is the vice chair of the Media Task Force of the National Campaign to Prevent Teen Pregnancy.

Further Reading

"Ann Moore Named President of the People Group," The Write News, November 13, 1998. Available online. URL: http://writenews.com/1998/110398.htm. Downloaded on May 2, 2001.

Guy, Pat. "'People' magazine—20 years and growing," *USA Today,* February 22, 1994, p. 6.

Siklos, Richard. "Up Front: Publishing Peek: A Really Simple Plan." *Business Week,* November 8, 1999, p. 6.

Time, Inc. "Press Release: People Online to be exclusively available on AOL," Time, Inc. New Media on the Web. Available online. URL: http://www.pathfinder.com/adinfo/pressrelease/view/0,2435,30,00.html. Posted October 19, 1998. Downloaded October 16, 2001.

MUSGROVE BOSOMWORTH, MARY (Cousaponokeesa)
(1700–1765)   *Trading Post Operator, Landowner*

Mary Musgrove Bosomworth was a well-known interpreter, diplomat, and businesswoman in colonial Georgia. Her deerskin- and fur-trading businesses and land holdings eventually made her the wealthiest woman on the Georgia frontier.

The daughter of a white trader and Creek woman of royal blood, Musgrove was born in 1700 into the Wind Clan, which lived in Coweta, located in present-day Alabama. At birth, she was named Cousaponokeesa. Her family sent her to live with a white family and attend school in South Carolina when she was seven years old. There, she was baptized as a Christian and given the name Mary.

After marrying John Musgrove Jr., the son of an Indian woman and a white landowner, she worked with her husband to build a fur trade at a post near the mouth of the Savannah River. She bore three sons during this busy period. Her knowledge of English and of both Native American and English cultures made her a great asset to the business, as the Musgroves traded with diverse people. In 1736, John Wesley, the founder of Methodism, visited the region and said of Mary Musgrove: "She understands both languages, being educated amongst the English. She can read and write, and is a well-civilized woman. She is likewise to teach us the Indian tongue."

Mary Musgrove also served as an interpreter and adviser for John Oglethorpe when he arrived in the region in 1733 with the first English settlers. With her help, Oglethorpe made treaties with the local tribes that enabled the English to found settlements in Savannah and Augusta.

With some of their business profits, the couple bought land and accumulated a large tract during the early 1730s. After John Musgrove died in 1735, his widow managed their 500-acre plantation, which included substantial numbers of cattle and horses, and the deerskin trade. She was respected by both the Native American and white communities and known for her financial expertise and political skills. When English leaders in the region asked her to set up another trading post near the Florida border, she created Mount Venture.

Musgrove then married Englishman Jacob Matthews, a former indentured servant and the leader of a group of Georgia rangers who defended Mount Venture from Spanish attacks. When the Spanish and British began fighting in 1742, Musgrove persuaded the Creeks to remain allied with the British; together, they pushed the Spaniards out of Georgia.

After 1737, Musgrove, who became the oldest surviving woman in her clan, continued to accumulate land from her Creek relatives. Her holdings grew to include thousands of miles along the Savannah River and several islands off the Georgia coast. Yet when she requested an official title for these lands, the British contested her claim and said that all of Georgia colony belonged to the English Crown. At about that same time, she asked the English to pay her the wages they had promised for the years during which she served as Oglethorpe's interpreter, but they refused.

In 1745, Jacob Matthews died, leaving Musgrove a widow once again. She still had not settled her legal issues with the English government but continued to serve as an interpreter for the local military commanders. She married Thomas Bosomworth, an Anglican clergyman, in 1747, and he supported her claim to the lands that she had acquired from her Creek kin.

Meanwhile, the Creek resented the way the English were treating Mary Musgrove and their people in general. When she joined a group of Creek who marched into Savannah in 1749 in protest, Musgrove was arrested. However, the British feared the Creek would revolt on her behalf, so they soon released her.

Musgrove and her third husband sailed to London where they pleaded her case before the British Board of Trade, but the controversy remained unresolved until 1757. The English government offered a compromise that gave her legal title to St. Catherine's Island but required her to sell her other islands at public auction and accept the proceeds as payment in full. Even then, the British government did not recognize her as the legal owner of these lands; they merely said that she was receiving St. Catherine's and the auction proceeds for "services rendered by her to the province of Georgia." As a result of this agreement, Musgrove became the largest landowner in Georgia. This is also the only known occasion in which a royal land grant was made to a Native American.

Mary Musgrove died at age 63 and was buried on St. Catherine's Island. Creek tradition decreed that her property would pass to her Creek female relatives, but instead it went to her husband and his English kin. In 1993, Mary Musgrove Bosomworth was named a Georgia Woman of Achievement.

Further Reading

Coulter, Ellen Merton. "Mary Musgrove, Queen of the Creeks," Savannah, Ga.: Georgia Historical Society, 1927.

Georgia Women of Achievement. "Mary Musgrove Bosomworth." Available online. URL: www.gawomen.org/honorees/bosomworthm.htm. Downloaded on June 2, 2000.

Todd, Helen. *Mary Musgrove, Georgia Indian Princess.* Savannah, Ga.: Seven Oaks, 1981.

N

⊠ NATORI, JOSIE CRUZ
(Josefina Almeda Cruz)
(1948–) *Entrepreneur, Executive*

As president and chief executive officer (CEO) of the lingerie and evening-wear company she founded, Josie Cruz Natori enjoys the process of creating beautiful merchandise and building a business. She has said, "I am a natural salesperson. I come from the Philippines, where being a woman entrepreneur is very commonplace. Women are always selling something from the time they are very young. It comes very natural to me." Natori has also commented, "My heritage and my femininity gave me the right tools to succeed in this very competitive business."

Josefina (Josie) Cruz was born in Manila, the eldest of six children of Felipe and Josefina Cruz. The family owned a construction firm, and everyone took part in the business. They were devout Catholics and Josie attended Catholic schools. As a child, she enjoyed drawing and painting and was devoted to the piano, which she began playing at age four. When she was nine years old, Josie appeared in concert with the Manila Philharmonic Orchestra. She planned to become a professional pianist but later decided to go into business.

At age 17, Cruz left for New York City to enter Manhattanville College, where she received two bachelor of science (B.S.) degrees—in economics and in music (piano). After college, she worked in corporate finance at Bache Securities. Bache sent her to Manila to open and run a brokerage office, and she gained valuable experience in sales. Two years later, she moved back to New York and became the first female investment banker at Merrill Lynch. Natori rose to the position of vice president at Merrill Lynch and earned a six-figure salary. She later said that she learned a great deal about corporate finance at Merrill Lynch and that knowledge has helped her to run her own company.

While working at Merrill Lynch, she went on a blind date with Ken Natori, a third-generation Japanese-American who was then working as an investment banker at Smith Barney Harris & Upham. The two fell in love and were married in 1973. Their son, Kenneth Jr., was born in 1976.

The Natoris wanted to open their own business and considered several possibilities, including a car wash, McDonald's restaurant, and import-export.

Designer and entrepreneur Josie Natori has said that her ability to understand how women want to look and feel in their clothing has helped her to succeed in this competitive field.
(Photo courtesy of Natori Company)

Josie Natori tried selling basketry and furniture from the Philippines without much success. Next she imported embroidered blouses from her homeland and showed them to a buyer from Bloomingdale's department store, who suggested she change the blouses into nightshirts. That idea made sense to Natori, who thought there was room for innovation in the lingerie market. In her opinion, much of the lingerie available at the time was either plain or vulgar. She wanted to introduce new designs in lingerie and at-home clothing, and evening wear that would be tasteful, elegant, and sensuous.

Although she had no experience in the fashion industry, Natori was eager to learn, and she appreciated good design and beautiful things. She later recalled, "But I learned that having an idea is one thing and executing it is another. Headaches came along the way, of course." Nonetheless, she was convinced she had a winning idea and says, "I think I understand how women want to feel. They are independent and they want to feel very feminine."

The Natori Company, which operates a factory in the Philippines, focused on creating and selling lingerie with embroidered designs and detailing that became her trademark. At first, the designs were usually floral, but they became more diverse. The colors were often vibrant. Sales grew steadily during the 1980s, a time when many people in the United States and other countries were spending money on luxury items. Natori later expanded her products to include perfumes, handbags, slippers, jewelry, and bridal gowns. In 1985, Ken Natori became chairman of the company.

The company adapted to changes during the 1990s, when, says Natori, customers became more value-minded. A less expensive line called Josie was introduced with more modern designs, geared for fun-loving and carefree customers. The colors and prints are bolder than in Natori's other lines, Natori Black Label and Natori White Label, but are still meant to be luxurious. The line was quite successful, especially with younger women.

During the late 1990s, Natori continued to develop exciting new products and accessories, including seamless brassieres. Embroidered pashmina shawls were among the most popular items in the collection. The company made plans to open more retail stores and boutiques and to develop a catalog.

Josie Natori is active in the arts and in various organizations. She is a member of the board of trustees of Manhattanville College, her alma mater, the boards of the Philippine American Foundation (which promotes rural development), the Asian Cultural Council, the Fashion Group International, and Council of Fashion Designers of America. Traveling is one of Natori's favorite activities, and she especially likes visiting Paris and Manila.

Natori has said that being a woman and a Filipina have been assets, and she expresses pride that she brought international recognition to a Philippines label. She advises other potential entrepreneurs to make sure that whatever they are doing comes "from deep within your soul." If you are passionate about what you are doing and respect that endeavor, says Natori, it will be reflected in your work.

Further Reading

"Josie Cruz Natori." Courtesy of the Natori Company, Public Relations and Marketing Communications.

Joven, Ginggay P. "Getting Intimate with Josie Natori," Philstar.com (Filipino Global Community). Available online. URL: http://www.philstar/archive.asp?archive=true&category id=18&content id=7048. Downloaded on June 14, 2000.

Kennedy, Danielle. "Tip Sheet: Top Entrepreneurs Share Their Hottest Sales," *Entrepreneur,* June 1998. Available online. URL: http://www.entrepreneurmagazine.com/Your Business/YB. Downloaded on June 4, 2000.

NELSON, MARILYN CARLSON
(1939–) *Executive*

Nelson, who has been called "the most powerful woman in travel," is chair and chief executive officer (CEO) of Carlson Companies. She leads one of the world's largest privately held companies, an international corporate and consumer services conglomerate that includes Carlson Marketing Group, Radisson Hotels & Resorts, Carlson Wagonlit Travel, T.G.I. Fridays restaurants, Regent International Hotels, and Country Inns & Suites by Carlson.

Her father, Curtis L. Carlson, was the son of Swedish immigrants and a self-made man. In 1938, he borrowed $55 to start the Gold Bond Stamp Company, where his wife Arleen helped market the new business. When Marilyn Carlson was born in 1939, the Carlson family business was beginning to prosper.

Marilyn Carlson Nelson studied at the Sorbonne in Paris and graduated with honors from Smith College in Massachusetts, where she earned her degree in international economics in 1951. After college, she was a securities analyst at Paine Webber, a financial services company, in Minneapolis, Minnesota. Nelson later recalled that her boss at Paine Webber asked her to use M. C. Nelson in her business correspondence so clients would not realize she was a woman.

After leaving Paine Webber in 1953, she joined her sister Barbara in buying and operating a small full-service bank in southern Minnesota. Having proven her abilities in nonfamily businesses, Nelson

After working as a securities analyst and banking executive, Marilyn Nelson joined the family business and now serves as CEO of the Carlson Companies, a leading provider of hospitality and travel services.
(Photo courtesy of the Carlson Companies)

joined the Gold Bond Stamp Company (the antecedent of Carlson Companies), where she held various assignments, then became director of community relations in 1968. The growing company owned and operated hotels and travel services. During the next 20 years, Nelson rose to new positions at the Carlson Companies before she became chief operating officer (COO) of the company in 1997 and then was named president and CEO in March 1998, which meant she controlled one of the world's leading providers of relationship marketing travel and hospitality services. In 1999, she was named board chair.

As the new CEO, Nelson declared that she hoped to double the company's profits within five years, saying that continuing expansion, along with "the human touch," would help them reach that goal. During her first year as CEO, Carlson Companies merged with Britain's Thomas Cook Group, another giant in the travel industry. Nelson made further changes by enhancing employee benefits and adding day care services. As of 2000, Nelson led about 190,000 people employed by Carlson brands and services in more than 140 countries, more than any other American woman executive. Carlson-related brands and services generated revenues in excess of $31 billion that year.

Nelson became national chair of the Travel Industry Association of America and was named Most Powerful Woman in Travel by *Travel Agent Magazine.* She was named seventh on *Fortune* magazine's 1999 list of the 50 most powerful women in American business. Nelson, who has also been recognized by *Business Week* and *Working Woman* magazines as a top businessperson, serves on the boards of Exxon Mobil and Qwest Communications International. She belongs to the World Travel and Tourism Council and is on the Council of the World Economic Forum.

Marilyn Carlson Nelson has also been honored for her dedicated work on behalf of charitable groups such as the United Way, both in her native Minnesota and the United States. In 1984, she became the first woman to chair a United Way annual fund drive in a major city. That year, the United Way of Minneapolis raised a record $28.8 million. She has also chaired numerous civic organizations and fund-raising efforts, and was recognized with the Woodrow Wilson Award for Corporate Citizenship from the Woodrow Wilson International Center for Scholars. Nelson has also been honored by other nations. The king of Sweden named her to the Royal Order of the North Star, First Class, and the president of Finland honored Nelson with the Order of the White Rose, Officer First Class.

Further Reading

Carlock, Randel S. "Filling Big Shoes at the Carlson Companies: Interview with Curt Carlson and Marilyn Carlson Nelson," *Family Business Review,* March 1999. Available online. URL: http://department.stthomas.edu/cfe/pub carlson.htm. Downloaded on June 11, 2001.

"Marilyn Carlson Nelson: Travel Titan," *Business Week,* February 1999, p. 64.

"Marilyn Carlson Ranks Seventh Among Fortune's 50 Most Powerful Women in American Business," Hotel Online, Special Report. Available online. URL: http://www. hotel-online.com/Neo/News/PressReleases1998 3rd/Sept98_MarilynCarlson.html. Downloaded on June 13, 2001.

Northwood University Outstanding Business Leaders Award: "Marilyn Carlson Nelson," Available online. URL: http://www.northwood.edu/obl/1996/nelson/html. Posted in 1996. Downloaded on May 25, 2001.

Summers, Mary. "Feminism, Power, and Happiness," *Forbes,* May 17, 1999, pp. 26ff.

✳ NEMETH, LANE
(1947–)   *Entrepreneur, Executive, Author*

Lane Nemeth founded and served as president and chief executive officer (CEO) of Discovery Toys, a company that makes and sells quality toys, books, games, tapes, educational software, and clothing. Through this endeavor, Nemeth has aimed to provide durable playthings that encourage children's creativity, imagination, and positive relations with others. She has said, "We choose and design toys that are nonviolent, and intentionally create cooperative game versions for most of our games that encourage children to work for a common goal."

Born in New York City on March 27, 1947, Nemeth received her bachelor's degree in English from the University of Pittsburgh and a master's degree in education from Seton Hall University in New Jersey. She embarked on a career in early childhood education. After she married Ed Nemeth in 1971, his employer transferred Ed to Concord, California, and she became the director of a state-funded day care center there. As her friends had children and her own daughter, Tara, was born in 1975, Lane Nemeth looked for the kinds of educational and developmental toys and games her staff had used at the day care center but could not find them in retail stores.

Nemeth was inspired to develop a company that would fill this need. From the family's home in Martinez, California, she began her business, stashing toys in various rooms, in 1978. She aimed to offer toys that would help children learn important life skills and interact in a positive way with other people. Her second goal was to invite parents to sell the products. By working from home on a flexible schedule, they would be able to pursue a career while raising children. Discovery Toys would be sold using the "party plan" method, in which its salespeople, known as educational consultants, order and buy stock, then display the items for groups of people, mainly parents and grandparents, who come together for a sales party. Through hard work and careful decision-making, Nemeth had a promising first year with sales of $280,000.

When her daughter entered first grade, Nemeth began working full time at her company. Her husband, a businessman, often arranged his schedule so that he could spend more time at home with their daughter.

Discovery Toys continued to grow during the 1980s and moved to new headquarters in Livermore, California, where it has its corporate offices and distribution and service centers. New products, including some created by Ed Nemeth, were introduced and sold well. By the early 1990s, the company had an estimated value of about $100 million and employed 30,000 educational consultants and 170 other staff members at its California offices. By 2000, the number of consultants had grown to 40,000. The company offered home-study parenting programs along with its toys, books, games, software, clothing, and personal care products for children.

In 1997, Nemeth sold the business to Avon Products, which has a similar sales model offering person-to-person service. Avon sold the company to private investors in April 1998. Nemeth remains on the board of directors of Discovery Toys.

After retiring as head of the company, Nemeth wrote a book about her experiences and her philosophy about children and families called *Discovering Another Way: Raising Brighter Children While Having a Meaningful Career* (1998). She has spoken to numerous organizations about ways to address the challenges of raising healthy, productive children and developing strong families in contemporary America.

Nemeth has received many awards for her achievements in business and education, including honors from the National Association of Women Business Owners, and she was named one of the Top 50 Business Women *Working Woman* magazine.

In her free time, Nemeth, who lives in Lamorinda, California, with her husband and daughter, enjoys collecting dolls from around the world and knitting, as well as swimming and bicycling in the morning before work. She is a popular speaker who appears at conferences and seminars on business, child development, education, and leadership. She has expressed concern about the need to build more self-esteem in children and to prevent the feelings of isolation that she feels can develop in a high-tech society. Sharing her business philosophy, Nemeth says, "Business is society. We touch an enormous number of people, and we have to touch everybody with care and concern, with gentleness and awareness."

Further Reading

Beyond Words Publishing, Inc. "Author Lane Nemeth." Available online. URL: http://www.beyondword.com/authors/nemeth1.html Downloaded on May 4, 2001.

Hallett, Anthony and Diane. *Entrepreneur Magazine's Encyclopedia of Entrepreneurs.* New York: John Wiley & Sons, 1997.

Matisoff-Li, Alexandra. "One Woman's Toy Story," Diablomag.com. Available online. URL: http://diablomag.com/archives/DM0003/sod.html Posted in 1999. Downloaded on May 1, 2001.

Nemeth, Lane. *Discovering Another Way: Raising Brighter Children While Having a Meaningful Career.* Hillsboro, Oreg.: Beyond Words Publishing, 1998.

✳ NIDETCH, JEAN
(1923–) *Entrepreneur, Executive, Author, Philanthropist*

Jean Nidetch founded Weight Watchers International, which became the world's largest weight control company. Honored as one of America's foremost entrepreneurs, Nidetch has said, "There will always be new opportunities for those of us who set no limit in our quest to accomplish our goals, and so we will realize our wildest dreams."

Jean Nidetch was born on October 12, 1923. After her marriage, she began raising a family in the Little Neck section of Queens, New York. In 1961, she weighed 200 pounds. She later said that she was an "overweight housewife obsessed with eating cookies." Although she tried dieting to lose weight, she found that it was difficult to stick with her diet alone and decided to find other women who wanted to meet regularly and support each other's weight-loss efforts. They began meeting each week in her living room, and Nidetch made weight plans for herself and the other women. Nidetch lost 70 pounds in one year. She was convinced that weight loss depended on more than just cutting calories and that people needed to change their habits and find sources of support to reach their goals.

Having demonstrated that a supportive group was a powerful tool, Nidetch, who called her group Weight Watchers, began holding meetings in a movie theater basement. Members initially paid two dollars a week in dues. She later said that her vision was "to bring together people with a need—a need to discover how capable they are, to inspire, to encourage, to stimulate, to teach, and to help people realize their dreams." She later described the company's humble beginnings:

> In 1963, Weight Watchers was born with no money and classes were held anywhere. My family and I spend our Sundays in those early years putting rubber thumbtacks on the bottoms of folding chairs so they wouldn't slide when a member of Weight Watchers sat down on a linoleum covered floor. It's true—we checked the bannisters for loose screws that had to be tightened, and we cleaned the rooms to be ready for every Monday morning.

Weight Watchers members were taught how to lose weight gradually through healthy eating plans and exercise. The group members offered each other support to stick with the program, applauded each other's successes, and offered encouragement when people experienced setbacks. As the group grew larger, Nidetch arranged to hold meetings in a loft over a movie theater in New York. The loft had 50 chairs, which meant 50 people could attend at one time.

To spread the word about Weight Watchers, Nidetch began visiting nearby communities to publicize the weight-loss program that had worked for her and her friends. In 1962, she met Albert Lippert, who joined one of her groups in Baldwin, on Long Island, New York. Using Nidetch's plan, Lippert had shed 53 pounds and his wife had lost 50 pounds. Lippert, who had been working in the retail clothing business, agreed with Nidetch that the Weight Watchers program was effective and would appeal to many other people who wanted to lose weight. In 1964, at Lippert's suggestion, Nidetch incorporated her business. Nidetch then partnered with Lippert to start building the business, and he joined it full time in 1968. They then took the company public with a stock offering.

The company experienced tremendous growth during the next decade. Nidetch was gratified when 17,000 Weight Watchers members from around the world gathered in New York's Madison Square Garden in 1971 to celebrate the organization's 10th anniversary. She later said, "we all rejoiced as we realized our dreams of enjoying our lives without the handicap we thought we could never overcome."

In 1973, Nidetch resigned as president of the company but remained involved with Weight Watchers as a consultant. Five years later, it was sold for $72 million to the Heinz Company.

Although she was no longer in charge of Weight Watchers, Jean Nidetch remained very active in the weight loss industry, appearing on dozens of radio and television programs and speaking to organizations throughout the United States and around the world. Nidetch also wrote several best-selling books about her experiences and the Weight Watchers program. For years, she wrote a monthly syndicated column that appeared in more than 300 newspapers. Her books include several cookbooks, as well as a memoir, *The Story of Weight Watchers*, which sold more than 2 million copies.

During the 1990s, Weight Watchers remained the largest weight control company in the world and had served more than 25 million members as of 1991. As of 1997, about 1 million people were attending a meeting weekly in 28 countries around the world. It was estimated that the company had a worldwide attendance of more than 42 million people in 1998.

The company continued to grow and develop new approaches, such as its 1-2-3 Success Plan, which was launched in 1997. The 1-2-3 plan allows people to eat foods based on a point system, using up a certain number of points per day.

Nidetch has received hundreds of awards and other recognition for her business achievements. *Ladies' Home Journal* magazine named her one of the most important women in the United States. In 1989, she won the Horatio Alger Award given by the Horatio Alger Association. Two years later, Nidetch received Northwood University's Outstanding Business Leader award. The London *Sunday Times* has called Nidetch one of the 1,000 Makers of the Twentieth Century.

Her own experience convinced Jean Nidetch that people could lose weight more easily if they had ongoing support from others, along with a healthy eating plan.
(Photo courtesy of Weight Watchers International, Inc. Weight Watchers is the registered trademark of Weight Watchers International, Inc.)

Nidetch is also known for her philanthropic activities. She funded the Women's Resource Center in Las Vegas at the University of Nevada. Located in the Reynolds Student Services Complex, the center provides services to both men and women students, including counseling, academic support, and help in entering college for the first time as an adult. She established the Jean Nidetch Foundation to help economically disadvantaged teenagers continue their education and funded a scholarship program at University of California, Los Angeles to support postgraduate education in political science.

As of 2002, Jean Nidetch was retired and living in Las Vegas, Nevada.

Further Reading

Nidetch, Jean. *The Story of Weight Watchers.* New York: New American Library, 1979.

Schuch, Beverly. "Weight Watchers CEO," Business Unusual, CNNfn, December 13, 1997.

Unger, Michael. "Cash-Hungry Heinz to Sell Weight Watchers' LI Unit," *Newsday,* February 18, 1999, p. A47.

Winslow, Olivia. "Albert Lippert, Early Partner in Weight Watchers," *Newsday,* March 3, 1998.

O

OMLIE, PHOEBE FAIRGRAVE
(1902–1975)   *Entrepreneur,*
Aviation Pioneer

Aviator and aviation safety expert Phoebe Fairgrave Omlie overcame many obstacles to success. She was the first woman to form her own air show, and she helped to found the first airport in Tennessee, as well as one of the first U.S. flying schools.

Phoebe Fairgrave was born in Des Moines, Iowa, on December 21, 1902, and her family moved to St. Paul, Minnesota, when she was 15. Although she was interested in flying while she was still in high school, when she graduated high school in 1920, she could not find a flight instructor who would give her lessons. During the 1920s, flying was still regarded as a man's activity.

To earn money and become part of aviation, she learned to perform air stunts—wing walking and jumping with a parachute. Fairgrave had been fascinated by the parachutists, stunt pilots, and wing walkers she had seen at air shows. However, when she tried parachuting herself, she had trouble lifting the heavy pack containing the parachute. She embarked on a program to build up her arm and shoulder muscles by exercising, lifting weights, and other types of strength training.

When she made her first jump on April 17, 1921, she landed in some trees, but she continued to practice and became proficient. Fairgrave joined the Glenn Messer Flying Circus and barnstormed throughout the Midwest at state fairs, impressing spectators with her daring jumps. She set a new record for women when she jumped from 15,200 feet on July 10, 1921. She then began working on double-parachute jumps, in which she would jump, cut the first chute after it opened, and go into a free fall before releasing her second chute.

At age 20, Phoebe Fairgrave launched her own air show, making her the first woman to form a flying troupe—the Phoebe Fairgrave Flying Circus. Her chief pilot was Vernon Omlie, who taught her to fly. In 1922, they were married. Phoebe Omlie became the first American woman to earn a federal pilot's license, in 1927.

The couple continued to perform air stunts. They saved their money in order to start their own flying school and aviation business, Mid-South Airways, in Memphis, Tennessee. The Omlies also used their skill as pilots to perform rescue missions. In 1927,

Aviator and aviation school founder Phoebe Omlie is shown powdering her nose shortly after winning the National Air Race Transcontinental Sweepstakes Handicap Derby in August 1931.
(Photo courtesy of Library of Congress)

when the Mississippi River overflowed, the couple flew supplies to flood victims during the crisis.

The next year, Phoebe Omlie became the first woman to complete the National Air Reliability Tour. This race lasted more than a month and covered 5,304 miles, 13 states, and 32 cities. Omlie also flew in the United States, Canada, and South America demonstrating the Monocoupe, a plane produced by Mono Aircraft that she had flown in the National Women's Air Derby of 1929 when she won first prize in the CW class. The race included several legs, beginning with a run from Santa Monica to San Bernardino, California. The next leg went from San Bernardino to Yuma, Arizona. From there, the pilots flew to Phoenix, then to Douglas, Arizona. In Texas, they stopped at El Paso, then Pecos.

Some people opposed the race and said women were not capable of piloting airplanes. A Texas oil-

man named Hailliburton claimed that women had "been dependent on man for guidance for so long that when they are put on their own resources they are handicapped." Omlie and the other women were determined to prove him wrong. They continued on to Midland, Texas, then Abilene. Omlie was clearly in the lead in her class at this point. The rest of the race included stops at Tulsa, Oklahoma; Wichita, Kansas; East St. Louis, Missouri; and Terre Haute, Indiana. In Ohio, the pilots stopped in Cincinnati, Columbus, and Cleveland. The last day of the race was August 26, 1929, when they took off for Cleveland. Fourteen of the original 20 women pilots arrived. Omlie, the winner in her class, had an elapsed time of 22:14:32.

To promote women in aviation, in 1929 Omlie helped form a club for women pilots. Called the Ninety-nines because there were 99 members, the group aimed to support women aviators and educate the public about their achievements. During the 1920s, Omlie became the first woman to earn an aircraft mechanic's license. She continued to participate in air races and broke speed records during the 1920s.

Omlie also took part in the presidential election of 1932, when Franklin Roosevelt, the Democratic candidate, asked her to help fly him from place to place during the campaign.

In 1933, President Roosevelt, who greatly respected Phoebe Omlie's abilities, appointed her as liaison between the National Advisory Committee for Aeronautics and the Bureau of Air Commerce. The president encouraged Omlie to develop a program for pilots based in Washington, D.C. Her pilot-training program, which she promoted throughout the United States, emphasized air safety. Omlie came up with the idea of marking the flat roofs of buildings with large letters showing the name of the city so that pilots could identify their location more clearly before landing. She also convinced the Airport Marking and Mapping Section of the Bureau of Air Commerce to get cooperation from all the states so that pilots would have consistent signals when flying from place to place.

When hiring people to work in the Bureau of Air Commerce's National Air Marking Program, she chose only woman employees, saying that they would work harder. In 1935, Omlie chose five leading women pilots as field representatives for the program. They were Louise Thaden, who was the first woman pilot to beat men in a cross-country race; Helen Richie; Blanche Noyes; Nancy Harkness (Love), who would later head the U.S. Air Transport Command in World War II as part of the Women's Airforce Service Pilots (WASPs); and Helen McCloskey.

Omlie remained active in her field throughout the war and then served in the Civil Aeronautics Administration throughout the 1950s. With her husband Vernon, she operated a pilots' training school in Tennessee, the first program of its kind in the United States.

In 1975, Omlie died in Indianapolis. The Phoebe Fairgrave Omlie Scholarship was established in her honor by the Federal Aviation Administration Mid-South Chapter Federal Women's Program (MSCFWP) and the Women in Aviation, International Memphis Belles Chapter. The scholarship is awarded annually to "a student or students demonstrating academic potential and ability to overcome obstacles."

Further Reading

Adams, Jean, and Margaret Kimball in collaboration with Jeanette Eaton. *Heroines of the Sky*. Garden City, N.Y.: Doubleday, Doran & Co., 1942.

Brooks-Pazmany, Kathleen. *United States Women in Aviation 1919–1929*. Washington, D.C.: Smithsonian Institution Press, 1991.

Holden, Henry M., and Captain Lori Griffith. *Ladybirds: The Untold Story of Women Pilots in America*. Freedom, N.J.: Black Hawk Publishing, 1991.

✾ OWADES, RUTH MARKOWITZ

(ca. 1948–)   *Entrepreneur, Business Owner, Executive*

Ruth Markowitz Owades founded Calyx & Corolla, a direct mail-order florist service, in 1988.

Her innovative idea, coupled with effective marketing and shipping methods, blossomed into a $25 million business that now serves customers in several countries. In an interview for the September 1999 issue of *Working Woman* magazine, Owades said, "The best qualities for an entrepreneur are tenacity and the ability to stay focused on what you want to achieve."

A native Californian, Owades received her bachelor's degree from Scripps College in Claremont, California, and earned her master's of business administration (M.B.A.) from Harvard University in 1975. She achieved a major success in the mail-order catalog business when she launched the Gardener's Eden catalog in 1979, selling upscale gardening accessories to consumers. In 1982, Williams-Sonoma purchased the business.

The idea for a direct-mail flower business came when she noticed that the wholesale flower market in San Francisco seemed to be exceptionally busy during the early 1980s. When Owades first considered going into the direct-mail floral business, she spent six months researching her idea, studying distributors, wholesalers, customer demand, and the competition. She later said, "I discovered that flowers go through a lot of middlemen and that if I could go from the grower to customer overnight by Federal Express, we could deliver a fresher product." Typically, flowers go from farms to a wholesaler who transports them to a distributor who then moves them to stores. Owades concluded that because the flowers in the average floral shop may be stored for 7 to 10 days on average before purchase, they have a short vase life as cut flowers.

She thought a segment of the American population would appreciate the chance to buy a variety of fresh flowers that were beautifully packaged and delivered in peak condition. Although some people discouraged her idea and pointed out the problems of dealing with a perishable commodity, Owades launched her business in 1988 in San Francisco. Its name, Calyx & Corolla, refers to the outer and inner parts of a flower. She aimed to eliminate steps in the process of buying flowers and deliver fresh-cut flowers the day after they were ordered. By computer, Qwades sent orders directly to flower farms where flower arrangers she had trained put the orders together on site.

By 1990, the company had exceeded revenues of $10 million and filled more than 150,000 orders. As the business grew, Owades added new products and offered customers the chance to purchase flowers and plants that were not always available in their local shops, such as tropical flowers and herbal bonsai plants. In 1993, Calyx & Corolla achieved $13 million in revenue and filled more than 300,000 orders.

As the head of the business, Owades has overseen the steady growth of Calyx & Corolla and has overcome the routine problems that most businesses encounter, as well as some unusual situations. For example, on Valentine's Day 1994, a blizzard prevented shipments from going out on time during one of the year's busiest "floral gift" days. Owades decided that her staff would personally contact every customer and gift recipient to explain what had happened and apologize. The company also sent written apologies along with a gift certificate. Although the process was expensive, Owades said it kept her customers loyal and was worth the cost.

Owades also wants employees to work in comfortable surroundings as they speak with customers and take phone orders, because she believes that comfortable employees are more likely to give good service. Employees at Calyx & Corolla sit in sunny rooms at desks that are angled so people are not isolated from each other, and the room is abundantly decorated with fresh flowers and plants. The company's lunchroom window looks out on scenic San Francisco Bay. Owades says that these kinds of surroundings reflect what the company stands for: "good taste, simplicity."

By the late 1990s, the company's annual sales exceeded $20 million, and in 2000 they reached $25 million. Owades was managing a business with several hundred employees and working with 25 domestic and four foreign growers. Each year, Calyx and Corolla sends out 15 million catalogs and serves 15 million customers. In addition to its print cata-

log, Calyx & Corolla operates a website where some of its selections can be seen and purchased.

Owades has been honored for her achievements as an entrepreneur and for her contributions to the catalog industry. In 1996, she received the Magnificent Seven Award from Business and Professional Women/USA. The organization stated that Owades had advanced "the cause and reputation of all women in business." Owades serves on the advisory board of *Catalog Success Magazine.*

Further Reading

"About Us." Calyx & Corolla on the Web. Available online. URL: http://www.calyxandcorolla.com/about/. Downloaded on October 17, 2001.

Carlsen, Clifford. "Women's Group Finds Flower Seller's Talent in Full Bloom," *San Francisco Business Times,* August 9, 1996. Available online. URL: http://sanfrancisco.bcentral.com/sanfrancisco/stories/1996/08/12/newscolumn2.html. Downloaded on June 2, 2001.

"Entrepreneurs Profits in Bloom," *Time,* February 18, 1991, p. 57.

Herbers, Jim. "Velvet Cubicles (And Other Great Workspaces)," *Fortune,* November 1999.

Meyer, Michele. "8 ways to get everything you want in life," *Cosmopolitan,* April, 1997, pp. 152–53.

Panepinto, Joe. "Special Delivery," *Computerworld,* March 7, 1994, p. 79.

OWEN, DIAN GRAVES
(Dian Graves Owen Stai)
(ca. 1939–   )   *Entrepreneur, Executive, Philanthropist*

Regarded as one of America's top business leaders, Dian Graves Owen cofounded Owen Healthcare Group, Inc. As chairman of the board, she oversaw the growth of this hospital pharmacy management company into a multimillion-dollar business. Describing her leadership style, Owen has said, "My management style is through an executive circle. . . . I set the goals. Management tells me how we're going to reach them."

Growing up in Abilene, Texas, Dian Graves admired her mother and the example she set. She later said, "It was she who taught me the value of work and the importance of patriotism."

With her husband Jean Owen, a pharmacist, she founded the pharmacy management company in 1969. Dian Owen later said that the company was founded out of "adversity," because Jean Owen had recently lost his job and was looking for a new line of work. The type of service he envisioned—managing an in-house pharmacy—was unusual. While Jean, a pharmacist, managed the company, Dian Owen was in charge of promoting sales and marketing their services to hospitals. They set out to build a business that owns and operates retail pharmacies and manages hospital pharmacies. It now also develops and markets computer software for pharmacies so they can manage their operations more efficiently.

Within seven years, Owen Healthcare had sales of about $6.6 million. After Jean Owen died in 1976 in an airplane crash, Dian received several buy-out offers but decided to run the company herself. When several important clients decided to leave Owen and sign up with a competitor, she was able to overcome that setback by signing on new clients to keep the business going. Owen later said that she and her team at the company overcame numerous obstacles: "My associates and I together have faced potentially damaging legislation, negative trends, and all of the other challenges of doing business in our industry, and indeed any industry, for the last twenty-seven years. Talent, hard work, confidence, and yes, luck have served us well."

Under Owen's leadership, the number of hospital clients rose from 24 in 1976 to 100 by 1982. By 1984, Owen Healthcare had become the largest company of its kind in the nation. Gross revenues also rose consistently, gaining more than 25 percent each year during the late 1970s and 1980s. From revenues of $6.6 million in 1976, revenues grew to $240 million in 1992, at which time Owen Healthcare employed more than 2,000 people, who served more than 250 hospitals in 40 states.

Owen oversaw this expansion and also made changes within the company. Attuned to the needs of its employees, especially working mothers,

Owen offered a day care service for their children. During the mid-1980s, the company also added new services and developed new technology. In 1984, it added its Hospital Materials Services Division; the next year, it added Owen Home Infusion Services. To keep costs down, Owen offered technology to help clients better manage their resources, purchases, and record-keeping.

In 1994, revenues at the company reached the $320 million mark. That year, the company had more than 2,000 employees who were servicing more than 500 hospital agreements in 41 states.

In March 1997, Cardinal Health, Inc., a company based in Dublin, Ohio, bought Owen Healthcare. Dian Owen left as chairman when that acquisition was finalized. She became Dian Graves Owen Stai that year when she married pharmacist and businessman Harlan Stai. As of 1998, Owen Healthcare had 3,600 employees nationwide and was serving over 72 percent of the acute care hospitals that hire outside pharmaceutical management.

In addition to her many business responsibilities through the years, Dian Owen has devoted a great deal of time to community service. She has served as a board member of the Muscular Dystrophy Association, the West Texas Rehabilitation Center, McMurry College, and St. John's Episcopal School in Abilene. She was the first chairperson of the Texas Department of Commerce and served as chairperson of the board—the first woman to hold that position—for the Abilene Chamber of Commerce in 1993–94. She has also been a member of the board of directors of the First National Bank, the Petroleum Club, the Muscular Dystrophy Foundation, and the Committee of 200, among others. Her Dian Graves Owen Stai Foundation contributes to various philanthropic causes.

She has been honored by many organizations, including the Northwood Institute as an Outstanding Business Leader (1996). During her acceptance speech, Owen said: "To have worked with wonderful associates, to have been paid well for that work, to have had more fun doing it than I would ever have dreamed possible, and then to receive an award for doing it, is pure delight. How privileged I have been to be part of Owen Healthcare and to have seen from my unique position a private view of the American dream and the free enterprise system."

In 1997, Owen was inducted into the Texas Women's Hall of Fame. Congressman Bob Hunter (R-Abilene) presented her with a copy of the resolution that accompanied her induction, saying, "No one could be more deserving than Dian Owen for this great honor. She has distinguished herself as a civic leader, philanthropist, astute business woman and a friend to hundreds of people across this state and nation."

Further Reading

Ray, Steve. "Dian Owen Inducted Into Texas Women's Hall of Fame," *The Abilene Reporter-News.* Available online. URL: http://www.texnews.com/news/owen01397.html. Downloaded on May 23, 2001.

Silver, A. David. *Enterprising Women.* New York: AMACOM, 1994.

P

PENNINGTON, MARY ENGLE
(1872–1953)   *Scientist, Engineer,*
Entrepreneur, Business Consultant

Mary Pennington developed effective methods of food preservation and refrigeration and became the first woman member of the American Society of Refrigeration Engineers. She pioneered the effort toward safe food storage and once referred to herself as "an expert in the handling, transportation and storage of perishables and the application of refrigeration."

Pennington was born on October 8, 1872, into a Quaker family in Philadelphia, where her father was a label manufacturer. (Members of the Society of Friends, a religious denomination, are known as Quakers.) She later recalled that she first became interested in science at age 12, when she read about nitrogen and oxygen in a chemistry book. In 1890, Pennington entered the Towne Scientific School at the University of Pennsylvania and completed the requirements for a bachelor of science (B.S.) degree in two years. However, because she was a woman, the university would not grant her the B.S. degree; instead, they gave her a certificate of proficiency.

Nonetheless, Pennington's professors allowed her to pursue graduate studies, and in 1895 she was awarded a Ph.D. The next year, she held a postdoctoral fellowship at Yale University.

In 1898, Dr. Pennington returned to her hometown. Two years later, she established the Philadelphia Clinical Laboratory, which performed bacterial analyses for physicians. She was appointed director of the bacteriological laboratory for the Philadelphia Department of Health and served there from 1904 to 1907. That year, she began conducting more studies of food.

In 1907, using the name "M. E. Pennington," she took the civil service exam in order to work for the U.S. Department of Agriculture. Not realizing she was a woman, the department offered her a job. Soon she was named director of its newly formed Food Research Laboratory, which was created in 1908 to implement the Pure Food and Drug Act, which Congress had passed in 1906. During those years, food-borne illnesses were a particularly serious problem. Often, food was processed, stored, and handled in unsanitary conditions, and few laws had been enacted to regulate these processes.

In her new job, Pennington studied the effects of temperature on milk, eggs, and other perishable foods. With this information, she was able to determine which methods of handling, processing, and preserving foods would make them safer and also better tasting. Pennington then helped to develop laws requiring government inspection of perishable foods.

Although millions of Americans drank milk and gave it to their children, there were no clear standards for storing it or preserving it safely. Pennington was the first person ever to study ways to preserve a perishable food (milk) in cold storage. The standards she developed for milk inspection were adopted universally.

Known to colleagues as "Auntie Sam," she also wrote pamphlets about food refrigeration for consumers and people in food-related businesses. During her time at the department, she helped to produce more than 30 bulletins, 25 articles, and a book about eggs.

Pennington's work took her on railroad trips around the country, as she examined how different types of insulation and air circulation affected foods while they were being shipped in refrigerated cars. The standards she developed for railroad refrigerator cars during World War I remained in effect for more than 25 years. Pennington also recommended ways to safely freeze and store fish, and she designed egg packing cases that protected these fragile items and thus reduced breakage. As a result of her efforts, foods could be shipped far from their source without spoilage, and they could be stored from one season to another, which helped to reduce seasonal and regional scarcities.

After she left government service in 1919, Pennington worked at American Balsa Company, a manufacturer of insulated containers. In 1921, she opened her own private consulting business as a refrigeration engineer. For more than 30 years, she traveled widely, sharing her expertise about frozen food processing methods and showing commercial companies how to design and construct refrigerated warehouses and refrigerators for commercial and household use.

Pennington maintained a business office at the Woolworth Building in New York City and lived on Riverside Drive. A 1941 *New Yorker* magazine profile noted that Pennington's kitchen was decorated in Pennsylvania Dutch style and that she enjoyed using frozen foods and serving them at dinner parties. Each month, Pennington also made time in her busy schedule to have her hair waved at a beauty salon in the Stevens Hotel in Chicago, Illinois.

In, Mary Pennington became the first woman admitted to the American Society of Refrigerating Engineers. In addition, she was active in the American Association for the Advancement of Science and the Institute of Food Technologists, was inducted into the Poultry Historical Society's Hall of Fame, and was one of only a few women members of the American Chemical Society (ACS) during the 1940s. She was inducted into the ACS in 1940. In 1940, she also received the Francis P. Garvan medal, the highest award the ACS bestows on women. Pennington continued working and studying until she died in 1953.

Further Reading

Alic, Margaret. *Hypatia's Heritage*. Boston: Beacon Press, 1986.

DeLong, Lois. "Mothers of Invention," National Engineers Week [for the media], February 18–24, 2000. Available online. URL: http://www.eweek.org/2000/News/Features/moi.shtml. Downloaded on August 30, 2000.

"Mary Engle Pennington (1872–1953)," Women's Biographies at University of Pennsylvania. Available online. URL: http://www.archives.upenn.edu/Women_at_Penn/. Downloaded on December 2, 2000.

Swoboda, Alexis. "Pioneer in Safe Food Storage: Mary Engle Pennington," *SWE (Society of Women Engineers) Magazine,* November/December 1994, p. 16.

PHILIPSE, MARGARET HARDENBROECK DE VRIES
(ca. 1639–ca. 1690)   *Merchant, Shipowner, Business Agent*

Margaret Philipse was probably the first female business agent in America, and one historian called her "perhaps the most enterprising of all the Dutch colonists, male or female."

She arrived in the colony of New Amsterdam when she was still in her teens with her first husband, Peter De Vries. They bought a plantation on Staten Island and helped to start a new settlement there. After De Vries died, Margaret De Vries sold their land and invested the money in ships. She may have started the first "packet line," ships making regular trips to carry passengers and goods, between America and Europe.

As the wife of a merchant who traded between the colony of New Amsterdam and the Netherlands, she had learned a great deal about this business and proved to be a capable business agent. At times, she even sailed with the ships and oversaw the loading and unloading of cargo, as well as the buying and selling of goods.

In 1661, she married Frederick Philipse, who had been a passenger on one of her ships to Europe, where he planned to sell a supply of furs. Working together and, later, with their son Adolph, the Philipses amassed a fortune as shipping merchants. Their ships carried paying trans-Atlantic passengers as well. In 1670, Margaret Philipse and her husband used some of her capital to buy 300 acres of land in the area that is now called Yonkers (part of present-day Westchester County in New York State). There they built an estate called Philipse Manor in 1693. They also purchased land in Manhattan that later increased greatly in value.

Margaret Philipse died in about 1690.

Further Reading

Biemer, Linda Briggs. *Women and Property in Colonial New York: The Transition from Dutch to English Law, 1643–1727.* Ann Arbor, Mich.: UMI Research Press, 1985.

Dexter, Elizabeth Anthony. *Colonial Women of Affairs, Before 1776.* Clifton, N.J.: Augustus M. Kelley Publishers, 1972.

Ritchie, Robert. *The Duke's Province: A Study in New York Politics and Society, 1664–1691.* Chapel Hill: University of North Carolina Press, 1977.

PINCKNEY, ELIZA LUCAS
(1722–1793)   *Business Manager, Entrepreneur*

During the mid-to-late 1700s, Eliza Lucas Pinckney ran several large South Carolina plantations and developed indigo as an important new crop in her region.

Eliza Lucas was born in 1722 in Antigua, in the West Indies, where her father, Lt. Col. George Lucas, was stationed with the British army. She was educated in England and learned to speak French fluently. In 1737, the family moved to Wappoo Creek, near Charles Town in the colony of South Carolina, where Lieutenant Colonel Lucas hoped the climate would improve the health of his wife, an invalid. He began running a plantation but was summoned to duty in 1739 when war broke out between Britain and Spain. Her father left the estate in the hands of 16-year-old Eliza, who was also expected to care for her mother and younger sister, Polly.

Eliza Lucas took over running the 600-acre main plantation, which was home to 20 slaves, and added two smaller farms that were planted with rice, the chief crop in South Carolina at that time. Her responsibilities included recording planting information, shipments, payments, and legal matters. In her correspondence, Lucas wrote about her busy days:

> I rise at 5 o'clock in the morning, read till seven, then take a walk in the garden or field, see that the servants are at their respective business, then to breakfast. The first hour after breakfast is spent at my musick [sic], the next is constantly employed in recollecting something I have learned for want of practise it should be quite lost, such as French or shorthand. After that I devote the rest of the time till I dress for dinner to our little Polly and two black girls who I teach to read, and if I have my papa's approbation (my Mama's I have got) I intend them for school mistresses for the rest of the Negro children.

During those years, rice prices were falling, so the family was considering different crops to cultivate, such as figs, cotton, alfalfa, and ginger. Eliza Lucas's father had sent her some indigo seeds. (Indigo yielded a blue dye sought by British customers.) Indigo was imported from the French colonies in the West Indies but had not grown well in the British colonies. Lieutenant Colonel Lucas urged Eliza to plant the seeds.

In 1744, after three years of poor indigo harvests, Lucas finally produced a good crop and found an effective method of making dye from blocks of indigo cakes. She sent a sample of the dye to some London merchants. The British parliament was then offering a monetary bonus for indigo grown in their colonies so they would not have to buy it from their enemy, France. French officials realized they would no longer be the exclusive source of indigo, and they made it illegal for people in the West Indies to export seeds, but by then Lucas already had a store of seeds to use for future plantings.

Lucas, who married widower Charles Pinckney in 1744, continued to grow indigo, and she distributed seeds to other South Carolina planters, who cultivated indigo on their plantations. The crop flourished, and colonists shipped 40,000 pounds of indigo to England in 1746. Within 20 years, Carolinians were exporting more than 1 million pounds of dye, making this a lucrative business for the colony.

The Pinckney family, which grew to include four children, divided its time between London and South Carolina. After her husband died of malaria in 1758, Eliza Lucas Pinckney began managing his seven plantations. Pinckney also continued to experiment with plants, especially hemp and flax, and she encouraged the growth of the silk industry in South Carolina. In addition, she continued to rear her children—Charles, Thomas, and Harriot—with whom she resided in her later years. Her fourth child had died in infancy. Charles was an aide to General George Washington during the American Revolution and later ran for president on the Federalist party ticket in 1804 and 1808, while Thomas, served as governor of South Carolina in 1787 and was later minister to Great Britain.

Pinckney died of cancer at her daughter Harriot Horry's home in Philadelphia in 1793. President Washington held her in such high esteem that he asked to be one of the pallbearers at her funeral. In 1989, she was inducted into the South Carolina Business Hall of Fame.

Further Reading

Brooks, Geraldine. *Dames and Daughters of Colonial Days.* New York: Crowell, 1900.

Graydon, Nell S. *Eliza of Wappoo: A Tale of Indigo.* Columbia, S.C.: R. L. Bryan and Co., 1967.

Pinckney, Eliza Lucas. *The Letterbook of Eliza Lucas Pinckney, 1739–62.* Edited by Marvin R. Zahnizer. Charleston: University of South Carolina Press, 1997.

The South Carolina Business Hall of Fame. "Pinckney, Eliza Lucas." Available on line. URL: http://www.theweb. badm.sc.edu/ja/jaelp.htm. Downloaded on August 4, 2000.

�֎ PINKHAM, LYDIA ESTES
(1819–1883)   *Entrepreneur, Herbalist, Author*

Pinkham developed and marketed Lydia E. Pinkham's Vegetable Compound, a concoction to treat "female complaints," and used advanced advertising methods, such as testimonials, to promote her product. Her grandmotherly image appeared in ads and on the product labels, marking the first time a woman's photo had been used for advertising purposes.

Lydia Estes was born on February 9, 1819, in Lynn, Massachusetts. She was the 10th of 12 children in a prosperous Quaker farming family that was actively involved in social causes, including the abolition movement. (Members of the Society of Friends, a religious denomination, are known as Quakers.) During her youth, Lydia met famous abolitionists, both black and white, and she also became active in the abolitionist movement. At age 16, she joined the Lynn Female Antislavery Movement and later helped to found the Freeman's Institute, an abolitionist group that also supported women's suffrage.

After graduating from Lynn Academy, she became a schoolteacher. Tall and slim, with auburn hair and dark eyes, she was known for her calm and composed manner.

In 1843, she married Isaac Pinkham, a 29-year-old widower with a five-year-old daughter. Lydia Pinkham gave birth to the first of their five children in 1844, and four of them survived childhood. Isaac Pinkham had been a shoe manufacturer, but in 1845 he began speculating in various businesses and tried his luck as a produce dealer, farmer, trader, and builder, among other things. The family moved frequently, and their economic situation was unstable and often precarious as Isaac borrowed money for new ventures that usually failed.

Like many other women of her day, Lydia Pinkham had long been interested in herbal treatments, and she kept a notebook that described how plant products could be used to alleviate various health problems. Throughout her neighborhood, she served as a midwife and nursed people who were sick. Women appreciated the herbal preparation she had been making and giving to friends and family for years. Her concoction contained unicorn root, fenugreek seed, black cohosh, and other herbs and roots, and it was reputed to help women with what were called "female complaints," such as menstrual pain and menopausal symptoms.

During the economic depression of 1873, Isaac Pinkham went bankrupt and his health gave out. Women from neighboring communities had been asking to buy Pinkham's herbal compound, so the family decided to sell the product. Numerous remedies were sold door to door and in drugstores in those days, and the government did not regulate their manufacture or sale. Pinkham brewed a large batch in her cellar kitchen, adding about 18 percent alcohol as a solvent and preservative. Her children contributed to the business in various ways, by providing money for supplies and ideas for the ads and by helping to distribute the product.

Pinkham and her son Will wrote ads about their product, which they named Lydia E. Pinkham's Vegetable Compound, a simple name that made no particular claims about what the product would do. Pinkham sincerely believed in her product and used it herself. She regarded it as safer and more effective than many of the remedies medical doctors offered to women. In truth, the concoction was much safer than many other home remedies that were being sold at that time, some of which contained such toxic materials as mercury, arsenic, and nitric acid.

The compound was on the market by 1875. Will and Dan Pinkham distributed thousands of advertising pamphlets to homes throughout the Boston area, and Dan also covered New York City.

Each bottle of the remedy came with instructions to take four spoonfuls a day, as well as a

During an era when most physicians were men, Lydia Pinkham produced a herbal remedy for women and addressed their specific health concerns in her writings and letters.
(Photo courtesy of the Lynn Museum, Lynn, Massachusetts)

165

four-page brochure titled "Guide for Women." Interestingly, despite the compound's 18 percent alcohol content, the Pinkham family supported the temperance movement, which advocated against the use of alcohol. Some of the people who wrote testimonials for the product were temperance movement leaders as well. However, the Pinkhams believed that taking alcohol in a medicinal preparation was not the same as drinking an alcoholic beverage.

In 1876, the family organized the Lydia E. Pinkham Medicine Company. In order to avoid any claims against the business by Isaac's creditors, they named Will Pinkham as the sole proprietor. Pinkham's sons vigorously promoted her product, using handbills and newspaper ads. In the beginning, sales were slow, and the family even mortgaged their home to pay for the newspaper ads, which called the product "a Positive Cure for all those Painful Complaints and Weaknesses so common among our best female population." One ad claimed, "If a woman finds that her energies are flagging, that she gets easily tired, dark shadows appear under her eyes, she has backaches, headaches, bearing down sensations, nervousness, irregularities or the 'blues,' she should start at once to build up her system by a tonic with specific powers, such as Lydia E. Pinkham's Vegetable Compound."

The family decided a picture would help sell the product. Lydia Pinkham was a healthy-looking person, and in 1879 her sons convinced her to put her own photograph on the ads and the labels that went on the bottles. Her kindly face, gray hair styled in a bun, and simple black dress with a lace fichu soon became recognized throughout the country. People made up songs and rhymes about Lydia Pinkham and her compound, which gave the company even more exposure. In Great Britain, medical students sang this song:

And so we drink, we drink, we drink to Lydia Pink,
The saviour of the human race,
She invented the Vegetable Compound,
Most efficacious in every case.

Pinkham gained additional customers after she wrote a book describing her views on how women could bolster their health through proper nutrition, exercise, fresh air, and cleanliness. Her advice to women included such statements as the following: "Bathe yourself all over every night in hot water. . . . Eat farinaceous foods and broths. . . . Ride out and walk out; dig, use the trowel. When in the house sit by [an] open window (well-protected) that you may inhale all the outdoor air possible." Her book also discussed menopause and other topics that many women felt uncomfortable discussing with their doctors, most of whom were men and were not trained to deal with women's special needs. Women praised Pinkham's straightforward approach, and millions of copies of her book were sold. She also broke down barriers by writing a book for married women and those who were preparing to marry that discussed sexuality, and she answered questions sent to her by thousands of customers.

By 1880, sales had increased greatly, and Pinkham received a $100,000 offer to buy her trademark, which she refused. The next year, sales exceeded $200,000 when the company sold more than 200,000 bottles. However, Lydia Pinkham faced two personal tragedies that year when her son Dan died of tuberculosis at age 32 and Will, who had just been married, died of consumption later that same year. Both sons had traveled away from home and worked long hours, depriving themselves of adequate food and rest, while they were building up the company.

Lydia Pinkham herself died on May 17, 1883, several months after suffering from a severe stroke. Newspapers reporting her death hailed her as the "savior of her sex," and claimed she had given women practical advice and help so that they could improve their own health.

Her descendants continued to run the business, which attained a peak revenue of $3.8 million in 1925. They also continued to answer customers' letters in Lydia Pinkham's name. Sales were high in Europe as well as North and Central America. Although the federal Pure Food and Drug Act of 1938 made it necessary for the company to cease making some of the advertising claims, the product itself was deemed safe for consumers. In 1968, the family sold the rights to Lydia Pinkham's formulas and trademark to Cooper Laboratories.

Further Reading

Kett, Joseph H. *The Formation of the American Medical Profession: The Role of Institutions, 1780–1860.* New Haven: Yale University Press, 1968.

Stage, Sarah. *Female Complaints: Lydia Pinkham and the Business of Women's Medicine.* New York: W. W. Norton, 1979.

Sutcliffe, Jenny, and Nancy Duin. *A History of Medicine.* New York: Barnes and Noble, 1992.

R

※ ※ ※ ※ ※

※ ROSENTHAL, IDA COHEN
(Ida Kaganovich)
(1886–1973)   *Entrepreneur, Business Owner, Business cofounder*

Ida Cohen Rosenthal cofounded the Maidenform Brassiere Company, which grew into one of the world's largest producers of intimate apparel.

Ida Kaganovich (later changed to Cohen) was born on January 9, 1886, in Rakov, near Minsk in Russia, where her mother ran a general merchandise store and her father was a Hebrew scholar. The family included seven children. While growing up, Ida was an excellent student, and she was apprenticed to a local dressmaker where she learnt sewing skills. At age 18, she immigrated to the United States, where her fiancé, William Rosenthal, another Russian immigrant, had arrived a few months earlier. They were married in 1906 and opened a dressmaking shop in Hoboken, New Jersey. Within five years it became the city's most prestigious dressmaking business. Ida was in charge of sales and finances, while William oversaw the design and tailoring of the dresses. The store employed six workers and became so prof-

itable that Ida Rosenthal was able to bring the rest of her family to America.

In 1918, the couple moved to New York City, where they opened a new dressmaking business. With a partner, dressmaker Enid Bissett, they operated a store called Enid Frocks on 57th Street in a fashionable shopping area beginning in 1921. Rosenthal and Bissett realized their custom-made dresses would hang better on their customers if they changed the shape of the brassieres women wore. In those days, brassieres were mere bandeau strips of cloth with hook fasteners in the back, forming a sort of flat belt around the breast instead of showing its usually rounded shape. Bissett and William Rosenthal experimented with new designs that had two cups separated by a center piece of elastic. The two dressmakers sewed tucks in the fabric to make pockets and the strip of elastic in the center held each breast separately. They built these brassieres into the dresses, costing between $125 to $300, they made for their customers.

Customers began requesting the new brassieres as a separate item of clothing, so Rosenthal and Bissett formed the Enid Manufacturing Company in 1923. The company made only brassieres (also called foundations), and William Rosenthal filed for a patent for a brassiere design that supported the bust in a natural position. He managed the design department and created a standardized sizing system for brassieres in sizes "small," "average," and "full figure." Ida Rosenthal was in charge of sales, a job that entailed traveling throughout the United States, and, eventually, other countries. She was also in charge of finance, while William Rosenthal served as president and chief designer.

By 1925, Bissett and the Rosenthals stopped mailing dresses and focused exclusively on the brassiere business. As sales grew, the company expanded and moved its manufacturing plant to Bayonne, New Jersey. In 1930, the name was changed to the Maiden Form Brassiere Company. A national sales team consisting of 30 men sold the bras to stores throughout the United States, and the Rosenthals advertised their products in newspapers and magazines, as well as on buses, billboards, windows, and counter displays and over the radio. By 1930, Enid Bissett was no longer active in the company.

Ida and William's daughter, Beatrice, (born in 1916), joined the company after she graduated from Barnard College, starting out on the production line and moving up into various positions. She married Dr. Joseph Coleman, who also eventually joined the company. The Rosenthal's son, Lewis, (born in 1907) died while he was a student at Columbia University Law School. In his honor, they donated Camp Lewis in New Jersey to the Boy Scouts of America in 1938. Their other philanthropic activities included establishing the Ida and William Rosenthal Foundation in 1953, a charitable institution that is still active today.

During the 1930s, sales at Maiden Form rose dramatically, aided by the shapelier clothing designs that were popular during that decade. More than a million of its "Variation" style brassieres were sold at one dollar apiece within 10 years after Maiden Form was created. In 1942, William Rosenthal patented a strap fastener that could be adjusted and then set in a fixed position, a feature that made bras fit better and was copied throughout the industry.

Ida Rosenthal, cofounder of Maidenform Company, is shown here with displays of the company's famous "I Dreamed . . ." advertising campaign.
(Courtesy of the Maidenform Museum and Catherine Coleman Brawer)

During World War II, fabric was rationed and elastic was not available but the company was able to find substitutes for materials, such as Mexican cottons and ginghams. Studies showed that women who wore an uplift-style bra had less muscle fatigue than women who did not, and many women were working in factory jobs devoted to the war effort so their stamina and comfort was important. The company also made parachutes, carrier pigeon vests, and other products for military use.

In 1949, the Rosenthals approved a famous and innovative ad campaign by their New York advertising agency that reflected women's increasing desire for independence and personal achievement in the postwar era. It featured a woman wearing a bra with the slogan: "I dreamed I went shopping in my Maidenform bra." This classic ad campaign continued for more than 20 years, as women wearing Maiden Form bras dreamed of boxing, riding a fire truck, soaring in a hot-air balloon, and fighting a bull, among other things. The ads were seen in countries around the world, including France, England, and China.

After William Rosenthal died in 1958, Ida became first the president, then the chief executive officer. In 1960, the company name became Maidenform Inc. Ida Rosenthal was a forward-thinking executive who used her understanding of production, finance, and sales to build the business. Maidenform bras were sold in more than 100 countries around the world, and more women recognized and wore bras with the Maidenform label than any other brand. In 1963 Ida Rosenthal said, "Our responsibility at Maidenform is to consider every woman as an individual, not as a part of a mass market, and to provide her with lingerie of the finest quality that gives her fashion, fit, and comfort—regardless of price."

For many years, Ida Rosenthal continued to work in her New York office. She suffered a disabling stroke in 1966 at age 80 and died seven years later. Her daughter, Beatrice Coleman, took over management of the company in 1968 after the death of her husband Dr. Joseph Coleman. During her tenure, Maidenform remained the largest privately held company of its type.

Further Reading

Bird, Caroline. *Enterprising Women.* New York: W.W. Norton, 1976.

Brawer, Catherine Coleman. "Ida Rosenthal." In *Great Lives From History: American Women Series.* Vol 4. Edited by Frank N. Magill. Pasadena, Calif.: Salem Press, 1995.

Brody, Seymour. *Jewish Heroes and Heroines of America: 150 True Stories of American Jewish Heroism.* Hollywood, Fla.: Lifetime Books, 1996.

Maidenform Company. "Timeline." Available online. URL: http://www.maidenform.com/timeline/time. Downloaded on May 5, 2000.

✲ ROWLAND, PLEASANT T.
(1941–   ) Educator, Entrepreneur, Business Owner, Executive Philanthropist

Pleasant Rowland founded Pleasant Company, a direct-marketer, children's publisher, and retailer nationally know for the American Girl brand, featuring beautifully made dolls, clothing, toys, books, and accessories to inspire children's imaginations and sense of pride and possibility within themselves. The company states that its mission is "to educate and entertain girls with high-quality products and experiences that build self-esteem and reinforce positive social and moral values."

Pleasant Rowland was born in 1941 in Chicago, Illinois, where her mother was a homemaker and her father was a self-made advertising executive. She majored in English and art history at Wells College and received her bachelor's degree in 1962. For the next six years, she taught elementary school students in Massachusetts, California, New Jersey, and Georgia. As a teacher, she was disappointed by the lack of creativity in the educational textbooks she was using. To spark her students' interest, she created her own teaching tools that aimed to make learning more enjoyable.

After she left teaching in 1968, Rowland spent three years working as a television reporter for station KGO-TV in San Francisco. While discussing bilingual education during an interview with a publisher, Rowland described her own teaching experiences, and the publisher offered her a job at his company, Boston Educational Research Company, developing new reading texts based on her ideas. Rowland worked for the company from 1971 to 1978 and held the position of vice president. Her reading programs for the publishers Macmillan and Addison-Wesley received high praise from educators.

In 1981, she became the publisher of *Children's Magazine Guide,* an index describing the magazines available for elementary schoolchildren. She sold the business to R. R. Bowker, Inc., in 1989, so that she could spend more time managing the Pleasant Company, which she had launched in 1985.

Rowland had gone into the doll business in order to offer children an alternative to the Barbie doll and other "grown-up-looking" dolls. She set out to create dolls that actually resembled girls ages seven to 12 and which had historical and educational interest. She later said that she wanted "to provide girls with beautiful books, dolls, and pastimes that celebrate the experience of growing up as an American girl. As an educator, I wanted to give girls an understanding of America's past and a sense of pride in the traditions they share with girls of yesterday." In 1986, her American Girls line debuted, featuring three childlike dolls dressed in realistic historic costumes and priced at $75 each. The dolls come with a wardrobe of clothes and accessories, furniture, and books with stories about their lives—at home, in school, on vacation, and during special occasions.

Rowland sold her products directly to consumers via large, colorful catalogs that were mailed directly to homes. As business grew, Rowland added a fourth doll in 1991 and a magazine, *American Girl,* which reached a circulation of more than 700,000 subscribers in 1998.

That year, with sales of $300 million, Pleasant Company became one of the top 20 consumer direct-mail companies in the nation, as well as one of the top 16 juvenile publishing houses and publisher of one of America's top 10 juvenile magazines. In June 1998, Rowland sold her company to Mattel for $700 million and was named a vice chairman and a member of the board of directors. She said that the merger with Mattel would provide new growth opportunities for the company. Pleasant Company, which continues its independent operation from the headquarters in Middleton, Wisconsin, has introduced some popular new products over the years. During the late 1990s, the company added History Mysteries "A.G. Fiction," and "Amelias" to its selection of books.

In July 2000, Rowland retired from actively running the business. She lives in Madison, Wisconsin, with her husband Jerry Frautschi, and has been spending more time on her philanthropic activities. Through the Pleasant T. Rowland

Foundation, she has donated money to the arts and to educational institutions, including Wells College, and has contributed to programs that benefit children with developmental disabilities and senior citizens, among others. She says, "I have tried to help good people, dedicated to worthwhile causes, make a difference in places of importance to them."

Rowland has received many honors during her career. The Institute of American Entrepreneurs named her one of 12 outstanding entrepreneurs in 1990; in 1992, she was appointed to the institute's board of directors. She was also named one of *Working Woman* magazine's Top 50 Business Owners from 1993 to 1998. In 1999, she received the Golden Plate Award from the American Academy

Pleasant Rowland's strong interest in education and history prompted her to create the "American Girls" line of dolls, accessories, and books.
(Photo courtesy the Pleasant Company)

of Achievements and the Governor's Award from the Wisconsin Foundation for the Arts.

Further Reading

"Forbes 400: Pleasant Rowland," *Forbes,* October 12, 1998, p. 314.

Grove, Smith, et al. *Forbes: Great Minds of Business.* New York: Simon and Schuster (audio), 1997.

"Mattel Agrees to Acquire Pleasant Company." Mattel Company: Press release. Available online. URL: http://www. mattel.com/corporate/company/news_media/press_ releases.asp?chapter=603. Posted on June 15, 1998.

Mattmiller, Brian. "$2 Million Gift Supports Early Childhood Programs," News@UW-Madison (University of Wisconsin). Available online. URL: http://www.news. wisc.edu/view.html?get=5965. Downloaded on May 5, 2001.

"Pleasant T. Rowland, Biography." Pleasant Company on the Web. Available online. URL: http://www. americangirl.com/corporate/html/customers/html. Downloaded on May 23, 2001.

"The Pleasant Company." Available online. URL: http://kidsbooks.about.com/library/PubFocus/ blpleasantco.htm. Downloaded on May 4, 2001.

✳ RUBINSTEIN, HELENA
(1870–1965)   *Entrepreneur, Executive, Philanthropist*

Helena Rubinstein was one of the first and most successful people to found and operate a large beauty products business, and she developed many product "firsts." At the time of her death, she had amassed a fortune of about $100 million and was well-known for her philanthropy as well as her cosmetics empire. Rubinstein believed any woman could improve her appearance by taking the time to use the right products. She once said, "There are no ugly women, only lazy ones."

Born in Krakow, Poland, on December 25, 1870, Rubinstein was one of eight daughters in a lower-middle-class family. She originally planned to become a physician and began studying medicine in Switzerland.

During her early twenties, Rubinstein left Europe to visit relatives in Australia. There, people admired Rubinstein's smooth, clear complexion and wanted to know about the skin cream she had brought with her from Poland. The cream, which had been created by a Polish chemist, contained herbs and almond oil. Rubinstein's mother had been using it for years and had shared this beauty secret with her daughter. Seeing the demand for this cream, Helena Rubinstein began selling it from a small store in Melbourne.

In 1902, Rubinstein was able to open her own beauty salon, where she gave facial treatments. She offered women a skin analysis service in which she studied their skin type and recommended cleansers, creams, and treatments. At the salon, she sold her Crème Valaze for one dollar a jar. She had been importing her products from Europe but, as the business grew, she had them made in Australia.

During those years, women dusted rice powder on their faces to get rid of the shine caused by facial oil glands, but this powder could block the pores. In addition, it had a whitish color that did not flatter most complexions. Rubinstein decided to develop her own flesh-tinted powders, finding materials with a lighter texture that did not clog pores. Customers appreciated the more natural appearance of Rubinstein's powders.

In 1908, Rubinstein married Edward Titus, an American journalist. During the next few years, she gave birth to two sons. By 1908, she had saved thousands of dollars and wanted to expand her business. Rubinstein moved to Europe in order to study the latest techniques in cosmetology while her sister Ceska took over the Australian business. By studying the makeup techniques of stage actresses, Rubinstein learned how to use eyeshadow and taught her clients to apply this cosmetic. She also studied the science behind skin care and worked with several prominent dermatologists. The lavish new salon she opened in London attracted a wealthy clientele, as did the Paris salon she opened in 1912.

When World War I broke out in Europe in 1914, Rubinstein moved to New York City where she opened a new and larger cosmetics business and salon and began a wholesale distribution business. Rubinstein hired chemists and researchers to

In this 1950 photo, cosmetics company executive Helena Rubinstein is shown modeling some jewelry. (Photo courtesy of Hulton Archive)

create new products, including the first line of medicated cosmetics ever made. She also developed her manufacturing business.

Rubinstein added numerous salons in various countries. People all over the world recognized her name and considered her to be one of the world's top cosmetics experts. Her main competitor, ELIZABETH ARDEN, was likewise regarded as an international expert on beauty. The two women had a personal rivalry and did not appear at the same social events.

During the 1920s, the Helena Rubinstein Company offered women more than 600 cosmetics, including 115 shades of lipstick, face powder, foundation, eyeshadow, mascara, eyebrow pencil, perfume, bath products, and other items. Rubinstein made personal appearances around the world and wrote books about her field, including *The Art of Feminine Beauty* (1930), *This Way to Beauty* (1936), and *Food for Beauty* (1938). She dispatched beauty advice, such as the following: "Whether you are sixteen or over sixty, remember, understatement is the rule of a fine makeup artist. Adjust your makeup to the light in which you wear it. Daylight reveals color; artificial light drains it." Her diet advice included this tip: "Leave the table while you still feel you could eat a little more." Another of her oft-quoted remarks was, "I don't sell perfume; I sell hope."

Rubinstein, who had divorced her first husband in 1937, married a Russian prince 20 years her junior in 1938. Continuing to develop new products, she named a line of men's grooming products after her husband, Prince Artchil Gourielli-Tchko-nia, who died in 1956.

Rubinstein continued to launch new beauty products during the 1940s, 1950s, and early 1960s. They included the first products designed for different skin types—oily, normal, and dry. By 1950, the Helena Rubinstein Company had manufacturing plants on five continents. Rubinstein also introduced more dramatic eye makeup and demonstrated these products on the faces of the actresses she made up for their movie roles.

In her personal life, the petite Rubinstein was known as a frugal person, yet she loved high-fashion clothing and international society. She often entertained famous people at her five homes, located in Europe and the United States. When she had first tried to rent an apartment on Park Avenue, the owners refused her because she was Jewish. Rubinstein went on to buy the whole building, where she designed a triplex for her own use. Later, Revlon founder Charles Revson bought Rubinstein's apartment.

The Helena Rubinstein Foundation, set up in 1953, donated millions of dollars to various philanthropic causes, including museums, educational institutions, and organizations that benefited the poor, especially women and children. Rubinstein also supported Jewish charities and helped to fund the arts in Israel.

Rubinstein died on April 1, 1965. The cosmetics firm she had founded was sold to Colgate-Palmolive Company. The Helena Rubinstein Company was resold to the French cosmetics conglomerate L'Oréal, which relaunched the brand in the United States in 1999, after a 15-year absence from the U.S. market, as an exclusive luxury cosmetic line.

Further Reading

Fabe, Maxene. *Beauty Millionaire: The Life of Helena Rubinstein.* New York: Crowell, 1972.

Rubinstein, Helena. *My Life for Beauty.* London: Bodley Head, 1965.

Tobias, Andrew. *Fire and Ice: The Story of Charles Revson, the Man Who Built the Revlon Empire.* New York: William Morrow, 1976.

RUDKIN, MARGARET FOGARTY
(1897–1967)   *Entrepreneur, Executive*

Margaret "Peggy" Rudkin built a home bakery business into the Pepperidge Farm Company, a corporation that produces breads, pastries, and other foods.

Born on September 14, 1897, in New York City, Margaret Fogarty was educated in Flushing, Queens. She wed stockbroker Henry Rudkin in 1923. With their three young boys, the Rudkins moved into a home set on 120 acres in Fairfield, Connecticut, in 1929. It was called Pepperidge Farm because many sorghum trees, known as pepperidge trees in their community, grew there. Rudkin enjoyed growing her own vegetables and fruits and raised livestock to provide fresh food for the family.

In 1937, when one of her sons was ill with asthma, the pediatrician told her he might be allergic to the synthetic additives in store-bought foods, especially white bread. She began reading more about nutrition and decided to bake her own preservative-free bread in order to produce healthy loaves for him. The bread, which contained stone-ground whole-wheat flour, whole milk, molasses, honey, and butter, was based on her grandmother's recipe. The first loaves were hard and did not rise much in the pan, but she finally developed a loaf that her son loved. It was so tasty that the family doctor and others who tried it wanted some too.

Rudkin began selling the bread from her own home as a mail-order product. She installed an oven in the garage and then in the stables in order to produce quantities of her whole-wheat bread. Soon, local grocers also wanted to stock the bread, and by 1940 she was receiving so many orders that the bakery expanded and was moved to nearby Norwalk, Connecticut. Thousands of loaves were sold each week even though the bread cost 30 cents, about three times the price of the average store-bought loaf.

During World War II (1939–45), business was difficult because many food ingredients were rationed, but the company was able to expand again during the postwar years. Rudkin's husband, Henry, became marketing manager of the company. In

1947, the first modern Pepperidge Farm bakery was opened in Norwalk. Within six years, the company was producing 77,000 loaves of bread each week and had bakeries in Illinois and Pennsylvania, as well as Connecticut. Pepperidge Farm added cookies to its product line and found that cookies flavored with high-quality chocolate were especially popular. Rudkin noted that Pepperidge Farm customers were willing to pay higher prices for products made with more expensive ingredients.

Rudkin was actively involved in running the business and appeared on television ads to promote Pepperidge Farm products to homemakers in a friendly style. She paid her employees higher-than-average wages and offered more benefits than most other employers. In return, Rudkin expected quality work and loyalty and acknowledged that she was a perfectionist.

By 1960, Pepperidge Farm had sales of $32 million. The Rudkins sold the business to the Campbell Soup Company in 1961 for $28 million in the form of Campbell's stock. Margaret Rudkin remained as president, supervising day-to-day operations. In 1963, she published *The Margaret Rudkin Pepperidge Farm Cookbook,* a best-selling collection of her family recipes. Rudkin continued to work in the company until a year before she died in 1967, after an 11-year battle with breast cancer. The Pepperidge Farm Company is still based in Norwalk, Connecticut. In addition to breads, it produces rolls, cookies, snack foods, and frozen pastries.

Further Reading

Connecticut Women's Hall of Fame. "Margaret Fogarty Rudkin." Available online. URL: http://www.ctforum.org/cwhf/rudkin.htm. Downloaded on February 9, 2001.

The Entrepreneurs: An American Adventure, Pt. 1. MPI Home Video, 1986.

Rudkin, Margaret. *The Margaret Rudkin Pepperidge Farm Cookbook.* New York: Erik Blegvad, 1963.

Schleier, Curt. "Entrepreneur Margaret Rudkin." *Investor's Business Daily,* March 13, 2000.

S

SANDLER, MARION
(1930–   )   *Executive, Business Owner, Philanthropist*

As the co–chief executive officer (CEO) and cochairperson of the board (with husband Herb Sandler) of Golden West Financial Corporation, Marion Sandler is one of the nation's top female banking executives.

After Marion Sandler received her master's degree in business administration (MBA) from the Leonard N. Stern School of Business at New York University, she looked for a job on Wall Street. She later said, "When I was looking for a job, I was offered a secretarial job. I was offered the job as assistant to a customer's man even though I was highly educated and had all the qualifications of a man."

Sandler began her career as a securities analyst at a New York City firm but became convinced that she would not receive any opportunities to advance in the company. She thought she and her husband, Herbert, an attorney practicing in New York, should get into the banking business, and she proceeded to find a small savings and loan business that was for sale in California.

In 1963, Marian Sandler and her husband founded Golden West Financial Corporation, a holding company, in Oakland, California. Sandler later said, "When we first started, we did everything ourselves. [For] our first branch application, I did the research, I typed it. I did the math." The business grew rapidly after the couple bought World Savings Bank. During the next 30 years, the Sandlers built up a savings and loan company that now sells savings accounts and residential mortgages through approximately 400 branches of its World Savings Bank. In 1999, the company had revenues of $2.8 billion. As of 2000, two-thirds of the top management and five members of Golden West's board were women. The company's assets that year were estimated at $40 billion.

Among other things, Marion Sandler is responsible for the company's marketing efforts. During the year 2000, she spent much of her time developing the company's Internet site.

The Sandlers, who live in Lafayette, California, share both the CEO position and chairperson of the board position at their company. Business analysts have praised the couple, who sometimes eat sandwich lunches at their desks, for their practical, down-to-earth management style, which includes simply furnished, plain executive offices. Sandler also says she and her husband have functioned as full partners both in the business and at home.

Through their Sandler Family Supporting Foundation, the Sandlers have contributed millions of dollars to various causes, including basic science research. In both 1997 and 1998, they gave $1 million to basic science research at the University of California at San Francisco (UCSF). In 1999, they initiated the Sandler Challenge, pledging to give up to $1.5 million per year in matching, one-for-one funds to the UCSF School of Medicine for basic research purposes.

Further Reading

Boroughs, Don. "Eating Humble Pie, Making Lots of Bread," *U.S. News & World Report,* April 6, 1992, pp. 50–54.

Cavuto, Neil. "The Cavuto Report: Golden West Financial—CoChairman Interview," *The Cavuto Business Report,* Fox News Network. Transcript. September 6, 1999.

Feigenbaum, Randi. "A White Man's World: Diversity in Management/Banking on Change/Women See Slow But Sure Gains in Financial Service," *Newsday,* April 14, 2000, p. 14.

UCSF Foundation. "The Sandlers Promote Basic Science Research." *Impact, the UCSF Foundation's Online Magazine.* Available online. URL: http://www.ucsf.edu/ foundation/foundation_news/1999/fnsandler.html.

✳ SEYMOUR, MARY FOOT
(1846–1893) *Entrepreneur, Publisher*

Mary Foot Seymour helped to build the secretarial profession and offered women training in stenography and typing, which gave them job opportunities that had not previously been available. In 1879, she opened the first typing school for women.

Seymour was born in 1846. She taught herself stenography and learned how to type on early versions of the typewriter. During the Civil War, more women held office jobs, and they continued to seek these kinds of jobs after the war. After the first really efficient typewriters were invented in the early 1870s, Seymour saw that more women would find rewarding new careers in the secretarial field and as clerks and stenographers if they had appropriate training. By combining stenography, a form of shorthand, with typewriting, secretaries could complete their correspondence and other work more quickly. In 1879, Seymour opened the Union School of Stenography; later, she opened another school, the Union Stenographic Company, which employed 25 typists and operated an employment agency for typists and stenographers.

She also opened her own publishing company and founded a bimonthly magazine called *Business Woman's Journal,* launched in 1889. The journal stressed the development of skills and informed women about new job opportunities and laws that could affect their careers. Seymour also gave advice about practical matters, such as office clothing. She urged women to regard themselves as equal to men in their workplaces. All the officers at her company, Mary F. Seymour Publishing Company, were women. The journal was a success, and she founded a larger magazine, the *American Woman's Journal,* to help women better manage their finances as well as their jobs. The magazine included columns and articles about jobs, investments, and insurance.

Seymour died in 1893. By 1900, more than 75 percent of all clerical workers were women, as compared to 3 percent in 1870.

Further Reading

Banner, Lois W. *Women in Modern American: A Brief History.* New York: Harcourt, Brace, Jovanovich, 1974.

Brounlee, W. Elliot, and Mary M. Brounlee. *Women in the American Economy.* New Haven, Conn.: Yale University Press, 1976.

✳ SHAVER, DOROTHY
(1897–1959) *Executive*

Dorothy Shaver was the first woman president of a major retail corporation, and she earned the highest salary ever paid to a woman as of that time— $110,000 a year during the early 1930s.

As Lord & Taylor's first woman president, Arkansas native Dorothy Shaver promoted American designers and charmed customers with innovative window displays, storewide themes, and in-store boutiques.
(Photo courtesy of Lord & Taylor)

Shaver was born in Center Point, Arkansas, on July 29, 1897. She and her sister moved to New York City together, hoping to market some dolls that her sister had designed. After she arrived, Dorothy Shaver decided to work in the growing retail industry. In 1924, she was hired as a compar-

ison shopper at Lord & Taylor, a high-quality department store on Fifth Avenue founded in 1826 by Samuel Lord and George Washington Taylor, who aimed to develop a unique store known for its elegant atmosphere. For example, they decided not to hire staff to stand outside and encourage people to enter the store, a practice that was common in those days. Soon after Shaver arrived at the store she showed her knack for selecting merchandise that appealed to consumers.

Shaver contributed enormously to the growth and success of the business by implementing creative and effective sales and marketing techniques. During her first year at Lord & Taylor, Shaver suggested that the store offer customers a personal shopping service. Her other innovations included the first junior department and a shop for petite women. By 1927, she was a member of the store's board of directors, and she was named vice president four years later. During the 1930s, Shaver continued to find innovative ways to serve customers and to promote the merchandise. During those years, she also developed the store's bureau of fashion and decoration to study and create fashions.

Shaver also introduced the idea of arranging the store into separate shops, or boutiques for various items—the first time anyone had ever organized store merchandise this way. She created dramatic displays in the Fifth Avenue window and came up with appealing storewide themes that drew customers into the store.

In 1931, Shaver was named president of Lord & Taylor, and her annual salary rose to $110,000, the highest paid to a woman at the time. She is thought to be the first woman to head an American retail enterprise of this size. Under her direction, the main store in New York City was enlarged. She selected a new store symbol: the long-stemmed American beauty rose, which is still used on the store's shoeboxes, wrapping paper, and in ads, among other things.

In addition, Shaver showcased the creations of American designers. Beginning in 1932, she declared that the designer's name should appear on the labels of their clothing, instead of the Lord & Taylor labels that had been used. She also played a key role in promoting sportswear for women. After she became vice president in 1937, Shaver was in charge of advertising, fashion promotion, public relations, and displays. That year, she founded the Lord & Taylor Award for Americans whose creative achievements contribute significantly to their community, to the nation, or to the world. The first awards, given in 1938, went to designers Clare Potter and Nettie Rosenstein.

During the 1940s, Shaver organized in-store presentations to showcase designers' work, which helped to build up the nation's design industry. Shaver said that American designers were equal to those in Europe, and she passionately promoted the talents of CLAIRE MCCARDELL, Tom Brigance, Bonnie Cashin, LILLY DACHÉ, and others. These designers created their own unique looks. For instance, Cashin, a native of San Francisco, introduced a layered look, featuring shawls and stoles over dresses and jackets, and she created ponchos and draped looks. She also made robes and kimonos, inspired by the Asian culture she had experienced while growing up on the West Coast.

As the demographics of America changed after World War II, Shaver thought the store should expand into the suburbs. She developed the branch department-store system that spread Lord & Taylor stores throughout the nation, placing them primarily in upscale shopping centers.

Working with the fashion publicist Eleanor Lambert, Shaver helped to establish the Coty American Fashion Critic Awards, which were first given out in January 1943 at the Metropolitan Museum of Art. Fashion designer Norman Norell was the first honoree, and Lilly Daché and John Fredericks received special awards as hat designers.

Shaver continued to run the New York store until she died in 1959. She was the only woman president in the Lord & Taylor department store chain's 175-year history, until 39-year-old Jane Elfers was promoted to that position in 2000.

Further Reading

"Dorothy Shaver: Biographical Notes." Courtesy of Lord & Taylor Public Relations Department. n.d.

"Flashbacks," *Forbes,* August 18, 2000. Available online. URL: http://www.forbes.com/forbes/98/0921/6206018b.htm. Downloaded on November 30, 2000.

Raynor, Polly. "American Designers Make Names for Themselves," *Morning Call*. Available online. URL: http://www.mcall.com/html/decades/38404.htm. Downloaded on October 18, 2001.

Stamberg, Susan, Robert Siegel, and Noah Adams, "Sportswear Museum," *All Things Considered*, National Public Radio, April 8, 1998. Transcript.

SIEBERT, MURIEL F. (Mickey Siebert)
(1932–) *Financier, Entrepreneur, Executive*

In 1967, Muriel "Mickey" Siebert became the first woman to buy a seat on the New York Stock Exchange. She then founded and became president and chief executive officer (CEO) of Muriel Siebert & Company, an investment firm. In 1999, Fox News Network business correspondent Neil Cavuto said of Siebert, "She's got her own company. She's got her own online brokerage business and she is someone *Smart Money* magazine has just called the number one broker on the block."

Siebert was born in Cleveland, Ohio, on September 2, 1932. From 1949 to 1952, she attended Western Reserve University but left before she completed the requirements for a degree. Two years later, she moved to New York City, where she applied for a job at the United Nations but was turned down. She decided to apply for a job at Merrill Lynch, a stock brokerage firm, but did not obtain that job, either. Despite these disappointments, Siebert persisted. At another brokerage firm, Bache & Company, she was offered a choice of two jobs. One job, in accounting, paid $75 a week; the other job was in training and research and it paid $65 a week. Siebert later recalled, "I made what was the right career decision for the time, and took the lower paying job. You could get by on $65 a week then. Today I pay more to garage my car than I paid for apartments for years." Although the job paid less, Siebert had more opportunities to learn important skills in training and research.

Siebert advanced at Bache to become a research analyst who studied companies and wrote reports for investors and institutions. In the beginning, the companies that Bache assigned to her were what she later called "Wall Street men's castoffs." She began to sell stock in companies she had carefully examined and to invest her own money in these companies. The firm recognized her ability and promoted Siebert to the rank of partner, a position she held at three different brokerage firms.

In 1967, Muriel Siebert became the first woman to buy a seat on the New York Stock Exchange. At that time, there were 1,366 seats on the exchange, and none had ever been held by a woman. The people who opposed admitting women to the exchange claimed the language was too rough and that there were no rest rooms for women on the main floor. A friend encouraged Siebert to bid on a seat, and, on December 28, her bid of $445,000 was accepted. For nine years, she was the only woman with a seat on the exchange, and she had to work hard to overcome the bias against women in her field.

In 1967, she had also formed her own brokerage firm, Muriel Siebert & Company, which conducted research and bought and sold analytical reports for institutional investors. However in May 1975, the company changed direction, becoming a discount service for investors. It cut commissions on the purchase and sale of securities and no longer conducted research or advised customers what securities to buy. Once again, Siebert had achieved a "first," because commissions on the New York Stock Exchange had not been negotiable before she offered the service.

Muriel Siebert broke another barrier in 1977 when she became the first female banking superintendent in New York State. Governor Hugh Carey appointed her to that position, which carried the responsibility for regulating all the banks in the state. Siebert later said, "The banking department in New York regulates about $500 billion, which is more than all of the other states put together. New York's biggest banks are bigger than any state agency because we've got the foreign banks, a lot of money center banks, and New York is the center of financing." She took a five year leave of absence from her company to serve in this position.

Between 1977 and 1982, Siebert also served as the director of New York City's Urban Development Corporation and as director of the city's Job Development Authority. In 1982, she resigned to run for a seat in the U.S. Senate but lost the election. Afterward, she returned to her brokerage company, where she has served as both chairman and president since 1983.

In 1999, Siebert's net worth was estimated at $1 billion dollars. This marked the first time an American woman had become a billionaire without having inherited at least part of the money.

She went on to buy and develop a financial site on the Internet geared toward women: the Women's Financial Network. Siebert said, "I am starting this business because women today know that they have to take, at one time or another . . . control of their financial future and their current finances." Her site offered serious financial information and planning tools for investors. It was widely praised for its efficient design, which made it easier to use than many other websites.

Siebert has donated time and money to several organizations, especially those that benefit women. In 1990, she founded the Siebert Entrepreneurial Philanthropic Program (SEPP), which donates half of her firm's commission to charity when Siebert's company underwrites a new public stock offering for a stock issuer or institutional investor. Between 1990 and 2000, SEPP gave more than $5 million to charities. In 1998, Muriel Siebert was elected president of the New York Women's Agenda, a nonpartisan coalition of women's organizations, and she is active in the National Women's Business Council and the Women's Forum.

Siebert also serves on the boards of the Metropolitan Museum of Art, the Guild Hall Museum, the New York State Business Council, and the Greater New York Council of the Boy Scouts of America. In 1994, she was inducted into the National Women's Hall of Fame. She won the

Sara Lee Foundation's Frontrunner award in 1998.

To mark the 30th anniversary of her arrival at the New York Stock Exchange, Muriel Siebert was invited to ring the buzzer that closes the Wall Street trading day, on December 28, 1997, and she accepted the invitation. By the late 1990s, more women were working on Wall Street as stock, bond, and currency traders and investment bankers than ever before.

Further Reading

Cavuto, Neil, "Siebert and Company—CEO Interview," *The Cavuto Business Report,* Fox News Network. Transcript. May 18, 1999.

Erdman, Andrew. "Fortune People: Muriel Siebert Seeks to Toll Bell," *Fortune,* December 14, 1992, p. 177.

Fisher, Anne B. *Wall Street Women: Women in Power on Wall Street Today.* New York: Knopf, 1990.

Gjertsen, Lee Ann. "Siebert Creating Financial Web Site for Savvy Women," *American Banker,* October 16, 2000, pp. 8ff.

Harrison, Patricia, ed. *America's New Women Entrepreneurs.* Washington, D.C.: Acropolis Books, 1986.

Mack, Consuelo. "Chmn. & CEO, Siebert Financial—Interview," CNBC/Dow Jones Business Video, October 11, 2000.

Osgood, Charles, and Ray Brady, "Woman on Wall Street," *CBS News Sunday Morning,* March 28, 1999. Transcript.

Women's Financial Network at Siebert. "About WFN." Available online. URL: www.wfn.com. Downloaded on October 18, 2001.

✳ SNIDER, STACEY
(1960–) *Executive, Film Producer*

As chairperson of Universal Pictures, Stacey Snider is one of only three women in Hollywood to head a major film studio as of 2001. Under her direction, Universal Pictures has surpassed all previous domestic and international box-office records.

Snider received her bachelor of arts (B.A.) degree from the University of Pennsylvania in 1982 and earned her law degree from University of California at Los Angeles in 1985.

After completing her law studies, she embarked on a career in the entertainment industry. She worked in the mailroom of the Triad Agency and was promoted to the position of assistant, then worked as an assistant at Simpson-Bruckheimer Productions. Snider then joined Guber-Peters Entertainment Company (GPEC) in 1986 as director of development. As executive vice president for GPEC, she oversaw development of a hit thriller, *Single White Female* (1992), starring Jennifer Jason Leigh and Bridget Fonda, and acquired the film rights to *The Remains of the Day* (1993) which was released to critical acclaim.

Snider became the president, production at TriStar Pictures in January 1992. At that studio, she developed and produced several hit films, including *Sleepless in Seattle* and *Philadelphia* (both 1993), *Jumanji* (1995), *Jerry Maguire* (1996), and *As Good As It Gets* (1997).

In 1996, she joined Universal Pictures as copresident, production. She was promoted to head of production in April 1998, then named president of production later that year in November. She was named chairman of production at Universal Pictures in November 1999.

At Universal, she is responsible for film production, marketing, and the domestic distribution activities for Universal films, as well as for finance, legal affairs, overseas operations, and home videos. In the late 1990s and early 2000s, Snider developed a string of hit films, including *The Bone Collector, American Pie, Notting Hill, Man On the Moon* (all released in 1999), *Erin Brockovich, The Family Man, Meet the Parents, Gladiator, The Nutty Professor II: The Klumps,* and *Dr. Seuss' How the Grinch Stole Christmas* (all released in 2000). *How the Grinch Stole Christmas,* starring comedian-actor Jim Carrey, broke all previous box-office records with its $55.1 million opening in 2000 and may have earned more money than any other film that year. *Gladiator* was one of the most celebrated films of 2000; it won the Academy Award for best picture, along with several other Oscars. Since then, she has overseen production of *Captain Corelli's Man-dolin, Spy Game, Jurassic Park III, A Beautiful Mind,* and others.

In 2000, domestic ticket sales for Universal films surpassed $1 billion, another first for the company. The previous record, set in 1999, was $935 million. Universal became the first studio in modern history to open five films in a row that became number one at the box office. Snider said, "It has been an incredibly gratifying year for us in which a lot of hard work has paid off."

Snider, who was ranked as the 31st most important person in Hollywood by *Premiere* magazine in May 2000, was named as one of America's 50 most powerful women in business in 2000 and 2001.

She has been honored by Special Olympics of Los Angeles and other organizations for her charitable work. Snider received the 2001 H.E.L.P. Humanitarian Award for her work with H.E.L.P, an organization that serves children challenged by learning disabilities, autism, Asperger's syndrome, emotional development problems, mental retardation, and abuse and neglect. Ron Meyer, president and chief operating officer (COO) of Universal Studios and cochair of the 2001 H.E.L.P. fund-raising luncheon, said, "Stacey is a true leader in everything she does. In recognizing her, the H.E.L.P. group has chosen a great role model whose compassion and commitment to children is exemplary."

As of 2001, Stacey Snider lived in Los Angeles with her husband and two children.

Further Reading

Premiere. "The Power List," Premiere Magazine Online. Available online. URL: http://premiere.hfnm.com/power100c.html. Downloaded on May 8, 2001.

Universal Pictures. "Universal Pictures' Stacey Snider to Receive The H.E.L.P. Group's Humanitarian Award at the 24th Annual Teddy Bear Picnic on Thursday, June 7." Press release. Yahoo PR Newswire. May 22, 2001. Available online. URL: http://biz.yahoo.com/prnews/010522/latu099.html. Downloaded on May 12, 2001.

Universal Studios. "Stacey Snider, Biography." Available online. URL: http://www.universalstudios.com/homepage/html/bios/stacey_snider.html. Downloaded on May 14, 2001.

STEWART, MARTHA (Martha Kostyra)
(1941–)   *Entrepreneur, Executive, Author*

As a lifestyle expert and the founder of Martha Stewart Living Omnimedia, Martha Stewart has influenced homemaking and decorating practices in the United States and around the world. In 1988, *Time* magazine called her the "guru of good taste (and taste buds) in American entertaining." When asked to describe her vision of her company, Stewart has said, "We are the leading authority for the home."

Martha Kostyra was born on August 3, 1941, in Jersey City, New Jersey, the second of six children in a Polish-American family. Her father, Edward Kostyra, was a physical education teacher who later became a pharmaceutical salesman in order to boost the family income. Martha Ruszkowski Kostyra, a teacher, had left her profession to raise her children, then returned to teaching when the youngest entered school.

The family moved to a modest three-bedroom home in Nutley, New Jersey, when Martha was three years old. Everyone helped with the household chores, and as the oldest girl, Martha learned to cook, garden, and sew her own clothes. She learned to make soups, preserves, breads, tarts, candies, and Polish specialties. During those years, her father, who worked in New York City, sometimes brought home pomegranates, persimmons, and other foods from the city markets that were unusual to many Americans. She later said, "We were brought up unpretentiously but with a lot of spirit and a lot of 'you can do anything you want to do' hammered into our heads."

Her father was an avid gardener, and Martha helped him to cultivate vegetables, fruits, and flowers in their backyard and an adjoining field. Each spring, they started plants indoors from seeds. Martha, who loved flowers, won a blue ribbon in a local flower show for one of her floral arrangements.

Hardworking and detail-oriented, Martha was a good student and active in numerous extracurricular activities, including planning and preparing a breakfast for the high school football team. She also worked part time as a model in New York City, doing television commercials and modeling clothes at a department store. As a senior, she chose this caption for her yearbook: "I do what I please and I do it with ease."

After graduation in 1959, she majored in history and architecture at Barnard College, where she received a partial scholarship, and continued modeling. During her freshman year, Kostyra moved to an apartment on Fifth Avenue in New York, where she worked as a live-in cook in exchange for housing. Near the end of that year, she met Andrew Stewart, a law student at Yale University in New Haven, Connecticut, and they were married on July 1, 1961.

After the Stewarts settled in an apartment near Yale, Martha continued to model in New York and attend college, earning her degree in history in 1964. After earning his law degree, Andrew Stewart practiced in New York City, where the couple lived in an apartment furnished with "finds" from auctions, antique shops, and flea markets. In 1965, their daughter, Alexis was born. Between 1965 and 1970, the family spent weekends and summer days at a country house in Massachusetts, where Martha Stewart enjoyed gardening. In 1967, she became a Wall Street stockbroker, a job that let her develop business skills.

She left Wall Street six years later to spend more time with her daughter and on home-based activities. In 1972, the Stewarts had purchased a run-down farmhouse in Westport, Connecticut, and they began living there full time. Martha Stewart began remodeling the house and planted an orchard and large garden, adding henhouses, another barn, and beehives. The Stewarts raised goats, chickens, turkeys, and geese, and kept several dogs and cats as pets. Stewart later said, "I loved the garden. I loved decorating, designing, cooking."

Stewart began conducting cooking classes, and in 1976 she opened a take-out gourmet food shop in Westport called the Market Basket. As the business expanded, she began to operate a professional catering business from her home. The business, called The Uncatered Affair, became quite successful. Stewart created Martha Stewart, Inc. She continued to teach a cooking class and began writing magazine articles about cooking and entertaining. In 1981, she created a larger kitchen next to her home where she worked with her staff to operate the catering business. They prepared and served food at dinner parties and large receptions that might include hundreds or even 1,000 guests.

In 1982, Stewart's first book, *Entertaining,* was published to excellent reviews. With its large, coffee-table format, it was the first full-color how-to book of its kind. The book sold well and would go into 30 printings by 1998. By 1985, Stewart had published four more cooking and entertaining books, was still operating the catering business, and also ran seminars at her home, where people could watch her cook and visit the farmhouse and grounds.

The year 1987 brought a new book, *Weddings,* and a $5 million, five-year contract to serve as Kmart's home-and-lifestyle consultant. Stewart would later produce a line of house paints and housewares for the chain. She gave up her catering business in order to pursue that commitment, write more books, and make instructional videotapes. That year, she and her husband separated, and they were legally divorced in 1990.

During the 1990s, she launched *Martha Stewart Living* magazine, published by Time Warner, and several other projects, including a radio show, syndicated newspaper column, and mail-order catalog called Martha By Mail. She also completed two books, *Martha Stewart's Gardening Month by Month* and *Martha Stewart's New Old House,* which described the process of restoring and decorating a 152-year-old farmhouse she had bought in 1988. Her television show debuted in 1993.

In 1995, Stewart negotiated a new contract with Time Warner that gave her more control over her business interests. She was named chairman and chief executive officer (CEO) of the new corporation, Martha Stewart Living Enterprises, which included a publishing division for her magazine and books, a television division, an interactive media division, and merchandising division. Stewart shared the ownership with Time Inc. Ventures. Stewart had built a media empire and become one of the most successful businesspeople in America. During a 1996 interview, journalist Barbara Walters called Stewart "the most fascinating business person of the year." In 1997, *Time* magazine named Stewart as one of its 25 most influential people.

By then, Stewart wanted to own and run her own company and she raised enough money to buy most of Time's shares. She announced that the new company would be called Martha Stewart Living Omnimedia. Time Warner, which retained an interest of less than 20 percent in the company, continued to help distribute Stewart's magazine. Stewart also introduced her website, which features information about her products and television programs, in September 1997.

In 2000, *Forbes* magazine named Stewart 274th on its list of the 400 richest Americans, which included 46 women. The article, which stated her net worth at $1 billion, said, "She built an empire by tapping into American desire for picture-perfect domestic life, or at least the desire to gaze at it from afar."

Stewart, who has expanded to international markets, sells products in England, Germany, Japan, and Brazil, where she has a television show. She also introduced her Martha Stewart Everyday Kitchen line of products to Kmart in 2000. Revenues for 2000 were expected to climb 20 percent. On sales of about $286 million, the company expected to post profits of $20 million in 2000, an increase of 73 percent from 1999. For the nine months ending September 30, 2001, total revenues at the company rose 5 percent to $210.6 million, and the net income rose 5 percent to $16.2 million. In 2002, Kmart filed for Chapter 11 protection from bankruptcy. Stewart said that the chain would continue selling her products "for the foreseeable future."

Shortly after her company went public, an interviewer for *People* magazine quoted Stewart as saying, "We don't know of another woman who built a company from the basement, like I did, who took it public, who is chairman and CEO and is a billionaire on the first day of trading."

Stewart looks for creative ways to inform her TV audience and often visits restaurants, farms, factories, and other places that raise, make, or sell things for the home. Her interests have led her to many places, including Alaska, where she hiked, went dogsledding, and made sourdough waffles from a recipe that dated back to the gold rush era.

Further Reading

Casciato, Don. "Stewart On Forbes List of 400 Richest," *Westport (Ct) News,* October 13, 2000, p. C-1. Martha Stewart Interview, *The Charlie Rose Show,* PBS-TV, September 15, 1995, transcript #1466.

Casciato, Don. Martha Stewart Interview, Larry King Live, CNN, April 23, 1990, transcript #28.

O'Neill, Anne-Marie and Sue Miller, "Biography: Martha Stewart," People Profiles, *People* Online. Available online. URL: http://people.aol.com/people/pprofiles/biography/biography/0,3375,64,00.html. Downloaded on October 18, 2001.

Reilly, Patrick M. "Martha Stewart Takes Over Control of Her Empire in Split With Time, Inc.," *The Wall Street Journal,* February 5, 1997, sec. B, p. 5.

Sahatjian, Elizabeth. "Martha Stewart Entertaining/Decorating Maven," *Cosmopolitan,* August 1990, pp. 12ff.

"The Top 25 Managers of the Year," *Business Week,* January 8, 2001, pp. 61–80.

Williams, Mary Elizabeth. "She's Martha and You're Not," *Salon* February 16, 1999. Available online. URL: http://www.salon.com/people/bc/1999/05/04/oprah/index/htm. Downloaded on June 13, 2000.

❋ SUI, ANNA
(1955–) *Designer, Entrepreneur*

Designer Anna Sui is known for her innovative and fun-loving fashions—what one critic calls "glamours yet wearable"—and her creative fragrance and cosmetic lines.

Born in Detroit to Chinese-American parents, Sui attended the Parsons School of Design in New York City after she graduated from high school. She worked as a fashion stylist for photographer Steven Meisel and designed junior sportswear before launching her own fashion collection. At first, Sui designed her clothes from a room in her apartment. Her first collection was presented in 1980 and received rave reviews, especially from younger critics.

Sui's collections have often drawn on styles from the past, mixed in ingenious ways with modern designs. They feature vivid colors and different textures and unexpected uses for fabrics and trims, such as crochet. Among the fashions she has reinterpreted for contemporary women are the baby doll dress, handkerchief hem, and patchwork.

During the 1990s, Sui added new product lines to her company's offerings. In 1997, she developed a line of evening clothes called Anna Sui Party and she has also begun designing menswear. She launched a fragrance, Anna Sui, and another fragrance, Beauty, which was advertised as capturing "the edge of urban cool." In 1997, Sui signed an agreement with Ballin, an Italian-based company, to manufacture her shoe collection.

Further Reading

Altculture. "Sui, Anna." Available online. URL: http://www.plastic.com/altculture/01/04/11/1749252.shtml. Downloaded on May 30, 2001.

TAGGARES, KATHY
(1952–) *Entrepreneur, Executive*

Taggares is the founder and president of K.T.'s Kitchens, Inc., a multimillion-dollar food processing business. Taggares has said, "[T]here are plenty of people in this company who are better educated than I am. But the reason I am sitting in the president's seat and they aren't is because I am gutsy, I am tenacious, I stir things up, and I am a very, very hard worker."

Kathy Taggares was born on June 28, 1952, and grew up on a potato farm in Othello, a small town in eastern Washington's Columbia Basin. Her father, Peter J. Taggares Sr., was the son of Greek immigrants and had begun farming in his hometown of Prosser, Washington, in the 1950s, then started his small farm in Othello after the family moved there in 1956. During the next two decades, he developed his farm into a large agribusiness. Kathy Taggares admired her mother and later said that her mother's example of hard work and encouragement inspired her to succeed throughout her life.

While growing up, Kathy worked hard on the farm, pulling weeds when she was young and learning to use heavy equipment as she grew older. She saved some of the money she earned working in the fields and used it to buy some Black Angus steers when she was in her mid-teens. As a member of 4-H, an organization for young people in rural areas, she raised steers as a project, then exhibited her steers and sold them at the annual county fairs. With her profits, she purchased more steers, and soon she was raising and selling several each year.

When she graduated from high school, Taggares decided to move to New York City. She attended New York University but was not sure what career she wanted to pursue. During her six years in the city, she held several jobs, including waiting tables and tending bar. Often, she attended classes, then worked at two different jobs.

In 1976, she left New York to visit an aunt who lived in Sun Valley, Idaho. Her mother had moved to Seattle, Washington, and Taggares also had friends living there, so she decided to relocate. At the University of Washington, she completed the requirements for a degree in history and graduated Phi Beta Kappa. After graduation, she worked for two major producers of frozen french fries—Chef Reddy Corporation and RDO Foods. Within a few years, she

Kathy Taggares overcame major challenges to turn a nonoperational factory in California into a successful food products business.
(Photo by Bonnie Schiffman, courtesy of K.T.'s Kitchens)

was promoted to vice president of sales and marketing, a job that involved a great deal of traveling.

Nine years after finishing college, she felt dissatisfied with her future prospects and confided in a friend and fellow employee that she wanted to run her own company. With her expertise in the food products business, Taggares began looking for a food business she could buy and run. Marriot Corporation was selling a food products factory in Los Angeles, California, and Taggares decided to buy the business, which produced salad dressings for private labels.

After four months of negotiations, Marriot agreed to sell for $6 million, with a down payment of $1 million. Taggares sold her condominium and some other assets to raise $200,000 and tried to get a bank loan for the rest. She later recalled,

> I put together a business plan—I copied it nearly word for word from a library book—and shopped it around to all the banks in town. They all said, "no, no, no," except for one that recognized how good and steady the salad dressing revenues were.

That bank lent her $600,000 but she still needed $200,000 more. Taggares convinced a local bagel manufacturer to give her that amount in exchange for a hamburger processing machine that she would own as soon as the transaction for the Marriot factory was complete. She received that last $200,000 just in time, on the day Marriot had set as the deadline. They told Taggares she must bring them a cashier's check for $1 million or lose her opportunity. She raced into the room five minutes late but was still able to conclude the sale.

Taggares encountered many challenges after she bought the business. The only employees who were still working at the plant were the line workers, and they spoke Spanish, a language she did not speak. There were no supervisors or administrative staff still working at the company, so Kathy and her friend Joan Paris, who had come to work for the company, had to learn all about the business. The factory's employees soon saw that Taggares was willing to work hard and do various jobs, including loading trucks. The first year, sales remained stable, at about the same level they were before the company changed hands.

Taggares was eager to add a new product, and she tried making a low-fat salad dressing, which turned out to be a poor investment. However, her next idea, to go into the pizza business, was very successful. She bought a pizza crust bakery and solved several problems as she worked to make that business a success. One of the bakers on her staff developed a hand-stretched pizza crust that caught the attention of Wolfgang Puck, a restaurant owner and well-known chef who had decided to mass-produce the gourmet pizzas he served at his famous Spago restaurant in Los Angeles. Taggares's company began making the crusts.

Next, Taggares decided it would make sense to buy equipment for making entire pizzas, not just the crusts. She found a pizza factory in Canada that was closing and arranged to buy its used equipment. After her salad dressing expert developed recipes for pizza sauce, they were ready to start production. One of her salad dressing customers, Costco, a chain of warehouse stores, liked her pizza samples, so Taggares began selling frozen pizzas to Costco. As time went on, other private-label customers and schools also became pizza customers. The growth of this business enabled Taggares to buy modern, high-tech pizza-making equipment.

Taggares is known as a caring employer whose workers express loyalty to their boss. Although she often spends 80 hours a week at her job, she is also active in her community and in various business organizations. Taggares, who lives in Los Angeles, also appears on television to share her ideas about business and the techniques that brought her success.

Further Reading

Enkelis, Liane, and Karen Olsen. *On Our Own Terms.* San Francisco: Berrett-Koehler Publishers, 1995.

Hagey, Jason. "Basin Farmer Taggares, 67, Dies," *Tri-City Herald,* February 23, 1999. Available online. URL: http://www.tri-cityherald.com/news/1999/0223.html. Downloaded on October 4, 2000.

Useem, Jerry. "The Art of Lying: Can It Be a Good Thing?" *Fortune,* December 20, 1999, pp. 278ff.

TIMOTHY, ELIZABETH
(ca. 1700–1757) *Business Owner, Newspaper Publisher, Printer*

Elizabeth Timothy was America's first woman newspaper editor and publisher and one of the first female journalists in the world.

Born in Holland around 1700, she was apparently well-educated, although little is known about her early life or her family of origin. She was married to Louis Thimothee, a French Huguenot who had settled in Rotterdam to avoid religious persecution in his homeland, and she gave birth to four children: Peter, Louis, Charles, and Mary.

In 1731, the family sailed on the *Britannia of London* to America, where her husband, who took the more English-sounding name Lewis Timothy, worked with printer Benjamin Franklin in Philadelphia. Franklin had sponsored the family's trip to America, and in exchange Timothy had agreed to work for him for a specified number of years. Timothy spoke several languages and began tutoring people in French and editing one of Franklin's newspapers, the *Philadelphische Zeitung.* This German-language paper debuted on May 6, 1732, but ceased publication on June 24, 1732. After that, Timothy served as a librarian of Franklin's Philadelphia Library Company and as a printer at Franklin's *Pennsylvania Gazette,* the foremost newspaper in the colony and later the most-read newspaper in colonial America.

Franklin was a civic-minded person who encouraged the growth of newspapers throughout the colonies. He had sent one of his former printers to move to Charles Town (later Charleston) and begin printing the *South-Carolina Gazette,* but that printer had died of yellow fever, so Timothy was sent to replace him. Using the press and other equipment Ben Franklin provided, Timothy agreed to operate the business for a certain number of years. Franklin was to pay one-third of the expenses and receive one-third of the profits.

In 1733, Timothy began publishing the *South-Carolina Gazette,* and Elizabeth Timothy and the children joined him in Charles Town the next year. Between 1733 and 1736, Timothy ran the press from an office on King Street, established a subscription postal service at his office, and obtained a land grant that included a lot in Charles Town and 600 acres outside town.

Lewis Timothy died suddenly, after an accident in 1738. With Franklin's approval, Elizabeth Timothy took over the printing operation in order to support her family, which had grown to include six children, with another child on the way. However, the *Gazette* masthead listed her 13-year-old son Peter Timothy as publisher. When she took over the business, Timothy informed readers that it was customary in Europe and in other colonies for a printer's family to work with a printer and that she and her son would be carrying on the business. She also printed a request for subscribers that read: "Subscriptions will be kindly pleased to continue their favours to the poor afflicted widow with six small children and another hourly expected." Timothy also wrote that she would "with the assistance of my Friends" make the *Gazette* "as entertaining and correct as may reasonably be expected."

Subscriptions increased during the time Timothy ran the printing business. Ben Franklin also wrote that he was quite pleased with her work and her business skills, saying that she was more efficient and kept better business records than her deceased husband. As the official printer for South Carolina, Timothy printed the acts and proceedings of the colonial assembly and legal tracts. She also printed books, pamphlets, and other publications. Timothy was praised for her contribution to the literary life of the colony and its cultural growth.

In 1746, when her son Peter turned 21, Timothy turned over the business operation to him but continued to run a book and stationery business in a store next to the printing office. She advertised her wares in the *Gazette,* and one such ad, which appeared in October 1746, listed pocket Bibles, primers, spellers, and some religious and health-oriented books for sale. She also sold copies of Ben Franklin's popular *Poor Richard's Almanack,* a humorous and informative book that sold thousands of copies each year in all 13 colonies.

Timothy left the colony sometime in the late 1740s but returned to Charles Town in 1756. She died in April 1757.

Peter Timothy, a patriot who supported independence from Britain, ran the printing business and newspaper until he and other well-known patriots were exiled after Charles Town fell to the

British in 1780, during the American Revolution. Two years later, he died while traveling on a ship that sank in the Caribbean. After his death, his widow, Ann Donavan Timothy, returned to Charles Town with her children, who numbered about 15, and carried on as her mother-in-law had done, operating the press and publishing the newspaper. Her son (Elizabeth Timothy's grandson), Benjamin Franklin Timothy, took over the business in 1792.

Years after her death, Elizabeth Timothy was recognized as the first woman in America to own and publish a newspaper. In 1973, she was inducted into the South Carolina Press Association Hall of Fame. Timothy was also inducted into the South Carolina Business Hall of Fame in 2000.

Further Reading

Sherr, Lynn, and Jurate Kazickas. *The American Women's Gazeteer.* New York: Bantam, 1976.

South Carolina Business Hall of Fame. "Elizabeth Timothy." Available online. URL: http://www.scetv.org/legacy/laureates/Elizabeth%20Timothy.html. Posted in 1999.

✳ TOTINO, ROSE CRUCIANI
(1915–1994) *Entrepreneur, Business Owner, Executive, Consultant, Philanthropist*

Through hard work, talent, and persistence, Rose Totino developed a successful pizza business that became a multimillion-dollar company and made her a corporate executive.

Born on January 16, 1915, Rose Cruciani was the fourth of seven children. Her parents were Italian immigrants who had settled in a section of Minneapolis, Minnesota, called Nordeast, which was populated mainly by families who had recently arrived from Europe, particularly Scandinavian countries.

Rose was 14 years old when the Great Depression struck in 1929. Like many families, the Crucianis struggled to make ends meet during the hard economic times that swept across the nation in the 1930s. Rose left high school at age 16 in order to contribute money to the family. She cleaned other people's homes for $2.50 a week and

helped her mother with the household chores, including cooking. During her teens, Rose learned to make traditional Italian dishes, including tomato-based sauces and breads.

In 1935, Cruciani married Jim Totino, another first-generation Italian-American, who had also quit high school and was working as a baker. The couple lived not far from their parents and were active members of their local Catholic church. They enjoyed entertaining friends, church members, and parent-teacher association (PTA) members at their small home and sometimes served their special pizza pies, which consisted of a layer of breadlike dough topped with combinations of cheese, sausage, tomatoes, herbs, and different sauces. People raved about Rose's pizza and looked forward to this treat when they visited the Totino family, which soon included two daughters.

During the 1930s, most Americans had not heard of the dish now known as pizza, and there were few pizza restaurants in the United States. Pizza had originated centuries earlier in Italy, where it had been a peasant's dish made from flat bread with tomatoes and herbs. A baker from Naples, Raffaele Esposito, has been credited with developing a modern version of pizza in 1889. To honor the visit of the Italian king and queen, Esposito added basil and sliced mozzarella cheese to the red sauce on the pizza to symbolize the three colors of the Italian flag—green, white, and red. Historians say the queen praised this patriotic dish.

Italian immigrants brought pizza to America during the late 1800s and adapted their recipes to the ingredients they found in the United States. The first modern pizzeria opened in New York in about 1905, and a few others appeared in large cities where Italian-Americans operated bakeries or food service businesses.

People urged Rose Totino and her husband to open a pizza restaurant. After discussing the idea, the couple decided to try. They calculated that they would need to borrow $1,500 from a bank to start such a business and that they could earn enough to pay their overhead expenses if they sold at least 25 pizzas every week. As the business grew, they hoped to earn enough income to pay off their business loan and earn a living.

Rose Totino worked long hours at the restaurant, Totino's Italian Kitchen, which was located on Central Avenue in Minneapolis, while Jim worked at both his regular job and the pizza business. Within a few weeks, their small business was making enough money that Jim Totino decided to work there full time. The Totinos developed a system: he made the pizza crusts while she prepared sauces and toppings. Within a few years, the couple had managed to save $50,000.

The Totinos faced new challenges when the costs of ingredients rose. They were already making as many hand-prepared pizzas as they could, so they could not increase their profits by selling more pizzas. For a while, the business seemed doomed. The Totinos sought loans to buy machinery that would produce more crusts faster so that they could serve more customers and also start supplying pizzas to supermarkets. However, the banks turned down their requests, and they had to wait months for a government loan from the Small Business Administration. After their loan came through, the Totinos began operating a plant with two shifts of workers and were even able to open a second plant. The pizzas made in these plants were sold wholesale to grocery stores as frozen pizzas.

Pizza became increasingly popular after World War II ended in 1945. U.S. Veterans who had served in Italy were eager to enjoy pizza at home. New pizza restaurants opened, and more people bought frozen pizzas from the grocery stores. During the 1950s and 1960s, Totino Frozen Pizzas became the leading brand of frozen pizza in the United States. Their motto was, "Nobody makes a pizza like Totino's."

Although the Totinos had once turned down a $1 million offer for their business, they did finally sell in 1971 after Jim Totino's health declined. Rose Totino preferred to sell their company to a local corporation, and she chose Pillsbury, a large food products business based in Minneapolis. In 1975, Pillsbury paid $20 million for Totino Frozen Pizza. Rose Totino remained with the business as an executive vice president, the first woman who

ever held that position at Pillsbury. Her annual salary was $100,000 a year.

Totino worked from an office in the company's technology headquarters and was in charge of quality control for the pizza products. She also worked to develop new products. She made public appearances around the country to promote Totino products and conducted business seminars. Her warmth and enthusiasm helped the business to grow. Despite her lack of formal education or business training, Rose Totino showed a keen understanding of how to develop and run a business, and she hired effective people. Employees said that Totino created a pleasant work atmosphere, and they praised her personal integrity and

Hard work and winning recipes enabled Rose Totino, shown here when she was an executive at the Pillsbury Company, to develop a business that became a leader in the frozen pizza industry.
(Photo courtesy of the Pillsbury Company)

generosity. In 1994, Paul Walsh, chief executive officer of Pillsbury, said, "[I]t was Rose Totino who captured our hearts. She was a brilliant business-woman, a loving wife and mother and the spirit behind our pizza operations."

Totino believed her good fortune was a gift from God and used her wealth and position to help others and enrich the community. She became a patron of the arts and contributed to Christian education and programs that helped young people in need. She also served on the boards of several educational, financial, and religious institutions. Totino donated $3.8 million to Northwestern College in Roseville, Minnesota, for a fine arts center, gave $500,000 to build a homeless shelter, and funded a local mental health center for adolescents. After she endowed a local Catholic high school, it was renamed Totino-Grace in 1980 in honor of Rose and Jim Totino. Totino gave her time as well as her money, and, according to her pastor, "She was the first person to volunteer to serve doughnuts or scrub tables."

During her lifetime, Totino received numerous honors for her business achievements and philanthropy. She was elected to both the Minnesota Business Hall of Fame and the American Frozen Food Institute (AFFI) Hall of Fame. In 1983, she received the Outstanding Business Leader Award from the Northwood Institute. During her acceptance speech, Totino said, "America is the spawning bed of incredible innovation, technology and creativity for the entire world and with that posture, automatically comes the awesome responsibility of management."

Totino died of cancer on June 21, 1994.

Further Reading

Chanen, David. "Pizza Pioneer, Philanthropist Rose Totino Dies at 79," *Minneapolis Star Tribune*, June 22, 1994, p. 1A.

Pillsbury Company. "History." Available online. URL: http://www.pillsbury.com/about/history.asp. Downloaded on January 12, 2001.

Pine, Carol, and Susan Mundale. *Self-Made: The Stories of 12 Minnesota Entrepreneurs.* Minneapolis, Minn.: Dorn Books, 1982.

Taylor, Russel R. *Exceptional Entrepreneurial Women: Strategies for Success.* Westport, Conn.: Praeger, 1988.

✺ TOWNSEND, ALAIR ANE
(1942–   ) *Publisher, Executive, Government Official*

As publisher of *Crain's New York Business,* Townsend is at the helm of one of the most influential business journals in the United States.

Alair Ane Townsend was born on February 15, 1942, in Elmira, New York, and graduated Phi Beta Kappa from Elmira College in 1962. She went on to earn a master's degree in sociology from the University of Wisconsin in 1964.

After graduating from college, Townsend pursued a career in government and served in various posts in Washington, D.C., including associate director of the Budget Committee of the House of Representatives, assistant secretary for management and budget of the United States Department of Health and Human Services, and staff director of the Subcommittee on Fiscal Policy of the Joint Economic Committee of Congress. She gained a reputation as an expert on federal budgeting and social welfare programs.

From September 1981 to February 1985 she served as budget director of New York City under Mayor Ed Koch. From February 1985 to January 1989, she served as the deputy mayor for finance and economic development for New York City. In that position, Townsend was responsible for developing and implementing policies that promoted economic growth and new jobs in the city.

In February 1989, Townsend became publisher of *Crain's New York Business,* a weekly newspaper that covers the New York City economy and business community, as well as regional, national, and international factors that affect them. After many years in government, she wanted to develop a career in the private sector.

Townsend has received numerous honors, including the 1989 Leadership Award from the New York City Building Congress; the Sara Lee Corporation's Frontrunner Award for "women who run the world"; and the Iphigene Ochs Sulzberger Award from Barnard College. A former governor

Alair Townsend (shown here with former New York City mayor Ed Koch), the publisher of *Crain's New York Business,* has also served in both local and federal government posts where she used her knowledge of finance and economic policy.
(Courtesy of Alair Townsend)

of the American Stock Exchange, she has served on the board of Fay's Inc., a drugstore chain, and now serves on the boards of Lincoln Center and the New York City Partnership/Chamber of Commerce. She is the chairman of the American Woman's Economic Development Corporation and belongs to the Women's Forum and the Economic Club of New York. Townsend was also a trustee at her alma mater, Elmira College, for a number of years.

Further Reading

Crain Communications Inc. "Alair A. Townsend, Vice President/Publisher, *Crain's New York Business.*" Available online. URL: http:www.crain.com/b_off/b1_bios/b19_atownsend.htm. Downloaded on June 13, 2000.

TUTTLE, JULIA D.
(1849–1898) *Real Estate Developer*

Landowner Julia Tuttle promoted her area of southern Florida and persuaded a railroad magnate to improve transportation to the region, leading to the development of the city of Miami.

A native of Cleveland, Ohio, she was the daughter of a legislator. She married the owner of an ironworks. Her father was then living in a part of Florida that would someday become the famous city of Miami, but at that time it was an Indian trading post. During the 1870s, Tuttle visited him three times and was fascinated with the region.

After Tuttle was widowed at age 42, she moved to the land her deceased father had owned in

Florida and used her inheritance to purchase 640 acres more on the north side of the Miami River. She then moved there with her two adult children. In 1890, she wrote to a friend, "It may seem strange to you but it is the dream of my life to see this wilderness turned into a prosperous country and where this tangled mass of vines, brush, trees and rocks now are, to see homes, surrounded by beautiful grassy lawns."

Years earlier, Tuttle had met Henry Flagler, a tycoon who was then building his Florida East Coast Railroad. Along the route, he had also constructed hotels to cater to tourists. He had said his line would terminate in Palm Beach, which he reached in 1894, because his primary goal had been to move his ailing wife to a warm climate. Tuttle wrote to Flagler urging him to continue the railroad to Miami, a distance of 66 more miles. Flagler refused, despite Tuttle's persistent letters.

Flagler changed his mind after the harsh winter of 1894–95 brought freezing temperatures to parts of Florida, including Palm Beach. Ninety-five percent of the citrus crop in Florida was destroyed. Flagler sent an aide to evaluate conditions in Miami. According to a popular story, Julia Tuttle met with Flagler's aide and sent him back to Palm Beach with fresh orange blossoms, or, in other versions, orchids. Flagler then visited Miami himself and met with Tuttle, who offered to sell part of her land to make way for the railroad. After other landowners in the region sold Flagler enough land, he extended his railroad to Miami. The first train arrived there in 1896, loaded with freight.

Julia Tuttle had been clearing her own land and laid out the first street in the city of Miami, which was founded and received a city charter in 1896. About 1,500 people lived there in the late 1890s. Tuttle became known as the Mother of Miami for her efforts to create the city, but she did not live long enough to witness its greatest period of growth. She had been suffering from serious headaches in 1897, and died, probably from a brain tumor, on September 14, 1898. Her real estate and other property were valued at about $400,000 at her death.

Bolstered by the railroad, Miami grew rapidly, and its population reached 5,000 in 1910. By 1920, that figure had grown to 30,000, and Miami was the center of a real estate boom during the first half of that decade.

Further Reading

Forbes, Malcolm. *Women Who Made a Difference.* New York: Simon and Schuster, 1990.

Hawes, Leland. "'Inventing Florida' Follows Burns' Formula," *The Tampa Tribune,* January 7, 2001, Baylife Section, p. 1.

Sheppard, R. Z. "Urban Razzle, Fatal Glamour: Four Authors Look at Miami, the Definitive City of the '80s." *Time,* September 28, 1987, p. 65.

V

✻ VANCASPEL, VENITA WALKER (Venita VanCaspel Brown, Venita VanCaspel Harris) (1922–) *Financier, Entrepreneur*

The founder and president of her own brokerage firm, VanCaspel & Co., Inc., Venita Walker VanCaspel was also the first woman member of the Pacific Stock Exchange.

Venita Walker was born on a farm near Sweetwater, Oklahoma, in 1922. As a child, she did farm work and picked cotton and was an excellent student at the local two-room school. She worked hard throughout her youth to pay her way through college and entered Duke University as a dual major in economics and business. Halfway through her program, she visited the University of Colorado and transferred there to complete her final two years of college, graduating Phi Beta Kappa with a degree in economics and finance in 1948.

VanCaspel, who had married her college sweetheart, was widowed when her husband died in an airplane accident. During that time, she began reading about how average Americans managed their finances and was surprised to discover that many households lacked the tools for making wise

financial decisions. She decided to use her background in economics and business to improve that situation, offering people financial planning and investment services. She knew that women, in particular, needed these services because many of them had traditionally left financial decisions to the man in the household.

During the 1960s, a time when few women held high positions in the world of finance, Van-Caspel opened her own securities brokerage firm, VanCaspel, Inc., in Houston, Texas. She was both president and chief executive officer (CEO) of the company. During the next three decades, she built the business through hard work and ingenuity, signing her first clients by giving seminars in department stores. She later said that most of these clients were married couples. Her clientele grew and her reputation spread outside Texas. In 1968, VanCaspel became the first woman to have a seat on the Pacific Stock Exchange.

Beginning in the 1970s, VanCaspel wrote articles and several books about financial planning and investing geared for consumers. She also began appearing on a national public television series, *The Money Makers,* which was shown on

184 stations across the nation, and another PBS series, *Profiles of Success.*

VanCaspel has written six best-selling books on money management and has appeared on numerous TV programs, such as *Good Morning, America* and *Moneyline,* as well as her long-running *Money Makers* series which aired during the 1980s. She is also a popular motivational speaker who has devoted time to projects that empower young people to work toward their goals. VanCaspel serves on the advisory board for the economics department at her alma mater, the University of Colorado, and on the boards of directors of the Horatio Alger Association of Distinguished Americans and the Robert Schuller International Ministries.

Listed in *Who's Who in Finance and Industry,* VanCaspel was honored as a Northwood University Outstanding Business Leader (1996) and the Outstanding Woman of the Year by the YWCA. She has received the Horatio Alger Award for Distinguished Americans in 1982 and the George Norlin Outstanding Alumnus Award from the University of Colorado. She was also chosen as Certified Financial Planner of the Year and was named Number One Financial Planner by 2,400 professionals in the industry.

Venita VanCaspel lives with her husband Lyttleton T. Harris IV in Houston, Texas, where they are active in church, community, and civic affairs.

Further Reading

Horatio Alger Association. "Venita VanCaspel Harris, 1982." Available online. URL: http://www.horatioalger.com/member/van82.htm. Downloaded on June 2, 2001.

Singell, Larry. "A Brief Biographical Sketch of Mrs. Venita VanCaspel Harris." University of Colorado, Department of Economics, Newsletter, spring 2000. Available online. URL: http://www.colorado.edu/Economics/newsletter/spring2000-singell.htm. Downloaded on June 1, 2001.

✳ VERNON, LILLIAN (Lilly Menasche)
(1927–) *Entrepreneur, Executive*

Lillian Vernon founded one of America's leading mail order catalog businesses, and her company has also expanded into outlet stores, business-to-business sales, and e-commerce.

Lilly Menasche was born on March 18, 1927, in Leipzig, Germany. Shortly before World War II, her family fled first to Holland, then to the United States to avoid the Nazi threat to the Jews in Europe, and they settled in New York City. There, Lillian attended school and worked for several years in her father's leather-goods business, which produced belts and handbags. She found she had a knack for designing popular items. She later said her father was an inspiration: "He never treated me as anything less than equal, and from that I learned a lot. His optimism and determination are part of his legacy to me."

After attending New York University for two years, she left to get married. As a young wife expecting a baby, she wanted to be able to stay home and rear her children but also earn some extra money. In 1951, she decided to sell belts and handbags through the mail, using as capital the $2,000 she and her husband had received as wedding gifts. She later said, "One morning, while leafing through magazines in my usual fashion, I was struck with an idea. Why couldn't I sell something through the mail out of my home?"

Although she had never run a business, she had ideas about what people needed and wanted and how they would like to order merchandise. She bought a stock of belts and handbags, along with an embossing machine to personalize these items with her customers' initials, then placed an advertisement costing $495 in *Seventeen* magazine to target teenage customers. When more than $32,000 in orders arrived at her home in Mount Vernon, New York, her mail-order business was born. It was named after the town where she lived and started her business and she became known as Lillian Vernon.

She proceeded to buy more items and advertise them in magazines. Prominent among her first products were jewelry and fashion accessories. Vernon offered monogrammed products which continued to sell well through the years, as the handbags and belts had in 1951. As time went on,

As the founder and CEO of Lillian Vernon Corporation, Vernon has been a pioneer and a leader in the mail-order business since the early 1950s.
(Photo courtesy of Lillian Vernon Corporation)

the company offered housewares, including dishes and other basics, decorative items, children's items, and various household organizers, all of which have sold well through the years.

While she was building her business, Vernon handled nearly all the work herself, including selecting and designing merchandise, writing ads, and filling orders. By 1954, the business had grown too large to run from her home, so the company moved to a storefront, and opened a warehouse.

In 1956, the first Lillian Vernon mail-order catalog was produced. The 16-page black-and-white catalog was sent to 125,000 people who had purchased merchandise from her ads. Sales steadily increased and reached the $1 million mark in

1970. One major reason for the catalogs' success was demography—more families had two wage earners, and mail-order shopping was convenient for busy people.

As chief executive officer and chairman of the company, Lillian Vernon remains active in the day-to-day running of the business and the selection of merchandise, which she finds while traveling to many countries. She has said that she wants to be "highly visible and available to my staff." The company keeps costs under control by finding economical sources for products, and its national distribution center, located in Virginia Beach, Virginia, is highly automated. Corporate headquarters are located in Rye, New York.

Although the catalogs target middle-class consumers, the company also claims the rich and famous among its customers, including Senator and former first lady Hillary Clinton, actress Betty White, singer Loretta Lynn, and actor Arnold Schwarzenegger. To further increase her business, Vernon developed spin-off catalogs and utilized new marketing opportunities. She launched her Lillian Vernon Gardening and Lilly's Kids catalogs in 1980. The company also has a website and has marketed its products over television's QVC shopping network.

In 1987, her company achieved a distinction: It was the first business founded by a woman to be listed on the American Stock Exchange. It has also been in business as long as, or longer than, most other mail-order businesses. Vernon told author Ann Sample, "We have stuck with our fundamentals. We continue to offer free personalization on most of our products, as well as practical and very sensibly priced items. And, most importantly, we offer exclusive products."

By 2001, Lillian Vernon catalogs reached more than 169 million people each year, and the company received more than 4.4 million orders annually.

The Lillian Vernon company has contributed both money and merchandise to numerous charities including social welfare agencies and educational and cultural institutions. For example, it has provided blankets for homeless people in New York City and gave 7,000 teddy bears to hospitalized children. In 2001, she funded the building of a Habitat for Humanity house to be constructed by Lillian Vernon staff.

Her dozens of honors include the Big Brother/Big Sisters National Hero Award and Ellis Island Medal of Honor. She has also received the International Women's Forum "A Woman Who Has Made a Difference" Award, the YWCA Bravo Award, the American Academy of Achievement Golden Plate Award, the Business and Professional Women Magnificent Seven Award, the YWCA Academy of Women Achievers Award, the Bonds for Israel City of Peace Award, and the Northwood Institute Outstanding Business Leader Award. Vernon has been inducted into the Connecticut Women's Hall of Fame and the Direct Marketing Hall of Fame.

Lillian Vernon serves on the boards of the Kennedy Center for the Performing Arts, the National Retail Federation, Lincoln Center, Citymeals-On-Wheels, the Children's Museum of the Arts, the National Women's Economic Alliance, and other organizations. She is also the author of *An Eye for Winners*, an autobiography that describes her techniques for developing a business.

Further Reading

Sample, Ann. "Catalogue Mogul Lillian Vernon," Women.com. Available online. URL: http://www.womenswire.com/watch/vernon3.html. Downloaded on October 18, 2001.

Silver, A. David. *Enterprising Women.* New York: AMACOM, 1994.

Lillian Vernon. "The Story of Lillian Vernon." Available online. URL: http://www.lillianvernon.com/Templates/herstory.tem. Downloaded on October 18, 2001.

Vernon, Lillian. *An Eye for Winners.* New York: HarperCollins, 1997.

W

✵ ✵ ✵ ✵ ✵

✵ **WALKER, MADAM C. J.**
(Sarah Breedlove McWilliams Walker)
(1867–1919) *Entrepreneur, Executive,*
Philanthropist

Despite formidable obstacles, Madam C. J. Walker created a tremendously profitable beauty-products business that employed thousands of women in manufacturing, beauty services, and sales, providing economic opportunities for employees and their families. Describing her success, Walker said, "I promoted myself. I had to make my own opportunity. . . . Don't sit down and wait for the opportunities to come." She advised other aspiring entrepreneurs, "If I have accomplished anything in life, it is because I have been willing to work hard."

Sarah Breedlove was born on December 23, 1867, in Delta, Louisiana, to a family of poor sharecroppers who had once been slaves. At age six, she was orphaned, and four years later, she went to live with her sister Louvenia in Vicksburg, Mississippi. However, Louvenia's husband, Jesse Powell, treated Sarah cruelly, and she left their home at age 14 when she married Moses (Jeff) McWilliams, with whom she had a daughter, Lelia, in 1885.

Widowed at 20, Sarah McWilliams had to find a way to support herself and her child. She moved to St. Louis, Missouri, where her four brothers were working as barbers. There she worked hard doing laundry, earning only about $1.50 per day, and she attended public night schools to further her education. She also saved as much money as possible so she could educate her daughter. To meet other African-American women who were striving to better themselves and the community, McWilliams joined the National Association of Colored Women and the St. Paul African Methodist Episcopal (A.M.E.) Church.

During this time, she suffered from a scalp problem that caused hair loss, and she tried various homemade remedies that were reputed to restore hair or help it grow. Some of these hair products were made by ANNIE TURNBO MALONE, a successful black entrepreneur. Then McWilliams tried making her own formula, trying different combinations of ingredients from about 1900 to 1905. She finally came up with a conditioning salve that improved her hair. Later, she told people that the idea for this formula, which may have contained sulfur, had come to her in a dream. Friends who

Beauty products entrepreneur and philanthropist Madam C. J. Walker stands on the steps of the Senate Avenue YMCA in Indianapolis, which she helped to build, for the dedication ceremony.
(Photo from Indiana Historical Society)

tried the mixture also praised its effectiveness, and McWilliams began selling it door to door.

In 1905, McWilliams moved to Denver, Colorado, and began selling her products there while also working as a cook. The next year, she married newspaperman Charles Joseph Walker and began using the name Madam C. J. Walker as she continued to sell her hair salve, called Madam Walker's Wonderful Hair Grower, door to door in black neighborhoods. Her husband worked with her to advertise the products, which expanded to include a coconut oil shampoo and other cleansing prod-

ucts, a salve for ringworm and eczema, and a product called Glossine, which helped to straighten and smooth the hair so that it could be styled in various ways. It was used with a special pressing comb that was heated beforehand.

As the business grew, Walker hired more and more saleswomen, called Walker agents, who were trained to give people at-home hair treatments and demonstrate the right way to use her products and the hot comb. She also started a mail-order business by placing ads in magazines and newspapers. African-American newspapers promoted Walker products, which soon grew to include skin cleansers.

In addition to creating and selling products, Walker influenced ideas about beauty and personal grooming. She claimed that cleanliness, good grooming, and pride in one's appearance were the essence of beauty, and these were available to people who properly cared for their hair and skin. Walker also strongly encouraged black women to appreciate their own beauty, challenging old biases that regarded Caucasian skin tones and features as better than those of other races.

By 1908, Walker had opened an office in Pittsburgh, Pennsylvania, where her daughter had moved in 1903. There, she founded Lelia College, which offered a $25 correspondence course for Walker "hair culturists." Two years later, Walker opened another training school, as well as a larger factory, the Madam C. J. Walker Manufacturing Company, in Indianapolis, Indiana, where she built her new headquarters. During a speech Walker later made to the National Negro Business League, she said proudly, "I have built my own factory on my own ground." At the factory, several thousand African-American women produced Walker hair and beauty products, including cleansers, shampoos, salves, pressing oil, and skin cream. These employees enjoyed better wages and working conditions than most African Americans of that era.

Walker was the sole shareholder of the company when it was incorporated in 1911, with its headquarters still in Denver. The next year, she and Charles Walker were divorced. She continued to expand her company and built beauty schools in various cities, including Indianapolis, and her large network of sales agents and representatives grew. Walker traveled throughout the East and South, lecturing on beauty products and the Walker methods. In 1913, she traveled in Central America and the Caribbean, demonstrating and selling her products.

In 1916, Walker moved to New York City, where she bought two adjoining homes in Harlem. Part of this space was turned into living quarters; the rest became a Walker school and a beauty salon. Her daughter, who now used the name A'Lelia, also lived in Harlem in the stunning townhouse that black architect Vertner W. Tandy had designed for the Walkers.

The company continued to prosper. Between 1911 and 1919, the business grossed more than $100,000 a year. In 1917, Walker earned about $276,000 from sales, speaking fees, and other business activities.

Madam C. J. Walker donated money and time to numerous humanitarian causes both in the United States and abroad. Among the recipients were the YMCA built for African Americans in Indianapolis, black churches and schools, the National Association for the Advancement of Colored People (NAACP), and the Tuskegee Institute. She also personally worked for social causes, such as the antilynching movement. In 1917, she joined a group of black leaders who took a petition to the White House seeking federal antilynching laws. She once said, "This is the greatest country under the sun. But we must not let our love of country, our patriotic loyalty cause us to abate one whit in our protest against wrong and injustice."

In addition, Walker gave special prizes and awards to Walker employees who engaged in community service and educational work. Walker training programs emphasized ways agents could benefit their communities. Once, after a speech Walker gave, a woman from the audience told her, "Your talk inspired me so that I was determined to see what good I could do in this world and for my people." She organized clubs for her agent-operators so they could help themselves and each other, as well as plan leisure and charitable activities. Members paid dues of 25 cents a month and received various services, as well as a $50 death benefit payable to their beneficiaries.

Although she maintained a home in New York City, Walker also built a mansion called Villa Lewaro in Irvington-on-Hudson, New York. Once again, she sought the talents of architect Vertner Tandy. The mansion, which cost about $350,000, included a swimming pool and formal gardens.

Madam C. J. Walker died at age 51 from kidney failure associated with hypertension (high blood pressure). During her lifetime, she had disputed the rumors that she was a millionaire. When she died in 1919, the value of her estate was estimated at about $509,000. In 1998, the U.S. Post Office issued a commemorative stamp in her honor as part of its Black Heritage series.

Further Reading

Bundles, A'Lelia Perry. *Madam C. J. Walker, Entrepreneur.* New York: Chelsea House, 1991.

———. *On Her Own Ground: The Life and Times of Madam C. J. Walker.* New York: Scribners, 2001.

Indiana Historical Society, Manuscripts & Archives: Madame C. J. Walker Collection, 1910–1980.

Peiss, Kathy L. "American Women and the Making of Modern Consumer Culture," *The Journal for Multi-Media History,* fall 1998 reprinted at http://www.albany.edu/jmmh/vol1no1/peiss-text.html.

WALKER, MAGGIE LENA (Maggie Lena Draper, Maggie Mitchell)

(1867–1934) *Executive, Bank President*

The daughter of a former slave, Maggie Lena Walker overcame poverty and discrimination against both her gender and her race to become America's first woman banker. When she died, newspapers hailed her as "one of the greatest Negro leaders in America."

Maggie Lena Draper was born on July 15, 1867, in Richmond, Virginia. Her mother, Elizabeth Draper, had conceived Maggie during a brief affair with a white abolitionist writer named Eccles Cuthbert. While working as a cook in a private home, she fell in love with William Mitchell, an African-American butler, and they were married in 1868. Together they had a son, John, and Maggie took Mitchell's last name. William Mitchell became a headwaiter in a hotel, and the family moved to its own home, but tragedy struck when he was killed in 1875 during a robbery.

Elizabeth Mitchell did laundry to support herself and her two children, and Maggie took on many household chores, including caring for her half-brother, John, and collecting and delivering the clothes her mother laundered. Nonetheless, she was an excellent student who loved school.

Maggie Mitchell also became interested in community activities. At age 14, she joined the Independent Order of Saint Luke, a national fraternal society that offered black Americans life insurance and promoted humanitarianism and self-help. As a senior in high school, she joined a group of classmates to protest the fact that African-American students were not allowed to hold their graduation exercises in the city theater, as white students did.

After graduating from high school in 1883, Mitchell became a teacher by day and attended accounting classes at night. She became more active in the Order of Saint Luke and visited sick members and collected membership dues, among other things. Soon, she rose to leadership roles in the organization and was assigned to organize new chapters.

In 1886, she married Armstead Walker Jr., a brick contractor. She resigned from teaching and devoted more time to Saint Luke, rising to the office of Left Worthy Grand Chief in 1890, the same year her first son, Russell Eccles, was born. A second son, Armstead Mitchell, was born in 1893 but died seven months later. Her third son, Melvin DeWitt Walker, was born in 1897.

Walker's energy, vision, and talent for working with people continued to benefit Richmond's African-American community. In 1895, she spearheaded a successful campaign to bring more children into the Order of Saint Luke so they could engage in community service projects and develop the values of thrift, industriousness, and studiousness that the Order espoused.

Four years later, in 1899, she was named Right Worthy Grand Secretary, the highest position in the organization. She faced several major problems, including a treasury that was nearly empty and debts totaling $400. Walker managed to boost the membership, raise enough money to pay off the debts, and add money to the treasury. In her 1901 address to the group, she said, "Since our last meeting, 1,400 new soldiers and 29 more councils [have joined our organization]. Into this army have come teachers, preachers, lawyers, doctors, businessmen, working men and women. We have invited all; and all have come." She proposed a weekly newspaper, the *St. Luke Herald,* which was launched in 1902; a few years later, she set up St. Luke Emporium, a retail store.

At the 1901 annual meeting, Walker had declared that the group should form a bank so that members could profit from their own economic enterprises. She said, "We need a savings bank, chartered, officered and run by the men and women of this Order. Let us put our moneys together; let us use our moneys; Let us put our money out at usury among ourselves, and reap the money ourselves." Walker became president of the Saint Luke Penny Savings Bank, which was chartered in 1903 and became a great success. The Walkers bought a comfortable home on East Leigh Street in the heart of the African-American community. After adding some rooms, they lived there with their extended family and often hosted community meetings and overnight guests.

Walker faced serious personal challenges in the years that followed. She injured her leg in 1908, and it never healed properly. Her husband died in 1915, and her son Russell died eight years later. By 1928, she could not walk at all.

Despite her physical disabilities, Walker continued her active life, staying mobile with the help of a wheelchair, chauffeured automobile, and an elevator in her home. In 1921, she ran for a state office, that of superintendent of public instruction, on the Lily Black ticket, composed entirely of African Americans, but was defeated. Other African-American banks merged with the bank during the 1920s, and it grew into a major institution called the Consolidated Bank and Trust Company. She served as president of the bank she had founded until 1931 and managed to keep it solvent after the Great Depression began in 1929.

Under Walker's leadership, the Order of Saint Luke grew to 100,000 members, with $100,000 in its treasury. The organization employed numerous people in its various enterprises.

Walker was particularly gratified that they created jobs for many African-American women, whom she had said were "circumscribed and hemmed in, in the race of life, in the struggle for bread, meat, and clothing." Likewise, she made important contributions to numerous civic groups and served on the board of directors of the Virginia Industrial School for Girls and the National Association for the Advancement of Colored People (NAACP), as well as on the Virginia Interracial Commission.

Maggie Lena Walker died on December 15, 1934, of complications of diabetes. Her home in Richmond has been declared a national historic site.

Further Reading

Bird, Caroline. *Enterprising Women.* New York: Norton, 1976.

Dabney, Wendell P. *Maggie Lena Walker, Her Life and Deeds.* Cincinnati, Ohio: Dabney, 1927.

Maggie L. Walker National Historical Site. "The Details," "Timeline of Maggie L. Walker's Life and Accomplishments," and "Address to the 34th Annual Session of the Right Worthy Grand Council of Virginia, Independent Order of Saint Luke." Available online. URL: http://www.nps.gov/malw/details.htm. Downloaded on September 1, 2000.

WANG, VERA
(1949–) *Entrepreneur, Fashion Designer*

Vera Wang, who founded a successful design company known for its luxury bridal wear and evening gowns, has in the eyes of many become the world's most influential bridal wear designer. According to fashion editor and consultant Polly Mellen, "From the moment that she went into it, Vera . . . single-handedly changed the wedding."

The daughter of Chinese immigrants, Vera Wang was born on June 27, 1949, and grew up on Park Avenue, in a wealthy section of New York City. Her father, Cheng Ching Wang, the son of a military general, built a successful chemical and pharmaceutical business in the United States. Her mother, Florence Wu Wang, came from a

Designer Vera Wang's creativity and vision have changed the bridal-wear industry.
(Photo courtesy of Vera Wang Company)

age 25 and remained as an editor until 1988. She then became a design director for Ralph Lauren but left in 1989 to open a fashion retail store in Manhattan's Carlyle Hotel.

In 1990, she opened her own boutique on Madison Avenue, offering expensive high-fashion wedding gowns. She later said that she was inspired to design bridal gowns because she had been disappointed with the designs she saw when planning her own wedding. Wang describes her business philosophy: "I wanted to build a fashion company starting with one market. I chose bridal wear. It was important to me to become an expert in this one market. And then expand into others." Two of the designers who inspired her were Geoffrey Beene and Giorgio Armani.

Wang gowns soon gained a reputation for being sophisticated and elegant, with distinctive silhouettes and details. In 1992, Wang began producing a less expensive line of ready-to-wear bridal gowns; the following year, she added evening gowns in a similar price range. Although she was already well-known in fashion circles, Wang became much better known among the general public when she designed the elegant and distinctive costumes worn by figure-skating champion Nancy Kerrigan in the 1994 Olympics.

Only six years after she opened her first store, Wang's business was thriving. Commenting on how she works on her designs, she has said, "It all starts with fabric but it's what you do with that fabric." Mille Bratten, an editor at *Bride's* magazine, says, "What Vera brought to market was her high-fashion background and a real sense of sensuality, that the bride could be feminine and modest and charming, but sensual too—and dress very fashionably." In 1998, revenues reached $20 million, and Wang employed 200 people.

Wang has designed for actors Sharon Stone, Holly Hunter, Alicia Silverstone, Halle Berry, Goldie Hawn, Jane Fonda, and Uma Thurman, and for singers, including Mariah Carey and Chynna Phillips. Because celebrities often choose to wear Wang's designs for major awards cere-

prominent landowning family, and she passed on to young Vera a love for the arts and for fashion as an art form. Wang later recalled that her mother owned beautifully designed clothes and accessories and that she sometimes went with her on shopping trips to buy designer clothing.

Growing up, Wang was a talented figure skater who considered pursuing a skating career. She changed her goal in 1968 after she did not win the women's title at the National Figure Skating Championships. As a hard-working student at Sarah Lawrence College, she had little time left to train in her sport. Wang earned a bachelor of arts (B.A.) degree in liberal arts from Sarah Lawrence but did not study fashion or design during those years. In 1971, she went to work for *Vogue* magazine, where she became senior fashion director at monies, such as the Academy Awards, Wang has been called Designer to the Stars. Her friend and client Sharon Stone wore a Wang design in pale pink chiffon for her wedding in 1998, and Wang also designed the gown that Victoria Adams, known as Posh Spice as a member of the Spice Girls musical group, wore at her wedding in 1999. Holly Hunter says, "Vera's designs are very simple but not boring. Her clothes celebrate the person, they never overwhelm."

As of 2000, Wang had begun designing shoes and planned to expand into women's sportswear and active wear and produce more accessories. In fall 2001 her first book, *Vera Wang on Weddings,* was released, and she continued to work on a bridal video. In February 2002, she launched Vera Wang Fragrance, with other fragrance and cosmetic products under development for the future. She plans to continue merchandising her name though such products as Vera Wang China, through Wedgewood USA; a luxury eyewear collection; and a new evening and bridal shoe collection by Stuart Weitzman. As she told journalist Cynthia Sanz, "We're not watching paint dry here. There's an energy in this little company that's extraordinary."

The mother of two daughters, Cecilia and Josephine, Wang lives in New York City with her husband, Arthur Becker, a businessman whom she married in 1989.

Further Reading

Gabor, Lisa. "Fashion/Style Guide: Designers' Picks: What gives a wedding gown its allure? The pros who make and (on occasion) wear them tell all," *In Style,* February 2, 1998.

McFadden, Cynthia, "Vera Wang's Royal Weddings of the Century," *Good Morning America,* CBS News, June 17, 1999. Transcript.

Sample, Ann. "Designer to the Stars: Vera Wang." Women's Wire. Available online. URL: http://www.women'swire.com/watch/wang.html. Downloaded on October 19, 2001.

Sanz, Cynthia, and Sue Miller. "Bio: Chic To Chic: Her sleek wedding gowns have made her a bride's best friend," *People Weekly,* July 7, 1998, p. 129ff.

✿ WATERS, ALICE LOUISE
(1943–) *Entrepreneur, Business Owner, Chef*

Through her influential Chez Panisse restaurant and cookbooks, Alice Waters has promoted a new kind of cuisine and has undertaken various projects to promote the idea of raising and using healthful and organic foodstuffs. The *New York Times* has called Waters the "patron saint" of organic farmers and the "Mother of American Cooking."

Alice Louise Waters was born in Chatham, New Jersey, on April 28, 1944. She attended the University of California at Berkeley, earning a degree in French cultural studies in 1967, then studied early childhood education at the Montessori Training School in London. The following year, Waters studied in France, an experience that sparked her interest in healthy eating and food preparation. She later said, "This was my first connection with farmers' markets and real food. I loved what I ate and I wanted that kind of food here."

Back in California, Waters worked as a teacher and began cooking dinners for friends. Out of these dinners grew the idea of Chez Panisse restaurant, which she opened in an old wooden house in Berkeley in 1971, aided by a $10,000 loan from her father. The restaurant, a French country-style bistro, was not an initially successful. Waters did a great deal of experimenting as the menu evolved, but maintained her focus on top-quality, fresh, seasonal foods.

Chez Panisse featured a fixed-price menu consisting of five courses. Waters changed the menu each day. Local farmers provided the ingredients for her recipes, which were prepared simply to highlight the natural flavors. One journalist described a typical menu: "a small watercress and beet salad; a bowl of vegetable broth; grilled fish; and for dessert, a single pear sitting on a plate. And every morsel, perfection." She popularized the use of fresh greens, particularly a mixture of baby salad greens called mesclun.

Waters promoted the use of pure foods and bought organic produce and other ingredients

Chef and restaurateur Alice Waters, shown here in the kitchen of her restaurant, Chez Panisse, has promoted the organic movement and influenced the way people prepare food and think about food production.
(Photo courtesy of Alice Waters/Chez Panisse)

"The sensual pleasure of eating beautiful food from the garden brings with it the moral satisfaction of doing the right thing for the planet and for yourself." She serves as director of the Chez Panisse Foundation, which donates money to nonprofit organizations that promote sustainable agriculture.

In 1980, Waters added a café to the restaurant, featuring an à la carte menu and wood-burning pizza oven. Café Fanny, a stand-up café serving breakfast and lunch, was opened four years later near the original Chez Panisse restaurant. Waters refused to franchise her restaurant or take part in certain other kinds of commercial endeavors, such as cooking shows or grocery store versions of her recipes, except for her Café Fanny Granola. She has written several cookbooks that changed the way many Americans prepared food. They include the *Chez Panisse Menu Cookbook* (1994), *Chez Panisse Vegetables* (1996) and *Chez Panisse Cooking* (2000).

A number of well-known chefs worked for Waters through the years. They include chef and restaurateur Paul Bertolli, who coauthored some cookbooks with Waters, and chef-restaurateur Mark Miller, known for Southwestern cuisine; Deborah Madison, a chef and cookbook author known for her vegetable dishes; and Jeremiah Tower, who opened Stars restaurant in San Francisco.

Waters has served on several boards, including the Public Voice on Food Safety and Health and the Advisory Board of the University of California at Berkeley. She is the director of the Chez Panisse Foundation.

Her community projects include the Garden Project, inspired by an organic gardening project that Catherine Sneed, a counselor at the San Francisco County Jail, organized at the jail, in 1992. The idea then spread to other parts of the city. In 1996 Waters founded the Edible Garden Project at the Martin Luther King Jr. Middle School in Berkeley where children learn to plant, grow, harvest, and cook fruits and vegetables. She was inspired to develop the project after learning that the school cafeteria had been replaced with a snack bar that sold packaged hamburgers, burritos, and pizza. In 1999, the students began planting the

from an expanding network of farmers and ranchers who produced fruits, vegetables, free-range poultry, and dairy products and meat from animals that are not treated with antibiotics or steroids or processed with chemicals. By 1999, Waters was purchasing ingredients from 75 different vendors.

Political ideals have strongly influenced Waters' approach to her business, and she has been an outspoken advocate of healthy food production, saying, "Wholesome, honest food must be the entitlement of all Americans." Waters has also said, first crops. The gardening project, which flourishes on a half acre, is interwoven with the school curriculum and lunch program. Other schools around the United States have developed their own programs based on the one in Berkeley.

Waters' professional influence has spread beyond the United States to various parts of Europe. The magazine *Cuisine et Vins du France* ranked her as one of the world's 10 best chefs. France invited Waters to open a restaurant in its Louvre museum in Paris, and that project is scheduled for completion in 2010. Waters has received many awards, including the *Cook's Magazine* Top 50 (1982); the James Beard Special Achievement Award (1985); the Restaurant and Business Leadership Award from *Restaurants & Institutions* magazine (1987); the Wine and Food Achievement Award (1989); James Beard Foundation's award for the Best Restaurant and Best Chef in America (1992); Humanitarian of the Year (James Beard Foundation, 1997); Pellegrino Artusi Award (2000), and Lifetime Achievement Award, *Bon Appétit* magazine American Food and Entertaining Awards (2000).

Waters, whose daughter, Fanny, was born in 1983, lives a few blocks away from Chez Panisse.

Further Reading

"Alice Waters: Biography." Courtesy of Chez Panisse.

Crawford, Leslie. "Alice Waters," *Salon.* Available online. URL: http://www.salon.com/people/bc/1999/11/16/waters/index.html. Posted November 16, 1999. Downloaded on August 3, 2000.

Online Chef. "Interview with Alice Waters of Chez Panisse." Available online. URL: http://www.onlinechef.com/chez.html Downloaded on August 3, 2000.

WHEELER, CANDACE THURBER

(1827–1923) *Entrepreneur, Artist, Interior Designer, Author*

Artist and textile designer Candace Thurber Wheeler found new ways to market handicrafts made by American women through her outlets and cooperatives and inspired many women to become self-supporting through their art. Author Mary Warner Blanchard writes that, through the decorative arts movement of the late 1800s, Wheeler was able "to move outward, to excel in the commercial world of men, and to dare to influence the images of nationhood."

Candace Thurber grew up on a farm in Delhi, in the western Catskill Mountains of New York State. One of eight children born to a deeply religious family, she was taught that women were best suited for the domestic life. Her mother taught her needlework, including cross-stitching, which she found interesting and creative. She also enjoyed making up fanciful stories, something her parents discouraged. Wheeler later recalled, "We were not only traditional, but actual Puritans, repeating in 1828 the lives of our pioneer New England forefathers a hundred years before."

Like other young women in her community, Thurber married young—in her case, at age 17, when she married Tom Wheeler, a New York businessman. The couple settled in Roslyn, New York, not far from New York City. Through her husband, Candace Wheeler became acquainted with city life, attending her first concerts and plays, and she met artists and writers whom he knew in the city. She gave birth to four children and became busy with her household and child-rearing responsibilities, as well as local charities. She became increasingly involved in the arts.

During her forties, Wheeler determined to become an artist herself and she studied painting in New York and in Europe. She was devoting herself to her new career when her daughter Candace died in 1876. To help ease her grief, she focused on helping others. That year, she saw an exhibit of needlework in Philadelphia that was on display to help women in need earn money to support themselves. Wheeler realized that many women were in this predicament, depending on others for support and with no way to earn their own living.

Wheeler decided to found a needlecraft school and sales outlet that would give such women the opportunity for self-support. By collaborating with other socially minded women of means and her artist friends, she formed the Society of Decorative Arts of New York in 1877. The society provided needlework classes and marketed women's handicrafts to stores and home-owners. Within a year, there were 30 branches of the society operating in towns across America. In 1879, Wheeler cofounded another society to help women who had no skills in needlework but could work in other areas: the Women's Exchange.

As a result of these efforts, Wheeler, who also designed fabrics, became known as an expert on needlework. Joining forces with noted stained-glass artist and designer Louis Comfort Tiffany, she developed a decorative arts firm called the Associated Artists. They worked under contract to design interiors and provide needlework and patterned designs for some of America's finest homes, including author Mark Twain's Hartford, Connecticut, mansion and some rooms at the White House. Wheeler and some of the young women artists she helped to educate designed fabrics for these jobs. Her partnership with Tiffany ended in 1883, and she continued the Associated Artists business with an all-woman staff.

At age 66, Wheeler was named the director of the Woman's Building at the Chicago World's Fair (Exposition) in 1893, where she displayed works by women artists from around the world. American women painted the murals in the building, and Associated Artists provided a large needlepoint tapestry, along with fabrics for the exhibit. Wheeler also wrote several books on household art.

In 1887, Wheeler and her brother Frank, who had become a wealthy grocer in New York City, founded the Onteora Colony in the Catskill Mountains, near their birthplace. In an area known for its natural beauty, it was one of the earliest summer retreats for writers and artists, initially visited by their own friends.

The Associated Artists firm was closed in 1907. During her last years, Wheeler enjoyed her homes in the Catskills and in Georgia and spent time with her family and gardens. Candance Thurber Wheeler died August 6, 1923. An exhibit surveying

Candace Wheeler's life and career opened at the Metropolitan Museum of Art in New York City in October 2001.

Further Reading

Naylor, Natalie M., and Maureen O. Murphy, editors. *Long Island Women: Activists and Innovators.* Interlaken, N.Y.: Empire State Books, 1998.

Sanders, Kathleen Waters. *The Business of Charity: The Woman's Exchange Movement, 1832–1900.* Urbana: University of Illinois Press, 1998.

Stern, Madeleine B. *We the Women.* New York: Schutte, 1963.

✳ WHITMAN, MEG (Margaret C. Whitman) (1956–) *Executive*

As president and chief executive officer (CEO) of eBay, Inc., the world's first online auction and trading site, Meg Whitman has played a major role in the 1990s boom in the sale of goods and services over the Internet. Many observers say that eBay has changed the way people in today's world buy and sell. Whitman told journalist Linda Himelstein, "We think of ourselves as sort of a community-commerce model. And what we've basically done is put in place a venue where people can be successful dealing and communicating with one another."

A native of Cold Spring Harbor, on Long Island, New York, Margaret (Meg) Whitman was born on August 4, 1956, the youngest of three children. Whitman entered Princeton University in New Jersey with plans to study medicine, but she became interested in business after she spent a summer selling ads for a campus publication. She also said that she learned a great deal during another summer job, working as a snack bar cook and general manager at a ranch in Valley, Wyoming. Her duties included baking brownies and cookies and buying various items to sell at the snack bar. Whitman said this job showed her that "You have to work hard to make things work right. It doesn't happen by itself."

In 1977, she received a bachelor of arts (B.A.) degree in economics, then went on to graduate studies at Harvard University in Cambridge, Massachusetts, and earned an M.B.A. (master's in business administration). During the next two decades, Whitman worked at several different companies. She began her career at Procter & Gamble Corporation in Cincinnati, where she worked in the area of brand management from 1979 to 1981. She spent the next eight years at a consulting firm, Bain & Company in San Francisco, where she served as a vice president.

In 1989, Whitman moved to southern California and became the senior vice president of marketing at Walt Disney Company's Consumer Products division. She remained at Disney until 1992, managing several key components of Disney's businesses and planning the company's entry into the publishing arena. One of the company's acquisitions during that time was *Discover* magazine.

From Disney, Whitman moved into the shoe business to work in Massachusetts for Stride Rite Corporation, where she was executive vice president of the Keds division, then president of the Stride Rite division. She spearheaded the development of Stride Rite's profitable Munchkin line of baby shoes. At Stride Rite, she also served as corporate vice president of strategic planning.

Whitman tackled the toy industry next by moving to Hasbro, where she was general manager for the preschool division and managed the global marketing of the Playskool and Mr. Potato Head lines of toys. The Playskool division had been losing money, but under Whitman, it became profitable again. From 1995 to 1997, Whitman was president and CEO of FTD (Florists Transworld Delivery); while there, she launched that company's Internet plan. During her tenure, the FTD changed from a florist-owned association to a for-profit, privately owned company, based in Downer's Grove, Illinois.

In 1997, Pierre M. Omidyar, the founder of eBay, an online auction site, offered her the job of president and CEO of his company. The company had been started to allow collectors to trade collectible Pez candy dispensers online, but it expanded to include many other kinds of items. At first, Whitman was reluctant to accept the offer to run eBay, which entailed moving back to California. However, after meeting with Omidyar, she became enthusiastic about the creative potential of the job. Whitman later said that eBay had developed a "really different consumer commerce paradigm" that intrigued her. She told reporters, "We are changing the face of traditional commerce by giving power to individual consumers." For his own part, Omidyar asserted that "finding Meg was crucial" to his company's success.

The eBay company went public with a stock offering six months after Whitman took over, and her stock holdings were reportedly worth about $1 billion dollars. Whitman fostered the online auction site's growth and took it into international markets. When she arrived, eBay's revenues were about $6 million a year. She established local sites in 53 U.S. cities and five countries: Canada, the United Kingdom, Germany, Japan, and Australia. In the years that followed, revenues were especially strong in Germany. Whitman worked hard to manage the company's cash and to eject fraudulent sellers who advertised items on the site. Bob Kagle, general partner at eBay investor Benchmark Capital, said of Whitman, "She has tremendous brand and customer instincts."

When eBay's website crashed several times during 1999, Whitman worked alongside the staff, sometimes all night. As of 1999, her stake in eBay was estimated to be worth at about $1.4 billion, making her one of America's richest people. That year, *Glamour* magazine named her one of its Women of the Year, saying, "In 1999, all of America caught eBay fever."

Meg Whitman had always expressed optimism about the company, but in 1999 she said, "It has surpassed my wildest expectations." That year, $2.8 billion worth of goods were sold on eBay. Revenues increased, and the company continued to meet its targeted earnings. Whitman described some of the changes that took place on eBay during that time: "In the beginning, this was strictly about individuals doing business with one another. What happened is that some of those individuals actually became small dealers. They quit their day jobs to sell full time on eBay."

Although many website-based companies, on dot-coms, failed in 2000, eBay continued to grow and make more profits. The company added autos to the site's list of products and, by year's end, they accounted for about 30 percent of eBay's gross sales. During the first quarter of 2000, revenues were up to $85.8 million and net income rose to $8 million, making eBay one of the most successful websites ever. That year, eBay showed profits of $60 million on sales of $420 million. This was an increase in revenues of about 92 percent. Gross revenues were up about 77.6 percent, while net revenues showed a rise of 11.19 percent over 2000. With $3.3 billion in sales and 16 million users, eBay remained the Internet auction leader, despite stiff competition from Yahoo!, Amazon.com, and Lycos. Whitman kept eBay's share of the person-to-person auction market at about 80 percent and improved the stability of the website.

Analysts gave Whitman a great deal of the credit for eBay's success. In 2000, she was third on *Fortune* magazine's annual list of the most powerful women in American business. *Time Digital* listed Whitman as fifth on its list, "The 50 Most Important People Shaping Technology Today." In its January 8, 2001, issue, *Business Week* magazine named her as one of its top 25 managers for 2000. Whitman says she has tried to create a fun and open environment at eBay and address customer's needs and expectations.

By 2001, eBay was the second most popular site on the Internet and was offering items in about 4,500 categories, including toys, books, antiques, and kitchenware. Whitman has made some business decisions that reflect her personal values: for instance, eBay refuses to sell antique guns (or any other guns) on its site, even though some people collect them. It also does not sell its customer list to other companies.

The mother of two sons, Whitman is married to Griffith R. Harsh IV, a neurosurgeon who practices at the Stanford University Medical Center. She enjoys fly-fishing with her husband and chil-

dren during her time away from work. Her other hobbies include skiing, tennis, and hiking. Whitman is also a collector herself and says that one of her prized items is a Burger King Mr. Potato Head.

Further Reading

About.com "Investing for Women: Meg Whitman," Available online. URL: http://womensinvest.about.com/money/womensinvest/blwhitman.htm. Downloaded on December 14, 2001.

Business Week Online. "Resume: Margaret C. Whitman." Available online. URL: http://www.businessweek.com:/1999/99_22/b3631009.htm?scriptFramed. Posted on May 31, 1999. Downloaded on November 29, 2000.

Business Week Online. "Q&A With eBay's Meg Whitman." Available online. URL: http://www.businessweek.com:/1999/99_22/b3631008.htm. Downloaded on November 29, 2000.

Guernsey, Lisa. "The Powers Behind the Auctions," *The New York Times,* August 20, 2000, Section 3, pp. 1, 11.

Kerstetter, Jim. "Empire Builders: Meg Whitman," *Business Week,* May 15, 2000, p. 86.

"Meg Whitman." *The Detroit News (Business).* Available online. URL: http://detnews.com/menu/stories/32861.htm. Posted on January 22, 1996. Downloaded on March 1, 2001.

"Meg Whitman, President and CEO." *The Industry Standard.* Available online. URL: http://www.thestandard.com/people/display/0,1157,1645,00.html. Downloaded on January 15, 2001.

"The 25 Most Influential Working Mothers," *Working Mother,* December 2000, p. 79.

✹ WILLIAMS, TERRIE M.

(1953–)   *Entrepreneur, Business Owner, Executive*

Williams founded the Terrie Williams Agency, a public relations and communications firm that provides services to some of the world's top entertainers, athletes, business leaders, and organizations. She once said of her work, "This business requires a constant stream of creative ideas. You can't stop thinking for a minute."

Terrie Williams was born in Mount Vernon, New York, in 1953. She attended Brandeis Univer-

Author and executive Terrie Williams founded and runs a public relations agency that has attracted major corporations and international celebrities as clients.
(Photo by Dwight Carter, courtesy
of the Terrie Williams Agency)

sity and graduated cum laude in 1975 with degrees in both sociology and psychology. She went on to receive her master's degree in social welfare from Columbia University in New York City and worked for the next three years as a medical social worker at New York Hospital.

She then entered public relations (PR), seeking more independence and a chance to use her creative talents while still being personally involved with people. Williams built up the PR department at *Essence,* a publisher of books and a popular magazine aimed at an African-American audience, and

211

she rose to become the director of corporate communications and the firm's youngest vice president. While she was working at *Essence,* Williams realized she wanted to start her own PR and communications company, and *Essence* said she could continue handling their public relations after she left.

In 1988, Williams launched the Terrie Williams Agency, opening her first office in Manhattan. She was the first African-American woman to open this kind of agency. Williams got off to a good start when film star and comedian Eddie Murphy and jazz artist Miles Davis, whom she had met while he was a patient at New York Hospital, signed on as her first clients. Williams developed offices on both coasts—one in New York and the other in Los Angeles.

Williams's agency handles public relations, media relations, and special events for people in entertainment, sports, politics, and business. Clients include large corporations such as Coca-Cola, Ortho Pharmaceuticals, Revlon, Time Warner, Inc., and Scholastic, Inc., as well as celebrities—among them, athletes Charlie Ward of the New York Knicks and track-and-field star Jackie-Joyner Kersee, actor Wesley Snipes, and singer Anita Baker. Large events hosted by the agency include the National Basketball Association's (NBA's) Stay in School Program.

Besides managing her agency, Williams is also a popular speaker and has presented her personal and professional ideas to numerous corporations and other organizations, including the New School for Social Research and the National Hockey League. She has also conducted business seminars for large corporations, such as Avon and Philip Morris. Her book, *The Personal Touch: What You Really Need to Know to Succeed in Today's Fast-Paced Business World,* was published in 1994 and became a best-seller. It has been used in business workshops, lectures, and corporate training programs.

Williams has won numerous awards, including the New York Urban League Building Brick Award, the Matrix Award from New York Women in Communications, the D. Parke Gibson Award from the Public Relations Society of America (PRSA), the PRSA New York Chapter's Philip Dorf Mentoring Award, and the Citizen's Committee for New York Marietta Tree Award for Public Service. In 1996, she was the first person of color to receive the Vernon C. Schranz Distinguished Lectureship at Ball State University in Muncie, Indiana. The lecture she prepared for this distinguished occasion has been reprinted in leading public relations journals and used in public relations classes around the world.

Williams, who is strongly interested in young people, is pleased that she has helped many of them develop their skills and talents. She said, "A lot of young people have come through the agency, either as interns or part-timers, to learn the business. Many of those people are now involved in many different aspects of the public relations business."

She has also worked on a personal level with young people as an active member of the Big Brothers/Big Sisters organization. Williams speaks and writes on the subject of troubled youth and has encouraged other adults to work with young people in detention centers, group homes, juvenile prisons, and other settings. She says, "There are so many small ways you can help a child have a better life and encourage him to be educated to his fullest; to be free of prejudice, hate, and fear; to be happy and productive. Just a little effort makes such a difference in how a child envisions her prospects." Williams wrote a motivational book called *Stay Strong: Life Lessons For Teens,* which was published in 2000.

In September 2000, *People* magazine and America Online invited Williams to join its Digital Heroes Campaign, which uses the Internet to expand the concept of mentoring to underserved youth. The e-mentoring program has enlisted other high-profile participants, including Arnold Schwarzenegger, U.S. Secretary of State Colin Powell, MARTHA STEWART, and Michael J. Fox.

Further Reading

"Distinguished Women, Terrie M. Williams," Governor George E. Pataki's Commission Honoring Distinguished New York Women. Available online. URL:

http://www.ny4women.org/tWilliams.html. Down-loaded on October 2, 2000.

Godfrey, Joline. *Our Wildest Dreams.* New York: Harper Business, 1992.

Silver, A. David. *Enterprising Women: Lessons From 100 of the Greatest Entrepreneurs of Our Day.* New York: AMA-COM, 1994.

Terrie M. Williams, President and CEO, The Terrie Williams Agency. Biography. Courtesy of The Terrie Williams Agency.

———. *Stay Strong: Life Lessons For Teens.* New York: Scholastic Books, 2000.

Williams, Terrie, Joe Cooney, and Jonathan Tisch (intro-duction). *The Personal Touch: What You Really Need to Succeed in Today's Fastpaced Business World.* New York: Warner Books, 1996.

✳ WINBLAD, ANN

(1952–) *Entrepreneur, Venture Capitalist, Computer Programmer*

Ann Winblad, one of America's top venture capi-talists, once described her job this way: "A venture capitalist is a person who invests money. Money, usually large pension funds and endowments—considered high-risk capital—in private compa-nies, in our case, mostly startups. And what we do on a daily basis . . . is help build those companies from small companies into big companies."

Winblad grew up in the small town of Farm-ington, Minnesota, where she was the oldest of six children. From age 6, she worked at a variety of paid jobs, including berry-picking, baby-sit-ting, and sewing doll clothes that she sold. Her mother was a nurse and her father was the foot-ball and basketball coach at the local high school. As a student there, Ann was a cheerleader and was active in numerous activities. An excellent stu-dent, she enjoyed science, math, and liberal arts courses and was the valedictorian of her graduat-ing class. During those years, she planned to become a biochemist.

Winblad enrolled at the College of St. Cather-ine and the College of St. Thomas in St. Paul, Minnesota, where she was one of 25 students in an experimental program in which they were allowed to help design their own course load. Winblad focused on math and business courses. The Con-trol Data Company had endowed St. Thomas with numerous computers, and Winblad took a strong interest in them. She later said, "Once I figured out there was such a thing as a computer and that programming was such fun, I was cornered." She took every computer course the school offered. While in college, she also worked at several differ-ent jobs, including waitress, bookkeeper, and cus-tomer service representative for Northwestern Bell.

When Winblad graduated from college in 1973, companies were eager to recruit qualified women with strong science and math skills, and she had a choice of several job offers. She took a job as a sys-tems programmer at the Federal Reserve Bank in Minneapolis. In 1975, after 13 months at the bank, she left and convinced three coworkers to work with her on a new project. Winblad founded Open Sys-tems, a software company, with an initial invest-ment of $500. Software was a new field at that time, so they were exploring new ground. Their company lost $85 the first year. Winblad later said, "I was very young and I had nothing to risk. I had no money. I didn't own anything, not even a car. So why not give this a try? Could I work for myself? Could I convince other people to work for me? Could I help define a product?" Winblad and her colleagues did programming jobs for other people during the daytime; at night, they worked on build-ing the company and its business software products. It became extremely successful and was sold in 1981 for $15 million in cash.

Although she could have retired, Winblad found that she enjoyed building a business and competing in the marketplace. During this time, technology was becoming a major force in the economy. Win-blad relocated to California and worked as a con-sultant for several major companies, including Microsoft, Apple Computer, and IBM. For about five years, she dated Bill Gates, the founder of Microsoft. She coauthored the book *Object-Ori-ented Software,* which was published in 1990.

In 1989, she cofounded Hummer Winblad Venture Partners with John Hummer, a former pro

213

basketball player, for the purpose of investing in software companies. Hummer, who had earned a master's degree in business administration (M.B.A.) from Stanford University, approached her with the idea. At that time, no other venture capital firms were focusing on high-tech startups. They were able to raise $35 million within 18 months after the company founded Hummer Winblad. The first venture they funded, with $30 million, returned $260 million to its investors, and it was followed by several more successes. As of 2000, the firm had more than $95 million invested in various software companies and had launched more than 70 startups.

Ann Winblad says that she looks for companies in strong markets that have outstanding chief executive officers (CEOs) who have "that ability to attract excellence." Winblad says that aspiring companies must convince her they can provide something important to their customers, because "I can't make customers buy things they don't want or need." Their most important asset, says Winblad, is their "intellectual capital."

Winblad has been a member of the board of directors of several firms, including Arbor Software, Berkeley Systems, Liquid Audio, Dean and Deluca, and Farallon Communications. *Vanity Fair* magazine named Winblad one of the top 50 leaders of the "New Establishment," and *Upside Magazine* listed her as one of the 100 most influential people in the digital age. *Business Week* named Winblad as one of its Elite 25 Power Brokers in the Silicon Valley and *Time* magazine listed her as one of its top 50 "Cyber Elite."

She offers this advice about succeeding in today's business environment, "Your commitment cannot be the assumption of knowledge, but the assumption that you'll always need to learn more."

Further Reading

"Ann Winblad on Women in the New Workplace." Business Week Online. Available online. URL: http://www.businessweek.com/bwdaily/dnflash/feb200/nf00217c.htm?scriptFramed. Posted on February 17, 2000. Downloaded on September 30, 2000.

Judge, Paul, editor. "Ann Winblad on Women in the New Workplace." *Business Week* Online Daily, February 17, 2000. Available online. URL: http://www.businessweek.com:/bwdaily/dnflash/feb2000/nf00217c.htm?scriptFramed. Downloaded on March 1, 2001.

O'Brien, Soledad. "Interview: Ann Winblad." Plugged In Spotlight. Available online. URL: http://www.womenswire.com/plug/sportlight/do721winbladTrans.html. Downloaded on February 21, 2001.

Townsend, Peg. "Ann Winblad, Partner Hummer Winblad Venture Capital," Techdivas. Available online. URL: http:techdivas.com/annwinblad.htm. Downloaded on February 8, 2001.

Winblad, Ann, Jill Wolfson, and Carla Sequeiros, "An Interview With Ann Winblad," The Tech Organization: Revolutionaries. Available online. http://www.thetech.org/revolutionaries/winblad/ia.html. Downloaded on October 19, 2001.

Winblad, Ann L., Samuel D. Edwards, and David R. King. *Object-Oriented Software.* Reading, Mass.: Addison Wesley Longman, 1990.

———. "More Than Data Processing." The Future of Software, winter 2000/2001. Available online. URL: http://www.futureofsoftware.net/aw0010aw0010.asp. Downloaded on March 10, 2001.

WINFREY, OPRAH GAIL

(1954–) *Executive, Actress, Talk-show Host, Publisher, Film Producer, Philanthropist*

The most powerful woman in broadcasting as of 2000, Winfrey is also one of the most versatile people in the media. She has succeeded as a talk show host, producer, actress, and philanthropist, and recently launched a multimedia venture called Oxygen Media, as well as her *O* magazine. Her talk show reaches more than 22 million people every week, and she is often called the most influential woman in America.

Oprah Gail Winfrey was born on January 29, 1954, in Kosciusko, Mississippi. Her parents, Vernita Lee and Vernon Winfrey, had intended to name her Orpah, after a Biblical figure in the Old Testament, but the name was misspelled on her birth certificate and read Oprah. Her mother, who was unmarried, worked as a maid and found it difficult to work full time while raising her child, so young Oprah sometimes lived with other relatives, including her paternal grandmother on a Mississippi farm and with her half-siblings in Milwaukee. A bright, verbal child, Oprah learned to speak and read early. At age six, she was living with her mother in Milwaukee, then was sent to live with her father, Vernon, and stepmother, Velma, in Memphis, Tennessee. They provided more structure and discipline than Oprah had experienced at her mother's house. For a few years, while living in Memphis, Oprah earned good grades in school and showed a talent for public speaking, both in church and on other occasions.

Although Oprah's life with her father had been more stable, her mother asked her to come back to Milwaukee. During those years, Oprah was abused by some male relatives and began to have problems in school and at home. She returned to her father's home in Memphis and once again excelled in school, earning a scholarship to a highly rated all-white suburban high school where she was elected president of the student council.

After high school, Winfrey entered Tennessee State University but left school at age 19 to join a Nashville news station as its first woman and first African-American anchor. Her next job was in Baltimore, Maryland, where she also worked for a TV station reporting the news. Winfrey much preferred her next job, as cohost of a morning show, because it gave her a chance to discuss the news and share opinions about current events.

In the early 1980s, Winfrey moved to Chicago, Illinois, to host a midmorning talk show. It was televised at the same time as the popular *Phil Donahue Show,* which had broken new ground during the 1960s by presenting a talk show in which the audience had the opportunity to take part in the interviews with Donahue's guests, who discussed various social, political, and self-help topics. Quickly, Winfrey attracted new viewers, and her show earned strong ratings. She attracted viewers across color lines and impressed people with her empathetic manner and willingness to share her own struggles, including childhood poverty and weight problems.

Viewers described Winfrey as a person who seemed approachable, someone they could regard as a friend. She later said that being alone on her show helped her to succeed: "The thing about working with a coanchor or a cohost is that it can be stifling, like a bad marriage. Somebody always has to surrender to the other person. And usually the person doing the surrendering was me."

The Oprah Winfrey Show was nationally syndicated in 1986 and began to top the ratings in its time slot. In the meantime, Winfrey had also become a respected actress and earned an Oscar nomination for her role in Steven Spielberg's *The Color Purple.* Her talk show soon was earning Emmys and other awards. Winfrey became a millionaire and role model for many people.

After forming her Harpo Entertainment Group, Winfrey became the first African-American woman to own her own production company and only the third woman to do so, after actresses Mary Pickford in the 1920s and Lucille Ball in the 1950s. Harpo has produced the miniseries *The Women of Brewster Place* for television, as well as other television productions, such as *Native Son,* and feature films, including a screen version of Toni Morrison's award-winning novel, *Beloved.*

In 1994, Winfrey decided to change the direction of her talk show and announced that it would not feature scandal, sensational themes, or exploitation—topics that were staples on most other daytime talk shows. Instead, said Winfrey, she would focus on topics and guests that promoted self-empowerment. Her guests have included psychologists, therapists, authors, money-management experts, and others who share ideas about how to improve communication and interpersonal skills, manage a home better, and rear children, among other subjects. Every month, Winfrey selects a book that embodies her philosophy and values and discusses it on the show as part of Oprah's Book Club. In addition, she formed Oprah's Angel Network to give money to people who are making a difference in their community.

Oprah Winfrey was the first woman to make the *Forbes* magazine list of the highest-paid American entertainers. She is also one of the 400 wealthiest Americans, with a net worth estimated at about $1 billion.

In 2000, Winfrey joined forces with some other top media executives, GERALDINE LAYBOURNE, MARCY CARSEY, Tom Werner, and Caryn Mandabach, to form a new multimedia venture called Oxygen, which includes a television network and website that, in Winfrey's words, will "create a new network that will focus on women and treat us like the busy, smart and complex people we are."

A dedicated philanthropist, Winfrey has provided significant support to educational institutions, including Morehouse College, Tennessee State University, the Chicago Academy of the Arts, and the Chicago public school system. She has also contributed to numerous programs that help children, especially battered or abused children, and to women's shelters. She helped to draft and lobbied for the passage of the National Child Protection Act, which was signed into law in 1994.

Winfrey has received numerous honors. In addition to 33 Emmys and the National Academy of Television Arts and Sciences Lifetime Achievement Award, she is a member of the National Women's Hall of Fame. In 1998, *Time* magazine named Winfrey one of the 100 most influential people of the 20th century.

Further Reading

Calio, Jim. "If You Knew Oprah Like I Know Oprah," *Redbook,* February 1998, pp. 62+.

Kanner, Miriam. "Oprah at 40," *Ladies' Home Journal,* February 1994, pp. 96+.

Mair, George. *Oprah Winfrey: The Real Story.* New York: Carol Publishing Group, 1994.

"Oprah's America," *TV Guide,* October 10, 1998, pp. 11–14.

Sellars, Patrick, "The Most Powerful Women in Business in an Age of Celebrity," *Fortune,* October 12, 1998, p. 76+.

Williams, Mary Elizabeth. "She's All Chat," *Salon.* Available online. URL: http://www.salon.com/people/bc/1999/05/04/oprah/index/htm. Posted on May 4, 1999. Downloaded on July 23, 2000.

Winfrey, Oprah, with Janet Lowe. *Life Lessons from the World's Most Influential Voice.* New York: John Wiley and Sons, 2001.

WOODHULL, VICTORIA CLAFLIN
(1838–1927)   *Executive, Publisher*

The first woman to run for U.S. president and speak to the U.S. Congress, feminist Victoria Claflin Woodhull was also the first woman on Wall Street, as cofounder of a brokerage firm that made both her and her sister Tennessee wealthy during the late 1800s. In addition, she published a newspaper to share her often controversial ideas about politics and human relationships.

Born in Ohio on September 23, 1838, Victoria Claflin was the seventh of 10 children. Her father was a drifter who put his children to work in a traveling medicine show where Victoria and her sister Tennessee conducted séances and put people in trances. While still in their teens, the two sisters struck out on their own and began working in states throughout the Midwest.

At age 15, Claflin married Dr. Cunning Woodhull, with whom she had two children. After he died, Victoria Woodhull married Col. James Blood, but left him to go to New York City where she and Tennessee became spiritual advisers to the aging industrialist Cornelius Vanderbilt. With his financial help, they opened a brokerage firm, Woodhull, Claflin & Company, on Wall Street in 1870. Nicknamed "the Bewitching Brokers" and "The Queens of Finance," they built a prosperous business and were able to move into a large, well-appointed offices. Using insider tips, most likely obtained from Vanderbilt, the sisters made profits of about $700,000. They bought a fine mansion in the Murray Hill district of New York City, where they lived with other members of their family.

Woodhull then made the startling announcement that she planned to run for president, making her the first woman ever to seek that office. She told audiences, "While others argued the equality of woman and man, I proved it by successfully engaging in business. I therefore claim the right to speak for the unenfranchised women of this country . . . and I now announce myself as a candidate for the Presidency."

During her 1872 presidential campaign, Victoria Woodhull often addressed noisy crowds such as this one.
(Photo courtesy of Hulton Archive)

She became more famous and controversial when, with Tennessee, she began publishing a journal, *Woodhull and Claflin's Weekly,* in 1871. The journal espoused radical political and economic ideas and called for the equality of women in the workplace, politics, and the home. They advocated the legalization of prostitution, short skirts for women, and "free love" (the acceptance of sexual relationships outside marriage), among other things. The sisters also exposed stock swindles, corrupt deals, and other scandals among members of Congress. More than 20,000 people subscribed to the paper, which was published for six years.

Woodhull and Claflin also took charge of the International Workingmen's Association, a marxist organization. They published the first American version of Karl Marx's Communist Manifesto in the *Weekly.*

As an outspoken advocate of women's suffrage, Woodhull was invited to present a speech before Congress in support of voting rights for women. Her speech was well received, and she impressed the more mainstream women's rights leaders, including Susan B. Anthony and Elizabeth Cady Stanton. Woodhull presented her lecture on constitutional equality at various women's rights conventions, where her charismatic personality inspired a large following. She urged women to seek economic independence, which she believed would give them even more power than the right to vote.

Critics, however, found fault with Woodhull. Her opponents included more conservative women's-rights leaders, who claimed Woodhull would harm their cause because of her controversial past and "immoral views." Abolitionist and author Harriet Beecher Stowe called her "Miss Audacia Dangereyes," and newspaper cartoonist Thomas Nast mocked her in a *Harper's Weekly* cartoon by portraying her as "Mrs. Satan."

During the 1872 presidential election campaign, Woodhull ran as the Equal Rights Party candidate against Democrat Horace Greeley and Republican Ulysses S. Grant. She published a 250-page collection of her essays on various topics and had support from suffragists, labor reformers, internationalists, and spiritualists, among others. Critics accused her of living with two husbands, among other misdeeds. In turn, Woodhull accused one of her most adamant critics, the prominent clergyman Henry Ward Beecher, of committing adultery with the wife of a well-known New York City editor. She was arrested for slander and sat in jail on election day, during which she won a few thousand votes.

Although Woodhull was later acquitted in this case, which caused quite a scandal at the time, she lost support from her financial backers and others. She and her sister were forced to defend expensive lawsuits against their newspaper by people who claimed they had been libeled. The paper was shut down, and Woodhull went bankrupt and lost her Murray Hill mansion. In 1876, she divorced Colonel Blood. She continued to make public speeches on various subjects but stopped criticizing marriage, instead calling it "a divine institution."

With Tennessee Claflin, Woodhull sailed for England in 1877, shortly after Cornelius Vanderbilt died. It was rumored that Vanderbilt's son William paid for their tickets and also gave the sisters $5,000 each so they would not testify during any court hearings over his father will. Woodhull resumed her lecturing career in Europe and married a wealthy English banker, John Biddulph Martin. His family did not approve of the marriage, and

British society never welcomed Woodhull. She died in 1927, after both her sister Tennessee (1923) and John Martin (1897).

Further Reading

Gabriel, Mary. *Notorious Victoria: The Life of Victoria Woodhull, Uncensored.* Chapel Hill, N.C.: Algonquin Books of Chapel Hill, 1998.

Puz, Susan Kullmann. "Legal Contender: Victoria C. Woodhull," *The Women's Quarterly,* fall 1988, pp. 16–17.

Underhill, Lois Beachy. *The Woman Who Ran for President: The Many Lives of Victoria Woodhull.* New York: Viking Penguin, 1996.

✱ WRIGHT, SUSANNA
(1697–1784)   *Farm Owner, Entrepreneur, Author*

One of the first women in to operate a business in early America, Susanna Wright was also an author, multilinguist, and self-taught physician. The owner of real estate in her own name, Wright ran a profitable farm, helped to operate a busy ferry business on the Susquehanna River, and was the first person to establish a silk business in Pennsylvania. In 1911, an article in *Harper's Weekly Advertiser* referred to Wright as "the original New Woman of America."

Born on August 4, 1697, in Lancashire, England, Susanna Wright came to the Pennsylvania colony in 1714 with her family who belonged to the Society of Friends, known as Quakers. She had been well-educated in her youth and continued to read and learn throughout her life, improving her skills in Latin, French, and Italian, as well as studying the sciences, literature, and other subjects that interested her.

The Wright family first settled in Chester, Pennsylvania, and then moved to a frontier area along the Susquehanna River in 1726. In this unsettled region, the family dealt with the hardships of living away from the city—challenges that included land disputes with the colony of Maryland. For about the first 60 years, the Wrights, Barbers, and Blunstons—the three Quaker families who were the area's first white settlers—

controlled more than 1,000 acres of land in what was called Wright's Ferry. In 1738, the Wrights built an English-style stone mansion, called Wright's Ferry Mansion, on the property, and that was Susanna Wright's home.

Susanna Wright owned more than 100 acres in her own name and cultivated hemp, indigo, and hops for sale, aided by German indentured servants. She and her two brothers established a ferry business, which became known as the Gateway to the West for travelers.

Her neighbors, many of them uneducated, respected Wright's problem-solving abilities and sometimes asked her to mediate with Native Americans, settle property disputes and other legal conflicts, and help them write documents, such as wills and contracts for indentured servants. She was also known for her medical skills. Strongly interested in politics, she encouraged her brother in his work as a representative to the Pennsylvania Assembly.

Wright became the first person to operate a silk industry in the colony. She reared silkworms and reeled and prepared the silk herself, then sent it to England, where it woven into cloth. Using plants and other natural materials, she dyed the cloth different colors. When Benjamin Franklin left Philadelphia in the 1770s to serve as a diplomat to Europe, he took a length of Wright's silk along as a gift for Queen Charlotte.

Throughout her life and especially in her later years, Wright wrote poetry, often calling for the equality of men and women. As a Quaker, Wright had been raised in a faith that claimed all people were equal in the eyes of God and that women could preach or speak out at religious meetings. She never married, claiming that it might hamper her desire to be independent and function as an equal with men.

Wright died in 1784. In 1788, when Congress considered situating the capital of the new nation on the eastern shore of Wright's Ferry, Susanna's nephew Samuel Wright laid out a plan for a town called Columbia. However, the capital remained in Philadelphia until 1800 and was later moved to New

Susanna Wright's mansion at Wright's Ferry in Columbia, Pennsylvania, is now a museum.
(Photo courtesy of the von Hess Foundation, Wright's Ferry Mansion)

York and then Washington, D.C. Wright's home has been restored and is a museum open to the public.

Further Reading

Harris, Sharon M., editor. *American Women Writers to 1800.* New York: Oxford University Press, 1996.
Logan, Deborah Norris. "Notice of Susanna Wright," *Analectic Magazine,* Volume 5, 1815. Reprint by courtesy of the Wright's Ferry Museum, Columbia, Pennsylvania.

WRUBEL, PRISCILLA
(1938–) *Entrepreneur, Executive, Environmental Activist*

Priscilla Wrubel cofounded the Nature Company, a chain of stores that sells products that people can use to explore nature and to learn more about the natural world. In addition, Wrubel works with environmental organizations to promote energy conservation and other environmental causes, and the company donates a percentage of its profits to nonprofit environmental groups and projects.

Priscilla Wrubel was born in 1938. She was teaching school in Geneva, Illinois, in 1961 when she decided to become a Peace Corps volunteer and was stationed in Monrovia, Liberia. There she met Tom Wrubel, an architect who was also working with the Peace Corps in Monrovia, and they were married during their tour of duty. They returned to the United States, where Tom earned a master's degree in African studies at in Los Angeles, California, and then they went back to Liberia. For the next three years, Tom ran the Fulbright Foundation office there while Priscilla Wrubel taught English. She later said, "I had been interested in natural history before I went over, but definitely everything in the rain forest was just so new and so amazing. It really broadened my perspective on the environment."

The Wrubels stayed with the Peace Corps for another three years before settling in Berkeley, California. By then they had children, and Priscilla Wrubel tried to find nature-oriented toys for them to play with. She was disappointed when she could not. A talented potter, she was planning to open a store selling pots and plants and had rented a space in Berkeley, but these plans were dashed when a chain plant store opened right down the street. The Wrubels decided to open a different kind of store in that rented space. As she later said, "[W]e decided 'let's sell something else in our store.' And that's when we came up with the idea of nature and kids and education."

When the store opened in 1973, its distinctive interiors displayed Tom Wrubel's skills as an architect and designer. Priscilla Wrubel had selected the merchandise, including binoculars, telescopes, nature field guides, rocks and minerals, and other materials that the Wrubels hoped would appeal to nature lovers and educators.

Sales were $52 on that first day and grew steadily thereafter. During the next 10 years, they opened four more stores in California and managed a growing mail-order business for customers who lived too far away to shop at the Nature Company stores in person. In 1983, when there were six Nature Company stores, CML Group, Inc., bought the business, and the Wrubels were able to keep growing and to expand into international markets. The Wrubels separated in 1985 but remained in the business together until Tom Wrubel died in 1988.

The Nature Company boasted $90 million in sales in 1991, compared to $70 million in 1990. In 1996, the diversified media giant Discovery Communications, Inc., owner of TV's Learning Channel, Discovery Channel, and Travel Channel, bought the Nature Company for $40 million. Beginning in 1997, the Discovery Channel began to rename the stores and change the product line, blending it with Discovery Channel products. Priscilla Wrubel worked with the chief executive officer (CEO) of the Nature Company and the Discovery Channel to help the company make this transition.

Further Reading

Bilello, Suzanne. "Ecology Goes Retail, Stony Brook is a Natural for Nature Co.," *Newsday,* September 1, 1992, p. 31.

Carlsen, Clifford. "Bay Area Retailers Bag Big Gains in So-So Season," *San Francisco Business Times,* January 17, 1997, n.p.

Cunningham, Patricia. "Naturally Inclined: Patricia Wrubel and the Nature Company," *The Peace Corps Times.* Available online. URL: http://www.peacecorps.gov/rpcv/community/wrubel.html. Downloaded on May 14, 2001.

Nelton, Sharon. "On Board for the Long Haul," *Nations Business,* October 1, 1995, pp. 55–56.

Z

☒☒☒☒☒

✹ ZIMMERMAN, MARIE CIESIELSKI
(1894–1973) *Radio Station Owner*

In 1922, Marie Zimmerman became the first woman to own and operate a radio station during a time when women were rarely heard over the airwaves.

The daughter of immigrants, Marie Ciesielski grew up on a farm in Jesup, Iowa, and married an electrician, Robert Zimmerman, in 1915. The couple lived in Vinton, Iowa, near Cedar Rapids. Radio was a new medium in the early 1920s and Bob Zimmerman was a big fan—an interest Marie Zimmerman soon shared. They enjoyed using their ham (amateur broadcasting) radio and talked about finding a radio station they could operate themselves. After saving up $150 and collecting $100 from backers to buy the transmitting equipment, Bob Zimmerman ordered the materials from Illinois and put the station together. The license was issued to Marie Zimmerman.

With no money to hire a staff, Marie Zimmerman operated the station (WIAE) and performed the various jobs that needed to be done. While Bob maintained the equipment, Marie planned the pro-gramming, hired performers, and handled all the paperwork required by licensing officials. They broadcast from their home, from rented offices, and sometimes from Bob's work truck. Stations usually did not broadcast every day in the 1920s, and the Zimmermans went on the air three or four times a week, presenting mostly music and news. Marie Zimmerman played records or featured local performers, many of whom appeared on the air for free, but she also introduced new kinds of programs. WIAE broadcast live from the county fairgrounds and went to other community events, and it aired speeches, including those of presidential candidates during the election of 1922.

The Zimmermans ran out of money to operate their station and did not renew the license after 1923. (In those days, few stations relied on commercial advertising for support.) A larger station with more funding began operating in the area during the mid-1920s. By the late 1920s, a few other women around the country had become station owners.

The Zimmermans later moved to Kenosha, Wisconsin. They remained interested in their ham radio and radio in general. Marie Zimmerman pursued another business career, this time in retail sales. She rose to the position of head buyer at a department store. In 1946, Bob Zimmerman died unexpectedly, and Marie Zimmerman returned to her family's farm in Jesup. She died in 1973.

Further Reading

Halper, Donna L. "Marie Zimmerman—Broadcasting's First Female Owner," Old Radio.com. Available online. URL: http://oldradio.com. Downloaded on November 21, 2001.

———. "Remembering the Ladies—A Salute to the Women of Early Radio," *Popular Communications,* January 1999.

✳ ZUBIZARRETA, TERE
(Teresa Arteaga Zubizarreta, Tere Zubi)
(1939–) *Executive, Entrepreneur*

Tere Zubizarreta founded Zubi Advertising Services, a full-service agency specializing in the Hispanic market. Zubizarreta, a self-made person who learned the advertising business from the ground up, has built her company into one of the five top Hispanic national agencies.

Teresa Arteaga was born on September 7, 1939, and raised in Cuba. She attended a Catholic high school in New Orleans, returning home for visits in the summer and on holidays. After graduating, she completed a course at a respected secretarial academy, the Tarbot School of English, in Havana. In 1960, 21-year-old Zubizarreta fled with her husband, Octavio Zubizarreta, and infant son, Joe, from Havana, Cuba, after the Cuban Revolution. They arrived in Miami, Florida, penniless, but ready to work hard to support the family and rebuild their lives.

Zubizarreta experienced some anti-Cuban discrimination in her search for work, but was hired for a $65-a-week job as a secretary at an advertising agency, McCann-Marschalk. She later said that one of the reasons she got the job was her honesty during the interview, when she admitted things she did not know but stressed, "I will learn." Zubizarreta was eager to learn as much as possible about the business, and she had a talent for mar-

As of 2001, the advertising firm that Tere Zubizarreta opened in 1973 was doing $80 million in billings with 60 employees, and Zubizarreta had received numerous awards for her business skills and community service.
(Photo courtesy of Zubi Advertising)

keting and working with people. Eager to advance, she regularly volunteered to work overtime and was promoted to higher positions at the company and the other agencies where she worked. However, after Zubizarreta was promoted to advertising director while working at EHG Enterprises, her job required a great deal of travel, something she did not want to do while her children were young, so she left the agency.

Some friends encouraged her to open her own business, but her first attempt, a business specializing in real-estate advertising, did not succeed. Undeterred, she opened another company, Zubi Advertising Services, Inc., in 1976. She later recalled that some people had discouraged her, saying that she had two major disadvantages—being female and Cuban. Zubizarreta chose to look at these factors as assets and later said, "I'm a Cuban. I know the culture of the Hispanic world. I have traveled extensively. So I know all the little idiosyncrasies of the various countries that make up this entire Hispanic world. So I said, 'These are assets. These are not weaknesses.' These are my assets. This is how I'm going to make it."

She targeted businesses in the Hispanic community. Her goal was twofold: to educate the marketplace about Hispanics and to educate Hispanics about important products and services in the marketplace. Friends loaned her a typewriter and office space to get started and printed some stationery for free. Her initial investment was $200 for telephone service. She signed some clients in the construction business, then worked with a Spanish-language newspaper, *El Nuevo Herald,* and her first client gave her a retainer fee of $465. As she proved her creativity and reliability, Zubizarreta signed on other clients, including Pepsi-Cola. More large corporate clients followed in the late 1980s and 1990s.

The agency scored another major account in 1998 when Mobil, a global oil, natural gas, and petrochemicals company, announced that it had selected Zubi Advertising as its national agency for Hispanic advertising and communicating with Hispanic consumers throughout the United States. Jan Crowe, the manager of Mobil's Global Marketing Communications, said, "Zubi more than met our expectations regarding strategic thinking and innovative strategies for reaching Hispanic consumers, who are a very important audience for us." Zubizarreta said, "We look forward to helping Mobil bring its messages to U.S. Hispanic consumers. We're pleased that this great global brand chose a South Florida agency for Hispanic marketing expertise." In 1998, Zubi Advertising Services, Inc., had $48 million in revenues.

By 2000, the company had satellite offices in Detroit, Michigan; Dallas, Texas; and Los Angeles, California, as well as its headquarters in Miami.

Clients have included the Ford Motor Company, Ford Division; Kraft Foods; First Union; Winn-Dixie, The Miami Heat, Hatuey Beer, Pizza Hut, American Airlines, and *El Nuevo Herald.* Tere Zubizarreta's son, Joe, and daughter, Michelle, also work in key positions in the business.

In 2001, the company was expected to surpass $100 million in billings. Joe Zubizarreta, who had just been appointed chief operating officer (COO), said, "This is a significant mark—a target that has been an ambition of ours since Tere Zubizarreta founded the agency 25 years ago."

During the decades she has worked to build her business, Tere Zubizarreta has also been active in the community. She has worked for numerous local and national charitable organizations, including the United Way, the Partnership for a Drug-Free America, and an organization that helps Cuban women immigrating to the United States to adjust to their new lives. Zubizarreta is the first Hispanic woman to be elected to the board of governors and committee chair of the United Way of America. She also serves on the board of directors of the Orange Bowl Committee, the Beacon Council (Miami-Dade County's economic development partnership), and the Miami Children's Hospital and is actively involved in the Association of Hispanic Advertising Agencies (AHAA).

She has won the Businesswoman of the Year Award from the Businesswomen Leadership Foundation and the Avon's Women of Enterprise award. In 2001, her company joined forces with other Hispanic-American leaders to launch New America Alliance: An American Latino Business Initiative, which is designed to strengthen the Hispanic community through education, political influence, and assistance to entrepreneurs.

As of 2002, Zubizarreta, who is now a grandmother, lives with her husband in Coral Gables, Florida.

Further Reading

Avon Women of Enterprise. "Tere Zubizarreta." Available online. URL: http://www.avon.com/about/women/mve/lead98.html. Downloaded on May 27, 2000.

Cantu, Hector. "Hispanic 'Power Club' Aims to Better Its Community," *The Arizona Republic,* January 17, 2000, p. D-2.

"Hispanic Entrepreneur: Latina Entrepreneurs Break New Ground," *Hispanic,* October 31, 1998, p. 80ff.

"Mobil Selects Advertising Agency for Hispanic Market," *Business Wire,* November 4, 1998.

Zubi Advertising. "Tere Zubizarreta, President & CEO," Zubi Advertising Services, Inc. on the Web. Available online. URL: http://www.zubiad.com/bio tere.html. Downloaded on January 31, 2001.

"Zubi Advertising to Exceed $100 Million Mark," Yahoo!Finance. Available online. URL: http://biz.yahoo.com/bw/010529/2071.html. Posted on May 21, 2001. Downloaded on June 29, 2001.

RECOMMENDED SOURCES ON AMERICAN WOMEN BUSINESS LEADERS AND ENTREPRENEURS

Abbot, Edith. *Women in Industry, A Study in American Economic History.* New York: Harcourt Brace, 1910.

Abramowitz, Rachel. *Is That a Gun in Your Pocket? Women's Experience of Power in Hollywood.* New York: Random House, 2000.

Adams, Jane. *Women on Top: Success Patterns and Personal Growth.* New York: Berkley, 1981.

Albertine, Susan, ed. *A Living of Words: American Women in Print Culture.* Nashville: University of Tennessee Press, 1995.

Alexander, Shoshana. *Women's Ventures, Women's Visions.* Santa Cruz: Calif.: Crossing Press, 1997.

Alic, Margaret. *Hypatia's Heritage: A History of Women in Science Since Antiquity.* Boston: Beacon Press, 1986.

Allen, Sheila, and Carole Truman, eds. *Women in Business: Perspectives on Women Entrepreneurs.* New York: Routledge, 1993.

Altman, Linda Jacobs. *Women Inventors.* New York: Facts On File, 1997.

Banner, Lois. *Women in Modern America.* New York: Harcourt Brace Jovanovich, 1974.

Bataille, Gretchen M., ed. *Native American Women: A Biographical Dictionary.* New York: Garland Publishing, 1993.

Baxandall, Rosalyn, Linda Gordon, and Susan Reverby, eds. *America's Working Women: A Documentary History—1600 to the Present.* New York: Vintage Books, 1976.

Berkin, Carol Ruth, and Mary Beth Norton. *Women of America: A History.* Boston: Houghton Mifflin, 1979.

Berkinow, Louise, in association with the National Women's History Project. *The American Women's Almanac.* New York: Berkley Books, 1997.

Bird, Caroline. *Enterprising Women.* New York: Norton, 1976.

Bolden, Tonya. *The Book of African-American Women: 150 Crusaders, Creators, and Uplifters.* Holbrook, Mass.: Adams Media Creations, 1996.

Brooks, Geraldine. *Dames and Daughters of Colonial Days.* New York: T. Y. Crowell, 1900.

Brooks-Pazmany, Kathleen, *United States Women in Aviation 1919–1929.* Washington, D.C.: Smithsonian Institution, 1991.

Brownlee, W. Elliot, and Mary M. Brownlee. *Women in the American Economy: A Documentary History, 1675–1929.* New Haven: Yale University Press, 1976.

Carter, John Mack, and Joan Feeney, comp. *Starting at the Top: America's New Achievers: Twenty-Three Success Stories Told by Men and Women Whose Dreams of Being Boss Came True.* New York: Morrow, 1985.

Carter, Sara. *Women as Entrepreneurs.* San Diego: Academic Press, 1992.

Catalyst Staff. *Advancing Women in Business, The Catalyst Guide: Best Practices from the Corporate Leaders.* San Francisco: Jossey-Bass, 1998.

———. *Census of Women Corporate Officers and Top Earners,* Vol. I. New York: Catalyst Inc., 1997.

———. *Census of Women Directors of the Fortune 500.* New York: Catalyst Inc., 1997.

———. *The CEO View: Women on Corporate Boards.* New York: Catalyst Inc., 1996.

———. *Corporations and Two-Career Families: Directions for the Future.* New York: Catalyst Inc., 1981.

———. *Cracking the Glass Ceiling: Strategies for Success.* New York: Catalyst Inc., 1994.

———. *Women in Corporate Management: Progress and Prospects.* New York: Catalyst Inc., 1996.

———. *Women in Corporate Management: Results of a Catalyst Survey.* New York: Catalyst Inc., 1990.

Center for Creative Leadership Staff, et al. *Breaking the Glass Ceiling: Can Women Reach the Top of America's Largest Corporations?* Reading, Mass.: Addison-Wesley, 1987.

Cline, Carolyn Garrett, et al. *The Velvet Ghetto: The Impact of the Increasing Percentage of Women in Public Relations and Business Communication.* San Francisco: International Association for Business Communication Foundation, 1986.

Cott, Nancy F., ed. *The Young Oxford History of Women in the United States.* 11 vols. New York: Oxford University Press, 1994.

Crittenden, Ann. "Up the Corporate Ladder: A Progress Report," *Working Woman,* May 1996, p. 22.

DaSilva, Rachel, ed. *Leading Out: Women Climbers Reaching for the Top.* Seattle: Seal Press, 1992.

Davis, Hillary. *A Million a Minute: Inside the World of Securities: The Men, The Women, the Money That Make the Markets Work.* New York: HarperBusiness, 1998.

Decker, Jeffrey Louis. *Made in America: Self-Styled Success from Horatio Alger to Oprah Winfrey.* Minneapolis: University of Minnesota Press, 1997.

DePauw, Linda Grant. *Founding Mothers: Women of America in the Revolutionary Era.* Boston: Houghton Mifflin, 1975.

Dexter, Elizabeth A. *Career Women of America, 1776–1840.* Francestown, N.H.: Marshall Jones Co., 1950.

———. *Colonial Women of Affairs: Women in Business and Professions in America Before 1776.* Clifton, N.J.: Augustus Kelley, 1924.

Driscoll, Dawn-Marie and Carol R. Goldberg. *Members of the Club: The Coming of Age of Executive Women.* New York: Free Press, 1993.

Enkelis, Liane, and Karen Olsen. *On Our Own Terms: Portraits of Women Business Leaders.* San Francisco: Berrett-Koehler Publishers, 1995.

Ericksen, Gregory K. *Women Entrepreneurs Only: 12 Women Entrepreneurs Tell the Stories of Their Success.* New York: John Wiley & Sons, 1999.

Fisher, Anne B. *Wall Street Women: Women in Power on the Street Today.* New York: Knopf, 1990.

Florence, Mari. *The Enterprising Woman.* New York: Warner Books, 1997.

Forbes, Malcolm. *Women Who Made a Difference.* New York: Simon and Schuster, 1990.

Gallagher, Carol, and Susan K. Golant. *Going to the Top: A Road Map for Success from America's Leading Women Executives.* New York: Viking, 2000.

Glazer, Penina Migdal, and Miriam Slater. *Unequal Colleagues: The Entrance of Women into the Professions, 1890–1987.* New Brunswick, N.J.: Rutgers University Press, 1987.

Godfrey, Joline. *Our Wildest Dreams: Women Entrepreneurs Making Money, Having Fun, Doing Good.* New York: HarperBusiness, 1993.

Goffee, Robert, and Richard Scase. *Women in Charge: The Experiences of Female Entrepreneurs.* Boston: Allen & Unwin, 1985.

Gonzalez, Cristine. "Ranks of Women Executives Grow," *The Oregonian,* November 10, 1998.

Greenwald, Carol S. *Women in Management.* Scarsdale, N.Y.: Work in America Institute, 1980.

Grove, Smith, et al. *Forbes: Great Minds of Business.* New York: Simon and Schuster (audio), 1997.

Hallett, Anthony, and Diane Hallett. *Entrepreneur Magazine's Encyclopedia of Entrepreneurs.* New York: John Wiley & Sons, 1997.

Hamm, Steve. "Why Women Are So Invisible," *Business Week,* August 18, 1997, p. 136.

Harris, Wendy. *Against All Odds: Ten Entrepreneurs Who Followed Their Hearts and Found Success.* New York: John Wiley & Sons, 2000.

Harrison, Patricia. *America's New Women Entrepreneurs: Tips, Tactics, and Techniques of Women Achievers in Business.* Washington, D.C.: Acropolis Books, 1986.

Helgesen, Sally. *The Female Advantage: Women's Ways of Leadership.* New York: Doubleday, 1995.

Herera, Sue. *Women of the Street: Making It on Wall Street—The World's Toughest Business.* New York: John Wiley & Sons, 1997.

Hine, Darlene Clark, Elsa Barkley Brown, and Rosalyn Terborg-Penn, eds. *Black Women in America: An Historical Encyclopedia,* 2 volumes. Bloomington: Indiana University Press, 1994.

Hudak, Leona. *Early American Women Printers and Publishers, 1639–1820.* Metuchen, N.J. and London: The Scarecrow Press, Inc., 1978.

James, Edward T., ed. *Notable American Women 1607–1950: A Biographical Dictionary.* Three Volumes. Cambridge, Mass.: The Belknap Press of Harvard University Press, 1971.

Jennings, Diane. *Self-Made Women: Twelve of America's leading Entrepreneurs Talk About Success, Self-Image, and the Superwoman.* Dallas: Taylor, 1987.

Kanter, Rosabeth Moss. *Men and Women of the Corporation.* New York: Basic Books, 1977.

Kwolek-Folland, Angel. *Incorporating Women: A History of Women and Business in the United States.* New York: Twayne Publishers, 1998.

Leavitt, Judith A. *American Women Managers and Administrators: A Selective Biographical Dictionary.* Westport, Conn.: Greenwood Publishing Group, 1985.

Leisey, Donald E., and Charles W. Lavaroni. *The Educational Entrepreneur: Making a Difference.* Los Angeles: Edupreneur Press, 2000.

Lerner-Robbins, Helene. *Our Power as Women: The Wisdom and Strategies of Highly Successful Women.* Berkeley, Calif.: Canari Press, 1996.

Lewis, Alfred Allan. *Ladies and Not-So-Gentle Women.* New York: Viking, 2000.

Lieber, Ron. *Upstart Start-ups: How 34 Young Entrepreneurs Overcame Youth, Inexperience, and Lack of Money to Create Thriving Businesses.* New York: Broadway Books, 1998.

Macdonald, Anne L. *Feminine Ingenuity: How Women Inventors Changed America.* New York: Ballantine Books, 1992.

Magill, Frank N. *Great Lives from History: American Women Series.* Pasadena, Calif.: Salem Press, 1995.

Majors, Monroe A. *Noted Negro Women.* New York: Gordon Press, 1972.

Marc, David, and Robert J. Thompson. *Prime Time Prime Movers.* Boston: Little, Brown, 1992.

Maret, Elizabeth, and Liz Carpenter. *Women of the Range: Women's Roles in the Texas Beef Cattle Industry.* College Station: Texas A & M University Press, 1993.

Markey, Kevin, et al. *100 Most Important Women of the 20th Century.* New York: Meredith Books, 1998.

Matthaei, Julie A. *An Economic History of Women in America.* New York: Schocken, 1982.

McCollough, Joan. *First of All: Significant "Firsts" by American Women.* New York: Holt, Rinehart, and Winston, 1980.

McHenry, Robert, ed. *Famous American Women: A Biographical Dictionary from Colonial Times to the Present.* New York: Dover Publications, 1980.

McVicar, Marjorie, and Julia F. Craig. *Minding My Own Business: Entreprenurial Women Share Their Secrets for Success.* New York: Putnam Group, 1981.

Meyers, William. *The Image-Makers: Power and Persuasion on Madison Avenue.* New York: Times Books, 1984.

Mikaelian, A. *Women Who Mean Business: Success Stories of Women Over Forty.* New York: William Morrow, 1999.

Moody, Patricia E., and Dick Morley. *The Technology Machine.* New York: Free Press, 1999.

Moore, Dorothy Perrin. *Careerpreneurs: Lessons from Leading Women Entrepreneurs on Building a Career without Boundaries.* New York: Consulting Psychologists Press, 2000.

Morrall, Patricia A. *Directory of Women Entrepreneurs: A National Sourcebook.* Atlanta, Ga.: Wind River Publications, 1991.

Morrison, A., R. White, and E. Van Velsor. *Breaking the Glass Ceiling.* Greensboro, N.C.: Center for Creative Leadership, 1987.

227

Moynihan, Ruth Barnes, Cynthia Russett, and Laurie Crumpacker, eds. *Second to None: A Documentary History of American Women.* 2 vols. Lincoln: University of Nebraska Press, 1993.

National Foundation for Women Business Owners (NFWBO). *1999 Facts on Women-Owned Businesses: Trends in the U. S. and the 50 States.* Washington, D.C.: NFWBO, 1999.

Oakes, Claudia M. *United States Women in Aviation, 1930–39.* Washington, D.C.: Smithsonian Institution, 1991.

O'Neill, Lois Decker, ed. *The Women's Book of World Records and Achievements.* Garden City, N.Y.: Doubleday, 1979.

Oppedisano, Jeannette M. *Historical Encyclopedia of American Women Entrepreneurs: 1776 to Present.* Westport, Conn.: Greenwood Publishing, 2000.

Peiss, Kathy. *Hope in a Jar: The Making of America's Beauty Culture.* New York: Metropolitan Books, 1998.

Perri, Colleen. *Entrepreneurial Women.* Kenosha, Wisc.: Possibilities Publishing, 1989.

Pestrak, Debra. *Playing with the Big Boys: Success Secrets of the Most Powerful Women in American Business.* Carlsbad, Calif.: Sun Publications, 2001.

Petsinger, Thomas. *The New Pioneers: The Men and Women Who Are Transforming the Workplace and Marketplace.* New York: Simon and Schuster, 1999.

Pine, Carol and Susan Mundale. *Self-Made: The Stories of 12 Minnesota Entrepreneurs.* Minneapolis, Minn.: Dorn Books, 1982.

Pinson, Linda and Jerry Jinnett. *The Woman Entrepreneur: 33 Personal Stories of Success.* New York: Upstart Publishing Co., 1992.

Read, Phyllis J., and Bernard L. Whitleib. *The Book of Women's Firsts.* New York: Random House, 1992.

Reilly, Philip J. *Old Masters of Retailing: A History of Merchant Pioneers and the Industry They Built.* New York: Fairchild Publications, 1966.

Rheem, Helen. "Equal Opportunity for Women: The Verdict Is Still Mixed," *Harvard Business Review,* July-August 1996, pp. 12–13.

Rimm, Sylvia B., et al. *How Jane Won: 55 Successful Women Share How They Grew from Ordinary Girls to Extraordinary Women.* New York: Crown, 2001.

Rizzo, A., and C. Mendez. *The Integration of Women in Management.* New York: Quorum Books, 1990.

Salem, Dorothy C., ed. *African-American Women: A Biographical Dictionary.* Hamden, Conn.: Garland, 1993.

Sherr, Lyn, and Jurate Kazickas. *Susan B. Anthony Slept Here: A Guide to American Women's Landmarks.* New York: Random House, 1994.

Sicherman, Barbara, and Carol Hurd Green, eds. *Notable American Women: The Modern Period: A Biographical Dictionary.* Cambridge, Mass.: The Belknap Press of Harvard University Press, 1980.

Siler, A. David. *Enterprising Women: Lessons from the 100 Greatest Entrepreneurs of Our Day.* New York: AMACOM, 1994.

Smith, Jessie Carney, ed. *Notable Black American Women.* Detroit: Gale Research, 1992.

Stoddard, Hope. *Famous American Women.* New York: Thomas Y. Crowell, 1970.

Taylor, Charlotte. *Women and the Business Game: Strategies for Successful Ownership.* New York: Venture Concepts Press, 1980.

Taylor, Russel R. *Exceptional Entrepreneurial Women: Strategies for Success.* Westport, Conn.: Praeger, 1988.

Uglow, Jennifer S., ed. *The International Dictionary of Women's Biography.* New York: Continuum Publishing, 1982.

Vare, Ethlie Ann, and Gregg Ptacek. *Mothers of Invention: From the Bra to the Bomb, Forgotten Women and Their Unforgettable Ideas.* New York: William Morrow, 1988.

Wilkins, Joanne. *Her Own Business: Success Secrets of Women Entrepreneurs.* New York: McGraw-Hill, 1987.

Wymard, Ellie. *Conversations with Uncommon Women: Insights from Women Who've Risen Above Life's Challenges to Achieve Extraordinary Success.* New York: AMACOM, 1999.

Yeager, Mary A. *Women in Business.* Northampton, Mass.: E. Elgar, 1999.

Zeidler, Sue. "Women Give Corporate America Top-level Make-over," Reuters, May 18, 2000.

ENTRIES BY FIELD

Advertising

Beers, Charlotte
Griswold, Denny
Lawrence, Mary Wells
Lazarus, Shelly
Zubizarreta, Tere

Agriculture/Ranching

King, Henrietta
    Chamberlain
Lewis, Tillie
Metoyer, Marie-Therese
Pinckney, Eliza Lucas
Wright, Susanna

Aviation

Beech, Olive Ann Mellor
Hopkins, Deborah C.
    (Debby)
Omlie, Phoebe Fairgrave

Building Contractor/ Construction

Alvarado, Linda
Gleason, Kate

Business Consulting

Husted, Marjorie Child

Moody, Patricia Ellen
Pennington, Mary Engle

Business School Owner

Gibbs, Katharine Ryan
Seymour, Mary Foot

Catalog Industry

Owades, Ruth Markowitz
Vernon, Lillian

Consumer Goods

Bissell, Anna Sutherland
Graham, Bette McMurry
    Nesmith
Handler, Ruth Mosko
Juliber, Lois D.
Owades, Ruth Markowitz
Pinkham, Lydia Estes
Stewart, Martha
Wrubel, Priscilla
Vernon, Lillian

Cooking Instruction/ Restaurants

Farmer, Fannie Merritt
Fertel, Ruth

Stewart, Martha
Totino, Rose Cruciani
Waters, Alice Louise

Cosmetics Company Entrepreneur

Arden, Elizabeth
Ash, Mary Kay
Ayer, Harriet Hubbard
Begoun, Paula
Bishop, Hazel Gladys
Lauder, Estée
Rubinstein, Helena
Walker, Madam C. J.

Decorative Arts/ Interior Design/Lifestyle

De Wolfe, Elsie
Stewart, Martha
Wheeler, Candice Thurber

Dressmaking/Millinery

Daché, Lilly
Demorest, Ellen Louise
    Curtis
Inman, Elizabeth Murray
    Campbell Smith
Keckley, Elizabeth Hobbs
Rosenthal, Ida Cohen

Educational Products

Davidson, Jan
Wrubel, Priscilla

Executive

Amonette, Ruth M. Leach
Arden, Elizabeth
Barad, Jill
Bartz, Carol
Bay, Josephine Perfect
Beech, Olive Ann Mellor
Bissell, Anna Sutherland
Boehm, Helen F.
Claiborne, Liz
Evans, Lettie Pate
    Whitehead
Fiorina, Carly
Fudge, Ann M.
Gordon, Ellen Rubin
Hopkins, Deborah C.
James, Betty
Juliber, Lois E.
Jung, Andrea
Knox, Rose Markward
McCormick, Nettie
Minyard, Liz
Owades, Ruth Markowitz
Owen, Dian Graves
Williams, Gretchen
    Minyard

Fashion Design

Claiborne, Liz
Daché, Lilly
Demorest, Ellen Curtis
Gray, Marie Hermann
Kamali, Norma
Karan, Donna Faske
Klein, Anne
McCardell, Claire
Natori, Josie Cruz
Sui, Anna
Wang, Vera

Film Industry

Lansing, Sherry Lee
    Heimann
Snider, Stacey
Winfrey, Oprah Gail

Finance/Banking

Ahmanson, Caroline
    Leonetti
Gleason, Kate
Hoffman, Claire Giannini
Miller, Heidi
Sandler, Marion
Walker, Maggie Lena

Food Processing/
Preservation

Jones, Amanda Theodosia
Lewis, Tillie
Pennington, Mary Engle

Food Products

Chin, Leeann
Fields, Debbi
Fudge, Ann M.
Gordon, Ellen Rubin
Haughery, Margaret
    O'Rourke Gaffney
Kellogg, Ella Eaton
Rudkin, Margaret Fogarty
Taggares, Kathy
Totino, Rose Cruciani

Furs/Trading Posts

Astor, Sarah Todd
Musgrove Bosomworth,
    Mary

Grocery

Minyard, Liz
Williams, Gretchen
    Minyard

Hair Care Products/Salons

Begoun, Paula
Harper, Martha Matilda
Joyner, Marjorie Stewart
Malone, Annie Turnbo
Miller, Sydell L.
Walker, Madam C. J.

Hotels/Travel Industry

Grossinger, Jennie
Nelson, Marilyn Carlson

Investment Management/
Brokerage Firms

Bay, Josephine Perfect
Siebert, Muriel F.
VanCaspel, Venita Walker
Woodhull, Victoria Claflin

Land Development/
Real Estate

Brown, Clara
Evans, Lettie Pate
    Whitehead
Haughery, Margaret
    Gaffney
Inman, Elizabeth Murray
    Campbell Smith
Mason, Bridget
Metoyer, Marie-Therese
Philipse, Margaret
    Hardenbroeck De Vries
Tuttle, Julia D.

Manufacturing

Gleason, Kate
Lukens, Rebecca Webb
    Pennock
Moody, Patricia Ellen

Modeling Schools/Agencies

Ahmanson, Caroline
    Leonetti
Ford, Eileen

Pharmaceuticals/ Health Care

Katen, Karen L.
Lewent, Judy
Owen, Dian Graves

Public Relations

Griswold, Denny
Williams, Terrie M.
Zubizarreta, Tere

Publishing/Printing

Aitken, Jane
Black, Cathleen P.
Franklin, Ann Smith
Goddard, Mary Katherine
Graham, Katharine Meyer
Moore, Ann S.
Rowland, Pleasant T.
Townsend, Alair Ane

Radio

Brunson, Dorothy Edwards
Zimmerman, Marie
Ciesielski

Retail

Astor, Sarah Todd
Auerbach, Beatrice Fox

Demorest, Ellen Louise
Curtis
Inman, Elizabeth Murray
Campbell Smith
Rosenthal, Ida Cohen
La Forge, Margaret Getchell
Shaver, Dorothy

Shipping

Bay, Josephine Perfect
Philipse, Margaret
Hardenbroeck De Vries

Software

Bartz, Carol
Davidson, Jan
Kurtzig, Sandra
Lopker, Pamela
Winblad, Ann

Technology/E-commerce

Amonette, Ruth M. Leach
Bajaj, Kavelle
Bartz, Carol
Fiorina, Carly
Hariton, Lorraine
Hopkins, Deborah C.
Laybourne, Gerry
Lopker, Pamela
Whitman, Meg
Winblad, Ann

Television

Brunson, Dorothy
Carsey, Marcy
Koplovitz, Kay Smith
Laybourne, Gerry
McGrath, Judith
Winfrey, Oprah Gail

Textiles

Bandy, Dicksie Bradley

Theatrical Companies/ Theatrical Agencies

Keene, Laura
Marbury, Elisabeth

Toys/Children's Products

Behrman, Beatrice Alexander
Handler, Ruth Mosko
James, Betty
Nemeth, Lane
Rowland, Pleasant T.

Venture Capital

Winblad, Ann

Weight-control Industry

Craig, Jenny
Lewis, Tillie
Nidetch, Jean

ENTRIES BY YEAR OF BIRTH

1600–1699

Philipse, Margaret Hardenbroeck De Vries
Franklin, Ann Smith
Wright, Susanna

1700–1799

Aitken, Jane
Astor, Sarah Todd
Goddard, Mary Katherine
Inman, Elizabeth Murray Campbell Smith
Lukens, Rebecca Webb Pennock
Metoyer, Marie-Therese
Musgrove, Mary Bosomworth
Pinckney, Eliza Lucas
Timothy, Elizabeth

1800–1849

Ayer, Harriet Hubbard
Bissell, Ann Sutherland
Brown, Clara
Demorest, Ellen Louise Curtis
Harper, Martha Matilda
Haughery, Margaret Gaffney
Jones, Amanda Theodosia
Keckley, Elizabeth Hobbs
Keene, Laura
King, Henrietta Chamberlain
La Forge, Margaret Swain Getchell
Mason, Bridget
McCormick, Nettie
Pinkham, Lydia Estes
Seymour, Mary Foot
Tuttle, Julia D.
Wheeler, Candace Thurber
Woodhull, Victoria Claflin

1850–1899

Arden, Elizabeth
Auerbach, Beatrice Fox
Bandy, Dicksie Bradley
Behrman, Beatrice Alexander
de Wolfe, Elsie
Evans, Lettie Pate Whitehead
Farmer, Fannie Merritt
Gibbs, Katharine Ryan
Gleason, Kate
Grossinger, Jennie
Husted, Marjorie Child
Joyner, Marjorie Stewart
Kellogg, Ella Eaton
Knox, Rose Markward
Malone, Annie Turnbo
Marbury, Elisabeth
Pennington, Mary E.
Rosenthal, Ida Cohen
Rubinstein, Helena
Rudkin, Margaret Fogarty
Shaver, Dorothy
Walker, Madam C. J.
Walker, Maggie Lena
Zimmerman, Marie

1900–1909

Bay, Josephine Perfect
Beech, Olive Ann Mellor
Bishop, Hazel Gladys
Daché, Lilly
Griswold, Denny
Hoffman, Claire Giannini
Lauder, Estēe
Lewis, Tillie
McCardell, Claire
Omlie, Phoebe Fairgrave

1910–1919

Ahmanson, Caroline Leonetti
Amonette, Ruth M. Leach
Ash, Mary Kay

Handler, Ruth Mosko
James, Betty
Totino, Rose Cruciani

1920–1929

Boehm, Helen F.
Claiborne, Liz
Ford, Eileen
Graham, Bette McMurry Nesmith
Graham, Katharine Meyer
Lawrence, Mary Wells
Nidetch, Jean
VanCaspel, Venita Walker
Vernon, Lillian

1930–1939

Beers, Charlotte L.
Brunson, Dorothy
Chin, Leeann
Craig, Jenny
Gordon, Ellen Rubin
Gray, Marie Hermann
Miller, Sydell L.
Nelson, Marilyn Carlson
Owen, Dian Graves
Sandler, Marion

Siebert, Muriel F.
Wrubel, Priscilla
Zubizarreta, Tere

1940–1949

Bartz, Carol
Black, Cathleen P.
Carsey, Marcy
Davidson, Jan
Fertel, Ruth
Juliber, Lois D.
Kamali, Norma
Karan, Donna Faske
Katen, Karen L.
Koplovitz, Kay Smith
Kurtzig, Sandra
Lansing, Sherry Lee Heimann
Laybourne, Gerry
Lazarus, Shelly
Lewent, Judy
Moody, Patricia Ellen
Natori, Josie Cruz
Nemeth, Lane
Owades, Ruth Markowitz
Rowland, Pleasant T.
Stewart, Martha
Townsend, Alair Ane

Wang, Vera
Waters, Alice Louise

1950–1959

Bajaj, Kavelle
Barad, Jill
Begoun, Paula
Fields, Debbi
Fiorina, Carly
Fudge, Ann M.
Hariton, Lorraine
Hopkins, Deborah C.
Jung, Andrea
Lopker, Pamela
McGrath, Judith
Miller, Heidi
Minyard, Liz
Moore, Ann S.
Sui, Anna
Taggares, Kathy
Whitman, Meg
Williams, Gretchen Minyard
Williams, Terrie
Winblad, Ann
Winfrey, Oprah Gail

1960–1969

Snider, Stacey

INDEX

Locators in **boldface** indicate main entries.
Locators in *italics* indicate photographs.